AF413810

The Truth About Transformation

Leading in the Age of AI, Uncertainty, and Human Complexity

Revised and Expanded Edition, 2025

Library of Congress Cataloging-in-Publication Data
Names: Novak, Kevin., Author
        Patton, Deborah., Author
Title: The Truth about Transformation / Kevin Novak
Description: Expanded Edition. | Amazon Publishing/Self-Published | Includes bibliographic references and index. |

Summary: "Any organization that seeks transformation desires to take advantage of new opportunities and growth. Most organizations turn to technology as the major driver of change. But technology is an enabler, not a silver bullet. Mistaking technology for transformation will lead an organization to failure. True transformative change requires an understanding of the human factors at play, how conscious and subconscious behaviors can derail any plan, and how society is influencing your organization. Change is the only constant. An evolving reality is emerging, one that will fundamentally change who we are, how we work, and how organizations will be relevant today and in the future. The truth about transformation is not what you may think. This guide to organizational transformation will surprise, confound, provoke, and challenge every ingrained belief. The future is out there, and the truth about transformation will change how you lead." --- Provided by Authors.

Identifiers: LCCN 2025924728 (print) | LCCN (eBook) .... | ISBN 979-8-9866201-2-1 (hardcover) | ISBN 979-8-9866201-3-8 (eBook)

Subjects: LCSH: Business | Organization Transformation | Human Behavior

Classification: LCC (print) | LCC (eBook) T1-995. T173.2-174.5 HD58.7-58.95

LC record available at: https://lccn.loc.gov/2022913453
LC eBook record available at: https://lccn.loc.gov/............

The Truth About Transformation

Leading in the Age of AI, Uncertainty, and Human
Complexity

By Kevin Novak
With
Deborah Patton

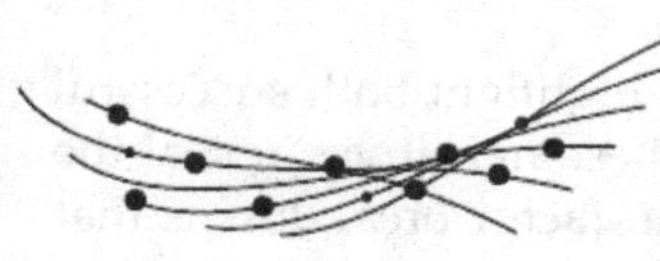

What's New in the Second Edition

Leading in the Age of AI, Uncertainty, and Human
Complexity

Revised & Expanded for 2025

This second edition reflects one of the most consequential periods of technological and cultural upheaval in recent history. Since the publication of the 2022 edition, the world has undergone rapid advances in artificial intelligence, unprecedented shifts in workforce expectations, and a dramatic acceleration in organizational disruption. These forces have reshaped how leaders think, how people work, and how transformation actually succeeds — or fails.

This revised and expanded edition includes:

• New analysis of AI's impact on organizational transformation

Substantial new sections explore the rise of generative AI, including the breakthrough moment marked by the release of ChatGPT, the rapid proliferation of language models, and the unintended consequences organizations now face as AI tools influence decision-making, information accuracy, and public perception.

• Updated frameworks for leading the AI-enabled workforce

New research and insights illustrate the psychological and behavioral impacts employees experience during AI adoption — including resistance, fear, cognitive displacement, and concerns about relevance. These updates provide leaders with actionable guidance for navigating the human-technology tension at the heart of modern transformation.

• New case studies and real-world examples

This edition adds contemporary case studies that highlight both successful and failed transformation efforts in the AI era. These narratives reveal the cultural blind spots, rushed decisions, and human-factor breakdowns that differentiate effective change from costly missteps.

• Expanded coverage of culture, workforce disruption, and generational change

Additional content examines how post-pandemic values, portfolio careers, shifting loyalty structures, and diverse expectations influence both organizational culture and transformation readiness.

• Deeper examination of data, bias, and digital decision-making

New material explores how humans shape — and distort — the systems they build, expanding the discussion of algorithmic bias, misinformation, and the risks of over-reliance on technology as a substitute for human judgment.

• Enhanced insights on identity, perception, and the emotional side of change

This edition strengthens the exploration of how rapid technological acceleration affects individual identity, societal cohesion, and human meaning — critical factors that influence transformation far more than strategy decks or technology investments.

Together, these updates make the second edition a significantly more comprehensive, contemporary, and practical guide for leaders navigating transformation in an AI-driven world.

While the core principles of the Human Factor remain constant, this edition integrates the technological, cultural, and psychological realities shaping organizational success in 2025 and beyond. With the aim and intent to help you and your organization change, adapt and transform in a complex world.

Field Notes

My Journey to Transformation

Kevin Novak

The genesis of this book is based on my career helping organizations manage the arduous and tricky passage to achieving digital and organizational transformation. I was fortunate that Deborah Patton was willing, able, and passionate about joining me in this adventure. Our worlds intersect in so many ways, and we have become writing partners with enormous levels of respect and admiration for each other.

This book ultimately represents a journey I have undertaken 2019. It began at a lunch with Tony Habash, the chief information officer, and chief business integration officer for the American Psychological Association. I have known Tony for over 15 years, having met him at a local CIO networking group when I was chief information and digital officer and head of new business development at the American Institute of Architects. Over the years we have stayed in touch at many lunches and conferences. I have always admired Tony for his intellect, critical thinking, and patience, particularly with organizational cultures and the people within those cultures.

In our times together, we often focused on our very geeky passions like data, technology, and using data and technology to create stakeholder and business value for an organization.

Although I don't often consider how to technically classify the variety of my professional experiences and interests, I do know I have walked the line between business and academia for most of my career. I have worked across public, private, and institutional organizations, each with its distinct and unique cultures and ingrained processes, most at the initial point of technology and internet adoption.

When I look back, one thing that all my professional and academic experiences share is that I have been, the "digital" guy, "marketing" guy, "technology" guy, "data" guy, "communications" guy, and the "business" guy.

And that's in addition to my roles as leader, facilitator, coach, teacher, and researcher. It has been an interesting ride and has helped me build the capability and capacity to see the patterns across the parts of all systems, the interdependence of the parts to each other, the criticality of humans in organizational cultures, and how those systems and cultures must come together productively and fruitfully to achieve strategies and goals.

Tony and I had another one of our lunches in the spring of 2019 that took its usual turn of healthy debate and tech-infused dialogues. At one point, Tony stopped me and said, "You know, you really need to write a book. You are one of a very few people that understand the variety of topics and how all those topics come together—and what organizations should really be doing." I chuckled at the time. But his comment stuck and regardless of how many ways I tried to dismiss it, it remained.

I started framing out an outline for the book and drafting some of the initial chapters. Leading a busy consultant and adjunct professor life, I often got distracted from working on the book with periodic returns until the summer of 2020 when some unexpected downtime was given to me during the lockdown.

It was at that time I re-engaged with Deborah Patton, who is the founder of Applied Brilliance, and asked her to be my co-conspirator. I have known Deborah for many years through my board roles with American Business Media Association and then having her as a part of my 2040 team. Deborah rocks. She is and has always been a tremendous counselor, debater, challenger, and strong supporter of mine. I knew what I would produce would be of significantly higher value with her involved. As we finalized the book my instincts proved true. I could not have done this without her.

For anyone who writes a book (if you're bold enough or crazy enough) it comes in fits and starts. I started with Tony's suggestion to write a book about the technological and data connections across technical systems and how those systems separately and together create value for an organization. But based on my own experience across ingrained cultures, always introduced to a new organization as the champion for change and transformation, I experienced a repetition of battles and retrenchments.

What each project had in common was that the most important part of any organizational change and transformation in today's dynamically changing society is not the technology.

Technology is important but is not a transformative solution on its own. It is the people, those across a workforce—the stakeholders and customers that make up an organization's culture—that are the most important parts. It is the human factor and dynamics at play, stemming from individual conscious and subconscious thoughts and behaviors that have the most significant influences, impact, and consequences.

The Truth about Transformation then became my passion. This book seeks to help you catalyze your own recognition and thoughts about the importance of the human factor and promises to ensure that you consider the human factor whether you are a CEO about to reorient an organization, a board director seeking to improve organizational performance, a manager seeking to align your team, or someone just starting a career, with all the passion for change that you bring. You also may learn some things about yourself that you didn't know.

I hope you find this book helpful, even comforting, knowing that change is hard, and that people can be unpredictable—but that there is an explanation for everything. The more you know and the more you are aware, the better prepared you are to meet organizational challenges with a sense of optimism and resolve. Curiosity and resilience will take you a long way.

That's what transformation is fundamentally about.

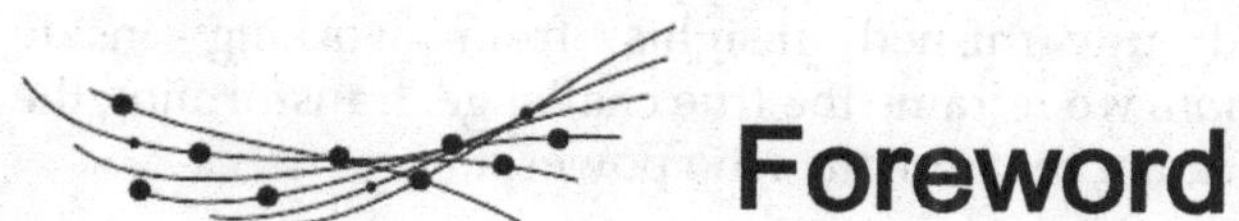

Foreword

An Insider's Guide

Foreword to the Revised & Expanded Second Edition

Leading in the Age of AI, Uncertainty, and Human Complexity

Most transformation initiatives still fail—and not because leaders lack strategy, funding, or sophisticated technology. They fail because organizations continue to underestimate the human dynamics that ultimately determine whether change takes root or collapses under its own weight.

The Truth About Transformation challenges the comfortable myth that change is primarily a technical or operational exercise. It exposes what actually happens inside organizations as they attempt to evolve: resistance packaged as practicality, misaligned incentives rewarded as "being realistic," capability gaps reframed as cultural problems, and deeply ingrained behavioral patterns that keep legacy thinking alive even as new technologies and structures are deployed.

Since the first edition, the world has entered a new era. Advances in artificial intelligence, automation, and decision systems have accelerated the pace and stakes of change. Yet despite these new tools, the same old transformation failures persist—because the core struggle was never technological. It was always human.

This revised and expanded edition reflects that reality. It incorporates the lessons learned from the rapid emergence of generative AI, shifting workforce expectations, and the profound uncertainty reshaping how organizations operate. But the central message remains unchanged: successful transformation requires confronting, understanding, and intentionally shaping the behaviors, assumptions, and power structures that define how people work.

This is not another book about "managing change." It is an insider's guide for leaders who operate in the messy, political, emotionally charged environments where real transformation happens. Through case studies, lived experience, and unvarnished insights from working inside organizations in transition, we reframe the true challenge: transforming the business means transforming the humans who power it.

The answer is not choosing between legacy wisdom and digital innovation—it is mobilizing the only asset that can make either of them work: your people.

Table of Contents

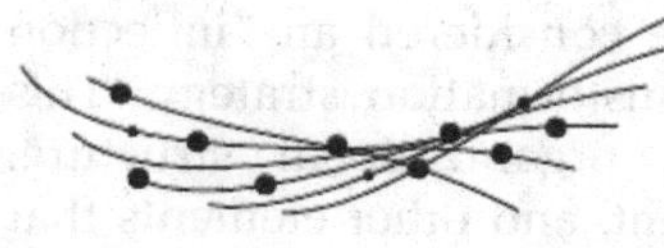

Part One: Resetting Context

Introduction: The 2040 Transformation Construct

Let's talk context. We are among those who believe that context is everything. It is the foundational pillar of any change and transformation. Without contextual analysis, transformation is merely theoretical. And without shared knowledge that results in shared organizational understanding and alignment, the exercise is meaningless.

Context is critical to prevent overlooking systems within systems and the impact our actions may have across systems when we consider organizational change and transformation. When we consider context, we must take into account how historical, social, societal, cultural, generational, political, and environmental factors impact and influence organizational change or transformation efforts. More precisely, a context-informed transformation strategy includes the market environment, organizational structure, technological infrastructure, human complement, and other elements that comprise a complete system dependent upon its interrelationship with immediate internal and broader external systems. These systems connect or diverge depending on the context of variables or factors. Context is complex because it is fluid and relates to each organization in specific ways with selected knowledge, data, and information points that feed into constructing strategies and tactics of change or transformation.

Organizational transformation is required when organizations reach a point in service delivery, product management, or market management where iterative improvements or innovations slow or cease and organizational positioning runs at odds with demand in the market (span of current or potential customers). If an organization recognizes these shifts before the situation erodes significantly allowing competitors to claim market share, transformation and change are real opportunities to reset processes, people, and culture.

When an organization arrives at what can be considered an "inflection point," it can employ a context-informed transformation strategy. This strategy includes the market environment, organizational structure, technological infrastructure, human complement, and other elements that comprise a complete system dependent upon its interrelationship with immediate internal and broader external systems.

Contextual analysis and creating a culture built on shared knowledge create an objective foundation for decision-making and spur transformation. In today's highly charged public and business discourses, making decisions that are based on objective criteria, not highly subjective, siloed, and biased opinions will provide the competitive edge you need to be relevant and meaningful to all stakeholders—including your customers and employees.

With contextual analysis, organizations can examine relevant factors and variables that determine roadblocks and impediments, as well as possibilities and opportunities for action. The contextual analysis first understands external trends and market changes that impact the organization. Then these factors are defined as variables and interpreted in context of the organization in terms of their influence and impact on transformation or change.

Technically speaking, contextual analysis is the systematic analysis— identification, sorting, organization, interpretation, consolidation, and communication—of data gathered in an inquiry to understand the factors and variables across the Macro (world, country, region, or locality), Meso (organization) and Micro (representing individuals and groups of stakeholders (customers, employees, etc.).

Here's a real-life example of contextual analysis based on the growth and changes in our world population. We may have the professional bias and perception that the population will continue to grow and therefore, there will always be new customers to acquire or new employees to hire. However, what is important to understand is where that population is or isn't growing. Then you need to determine if your customers are trending older and no longer aligned to your target market. We know birth rates around the world are in decline in developed countries while data shows that an estimated 2.5 million Alphas are born globally every week. Understanding in detail where stagnation is occurring and where growth is predicted is important. If we don't take the time to acquire, assimilate, and analyze data points, we may find ourselves drawing a conclusion that isn't based on reality.

Seven important factors comprise contextual analysis and can lead to an objective understanding of the factors and variables that represent what an organization needs to know which can lead to informed shared knowledge. These factors are critical for transformation in today's digital marketplace.

1. The Macro Trends: This is the environmental context in which the organization exists.

2. The Micro Trends: How are individuals and groups, which encompass all the stakeholders in your market, changing (values, perceptions, expectations, and preferences)?

3. Market Opportunity: Can growth occur with existing value? Is that growth sustainable? Who are the competitors, and can you compete?

4. Value and Shared Purpose: What are the unique value propositions of your products and services. Is the organizational structure and culture aligned to a shared purpose focused on growing the value proposition and maintaining orientation to the market?

5. Technology Trends: The major innovations, shifts, and opportunities that enable transformation and change that accords to the "market" and environment.

6. Capabilities: What orientation and organizational capabilities exist and what are the gaps? Is your workforce motivated to align to market orientation and a shared purpose?

7. Knowledge: Is it shared throughout the organization or stuck in silos and therefore inaccessible to everyone? Are the organization and its culture working from the same set of shared knowledge and the understanding it begets?

These seven factors, which go deeper than briefly summarized, are foundational to transformation and require rigorous critical thinking and inquiry within the context of the environment, market, and workforce.

It's one thing to build a strategy for change and anticipate what your stakeholders expect from you. It's totally another proposition to bring your teams along to make change and alignment to a shared purpose based on contextual analysis a reality.

Organizations evolve following the laws of Darwin's Evolution of the Species: simply stated, survival of the fittest. As in life, which is an interconnected system where a change in one part of one system has a dependent action/impact or catalyzing effect for change on other parts of the system, an organization has similar behaviors and survival mandates. Organizational evolution is subject to similar factors and variables and systems that comprise the market environment. An organization is tempted to transform, pivot, or effect change internally and proclaim that success has been achieved. But if the transformation is attempted without context of the external system in which the organization exists, the desired results may never come to fruition.

Context is critical to prevent overlooking systems within systems and the impact our actions may have across systems when we consider organizational change and transformation. Decision-making tends to be limited by wearing blinders to what is directly in front of us or in direct correlation to achieving goals. Context informs decision-making by mapping the interrelationships and interdependencies across all systems. Decisions, therefore, will not fail because of unintended and uninformed consequences that impact desired results.

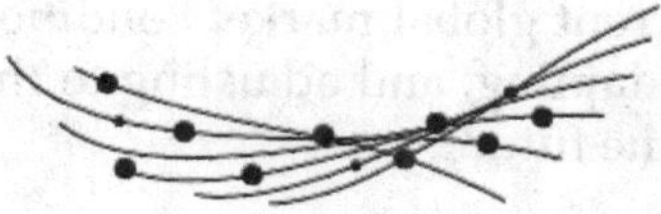

Chapter 1: Past as Prelude

"We should take lessons from the past to keep us mindful of what doesn't work. But when it comes to transformation and change, it is virtually impossible to rely on the past for direction. Predicting the future based on the past is as irrelevant as predicting the present."

Take Three Tenses

The past is not always a safe standard to inform the present or the future. Variables encompassing market forces, technology, socioeconomics, and more are constantly in a state of flux—as are we as individuals and society. Operating in current global market conditions requires a complex balance of responding, adapting, and adjusting to the present while trying to predict and prescript the future.

Think of this analogy: The physical environment is a system of parts that integrate to form the whole. An organization is one part within the environmental system, but also a system unto its own with its integrated parts. Operations and processes are parts of the organizational system and a change at the upper levels of the system (think new strategies, new goals, market pivots, and even organizational transformation) must encompass, determine, and assess whether operations, processes and even staff are at a point of "readiness" to support change and transformation.

Past performance isn't necessarily correlated to present or future performance in context of change or transformation initiatives.

The past is a challenging construct as what we majorly know and believe relies upon what we as individuals or as an organization have learned and experienced in the past. We look to the past for solutions to problems or for learnings about what has worked before. But the past is indeed the past; it cannot be changed or manipulated. The sets of variables and conditions that were present at some point in time in the past are no longer the same, nor will they be the same in the future. Making decisions, taking actions, or planning for change or transformation based on the sets of variables and conditions that existed in the past is an organization's folly.

Technological Determinism

The technological advances of the past 200 years have been accelerated in the last five years. The only constant is change, although we would like to keep consistency and predictability as to the norm because it allows for comfort and safety. Think: How often do you say or hear, "those were the days..."

Technological determinism offers a perspective on the ongoing challenge to understand how human behavior has been affected by technology.

Technological determinism (thought to be introduced by economist and sociologist Thorstein Veblen) is "a reductionist theory that assumes that a society's technology determines the development of its social structure and cultural values," as defined by Wikipedia. In other words, a society's technology determines its cultural values, social structure, and history. According to the theory, social progress follows an inevitable course that is driven by technological innovation.

When you dive into the theory, ironically, humans have created the technology that has radically shaped their behavior. As technology has evolved, our partnership has evolved with it. According to Dr. JT Kostman, psychologist, and technologist, "Humans have always had a symbiotic — or should I say SymbioTech — relationship with technology (Yakobovitch, D., (2021). From fire and the wheel, paper and pencils, pacemakers and prosthetics, eyeglasses, and iPhones, we've been the species that uses technology to augment and transcend our basic biology. Technology allows us to overcome dangers, drudgery, and dread diseases. And as we evolve technology, we evolve our species in the process, becoming more than we might ever otherwise be. Humans create and advance technology — and technology, in turn, advances us."

What is not often apparent are the consequences of this symbiotic relationship. Have we always had innate abilities or has the adoption of technology fundamentally changed humans? Look around you and consider your behavior change brought to bear by technology. Has the technology in your hands, your car, your home, and your office triggered new behaviors? Has technology fundamentally changed how you define yourself? These are existential questions that are worth asking to get a clear grip on the role technology plays in our lives.

As we seek to advance technology, and in the process evolve humanity, we rarely examine the consequences that will come in the near- or far-term, and the impact those consequences will have on each human. As we develop algorithms to enable us to find information more quickly by interacting with our networks, our intent may have been to save time and energy, but we may not realize the possible bias of the information presented to us based on machine learning tapping into our past behaviors. By the same token, we may not understand that we receive selected posts across our networks because algorithms reveal how others in our network have interacted with them.

These examples are the reason to be concerned about technological determinism.

We can easily be manipulated by algorithms and as a result, we don't know what we missed as the decision on what to show us was made without our involvement. It takes technological savviness and heightened awareness to understand how these systems work.

At an individual level, the impacts may not be significant, but when viewed at an organizational or societal level, the impacts are significant and can often be severe. We have become painfully aware of the impact of misinformation, disinformation, bias, and bullying online.

We operate in a constant flux of change, innovating and transforming as we go, often without precedent. Behaviorists would argue theoretically that as an organization seeks to bring about change or transformation made possible by technological enhancements, we do not definitively know how technology will change our workforce. It's too soon to know how AI, ML, and its popular application in "thinking" robots will pan out. The conundrum of artificial intelligence overtaking its human creators is a subject of much debate.

Generally speaking, the human factor flies directly into the face of the tech community that believes technology is the silver bullet; the answer to everything. In both organizations and society, technology is a tool created by humans to solve problems. How technology is changing organizational cultures and workplaces is a work in progress with positive and negative changes that will be significant.

Technology in Human Context

Our immediate past (the last 200 years) focused on manufacturing and industrialization. As new technologies were created, society adapted and assimilated the technologies and resulting practices to achieve its desire for progress. The technology we have created has unlocked countless new digital businesses and has enhanced every industry and market sector. Technology has been a fundamental superpower propelling industrial manufacturing and production. It also fueled a thought leadership industry built on best practices, business theory, and organizational design applied across all organizational types. We have moved through Six Sigma mantras, quality control theories, and project management to new agile software development practices applied to every situation and business need. Agile applies to manufacturing, production, and processes to establish predictability and reduce errors.

However, technology is not interchangeable and applicable to business solutions across the board. Technological tools cannot be directly repurposed from one organization to another unless those organizations are in the same line of business or manufacturing similar outputs. An assembly line with robotics is not a model applicable to the knowledge industry that uses its own set of AI and ML tools. So, managing a technology-enabled workforce is different in each organizational culture. For example, those focused on providing knowledge-based products via digital mechanisms or who are providing customer service and interacting with customers day to day cannot be directly correlated to a production line where robotics minimizes human errors.

Technology may be the most misunderstood suite of tools in a business. We often assume that when we seek to fill a knowledge gap, our existing networks and information sources are sufficient to fill those gaps—even if they are not relevant. When it comes to technology, information sources and research come with a focus on what has come before. Looking to the past and what worked satisfies our human need to minimize risk and ensure safety. Remember, change and transformation is uncomfortable and often come with risk. So, if we think the knowledge, we have gained ensures success, low risk, and safety, we will seek to emulate it. But watch out, it's like fitting a square peg into a round hole.

The point here is not to paint a negative perception of the relationship between technology and humans, but rather to demonstrate that we by nature tend to be too optimistic and over-generalize our perceptions of a solution. Our perception of reality is our reality based on our values, life experiences, and knowledge. We seek to categorize everyone into the groups we believe should exist and assume that everyone's thought processes are the same as ours. That is not a best practice when it comes to technology.

In fact, in terms of transformation and change when it comes to technology, the past is only a prelude only to the past. The rate of technological change that is influencing and changing human behavior is exponential. It's virtually impossible to plan change and transformation on past technological solutions. It requires rigor and dedication to be current and informed on new tools and how they can be applied to your organization. That said, the bigger challenge is to understand conceptually how technology will make your organization more competitive, internally, and externally. In this context, future CEOs of any business may be Chief Engineers.

Industrialization and Change

Transformation and change are the natural outcomes of industrialization. However, late 18th-century industrialization is an outdated model of how we want businesses to operate and behave today. Assembly lines and the people that worked on them were expected to produce a certain number of things each day, week, and month. Under the mandate of productivity and performance, workers were trained to operate on a predictability model of exactly what was expected in the workplace. Of course, manufacturing and assembly lines remain in major sectors of the economy, enhanced by AI, ML, and robotics. But our manufacturing economy has been replaced by the knowledge economy with new models, rules, cultures, and measures.

The Industrial Revolution certainly had innovators and change agents: risk-taking geniuses included Thomas Edison, the Wright Brothers, and later, Henry Ford, all of whom changed the course of history. Innovation generally improved the quality of life and industry, but it certainly was not celebrated and emulated among average workers who viewed it as disruptive to their routine and their desire for security, minimization of risk, and maintaining comfort. For the most part, workers accepted their status in the system and may have reluctantly gone along with the innovation. But most workers never experienced the full potential of innovation; they typically resisted change and wanted the system to stay the same.

Industrialization and the Worker

Work was just work in the Industrial Age. Today work for many also remains a means to an end. The Industrial Age defined the worker as an individual who needed to earn money to live. An individual who was chained to an organization must perform to acceptable standards or be fired. Individuals, therefore, were quickly and deeply classified as cogs in the wheel that could be easily replaced with others if performance standards were not met. A salaried job on a production line was highly sought and valued as it created predictability, safety, and consistency. Work was basic and achieving a higher level of self-actualization (Maslow's Hierarchy of Needs) was out of reach for the average worker.

The Industrial Age worker's relationship with technology was utilitarian, focused on physical outputs. The organization learned and formed its replicable model and approach.

Much of historical business theory and practice centers on the product: production, innovation, process improvements, and reduction of errors. The most significant change in today's workplace is the focus has changed from physical products to intangibles – even in popular bitcoin currencies.

The Legacy of the Industrial Age

What has survived from the Industrial Age is a hierarchical, command and control organizational model where the assumption is that all will follow the leader. This model is typically structured in siloed teams, departments, and initiatives. The Industrial Age organizational model is the antithesis of transformation or change. The Industrial Age model was about goals, not refining the process. The end justified the means.

In a vertical model, the inter-dependencies and touchpoints across business processes and activities in other areas of the organization are largely ignored. There are only shared services (HR, finance, and communications) that work across silos. Operating with a vertical model eliminates the power and potential of stakeholders contributing to shaping the future of an organization. Not unlike the Industrial Age assembly line, a pathway for success in a vertical model is created at a higher level and the workforce follows direction without personal strategic or operational contributions.

Management, Post-Industrial Age

Although manufacturing is still 16% of the global GDP (PR Newswire, 2022), the human factor as an assembly worker has been disintermediated by robotics. The human factor today has evolved to knowledge and expertise unleashed by the human imagination. Knowledge and expertise have become highly sought-after skillsets with premium compensation for intellectual thought, processing, and decision-making.

The Knowledge Age worker needs to be managed differently. However, the past has a stronghold and there are generations in the workforce today who grew up and worked in an Industrial Age model. The 18th-century values, life experiences, and conceptions of how organizations should be structured and how work and workers should be managed continue to permeate today's organizations, despite the shifts and changes of the multitude of variables and factors across the economy and society.

Our human default to seek out leaders and silently follow directions comes at a cost, as a constructive upstream and downstream dialogue is rarely a norm, given the leader's direction is followed and not questioned (or critiqued openly).

Innovators and leaders often overlook the differences among other individuals simply because of their motivations to effect change and their defaults and programming as Type A achievers. In Type A societies like the United States, assumptions and generalizations are made by leaders and those that are responsible for change and transformation. Leaders often categorize everyone into groups that have the same or similar motivations.

The intent is to follow a formula and have these groups produce high-quality work, take on increasing responsibility, improve the performance of the organization and gain increasing amounts of compensation.

What defines the differences between average workers and innovators who want to effect major change leading to transformation? For most workers, the desire for predictability, safety, and comfort transcends risk. For innovators, to transform is to take risks. To innovate requires questioning the status quo. To change a system or process necessitates independent and collaborative critical thinking. Each of which runs contrary to our human defaults across the spectrum of our workforces, seeking leaders to follow.

The changes in managing a workforce have been propelled by the next generations and older workers who are fed up with unfulfilled work and not having a voice. Under pressure from stakeholders, savvy leaders are now sitting back, critically, and objectively assessing what business they are in. They are being forced to consider their own personal defaults, biases, perceptions of reality, and conceptions of the worker. Diversity, inclusion, and stewardship of the community and environment have become table stakes.

The practices of the Industrial Age are ebbing, replaced by managing in an Information Age. We should take lessons from the past to keep us mindful of what doesn't work. But when it comes to transformation and change, it is virtually impossible to rely on the past for direction. Predicting the future based on the past is as irrelevant as predicting the present.

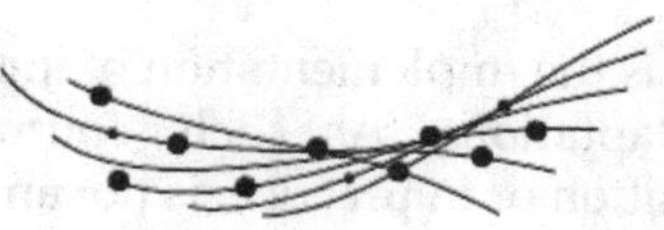

Chapter 2: Evolution and Revolution

"Over time as organizations grow, they become risk-averse, seeking to protect and ensure that organizational performance continues as expected and required through established, ingrained processes while appearing to be innovative."

Only Change Endures

Transformation is the implementation of innovation, improvements, and adaptations. As such, contrary to popular hype, transformation, by definition or in practice, is not an abrupt revolution. The journey of transformation requires a process for change agents to engage, collaborate, and get buy-in from those who will execute the changes. Tension and ultimate failure occur when each side of the human equation remains at opposite ends of the transformation spectrum. Even an urgent call for change requires an evolutionary process and can't be achieved overnight. Rarely do organizations consider the importance of transitions and transition management in transformation. More on that topic in Part Two.

Balancing Acts

To transform, a business needs equilibrium across each of the human components. To start, transformation requires the identification of all the parts of the system that are affected. This includes the human element, processes, and norms of the culture. It is important to recognize what can and cannot be changed and affected. Once an assessment and analysis are complete, an organization must evaluate its opportunities across all processes, technologies, and platforms. Then the team must chart the transformation journey and network all its parts holistically that play into the path forward and desired outcomes.

Be forewarned! Failure to manage transformation holistically using systems thinking and recognition of human behavior often results in siloed initiatives across marketing, sales, product development, and production. Transformation fails miserably when progress in one specific area is disconnected from other components needed for change.

Innovation Theater

Everyone talks about innovation, but how does it happen?

And what is the difference between authentic innovation and a pastiche of innovation that doesn't power true transformation or change?

As we all know, managing and operating an organization has many underlying parts that come together to create the whole system. A startup has the agility and flexibility to innovate and pivot as its size is small, focused, and often committed to solving a particular problem.

Once it becomes successful and grows, it requires, like every mature organization, the infrastructure to support finance, human resources, product management, communications, marketing, and the like. Creating and managing innovation within a more complex organization must evolve from a startup mindset. Success stories abound on how startups embed innovation and disrupt, but what is not widely reported is how they build a system dependent on processes and culture over time as they grow.

Ongoing innovation becomes as complex a task for startups as faced by mature organizations. Ironically, mature organizations seek to emulate what they believe is successful, making assumptions that their smaller, more agile counterparts know something they don't. What results is the attempt to adopt startup innovation strategies and tactics with an immediate, closed-loop approach that segregates the innovators from the rest of the organization. Although mature organizations think they can act like startups, they majorly miss the point that startups exist in a very different context, culture, and system. What happens? Innovation may surely start in a closed loop but will only succeed in catalyzing transformation if it gets incorporated into the larger organizational system—and the system itself understands how it will be changed. Otherwise, innovation becomes a square peg that cannot fit into a round hole.

There is a growing amount of surface noise about innovation that is more posturing and positioning than the real deal that begets true change and transformation as organizations seek to respond and adapt to the dynamically changing marketplace. This veneer of innovation is referred to as "innovation theater."

Innovation Theater Decoded

According to Alex Moazed, entrepreneur, author, and CEO of Applico, "Innovation theater is any innovation initiative that is done to signal that innovation is happening (somewhere in the organization) but that doesn't have a significant business impact or connectedness to the organizational system (Moazed, A., (Nd.).

These initiatives are often accompanied by large press releases with little tangible detail." Innovation theater then becomes a closed-loop effort that is taken on to please internal desires for a particular change, be responsive to shareholder criticism, or in recognition of a much larger problem whose solution seems elusive or too complex. Does this sound cynical? Maybe, but innovation is a much-abused concept.

The leadership perspective, even aspiration, is that a closed-loop innovation structure will protect the rest of the mature, larger organizational system by limiting risk. If it is successful, the innovation will serve as inspiration and "proof" that the organization can innovate, serving as the jumping-off point for larger-scale change across the organizational system.

If there is doubt that an organization can innovate, change and/or transform, an experiment in isolation doesn't remove the doubt, produce "proof," or address the organizational aptitude to embrace innovative practices. The faulty premise here is that achievement of innovation will be able to inspire, move and disrupt the organization from point A to point Z but ignore all the points in between.

An innovation theater approach doesn't take into account the processes, policies, and human element that must come together to support how the current work will evolve, catalyzed by the innovation. Further, it results in ignoring the need for transition management and setting forth how the innovation would be assimilated, plus how the organizational system would change and evolve in response to the innovation.

Innovation theater is often conceived and manifested in decisions made at upper levels of the organization, encased as a single-focused strategy without context of how the organization operationally and functionally meets its purpose (producing products, serving customers).

Steve Blank describes innovation theater in the Harvard Business Review as the temptation for "large organizations to focus on checking all the boxes in their top-down processes rather than improving the results — what they make, how they serve customers, and the prescribed means they take to achieve those ends." He adds, "As organizations get larger, they start to value the importance of process over the product (Blank, Steve. (2019)." Over time as organizations grow, they become risk-averse, seeking to protect and ensure that organizational performance continues as expected and required via established and ingrained processes while appearing to beget innovation capability.

Innovation cannot happen if the inter-relationships and co-dependencies of the parts of a mature organizational system are overlooked, purposely avoided, or considered outside of the scope, focus, or intent of the innovation. In this case, an organization has no choice but to work around the innovation system. The result is a binary system with each part revolving around the other but always remaining separate. As opposed to leading, managing, and operating one organization, the human system now must manage two systems.

A Global Pandemic and Transformation

Let's bring forward what happened and resulted from Covid-19 as a litmus test for how transformation can work. Society was thrust practically overnight into new routines, including moving most physical interactions to digital formats. As society continued to contend with Covid, we were forced to alter personal routines, community practices, and even how work was accomplished. In confronting such radical change that was enforced externally, there was strong pushback among many with the desire to return to what was routine, day-to-day work, and familiar activities. The push and pull of enforced change created rebellion among those that could not accept the sudden change. Many people were stuck in transition, confused by conflicting information, their own beliefs, and anxiety about the future. Transformation evolved too quickly in terms of how to manage a new normal, personally, and professionally. We were confronted by an ancient societal principle: the individual versus the demands of the group. This was reflected in the workplace, communities, at home and the larger social constructs with polarization about safety, education, and healthcare becoming politicized. Compliance became a personal issue and created politicized factions.

The normal evolutionary journey of transformation was accelerated, creating a very rough ride for a lot of organizations.

But here's something ironic. During Covid, innovators were suddenly catapulted to the top of their organizations, pushing forward ideas and plans they had been sitting on in the past, now in full steam ahead.

It was no revolution, as these ideas had been simmering on the back burner often for years. Implementing those ideas was another matter and often pushed organizational cultures to their limits.

It was a case of evolution unfolding in real-time in front of our eyes.

No Rewriting History

Remember, the past is comprised of its own situational, time-relevant variables and factors. When the situation changes, the variables and factors of the past are no longer relevant to the present or the future. A longing for the past is a longing for comfort and normalcy; a new normal can be uncomfortable and stress-filled with an unclear path forward. That's a lot to consider. In the case of Covid, the situation changed so quickly, few of us had any roadmap for navigating completely new terrain, and a desire for the familiar past often sidetracked forward progress in the face of a crisis.

Change can trigger resistance. The push and pull resulting in a strong desire to return to "normal" begins with accepting that the past was known and comfortable. And despite bumps in the road, we knew how to navigate the path forward. In our past, we were familiar with how tasks could be accomplished, social calendars managed, appointments completed, and work moved forward. Where there were unknowns, individuals used their personal or social networks to seek advice to fill gaps in knowledge and know-how. In today's post-Covid environment, everyone has been leveled with new knowledge and know-how tools to manage the many unknowns and gaps that cannot be filled.

Ambiguity is always present in life, but the unfamiliar, which no one has a true basis for understanding "fact" and "reality," results in an exponential increase in ambiguity where risk and the potential for failure increase in tandem. A recognition of the need for transition and how factors and variables in the present exist to form a new basis of reality that must be accommodated for self and group definition is hard to grasp for most. For a society or organization that looks to the past to model what to do in the present contending with different variables and factors, anxiety takes over.

Organizational Transformation Can Be Stressful

Fear and stress take center stage when change is being planned or has already begun. Outside of the leaders championing change, everyone else is in the same position with missing information about this new normal. What does it look like, how does one manage it, what will one leave behind, what will one gain, how does one navigate and transition through it, and in the end, how will it change (or not) one's life?

Identifying and evaluating the factors and variables in a changing environment via context analysis is critically important.

Without the exercise…the cycle of resistance and dysfunction continues. By human nature, we repeat the same cycles over and over again. Some relish change and crave it. Those that relish it tend to have entrepreneurial attitudes and attributes or are simply bored with repetition. In any case, they are majorly in the minority in an organization and even across an entire society.

Discomfort with change also crosses over into the market with members, subscribers, and customers.

The same process of paving the way for change needs to be managed for all stakeholders, not just the workforce. A typical example of not managing change is when organizations rebrand, change, or update offerings, or reduce product offerings or services without informing stakeholders. The organization's optimism in making improvements and changes that are believed to be opportunities to grow the market, further immerse current customers, and/or create greater customer loyalty can be highjacked without change management. Often the result is an upset in the market and customer base. Change has a downstream impact that can make the customer uncomfortable, especially if the changes don't match customer pain points and frustrations with current offerings or products.

The Dotcom Revolution

Many may remember the early stages of the Dotcom Era as a time of tremendous opportunity where all guardrails were removed to make way for a digital revolution of all business models. Entrepreneurs and innovators propelled their energies and ideas and catalyzed numerous existing businesses to transform.

New companies were created to offer digital versions of products, and services or to act as the point of service for ordering and delivering. Early in the era, the stock market grabbed on seeing the potential, believing the hype and the promise, and invested heavily in any shiny new idea, innovative company, or disruptive effort that seemed to offer promise. In many ways, we are seeing a similar situation today with the overvaluations of new technological entrants on the stock exchanges. It bears watching.

A lot of money was spent in the mid-1990s and those involved applied for their hard work and were paid handsomely.

Sadly, much of the promise was never realized and transformation failed. Many of the new businesses that were created went out of business, Pets.com was a dramatic example. An idea before its time, the premise was that customers were ready to purchase all their needed pet supplies online. Easy access and convenience were a market changer – a revolution that customers weren't ready for. Timing is everything. What Pet.com missed was customers weren't comfortable about changing their purchasing behaviors and sharing their payment information online. Fast forward to today and the proliferation of online pet supplies is staggering. This is a chronicle of an evolution that eventually found its natural timing, accelerated by Covid.

Amazon's Evolution that Sparked a Revolution

Many would argue that Amazon got it right straight out of the gate. Jeff Bezos understood the imperative of customer-first, and he had the vision and tech expertise to deliver. He changed an entire industry, changed consumer behavior, and put a lot of legacy brands out of business. Observers may judge Bezos as a revolutionary, but he was methodical in his transformation of retail into a platform, initially disintermediating brick and mortar and making the shift to digital consumption painless and frictionless.

To unpack the Amazon evolution, it's helpful to review how it happened. In its launch, it provided a new way to search for books online, allowing customers to purchase them and have them shipped for free to any home or business. Bezos recognized the need to start with a single focus, generating market interest among the male technical professionals who were comfortable buying online, solidifying a company and related technology, then actualizing his larger vision to expand, grow and basically dominate the electronic commerce marketplace. He wrote in his original 1997 Letter to Shareholders outlining the fundamental measures of Amazon's potential success," relentlessly focusing on customers, creating long term value over short-term corporate profit, and making many bold bets. This is Day 1 for the Internet," Bezos wrote, "and if we execute well, for Amazon.com." As he wrote to shareholders later in 2016, "Staying in Day 1 requires you to experiment patiently, accept failures, plant seeds, protect saplings, and double down when you see customer delight (Bezos, J., (1997)." In other words, the company treats every day like it's the first day of their new startup.

The rest is history. Amazon invested continuously in building the infrastructure needed to open new markets.

The key to their success was to be customer-centric, scale, and scale fast, overshadowing (or eliminating) any competitors. Wall Street bought it hook line and sinker and supported Amazon's growth through the years without profitability.

It takes confidence and an outsized belief in one's vision to pull this off.

So many others have failed because they neglected to anticipate the change in customer behavior enabled by technology. By the time they caught up to this shift, Amazon overshadowed every aspect of their businesses and sailed ahead. Bezos set the tone for transformation methodically and with the single focus of serving the customer. He keyed into the dopamine burst customers experience when making a purchase and having the product immediately in hand—without leaving home. Bezos had the vision to understand that humans could learn and adapt their behaviors to an online shopping experience that has evolved into a pantheon of services and products that continue to feed that dopamine hit. In the process, Bezos singlehandedly revolutionized the retail industry and then went on to disrupt web services, healthcare, commercial aerospace, fintech, the voice assistant, music, film, and gaming industries.

Technological Determinism Revisited

Digital transformation is an evolution that seems like a revolution. Those tech visionaries affecting change and leading the "new digital revolution" had already processed the moving parts, committed to the path forward, and understood the details. However, the consumer (and professional) market wasn't on the same change pathway or transformation curve as the disruptors.

As mentioned, Amazon could be described as a classic case of technological determinism. The company evolutionized technology and revolutionized the retail industry and in the process shaped/determined consumer purchasing behavior and expectations. But it took a highly trained and talented Jeff Bezos to know how to apply technology to fulfill his vision of changing consumers and the marketplace. One could argue it's a chicken or the egg case study of who or what is determining who or what.

Amazon is a great use case for the laws of evolutionary transformation. Its workforce of engineers and tech experts was years ahead of the consumer sector, and under Bezos's direction was focused on how immersive tech could change everything.

They introduced systems and processes to bring along the consumer to become comfortable with simple online transactions and at the same time seduce them with the power and potential of digital commerce to assist in search and discovery. The risk was minimized and a level of comfort among consumers unlocked the floodgates of what Amazon became after 24+ years in business. Two decades is not what we would define as a revolution, but the rest of the marketplace was so far behind it was revolutionized just by being so late to the party.

From a Macro perspective on technology, Gideon Litchfield, editor in chief at Wired says, "The lesson of the last 30-odd years is not that we were wrong to think tech could make the world a better place. Rather, it's that we were wrong to think tech itself was the solution — and that we'd now be equally wrong to treat tech as the problem. It's not only possible but normal, for a technology to do both good and harm at the same time. A hype cycle that makes quick billionaires and leaves a trail of failed companies in its wake may also lay the groundwork for a lasting structural shift (exhibit A: the first dotcom bust). An online platform that creates community and has helped citizens oust dictators (Facebook) can also trap people in conformism and groupthink and become a tool for oppression. As F. Scott Fitzgerald famously said, an intelligent person should be able to hold opposed ideas in their mind simultaneously and still function (Litchfield, G., (2022)."

The Change Within Us

Amazon's success was also due to its recognition of, and respect for human apprehension about change, particularly radical change. For over two decades, Amazon built the necessary infrastructure to be prepared for when the consumer market was ready for change. And change accelerated as consumers responded, and in turn fed back to Amazon about how they wanted a better customer experience. Innovation begat innovation rationalized by machine learning and advanced analytics.

All organizations are impacted by the human factor, both internally and externally. Visionaries, disruptors, and strong leaders like to conceptualize, even idealize, how they believe humans should act and respond. This extends to internal employees, partners, or current and prospective customers.

With advances in AI, these perceptions can be vetted (or nullified). Ultimately, human behavior dominates.

We aren't yet at the point where we can rely on machines to think for us or our organizations. Therefore, transformation is a very human process, and to be successful, we must understand the human equation in our efforts to evolve, transform or even revolutionize an organization.

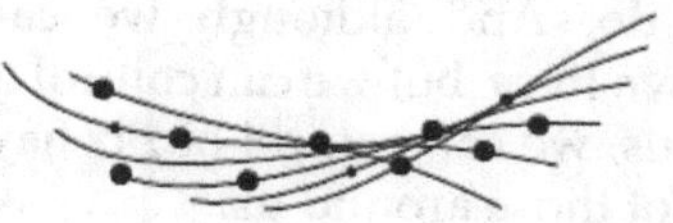

Chapter 3: Shapeshifting: Culture, Population, and Diversity

"Your market and workforce are going to look very different in the future. Demographic factors and variables must be considered in context of your organization, whom your organization serves, and whom your organization employs. Stresses and tensions to find the right individuals with the right skills in a constantly evolving competitive environment are made even more complex by shifting and changing cultural attitudes."

Living Change

Basic values don't change from generation to generation, but the circumstances of life do. And although we can't always control the circumstances of our own lives, but we can control how we respond to them and manage them. Thus, we can control our behaviors in many ways and adapt to the behaviors of those around us.

And that is the key factor needed to understand how to become more human-centric in this digital age, reinvent an organization's culture, develop new products and services and, most importantly, manage an organization effectively. It is the circumstances of life in the first quarter of the 21st century and how we as humans will respond to those circumstances that have forced organizations to dramatically shift their business models and attempt to meet the challenges of transformation.

The Covid-19 pandemic created constraints, challenges as well as opportunities that continue to have an influence—and may ultimately set up significant long-term changes and adaptations crossing all aspects of human lives. Without having a playbook to manage a global pandemic, each of us was living in uncharted territory, feeling, internalizing, and managing a new reality on a day-to-day basis.

As we look forward, much of what we have always known or depended on pre-Covid doesn't seem as relevant as it once was. Surviving in the pandemic, our strong, intuitive gut-driven decisions, often correlated to our institutional knowledge and values, were limited by our prior experiences. Almost overnight, we were propelled into a new world, and we tried to rise to the occasion with resilience, agility, and determination. But there was also plenty of anxiety, fear, and loss of control. We found ourselves vulnerable when we made decisions using past knowledge and experience that lacked the depth of understanding of a new Covid world. We were challenged to manage a customer base and workforce as we were learning and adapting on the fly. All of this brings us back to the fundamental importance of understanding people, processes, and culture and how all three were being redefined in real-time.

We accelerated the adoption of technologies to make us more connected and physically mobile. Innovators who were working on new tech applications quickly came to the forefront with critical solutions to keep society and businesses connected and moving ahead.

A global pandemic aside, the world continues to change in very impactful and influential ways that are going to require organizations to change and transform if they seek to sustain, remain relevant, and grow. Three perspectives, Micro, Meso, and Macro, all come into play in the consideration of world population dynamics, which influence and change transformation initiatives both internally (organization) and externally (customers, workforce, and the market environment).

- The Macrosystem is defined as the larger environment that the organization exists in and represents the world, the society, the economy, and/or the country and continent(s) the organization serves.

- The Mesosystem is defined as the organization and its organizational system comprised of its strategies, purpose, structure, workforce, operations, and all of the services and/or products it provides.

- The Microsystem is defined as the individuals and individual groups representative of the workforce, partners, customers, and prospective customers. Within the microsystem exists family structures as well as local/extended communities.

Overview: Demographic Trends

Let us consider the implications of the most significant demographic changes underway across the globe. Immigration, migration, changes in familial structures, the changing role of women in the workforce, increasing mobility, declining birth rates, growing diversity, and generational shifts are just a few of the factors and influences to watch and yes, understand. Each of these megatrends relates to your current and future workforce and customer base and should guide you in determining where your current or desired organizational complement may be heading.

According to Darrell Bricker and John Ibbitson, authors of *Empty Planet*, the global population will peak around the middle of this century and then begin to decline especially in what we consider to be the most affluent places on the planet. According to the authors, Japan, Korea, Spain, Italy and much of Europe are facing long-term reproduction rates that won't be able to sustain their current population levels.

And they believe this same leveling, and the subsequent downward trend will be seen in places such as China, Brazil, Indonesia, and even such fertility hot spots as India and Sub-Saharan Africa.

Optimistically, Ibbitson and Bricker believe that a smaller global population will result in some real benefits: "fewer workers will command higher wages; the environment will improve; the risk of famine will wane and falling birthrates in the developing world will bring greater affluence and autonomy for women (Bricker, D. J., & Ibbitson, J. (2019)."

They predict enormous disruption as well. Already in Europe and parts of Asia, "an aging population and worker shortages weaken the economy and impose crippling demands on healthcare and social security." Opportunity knocks for the innovators in wellness and healthcare services and products to serve the needs of an aging population and the institutions that serve them.

Population Shifts

Current population trends contradict ingrained historical perceptions, particularly with an older demographic whose basis of knowledge aligns with the past. And this older demographic currently holds most leadership positions across organizations and society. A legacy perspective will hold back any organization and stifle transformation.

Awareness of population shifts is critical in planning for the future. For example, decreasing birth rates and overall changes in population impact organizations who rely on population growth for their growth across a marketplace and the needs of that increasing population for organizational growth.

- A deeper look at the world population reveals that there are two billion children in the world today aged 0-15, according to the United Nations, and that number is expected to remain constant in 2100 (United Nations. (Nd.). As the overall population ages, a younger population is predicted to remain constant.

- According to the Brookings Institute, a staggering 60% of Africa's 1.25 billion people are under the age of 25, the youngest population in the world (Brookings., 2019.). The disconnect is that the median age of leaders in Africa is 62. Thione Niang, co-founder of Akon Lighting Africa states, "In many cases, the younger generation is more knowledgeable, equipped, and prepared to address the fast-moving issues of today than the establishment leadership (Niang, Thione. (2019)." The generational showdown is hovering on the horizon.

- We are exiting a time where population growth was strong and constant, adding nearly 5 billion individuals in 75 years. That growth was leveraged by organizations across the globe for their growth, expansion, and profit (United Nations. (Nd.).

- The world population now numbers over 7.7 billion. The US is currently 4.25% of the world's population. In contrast, China and India represent nearly 1.4 billion of the 7.7 billion current population, or 18.4% of the total population attributable to China and 17.7% to India (United Nations. (Nd.).

- Although the population has grown, each developed, industrialized country is experiencing a downward trend in overall population growth and youth where the average age is currently 28 but is forecast to reach 38 by 2050, says Worldometers (Worldometers. (Nd.).

- In high-level terms, people over the age of 60 currently account for about one-eighth of the global population today with an expected increase to about one-fifth in 2050, according to the UN (United Nations. (Nd.).

- Population in the world is currently (2019-2020) growing at a rate of around 1.08% per year (down from 1.10% in 2018, 1.12% in 2017, and 1.14% in 2016). The current average population increase is estimated to be 82 million people per year, according to Worldometers (Worldometers, (2021).

- The UN reports current global total fertility rate is estimated at 2.4 live births per woman, almost half of the levels observed in 1970-1975 (4.4 live births). Projections show that by 2015-2020 the highest fertility rates are likely to be in Sub-Saharan Africa (4.7 live births) and the lowest will be in Europe and Northern America (1.7 live births (United Nations. (Nd.).

It is important to mention that the areas of the world with the highest average and projected birthrate also have the highest rates of mortality for children under five years of age.

In summary, the birth rate is in decline while the percentage of deaths remains steady. Although the overall population appears larger than ever, the declining birth rate will begin to play a stronger role in decreasing population totals resulting in a high percentage of the overall population trending older.

Developing countries and regions remain the sources of the highest average birth rates. The highest child mortality rates are in emerging economies with governments challenged to improve healthcare, manage disease, improve living conditions, and better infrastructure. To put it into perspective, developing countries and regions in Africa today in some ways reflect conditions existing in the United States at the turn of the 19th century during the Industrial Age as America advanced technologies and infrastructure to support a growing society.

Although birth rates are high in Sub-Sahara Africa, so are infant and child mortality rates. What is different historically in industrialized countries where the services and infrastructure are built in anticipation of an expanding population. As such, infant and child mortality improved, and the population grew to meet the societal and market demands of the population and the organizations that required an expanding workforce. The trends show that Sub-Sahara Africa will be responsible for most population growth. It will benefit from advances in technology, biotech, healthcare, and education, so the region can leapfrog over the slow progress of the past.

Aging Population

As the trend data demonstrate, the world's population is aging.

- An older population requires and consumes higher levels of resources across society than younger generations do.

- An expanding older population increases demands on a shrinking younger generation resulting in need gaps, societal stress, and changed priorities.

- Life expectancy is increasing but the quality of life is unknown, resulting in new societal demands for care.

Improved healthcare in developed countries means humans are living longer. This phenomenon sets up a new paradigm in which the past is not an informed indicator of the present or predictive of the future. As such, life extension will change how economies are structured and what industries will comprise the market. During this transitional time, we are entering a period of ambiguity, which creates higher levels of risk related to change and transformation.

For example, there may be a scarcity of resources with more people living longer lives. A shrinking younger population may experience increased anxiety and stress as more responsibility is placed on them to drive economies, fund required social services, and develop care-based expertise and the skillsets to meet the needs of society.

Organizations don't immediately recognize the need to apply critical thinking to determine how population change will impact a business or even society across countries, regions, and continents. An older population creates challenges for acquiring and retaining the appropriate skills and expertise needed by an organization. A multi-generational workforce will be the norm. Younger workers might think, "The population is aging, ok, that means the population is getting older, there isn't any impact on me. I don't think it's a problem." The truth is that an older population will affect everyone. How we move through life stages personally and professionally shifts across the spectrum of ages, and if we are smart, we pay attention to these changes and learn from them.

Organizations today are already struggling to fill a variety of roles as they seek to take advantage of technologies to grow and transform. Planning a future workforce should start now to meet operational and growth needs. How we work will be different. The Industrial Age model is a relic; human workers are no longer cogs in the wheel. However, robots are. When humans are liberated from repetitive tasks the belief that all work must be physically conducted in a shared space, whether that be a factory or an office building, is being revised. Many older leaders want workers in the physical fold while many younger workers rebel as they have discovered new ways to perform with an improved work/life balance. The jury is out on how to find common ground between two different work views. Enlightened leaders will redesign an organizational model to embrace both perspectives without negative consequences to the maintenance and growth of a highly skilled workforce.

Economic structures will respond to societal demographic demands and meet the needs of the market and overall society. We can have a high degree of confidence that societal structures and economies will evolve to serve an older population and will be designed to achieve the greatest profit potential. At face value, the future will create an opportunity for those who want to seek lucrative bioresearch, medical, tech, fitness, and care-based careers. An aging population does not necessarily mean a deteriorating population. Bioscientific breakthroughs in genetics, stem cell, and AI research will lead to a vibrant older population for those who can afford it.

In summary, organizations and those that govern our society who focus first and foremost on short-term decision-making will miss the opportunities emerging from a massive population shift. Leveraging population data is an asset and will separate the winners from the losers.

Diversity, Ethnicity, and White Minority

While the world's population is growing more slowly than at a historical pace, diverse ethnicities and nationalities will drive the future's melting pot of culture, talent, and innovation. Countries, regions, and continents across the globe continue to become more diverse as a result of population shifts and urban migrations. Cultural advancements and shifts away from ethnic and national prejudices will support society and a workforce that is diverse and inclusive.

Although many attempts to create or maintain policies that erect barriers that limit diversity and keep a hold on the past, the world is not going to stop changing and becoming a melting pot where no one ethnicity dominates in any one country, region, or continent. The rapid advances in transportation and therefore cross-border movement of individuals and groups have increased human mobility and migration beyond anything previously noted across history. The ever-mixing melting pot across countries and regions will result in unknowns for the near present and future. At work, we need new insights and understanding of organizational performance with a diverse, inclusive workforce. All organizations should be catalyzed to determine how to benefit from projected population shifts in the countries and regions they serve.

The Changing United States

The United States, historically a melting pot, continues to experience dramatic changes in its racial and ethnic composition.

- The US population reflected a 0.62% annual change in growth in 2018 and 0.59% in 2019, continuing a steady decline from 0.76 in 2015, according to Worldometers (Worldometers. (Nd.).

- The US population growth from 2019 into 2021 stands at 1.5 million individuals while nearly 1 million of that growth represents migrants entering the United States. Migrants have consistently averaged 48% of all US growth per year over the past 5 years (United Nations. Nd).

- The 2020 United States Census confirms those identifying as "white" represent only 48% of the total United States population. Asians, Hispanics, and African Americans' growth across the country represent the expanding minority base of the population (United Nations. (Nd.). The white population has decreased by 8.6% since 2010 according to Pew Research Center and is forecast to only change by +/-1% over the next 30 years (PEW Research Institute., (2022).

- Growth in the Hispanic and Asian populations in the US is predicted to almost triple over the next 40 years, by 2055 (United Nations. Nd).

- Asian Americans recorded the fastest population growth rate among all racial and ethnic groups in the United States between 2000 and 2019. The Asian population in the US grew 81% during that span, from roughly 10.5 million to a record 18.9 million, according to a Pew Research Center analysis of US Census Bureau population estimates. Furthermore, by 2060, the number of US. Asians are projected to rise to 35.8 million, more than triple their 2000 population (PEW Research Institute., (2022).

- The Asian American population has increased in every state and the District of Columbia over the past two decades. California had an Asian population of roughly 5.9 million in 2019, by far the nation's largest. It was followed by New York (1.7 million), Texas (1.5 million), New Jersey (870,000), and Illinois (732,000). A majority of U.S. Asians (56%) live in these five states, according to Pew (PEW Research Institute., (2022).

- According to the most recent US Census, the Hispanic or Latino population grew from 50.5 million (16.3% of the US population) in 2010 to 62.1 million (18.7%) in 2020 (US Government, Census Bureau. (Nd.).

- Slightly more than half (51.1%) of the total US population growth between 2010 and 2020 came from growth in the Hispanic or Latino population (US Government, Census Bureau. (Nd.).

Global Shifts in Nationality, Race, and Ethnic Composition

During the 19th and 20th centuries, immigration into the US was principally from European countries. Newcomers were similar in culture and values to those already in residence who started arriving during the 17th century.

That pattern has been shifting dramatically, and the US is changing fundamentally in ethnicities, language, and culture. Data demonstrate that the United States and other regions of the world self-identify as multiracial. In 2020, the percentage of people in the United States who reported multiple races changed more than all the other racial groups, increasing from 2.9% of the population (9 million people) in 2010 to 10.2% (33.8 million people) in 2020 (United Nations. Nd).

The United States is not alone in its diversification. Immigration is becoming a force across all developed countries of the world and will surely become a factor in developing countries as they mature in infrastructure and economic terms. This change has occurred over a brief 10 years and is likely to continue its upward climb as countries and regions of the world become more diverse. The hope is that cultures will assimilate, and we will accept that ethnicities and races comprising humanity are more similar than they are different. However, it is their cultural differences that contribute to organizations and make them culturally richer and more relevant in terms of how they think, what they value, and how they align with all stakeholders.

- Growth in the number of international migrants has been robust over the last two decades, reaching 281 million people living outside their country of origin in 2020, up from 173 million in 2000 and 221 million in 2010. Currently, international migrants represent about 3.6 percent of the world's population, as stated by the UN (United Nations. Nd).

- In 2020, refugees accounted for 12% of all international migrants, up from 9.5% in 2000, as forced displacements across national borders continued to rise faster than voluntary migration. Between 2000 and 2020, the number that had fled conflict, crises, persecution, violence, or human rights violations doubled from 17 to 34 million according to the UN (United Nations. Nd).

- International migrants often make up a larger proportion of working-age persons compared to the national population. In 2020, 73% of all international migrants were between the ages of 20 and 64 years, compared to 57% of the total population. In the absence of international migrants, the ratio of persons aged 65 years or above per 100 persons aged 20 to 64 years, or the old-age dependency ratio, in high-income countries would have been nearly 3 percentage points higher in 2020, states the UN (United Nations. Nd).

- The United States remained the largest destination, hosting 51 million international migrants in 2020, equal to 18% of the world's total (United Nations. Nd).

- Germany hosted the second largest number of migrants worldwide, at around 16 million, followed by Saudi Arabia (13 million), the Russian Federation (12 million), and the United Kingdom (9 million), according to the UN (United Nations. Nd).

Immigration is a powerful trend and one that all organizations need to factor into their business plans. The nearly 50% average growth resulting from immigration should cause any organization to pause and reconsider what it believes its market represents.

The +/- 1% growth in the identified white population of the United States and the overall 50% growth representing immigration demonstrates that although the overall market (and population) is growing, the growth is segmented by different cultures, races, and ethnicities. The United States is becoming more representative of Latinos, African Americans, and Asians than White. While many Latinos, African Americans, and Asians may be immersed in the country's culture they hold unique values, preferences, and traditions from their near-term ancestors.

We are at a time in history where we cannot use the past to determine our approach to the present or the future; the factors and variables are not the same. Just as with population trends, the diversity of populations in countries and regions of the world is unprecedented. It would be a mistake to use the past performance of an organization if it is no longer representative of the current population, buying behaviors, needs, values, or beliefs. It would also be wrong to use general population statistics and apply them as a blanket to organizational goals or strategies. All organizations should reflect their customer base, including the workforce, leadership, and the board. Diversity and inclusion are a powerful combination to ensure the enterprise is and remains relevant and competitive.

The Shift of Women in the Population and the Global Workforce

The expanding entry of women into the workforce across the globe continues to influence population shifts, immigration, and migratory patterns as well as changing the perception of the family unit.

On a macro level, some female population shifts are attributable to the rise in women's status. Hans Rosling reported in *Factfulness* that 60% of girls in low-income countries finish primary school (Rosling, H., et. al. (2019). Women have the potential to become the transformation agents of the future. A widely held belief is that if you educate a woman, you have educated a village, and that has dramatic ramifications ranging from self-esteem to financial stability. Developing countries are beginning to catch up and may soon represent the same diversity across the employment sector as developed countries. This is an important factor all businesses must recognize in defining and building their workforce of the future.

Migrant women are also viewed as the catalysts of change, promoting positive social, cultural, and political norms within their homes and throughout their communities. Nearly half of all international migrants worldwide were women or girls. In 2020, the number of female migrants slightly exceeded male migrants in Europe, Northern America, and Oceania, partially due to women's higher life expectancy (United Nations. (Nd.).

Working mothers are most likely to be Gen X and millennials. These two generations value work-life balance above work achievement. They currently make up 68% of the workforce (United Nations. (Nd.).

In terms of education and preparation for work, women tend to obtain degrees in fields that lead them to lower-paid occupations (humanities, education, social sciences). As such, even though the percentage of degrees awarded to women is higher than that of men (36.6% for women compared to 35.4% for men in (2019), they are less likely to be the highest wage earner which significantly influences any decision for the working mother to leave the workforce compared to the working father.

Women still have a way to go in achieving parity with men in the workforce; the non-adjusted average salary of a woman is 79% of that of her male peer. And work styles are different between genders. Ashley Whillans of Harvard Business School and Grant Donnelly of Ohio State University write in the Wall Street Journal that "Women are likelier than their male colleagues to take on administrative tasks, which means they're often saddled with urgent deadlines rather than work they can complete on a flexible schedule. And women are less likely than male colleagues to request deadline extensions at work, per new research from Whillans and Donnelly. They looked at a group of college students studying business and found that the men were "nearly twice as likely" as the women to ask for an extension on a big assignment (Donnelly, G, Whillans, A. (2021)."

Of the top 100 wealthiest people in the world, 10 are women. Of the Fortune 500, 41 of the CEOs are women (Hinchcliff, E. (2021). Women-owned firms represent only 19.9% of the total (Census Bureau. (2021). Women make up 33% of the tech workforce (Finances Online. (2022). On the other hand, 86% of nurses are women (Zippia, (2022) and 76% of teachers are female, yet only 36.3% of doctors are women (Boyle, P. AAMC (2021). And 59.5% percent of college students are women. (Erudera College News. (2021). As of September 2021, 26 women serve as Heads of State and/or governments in 24 countries (UN Women. (2021). At the current rate, gender parity in the highest positions of power will not be reached for another 130 years.

Yet it is women who run households and control the money, educate the children, shop, cook, do most of the housework, and keep their communities stable. Women spend an average of five more hours on childcare and chores per week than men, as per a report from scholars at London Business School and Harvard Business School Giurgea, L. et. al., (Nd.). Erica Pandey writes in Axios, "Many teleworking women have had to give up their house's one home office to their husbands—forcing them to work in less-than-ideal spaces, adding to the stress and chipping away at productivity (Pandey, E., (2021)." There is a move among millennials to support universal basic income to pay women for the work they do, often in addition to holding down full or part-time jobs to provide financial security for their families.

Urbanization

Urbanization and the move to cities impact and challenge how to maintain and grow the workforce of the future as well as understand a customer base and market. During Covid, there was an opportunistic counter influence on urbanization as many used the move to remote work as an opportunity to move out of the urban environment. It remains unclear if this is a sustainable longer-term trend.

Today, 55% of the world's population lives in urban areas, a proportion that is expected to increase to 68% by 2050. Projections show that urbanization, the gradual shift in residence of the human population from rural to urban areas, combined with the overall growth of the world's population could add another 2.5 billion people to urban areas by 2050, with close to 90% of this increase taking place in Asia and Africa, according to a United Nations data set (UN DESA. United Nations. (2018).

- The 2018 Revision of World Urbanization Prospects produced by the Population Division of the UN Department of Economic and Social Affairs (UN DESA) notes that future increases in the size of the world's urban population are expected to be highly concentrated in just a few countries. Together, India, China, and Nigeria will account for 35% of the projected growth of the world's urban population between 2018 and 2050. By 2050, it is projected that India will have added 416 million urban dwellers, China 255 million, and Nigeria 189 million (UN DESA. United Nations. (2018).

- The urban population of the world has grown rapidly from 751 million in 1950 to 4.2 billion in 2018. Asia, despite its relatively lower level of urbanization, is home to 54% of the world's urban population, followed by Europe and Africa with 13% each (UN DESA. United Nations. (2018).

- Today, the most urbanized regions include Northern America (with 82% of its population living in urban areas in (2018), Latin America and the Caribbean (81%), Europe (74%), and Oceania (68%). The level of urbanization in Asia is now approximating 50%. In contrast, Africa remains mostly rural, with 43% of its population living in urban areas (UN DESA. United Nations. (2018).

- Tokyo is the world's largest city with an agglomeration of 37 million inhabitants, followed by New Delhi with 29 million, Shanghai with 26 million, and Mexico City and São Paulo, each with around 22 million inhabitants. Today, Cairo, Mumbai, Beijing, and Dhaka all have close to 20 million inhabitants. By 2020, Tokyo's population is projected to begin to decline, while Delhi is projected to continue growing and become the most populous city in the world around 2028 (UN DESA. United Nations. (2018).

- By 2030, the world is projected to have 43 megacities with more than 10 million inhabitants, most of them in developing regions. However, some of the fastest-growing urban agglomerations are cities with fewer than 1 million inhabitants, many of them located in Asia and Africa. While one in eight people live in 33 megacities worldwide, close to half of the world's urban dwellers reside in much smaller settlements with fewer than 500,000 inhabitants (UN DESA. United Nations. (2018).

When considering the dramatic implications of population shifts and urban migrations, one begins to understand the long-range ramifications these movements will have on an organization. We're not just talking about huge macro geo-trends; we're talking about changes in your local communities. These communities surround and support your organization and represent both a percentage of your customers and the majority of your near-term and future workforce.

The main takeaway from all these shapeshifting trends is that your market and workforce are going to look very different in the future. The factors and variables presented here need to be considered in context of your organization, whom your organization serves, and whom your organization employs. Stresses and tensions to find the right individuals with the right skills in a constantly evolving competitive environment are made more complex by shifting and changing cultural attitudes.

Transformation cannot be effective if the diversity of your workforce does not reflect different values and beliefs in how they respond to various stimuli, including changes in the workplace.

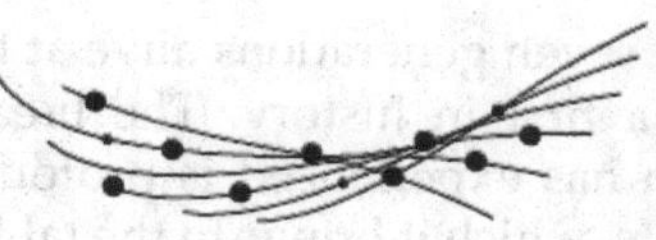

Chapter 4: Shifts in Generational Dynamics and Values

"Here's what won't continue to work: siloed, calcified cultures, stuck in tradition and habit. A hierarchical, command-and-control structure with aging leaders stuck in historical thought processes is a disaster in progress. Organizations that are rigid and focused on habit are based on our human desires for safety and comfort. This organizational structure results in habitual and predictable behavior. Enforcing what is safe certainly sublimates innovation."

The Seven Generations

Today we have seven generations alive at the same time and a six-generation workforce: a first in history. The breadth of innovation and change each generation has experienced is profound. Each group comes with its own set of beliefs, which it brings to the table in how it leads, makes decisions, embraces new ideas, has expectations, and collaborates with others.

Seven generations can be put into perspective by the First People's operating principle, based on an ancient Haudenosaunee (Iroquois) philosophy that is described by Indigenous Corporate Training as "The decisions we make today should result in a sustainable world seven generations into the future. Written somewhere between 1142 to 1500, has been adopted as a guideline for decisions being made about energy, water, and natural resources, and ensuring those decisions are sustainable for seven generations in the future. But it can also be applied to relationships—every decision should result in sustainable relationships seven generations in the future." (Indigenous Corporate Training, Inc. (2020."

From a more contemporary perspective, Alibaba Founder Jack Ma made news when he spoke at The World Economic Forum in Davos in 2017 (Huang. 2017.). He coined the 30-30-30 matrix as advice to government and business leaders. He said the next 30 years are critical to the entire world. "Every technology revolution takes 50 years. In the first 20 years, the companies/technologies are established. The implications of the technological developments will become evident in the following 30 years." Next, he says to watch the 30-year-olds. "They are the internet generation and will change the world. They will build a new tomorrow." And finally, watch companies that have fewer than 30 employees, the small businesses that make up the longtail. These innovative new business models and organizational cultures will play to the next generation in products, services, and a shared worldview (Economic Times. (2017).

According to Bloomberg, "almost one-third of the world's 7.7 billion people were born since '01." Gen Z (born after 1996) comprised 32% of the global population of 7.7 billion in 2019, moving ahead of millennials, who account for a 31.5% percent share. Generation Z will soon have more expendable income than their millennial predecessors, the oldest of which are now in their late thirties—often with teenage, Gen Z, or Generation Alpha, kids of their own (Lu, W. & Miller, L., 2018.)."

The generations before Gen Z comprise the aging global population. For the moment they outnumber both Generation Z and Alpha. Most workforces represent aging boomers nearing retirement, Generation X nearing maturity in upper-level leadership positions and most maturing millennials, and Generation Z representing younger talent.

- The Silents (born 1901–1927)

- The Traditionalists (born 1928–1945)

- Baby Boomers (born 1946–1964)

- Gen X (born 1965–1980)

- Millennials (born 1981–1995)

- Gen Z (born 1996–2010)

- Generation Alpha (born 2011–2025)

The Five Working Generations

Let's look at the five generations that make up our workforce today.

- **The Traditionalists**

The Traditionalists are the oldest employee group born between 1925-1945 and comprise only 2% of today's workforce. It is a generation of workers that values traditional benefits.

- **Baby Boomers**

The Baby Boomers were born between 1946 and 1964 and make up 25% of the workforce. Kiely Kuligowski of business.com says, "The Vietnam War, the first Civil Rights Movement, and Watergate were the major world events that helped shape the baby boomer generation. Many boomers do not have enough money saved for a comfortable retirement and may work into their 70s. When working with boomers, provide clear, specific goals and deadlines, offer them mentoring opportunities where they can share their experience, and place them in team settings (Kuligowski, K. Nd.)."

In terms of work characteristics, she adds, boomers are generally known for:

- Job loyalty
- Self-motivation
- High work ethic
- Being competitive
- Willing to make personal sacrifices for professional success

- **Generation X**

Gen X workers, born between 1965 and 1980 comprise nearly 33% of the workforce. According to Amwins, Generation X values work-life balance, such as flexible working hours, childcare, and financial protection, as they tend to carry the most dependents and oftentimes are caretakers to their parents or grandparents (Sackett, H. (2021). PricewaterhouseCoopers reports more than 53% of Gen X employees are worried about their financial wellbeing, as many are burdened with settling extensive student loans and paying for their children's education. This generation knows what they want and has the resources and skills to find what they need (PWC., (2022). Kuligowski states, "The major world events that shaped Gen X include the AIDS epidemic, the fall of the Berlin Wall, the invention of the internet, and the subsequent dot-com boom. In managing Gen X employees, aim to be efficient, provide direct feedback, and offer them plenty of independence (Kuligowski, K. Nd)." She says Gen Xers are known for being:

- Efficient
- Direct in their communication style
- Adaptable to new technologies
- Independent
- Steady and dependable

- **Millennials**

The millennials born between 1981 and 1996 are the fastest-growing segment of the workforce and the largest at 35%. According to Harvard Pilgrim, by 2025 millennials will take over a much larger market share and comprise 74% of the workforce (Harvard Pilgrim Healthcare. (2022). And according to Amwins, "Like Gen Xers, a primary concern for millennials is managing debt, as they have accrued an unprecedented amount of student loan debt. Millennials have adopted an 'anything can happen' mentality and are willing to pay for peace of mind to be financially stable.

Other desirable benefits for millennials include student-loan repayment benefits and flexible work hours. While millennials are known to frequently switch jobs, up to 34% do so because their positions lack work flexibility (Sackett, H. (2021). Kuligowski adds, "The major world events that defined the millennial generation include the Columbine shooting, 9/11, and the advent of the internet. Millennials started their careers during a recession in the 90s which has impacted how they view long-term careers. They care about their performance and are confident in judging their managers (Kuligowski, K. (Nd.)." When working with millennials, get to know them personally, communicate in-depth with them about their progress and output, and offer flexible work schedules." You also need to be transparent and honest with them. "More importantly, never judge their work by the hours they put in, but with their results. Millennials demand a work-life balance above everything else. Millennials assert themselves and question the status quo—suggesting a change to a policy that seems inefficient, for example—can also cause undue trouble," states Dr. Jeffrey Arnett, Developmental Psychologist (Chamberlin, J. (2009). Kuligowski adds, that millennial employees are:

- Competitive
- Achievement-oriented
- Tech-savvy
- Focused on work-life balance
- Open to seeking out unique work experiences

- **Gen Z**

Gen Z was born between 1997 and 2012 and is the first true tech native generation, born into a world with an evolved internet. Gen Z is known for being the most diverse generation in American history. Generation Z employees are especially concerned about job security, and they place value on benefits that support career growth and development (BridgeWorks., (2019). Additionally, Amwins says," Gen Zers are more likely to weigh supplemental benefits as part of total compensation, seeking out offerings like flexible paid time off (PTO), tuition reimbursement, pet insurance, and accident insurance (Sackett, H. (2021). Before the Covid-19 pandemic, this generation did not appreciate the full range of employee benefits but now are placing more importance on benefits that support their overall wellbeing like mental-health benefits and Employee Assistance Programs (EAPs)."

Kuligowski adds, "Major world events that defined Gen Z include exposure to violent events (Sandy Hook, the Boston Marathon bombing, worldwide terrorism), significant technological advancements, the Great Recession, and a global pandemic.

When working with Gen Z, give them opportunities to multitask, provide lots of autonomy and self-direction and offer a solid work-life balance." She says Gen Z's major characteristics are:

- Diverse
- Open-minded, progressive
- Tech-savvy
- Individualist and creative
- Self-directed

Stereotypes

As humans, we are controlled consciously and unconsciously by our personal biases. And according to Professor Megan Gerhardt, director of leadership development at Miami University's Farmer School of Business and author of *Gentelligence*, "What we value as individuals are often influenced by events completely out of our control, dictated by our experiences at the beginnings of our lives and our careers. Each generation enters the workforce under certain conditions, which ultimately helped to shape our sense of purpose, our preferences, and our drivers for success (Waldman, E. (2021)."

You can't manage what you don't understand. Gerhardt adds, "Many of the generational conversations in the news today rely on false stereotypes and clickbait headlines, rather than taking the time to understand the important differences that are a part of our generational identities. When we assign negative or overarching characteristics to each group, we imply that their values, beliefs, and goals are fundamentally flawed."

She advises challenging these harmful stereotypes:

- The Traditionalists: loyal but traditional
- Boomers: collaborative but averse to change
- Generation X: independent but bleak
- Millennials: driven but entitled
- Gen Z: progressive but disloyal

Millennials take on the brunt of stereotypical profiling. They are typically viewed as entitled, lazy, and narcissistic. Arnett says, "What is true is that they have high expectations of work; they expect it to be more than just bringing home a paycheck.

They are looking for identity-based work, something they enjoy that suits their abilities and interests. The problem is many profit-driven workplaces aren't designed to offer that type of self-fulfillment. Plus, some employers and older colleagues find the search for more meaningful work exasperating, viewing it as having a sense of entitlement. That's partly where the stereotypes come from. The fact that they are willing to question and offer criticism is something that can make an organization better. If you dismiss that, they will look for something else and probably find it."

Values

"Each generation has different values it prizes. For example, Gen X appreciates flexible working arrangements and promotional opportunities; boomers value individuality and material success; millennials like personal freedom and engaged workplaces; and Gen Zers prioritize creativity and progressive thinking. It can be challenging to meet everyone's differing values and provide them with a workplace that supports them," states Kuligowski.

Trends analyst Jasmine Glasheen adds, "Next-gens refuse to work the entry-level jobs for which their parents were grateful. Paying your dues isn't part of their reality. Instead, they see being stuck in a career they don't enjoy as being oppressed by the one percent. This makes it challenging for employers to fill entry-level positions and retain younger employees. Boomer and Silent generation employers can no longer treat entry-level employees as they were treated in the early days of their careers. The dissonance comes when employers expect next-gens to do grunt work, give away their ideas without recognition, and work in 'thankless' jobs for the long term. Employers that want next-gens to invest in a career their companies need to provide accelerated advancement opportunities, as well as authentic recognition and praise (Glasheen, J. (2021)." Deloitte found that 49 percent of millennials said they would quit their current job in the next two years if given the choice. "Pay/financial rewards" were the main incentive for the intended turnover (43 percent). However, "lack of opportunities to advance (35 percent)," "lack of learning and development opportunities (28 percent)," and "not feeling appreciated (23 percent)," "work-life balance (22 percent)," and "boredom (21 percent)" and "culture (15 percent)" also played a role for some (Deloitte. (2021).

Managing a Multigenerational Workforce

Look for innovation and actionable solutions resulting from cross-generational, cross-function teams. Keep everyone connected and ensure they feel included. Be mindful of the need for clarity.

Operate with purpose and enable employees to see there's a place for each of them. Provide meaningful work and professional growth. And be trustworthy; show employees that you care for their welfare. Create the kind of environment in which every person feels willing to ask for help, share their best ideas, and take risks. Gerhardt says you need to prioritize psychological safety. "People come to conversations with different experiences and varying levels of willingness to engage. The role of the manager is to provide ongoing opportunities to have discussions—not to force people to a particular point of view or to check a box."

"A multigenerational workforce provides opportunities for learning and innovation," states Kuligowski. "Employees of different ages offer plenty of opportunities to share experiences, ideas, and thoughts (Kuligowski, K. Nd.)." Combining multiple generations is a great way to effectively problem-solve and come up with creative solutions to challenges your company is facing. Each generational cohort has its unique characteristics, values, and outlooks, and familiarizing yourself with each generation can help you create a collaborative, productive workplace. Employees are unique, and you should treat your employees as individuals first and foremost.

1. Be flexible. The most important thing you can do with a multigenerational workforce is to be flexible, with everything from working hours to communication styles. Creating a culture of flexibility inspires your employees to be flexible as well, which can help resolve disagreements or differing thoughts on how things are done.

2. Understand your employees. Get to know your employees, not just their generational characteristics, but as individuals. "My best advice for managing a multigenerational workforce is to listen and understand how your teams do their best work," says Miles Beckler, founder, and entrepreneur at MilesBecker.com. "Certain workers are very visual, while others are auditory or even social. Assigning people tasks that harmonize with their personal style or putting them in teams that complement their skill sets, are important strategies for improving productivity (Beckler, M. (Nd.)."

3. Provide opportunities for employees to learn from each other. Each age group has a wealth of knowledge and experience—it's in your best interests to create channels where that knowledge can be shared, e.g., a mentorship program where boomers are paired with millennials or Gen Zers, or a mutual mentorship where members of two different generations work together as a team. This can promote team bonding, help your team members understand each other, and create higher employee engagement.

4. Avoid stereotypes. Muhammad Shabbar, HR manager at AI Manal Development, advises business owners and managers to "avoid generational conflict by removing stereotypes. Regardless of generation, work harmony can be achieved if these assumptions are removed (Shabbar, M. (2022)."

5. Customize your communication methods. Since each generation tends to have its favored methods of communication (in person for boomers, email for Gen X, collective messaging and text for millennials, text for Z), communicate with each of your team members according to their preferences. It may not seem like much, but it demonstrates your recognition of their preferences and that you value them.

Life Stages: Five Generations

While it's important to understand that human default behaviors result from personal factors and variables, it is also important to gain clarity on how life stages play a role in changing personal and professional beliefs, values, needs, and wants. Technically, nine life stages are defined chronologically.

1. Prenatal Development
2. Infancy and Toddlerhood
3. Early Childhood
4. Middle Childhood
5. Adolescence
6. Early Adulthood
7. Middle Adulthood
8. Late Adulthood
9. Death and Dying

But a life stage can also be described by life events that inform behaviors and beliefs. A few key examples include being a student, young professional, newly married, becoming a parent, a grandparent, entering retirement, and being critically ill.

As history demonstrates, generations are most influenced by the life events surrounding them when they are young. Those growing up in the depression of the 1920s were more frugal and resourceful, mindful of the scarcity of income and goods at the time. They were more suspicious of institutions, kept money close, and were more appreciative when times were good. Those growing up during World War II continued the frugal nature of their ancestors and took personal and family security more seriously as they or family members fought in the War. The atrocities of the War also beget a desire for greater societal respect and increased equality. Post-War, this generation sparked impressive growth in all aspects of society and were the parents of the boomers. All generations before X, millennials, Z, and Alpha trusted information sources via newspapers, books, broadcast television, and radio.

A life stage impacts thought, opinion, needs, and wants at specific points during a lifetime. Accordingly, life stages change over time, based on one's situation, and therefore changing attitudes, lifestyles, and values. An organization can manage a multi-generational workforce more effectively if it can categorize its workforce members into life-stage groups. This is also true for classifying the customers that comprise their market. Instead of seeing workers and customers as one homogenized group, we should recognize and appreciate the attributes that truly reflect distinct groups of individuals.

Snapshots: Gen Z and the Alphas

The two most recent generations are proving to be significant game-changers, culturally and in the workplace. Gen X and millennials will play supporting roles as the two younger generations become our future leaders. And their influence is pervasive. Gen Z and Generation Alpha will be different from any generation that has come before. In addition to being always connected and having a wealth of information and voices at their fingertips, these generations will have been the most impacted by the pandemic with drastic changes to their day-to-day lives across education, home, and social environments. Generations Z and Alpha will also bear the scars of societal conditions well into adulthood in ways we cannot anticipate.

- **Gen Z**

Nearly half of Gen Z (48%) are racial or ethnic minorities, so they expect to see diverse models that reflect their demographic in advertising. Ethnically diverse, gender-ambiguous models with large Instagram followings will come to replace the airbrushed elite that has reigned with their predecessors. Edgy is the new normal and organizations have more to lose by fitting in than by standing out, as reported by Refinery 29 (Cunningham, E. (Nd.).

Gen Z guides household purchasing decisions and they set the precedent for the level of real-time personalization that brands need to provide. Being addressed by name, with their purchasing preferences taken into account is the bare minimum, according to Gleeshan.

These young consumers were born squarely in the Digital Age and consider tech an essential survival tool. Gen Z has always been connected and has stimulated the growth of emerging social media brands, mobile-first consumption, streaming content, and voice-assisted communications. As digital natives, Gen Z played with smartphones in their strollers, communicate in a different vocabulary, and have expectations from work and managers that pale in comparison to the millennials who have been their digital forerunners.

According to CNBC, hiring Gen Z will require more of a marketing effort by companies (Morris, C. (2018). This group is looking more for meaningful day-to-day work experiences, so corporations need to prove that they can provide this through online recruitment initiatives to attract the next generation. And they will be more difficult to manage and train, according to a national survey by APPrise Mobile. (Morris, C. (2018).

Understanding what motivates them and what their expectations are will guide in building a business culture roadmap to transformation.

Gen Z is even more frugal, and more sustainability-obsessed than the generations that came before. A whopping 89% of Gen Z say planning for their financial future makes them feel empowered, while 64% have already begun researching the topic of financial planning. With dollars and cents on their minds, 72% say that cost is the most important factor when making a purchase.

Tech-savvy, 47% use their phones in-store to check prices and ask family or friends for advice, as reported by the World Economic Forum. In a 2019 survey published in Business Wire, Gen Z ranked as the demographic that's the most concerned about environmental and social issues (World Economic Forum. (2018). Right behind them, Generation Alpha wants all people to be "treated fairly no matter what they look like" and to make sure that "everyone has enough food to eat," according to Gleeshan.

- **Generation Alpha**

An estimated 2.5 million Alphas are born globally every week. By 2050 they will number almost 2 billion—the largest generation in the history of the world, according to Mark McCrindle, the Australian social analyst who coined the term Generation Alpha (McCrindle, M. & Fell, A. (2020). Alpha is a generation that has had a very different life experience than those preceding them. Most won't remember a world without Covid-19, an iPhone, or the threat of a climate collapse. Researchers report that many members of Generation Alpha will never use cash or own a car.

Similar to Gen Z, Alphas lead highly digital lives. Generation Alpha has been immersed in technology their entire lives. "With the oldest members of Generation Alpha approaching their teen years, it's fair to say that they don't know a world without technologies that most of us would consider advanced. We often talk about the negative impacts of technology exposure, but some of the benefits of technology exposure to the collective consciousness are arguably positive. The up-close-and-personal glimpse that the internet gives next-gens into the life experiences of others has led to an increase in global awareness, compassion, and sustainability," according to Glasheen.

She adds, "With the stress of technology's influence, it seems paradoxical that next-gens need a reprieve from technology, but they want more immersive technology experiences. The difference is in how technology is being used. Alphas want technology to create experiences that are physical, highly social, and celebratory in nature. They will live in the metaverse, seamlessly traveling between virtual and physical realities.

"Not only is Generation Alpha diverse and compassionate, but they're also ready to take action to create change. Alphas witnessed the power of social activism during the 2020 pandemic. The #blacklivesmatter and the #metoo movement showed them the power of social media to bring about social change. Generation Alpha is more racially and ethnically diverse than any preceding generation.

They're being parented by millennials – the first group to see the change that voting with your dollar can make, "adds Glasheen. She says, "Expect Alphas' purchasing behavior to continue to favor value-driven brands. This means that brands need to look at production, as well as marketing, to create a transparent, ethical supply chain."

As Generation Alpha is more diverse than any generation that came before them, they have a vested interest in brands that support inclusion. They will live on a planet ravaged by climate change, so they have a genuine interest in sustainable brands, according to Glasheen. And since they grew up with technology influencing every aspect of their day-to-day lives, they'll have different ideas about marketing etiquette than their predecessors. They want real-time app personalization from brands on social media. Brands that drag their feet on providing this run the risk of failing to connect with this influential demographic during their formative years — missing out on positive, lifelong brand sentiment and loyalty, she adds.

To ignore emerging Alphas is to ignore your future. They are going to continue to shape our global culture and physical world," Glasheen adds. McCrindle describes Alphas as unusually visual in how they consume content, highly networked in how they socialize, and global in their outlook and perspective. He adds, "brands can no longer design products for them and push them at them. They want a seat at the table." Generation Alpha has been dubbed "mini-millennials" because of the similarities in purchasing behavior between this demographic and their millennial parents. (Not unlike the similarities between Gen Z and their boomer grandparents.) (McCrindle, M. & Fell, A. (2020). As the most educated generation, Generation Alpha is already highly opinionated and are activists with fully developed positions on most current issues, explains Glasheen. The desire for collaboration, inclusion, and having a voice are legacies of millennials. Adweek reports that "global marketing giants are already in awe of Generation Alpha's might and using all their powers of social listening to tap into what they're thinking."

Next-Gens at Work

Gen Z now comprises the majority of any organizational workforce and is becoming the majority of an organization's customers. This generation brings a heightened sense of social justice and technology expertise. It has been reported ad nauseum about the cultural voices of millennials and Gen Z. They terrify traditional organizational leaders who have not yet mastered digital savvy, and next-gen workers' demand for the transition from command-and-control to collaborative management.

Generational frictions are becoming apparent in companies run by and catering to a largely millennial demographic. Gen Z is making work life for older millennials uncomfortable. Gen Z's expectations are more self-focused than millennials and Twenty-somethings roll their eyes at the habits of their elders.

There is a new boldness in the way Gen Z dictates taste. Millennials entered the office during and after the 2008 financial crisis and felt lucky to land any type of work. Gen Z, meanwhile, is starting their careers at a new moment of crisis—amid a pandemic that has upended the hours, places, and ways we're able to work. A fall 2021 survey of Gen Z job candidates from the recruitment software company RippleMatch found that more than two-thirds wanted jobs that will indefinitely stay remote," reports Emma Goldberg of the New York Times (Ripplematch. (2021) & Goldberg, E. (2021). Goldberg adds, "Gen Z has to protect their health, to seek some divide between work and life—but some are baffled by the candid way in which those desires are expressed. They're defiant of workplace hierarchy."

As digital channels amplify every employee's voice to the masses, there is no longer such a thing as "internal business practices." It's all transparent these days. Large corporations have been called to staff up with empowered advocates and eliminate irrelevant top-down management. In addition, legacy businesses have been put to the test by shifting from analog to digital, practically overnight.

Since corporate communities are now working with six generations, two speak a tech-infused language and have different reference points and digital worldviews that put them in a separate arena. Younger millennials and Gen Z employees may consider emojis fair game in work emails, for instance, while boomers and Gen Xers may find this type of language appalling in a professional context.

Millennial and Gen Z employees may also have a very different idea of what constitutes professional workwear. Keep in mind that younger generations place strong importance on their ability to express themselves, both through the brands they patronize and in working for a particular employer. As such, employers seeking next-generation talent may consider dress codes that are more inclusive of next-generation sensibilities.

Dress codes that require employees to hide tattoos and piercings, for instance, could cause organizations to lose out on in-demand tech and creative talent, who may view such a dress code as indicative of dated policies that could extend across organizational policy and the organization's work environment. With skilled talent in short supply, it is a buyer's market for jobs and organizations lose out on the skills they need the most.

Tensions rise in organizations when systems and processes are rooted in the past trying to replicate what was historically successful. Policies, processes, and structures that emulate a command-and-control hierarchy expect that those comprising the organizational system will follow the leader. Generation Z rebels in such systems recognize that the systems are not truly matched to their beliefs and perceptions of their societal reality. As they are innovators and drivers of change, given their expertise in technology and need for connectivity, they appear more in tune with what is possible not an organization that is lagging. Leaders need to stay close to the culture to communicate with and manage younger workers.

Gen Z's shared experience also brings to light how critical thought-based solutions stem from their deep knowledge of what technology enables. Gen Z produces outcomes impossible for prior generations who relied on shared experiences of learned analog behaviors and what worked in the past. Human behaviors are consistent, particularly in context of subconscious considerations that represent how we react, how we think, and how we make decisions. However, life experience and values play a strong role in differentiating actions, reactions, and thoughts across generations.

Inter-generational clashes occur on differences in beliefs about how work is accomplished, problems are solved, and how work is measured. Tensions also emerge because technology is fundamentally changing how we interact, relate, communicate, and accomplish work. The benefits of industrialization were not mentioned in the same breath as addiction, distraction, obsession, fear of missing out, and other psychological states and conditions because of technology. With advancements in mobility, work has become faster and communication easier. Younger generations are a new breed that is not easily compared to previous generations. They are both the beneficiaries and victims of technological determinism.

Here's what won't continue to work: siloed, calcified cultures, stuck in tradition and habit. A hierarchical, command-and-control structure with aging leaders stuck in historical thought processes is a disaster in progress. Organizations that are rigid and focused on habit stem from our human desires for safety and comfort.

This organizational structure results in habitual and predictable behavior. Enforcing what is safe has minimal risk, will yield less than stellar results, and certainly sublimates innovation.

What resonates with Gen Z and the future Alphas is an entrepreneurial, collaborative leadership model. Given their integration of connectivity, devices, and technology in nearly every element of their lives, they are acclimated to constant and collaborative communication, solution seeking, and decision-making.

The Generational Shift: Gen Z and the New Transformation Landscape

This new generational Z force now shapes transformation readiness for any organization. They bring different expectations, different thresholds for tolerance, and a different definition of work itself. They reject organizational theater—the endless meetings, overstated mission statements, and performative change language that older generations learned to tolerate. They want clarity, authenticity, psychological safety, and visible integrity. And when those elements are missing, they leave. Quickly.

This generation does not fear change; they expect it. But they resist transformation efforts that lack transparency or rely on legacy power structures. For organizations, this is not a generational problem to manage but a cultural accountability test. Gen Z's presence forces leaders to confront the contradictions between what they *say* they value and what the organization actually rewards.

The Holistic Approach

Therefore, when considering organizational change, transformation, or adaptations needed to grow a changing and more diverse population, one must take a holistic approach. Recognizing the contextual factors and variables provides insight into the transformation type and structure reflected across both the Macrosystem (world, country, region, and locality) and the Microsystem (individuals representing the customer market and the workforce). Understanding generational and life stage nuances, including factors of culture and individuality across ethnicity, nationality, and gender identification can inform an organization in context of its Mesosystem (the organization itself and how it is operated and structured).

This awareness is instrumental in redefining the current or desired customer base and how it builds, manages, and interacts with its workforce. The exercise will create confidence in how the organization (Mesosystem) needs to orient, change, and transform to adapt and be relevant in current and future societal terms.

Managing a multi-generational workforce does and will continue to require acknowledging each specific individual's life stages, values, and talents. Be forewarned, a siloed model is destined for antiquity. Organizations that believe they have plenty of time to change are going to fail; society is moving forward too dynamically and rapidly.

Time to get moving …quickly.

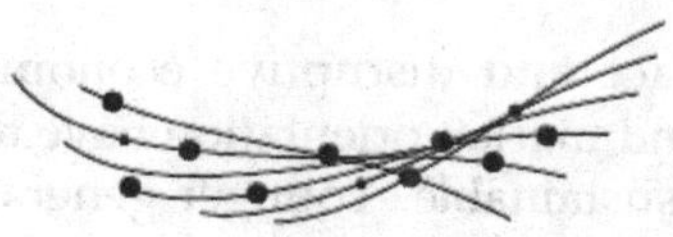

Chapter 5: The Changing Workplace and Acquisition of Talent

"Just think about the new job titles today: content engineers; customer activation specialists; engagement experts; content marketers; growth hackers, revenue officers, social directors, email marketers; database analysts; information security specialists, and chief metaverse officers. CEOs become replaceable if they don't put together a tech-talented and digital-savvy workforce that wants to work in an entrepreneurial and collaborative environment, contributing their necessary skills that define the future of any organization in a digital economy."

Intergenerational Diversity and Inclusion

In a dynamic marketplace and disruptive economies, an organization's workforce, workplace, and market orientation have to adapt and transform to remain relevant and sustainable. Younger generations have shifted the cultural and business conversation to hone into the deficits of many organizations that don't have a diverse and inclusive workforce—and that includes the C-suite and boards. It's one thing to change hiring practices, but another to run an organization that is authentically sensitive and responsive to a prism of perspectives and worldviews. This begs for a new type of training, one that is geared towards intergenerational diversity and inclusivity.

Any organization is the sum of its parts, and a healthy, effective workplace culture recognizes the fact that each generation brings a unique skill set to the table which is neither more nor less valuable than their cohorts. To be successful, an organization's workforce should reflect the diversity of their customers. Therefore, with so many different generations comprising a workforce, any attempt to maintain a rigid, non-diverse workplace culture is a death knell.

In a rigid organizational system, the Mesosystem (the interconnected relationships and interactions among the organization's various microsystems) can become disconnected from the realities of the external society. If an organization is led with the belief that all customers and employees should reflect only its leaders, culturally, ethnically, and in worldview, it is trying to fit a square peg in a round hole. Fast Company reports that recognizing the attributes of every generation that comprises a workforce and the marketplace will ensure that all employees feel safe in expressing their unique ideas. Younger employees who reflect the behavior of next-gen customers will have a voice along with long-term employees who won't feel that their position in the company is threatened by next-gen upstarts (Litt, M. (2018). It's essential to recognize and respect the diversity that also comprises the Macrosystem and Microsystem define an organization.

Collaborative Roadblocks

The value of teamwork and collaboration has been validated, but organizations often limit it to certain situations.

Undergraduate and graduate education programs typically focus on group projects to teach the social and work skills required in professional life. Yet this curriculum seems irrelevant to younger workers when they are in the trenches and are faced with Mesosystem hierarchical, command-and-control structures. The theory doesn't always bridge to practice in work situations. For example, when teams exist in silos within such a Mesosystem they do not connect across an organizational culture. Top-down project management has also become an accepted practice to get work done efficiently and achieve desired results. However, this approach runs counter to the collaborative structure that will yield better results ... results that also reflect the needs and demands of both the workforce and the customer base.

Historically, humans have tackled solving problems individually without connecting them holistically to a larger system. In business, this practice has been widely accepted as it addresses perceived problems by developing isolated problem-solving systems within the Mesosystem that aren't connected to the other parts of the larger organization. This is reinforced by professional education (training, seminars, courses) that typically doesn't recognize systems thinking and how behavior will change in the process of transformation.

Therefore, professional education systems (project management, Six Sigma, etc.) attempt to improve efficiency and profit structure in the hopes of removing the faults and defaults of the humans that comprise the system. The structure seeks to create rigidity to the point of overprocessing by aggregating all problems without understanding how work may fail to fully address the overall goal and each human's role in the process. What's missing here?

It's impossible to achieve transformation without a collaborative, systems-thinking approach to creating a customer- and human-centric model. It takes more than a village to balance the quantitative and qualitative expertise required to understand, gain context, and compete in the digital marketplace. Building rigid systems within systems and maintaining silos will only continue to manifest an operational past that has become irrelevant.

Technology Tools

Tech is not a silver bullet. It may be more of a Trojan Horse. As a business leader, it is important to understand the larger impacts technology has on customers and the workforce.

Technological determinism posits that technology fundamentally changes the behavior and outlooks of its stakeholders, regardless of age. Has the availability of technology changed society, or is it just another tool we have adopted to seek solutions? We have always relied on tools to help us do things and accomplish tasks and technology is just another tool in our toolbox of inventions and innovations.

Nonetheless, it's worth asking the question whether you recognize if technology has resulted in behaviors that have impacted your workforce and your customer base. You must keep one step ahead to ensure your transformation plans provide for tech advancements and adaptations, based on who your customers and workforce are today, and how they will evolve in the near future. Mohr's Law is in full operation, with a current torrent of new tech solutions that are consistently challenging and impacting how we work, not to mention how we live.

The adoption of technology, AI, devices, and internet access has fundamentally changed younger generations. Their information-seeking behaviors are a direct result of connectivity. Ditto their relationships and purchase behaviors.

However, the younger generation cannot be singled out as the only cohort that has been transformed and altered by technology. Many aging boomers are as tech dependent as their grandchildren.

Think about it: If you design tech solutions for the neediest in any society, you have solved the problems for society at large. Smartphones are the perfect example of serving all ages and groups with needs-based solutions, especially individuals who are members of our neurodiverse community.

Remote/Hybrid Work

The challenges of attracting a changing workforce and the acquisition and retention of talent are still residuals from the pandemic. We are living in a workplace in transition. Remote/hybrid work has been a legacy of the pandemic that will have a lasting impact on organizations. What happens when you have a decentralized workforce? "One of the bigger strategic changes that companies are going to have to make, is to make knowledge more formalized and make processes more formalized so that you don't need to rely on oral tradition at the company to pass down key knowledge," according to Adam Ozimek, a labor economist (Frick, W. (2021).

During the pandemic, almost overnight, companies had to become digitally savvy, from virtual organizational constructs and providing the secure technology required to run a remote workforce. From a human factor perspective, remote work has been a radical shift for many. And above all, organizations have had to find new ways to share processes and procedures without the traditional method of passing knowledge down in person, on the job.

Employees who are chained to their screens all day offsite have suffered from virtual overload. Teams have had to adjust to new organizational models. Creative teams have been affected by the lack of spontaneous ideation that happens randomly in the office.

Managers have had to learn new skills to promote innovation and ensure tasks get completed. Some team members feel more confident to express opinions and expertise on screen without the judgmental physical cues that are typical of group dynamics in meetings. The C-suite has had to forfeit frequent informal top-level meetings for more formalized appointment-based on-screen schedules. The IT team has had to ensure cybersecurity with a distributed network of computers, many of which are not encrypted or even set up for security.

Further, employees working remotely are made more accountable by record-keeping their daily screen time and monitoring what they are doing online. Financial managers are debating changes in pay structures if workers move to other locations with lower costs of living.

In effect, the adoption of remote/hybrid work has upended the organizational status quo. To transform sustainably, an organization must consider the performance of its workforce from the workers' perspective. Some CEOs have put it to group vote and designed a hybrid model that satisfies most employees. The elephant in the room is the fact that the resignation rate of employees who feel they are not being heard or valued is putting strain on keeping the wheels of business moving smoothly.

When an employee churn rate is high, legacy knowledge and expertise are at risk, and organizations increasingly are moving to digital and automated systems to ensure smoothly running operations. Although the metaverse may seem science fiction to some, many forward-thinking individuals believe that remote work can be enhanced by avatars in a metaverse world interacting with each other to simulate and satisfy real-life social needs.

The evolution of remote and hybrid work has moved well beyond temporary adaptation—it has become a mirror reflecting the maturity, adaptability, and values of leadership. What began as an emergency response to a global disruption is now an enduring test of organizational behavior. That said, in 2025 many organizations rethought a decentralized workforce and are calling employees back into the office. The results of this shift are mixed; many working mothers have chosen not to return, and some next gen employees are choosing life/work balance over a return to office.

The systems we built to survive have exposed how well—or how poorly— we understand the human factor. What follows is a reality check on where remote work has truly taken us, and what it reveals about our readiness to lead transformation in a permanently hybrid world.

Remote Work Reality Check

The early narrative around remote work was perhaps overly romantic. Many believed that digital proximity could replace human connection and that efficiency would rise in a frictionless, virtual workplace. Three years later, we have the data—and the emotional residue—to see the reality with greater clarity.

The shift to hybrid and remote structures wasn't temporary; it was transformative. According to McKinsey's *American Opportunity Survey* (2022), 58 percent of U.S. workers had the option to work from home at least one day a week, representing roughly 92 million people. More importantly, 35 percent did so full-time. These aren't outliers—they're the new majority shaping what work means. The implication is clear: transformation must now account for a workforce that refuses to be defined by geography.

Three years later reveals a nuanced story. When we talk with executives, the conversation often starts with metrics and ends with frustration. They see flexibility as a management challenge instead of a leadership opportunity. Between 2022 and 2024, the so-called "return-to-office wars" illustrated how misaligned leadership intent can collide with human reality.

Fortune's 2024 analysis revealed that companies enforcing mandatory office attendance saw, on average, 14 percent higher turnover than before their mandates (Fortune, 2024). The Scoop Flex Index (2025) confirms the pattern: nearly two-thirds of U.S. firms now operate with some form of location flexibility. In other words, most organizations have already surrendered to the hybrid majority—even if they refuse to admit it.

The deeper issue is trust. Remote work was never just about where we work; it was about whether leaders trusted people to perform without physical supervision.

When trust erodes, culture fractures. Amazon learned this the hard way. A Blind survey in 2024 found that 91 percent of its employees were dissatisfied with the five-day office mandate, and 73 percent considered leaving (Blind, 2024). By December, the Strategic Organizing Center reported that nearly half of Amazon's corporate employees had already applied elsewhere, and 68 percent expected to leave within a year (Strategic Organizing Center, 2024). That's not a staffing challenge—it's a credibility crisis.

The behavior is predictable.

Humans seek autonomy, and when autonomy is taken away, they disengage. Stanford researcher Nick Bloom found that while company policies increased office attendance requirements by 10 percentage points in 2024, actual attendance rose less than 2 points (Bloom, 2025). The term *coffee badging*—showing up briefly to be seen, then leaving—illustrates the disconnect between policy and purpose. Leaders wanted visibility; employees gave them performance theater.

The lesson isn't about who's right, it's about how our behavior adapts within systems. People always find equilibrium, even if it isn't the one management designed. The Association for Talent Development (ATD, 2024) reports that retraining a single employee costs organizations an average of 13.7 hours and $1,054 annually, not including lost productivity. Multiply that by turnover triggered by poor trust management, and you begin to see the financial cost of cultural myopia.

Hybrid work, then, isn't an HR policy, it's a behavioral contract. The data support this evolution. Owl Labs (2023) found that 68% of managers believe remote or hybrid workers miss out on informal feedback, while only 41% of employees agree. That gap tells us the real story: Perception drives bias more than evidence does. In hybrid systems, visibility bias becomes the new glass ceiling.

Some organizations are evolving intelligently. Atlassian, Airbnb, and HubSpot have adopted "event-driven" models, where teams gather for specific moments of collaboration rather than defaulting to full-time physical presence. Atlassian's Team Anywhere report (2024) found that 92 percent of its employees believe distributed work enables them to perform at their best. That's what a purpose-based model looks like in practice. It's not about the absence of an office; it's about the presence of trust.

Gallup's ongoing research (2023) shows that the vast majority of remote-capable employees prefer hybrid arrangements, with about one-third favoring fully remote work. FlexJobs' 2024 Generations at Work Report revealed striking differences in how age cohorts view remote work (FlexJobs, 2023):

- Gen Z (ages 20-30): Despite being "digital natives," only 40% support fully remote work, with 73% preferring hybrid arrangements (FlexJobs, 2023). Notably, only 22% said fully remote was their ideal, suggesting a hunger for mentorship, social connection, and structured learning that in-office time provides. They're the least likely age group to apply to remote roles, with a 35.5% application rate (Been Remote, 2025).

- Millennials (ages 30-45): The strongest advocates for remote flexibility, with 56% supporting remote/hybrid options and 45% saying fully remote is their ideal arrangement (FlexJobs, 2023). This cohort comprises approximately 35% of the US workforce (TeamStage, 2024) and includes many with caregiving responsibilities for both children and aging parents adding to this "sandwich generation's" pressures that make flexibility crucial.

- Gen X (ages 45-60): The most remote-leaning cohort, with 75% supporting remote/hybrid options and 62% preferring fully remote arrangements (FlexJobs, 2023). With established careers, proven track records, and often reduced caregiving demands, they have both the leverage and life circumstances to insist on flexibility.

These generational differences present a leadership challenge: One-size-fits-all policies inevitably fail to meet the diverse needs of a multigenerational workforce. The most effective leaders tailor flexibility to both role requirements and individual circumstances. These employees, regardless of generational assignment aren't rebelling against culture—they're redefining it. The organizations clinging to five-day in-office mandates are not preserving productivity; they're preserving hierarchy.

We are living through a cultural reset in which leadership maturity, not policy enforcement, determines success. Remote and hybrid models have exposed the quality of management thinking.

They've revealed which leaders understand systems and which still confuse supervision with engagement. As we continue to transform, the question isn't whether remote work works—it's whether our leadership systems do. Transformation has always been about adaptation. The hybrid workplace is simply the next iteration of that truth.

Project Management

Project management is a system and tactic that reduces risk and provides a sense of security. A rigid command-and-control system aspires to a predictability of what should be focused on and what needs to be done. However, these systems operate without the context of whether the tasks, activities, or actions are producing value. Unfortunately, rigid management systems still permeate organizational cultures; they represent the past and remain disconnected from the present.

In any project management practice, collaboration is compromised when the selection and implementation of technological systems to enhance work and manage details and processes become the focal point. Although it is tempting to rely on technology to enhance collaboration, connect individuals and groups across offices, the shortsightedness in this practice is the limitation of technology to address the human factor.

Technology is an enabler and can enhance human abilities, but it is not an answer to the challenges created when humans work together. Tasks and milestones on collaborative e-platform trackers and workflow charts are expedient in logging the technical work that must be accomplished. These systems are highly rational in noting line items for those responsible for work, measuring when training is needed, making documentation deadlines, and creating the overall project timeline. These efficiency tools often become the crutch organizations use to control workflow, but they neglect factoring in the human touch and behavior.

These task-based systems also lack actual details on exactly how the technology helps work get done and how it accommodates iterative improvements in processes. Although these tech systems are managed by humans who input the tasks and expected outcomes, the tech (so far) is not smart enough to self-update and self-iterate new tasks to amplify desired results.

As such, it enables human efficiency but cannot correct human behaviors. And to make matters more complex, technological systems can contain faults from the start based on who programmed them.

The critical point we're stressing in collaborative project management technology is that it does not recognize human behavioral defaults. Without considering the human factor, the technology is a drone tool that is only as strong as its input.

Futurists predict a marriage of humans and machines. These futurist intelligent machines will have to factor in a myriad of human behaviors, intuitions, and emotions so that the machine can reduce errors. This marriage is not based on reality; humans are genius at finding ways to work around a system, game it, find ways to control it, or force it to comply. This futurist dream mandates that a machine is as clever as a human being.

Identifying Talent

Gen Z and Alphas follow a North Star to seek organizations that match their beliefs and values and identify leaders who are adaptable, agile, and highly collaborative. Next generations want a seat at your table, and they're not going to let you forget it.

This demands that organizations be clear about the talent pool skill sets they need to recruit to succeed. Just think about the new job titles today: content engineers; customer activation specialists; engagement experts; content marketers; growth hackers, revenue officers, social directors, email marketers; database analysts; information security specialists, and chief metaverse officers. CEOs will become replaceable if they don't put together a tech-talented, digital-savvy workforce that works well in entrepreneurial and collaborative environments.

Admittedly there has been a tremendous amount of research, analysis, and thought applied to those comprising Gen Z, Generation Alpha, and GenAI. An organization must first and foremost understand and respect the diversity of the workforce and its current and desired customers. At the same time, catalyzing workforce changes appealing to younger generations without contextual analysis is not a smart strategy. As influential as Gen Z is becoming, it's wise to take a step back and put their attributes and workstyle trends into perspective. Yes, Gen Z is the majority of a future workforce, but building an organization just for them is not a panacea nor is it positioned for success. Succumbing to drastically changing an organization's approach and adapt it solely to this digitally savvy group is shortsighted and will limit overall transformational efforts.

Market Insights

When it comes to market alignment, any organization must consider important elements that are often missed or left out in a short-term decision making. This approach often results in a misaligned and malformed sense of urgency. First, consider the correlation between who your target market is today and who the market will be in the future. When organizations experience a stagnation of revenue, they often attempt to increase market penetration without the recognition that the same or similar customers may not exist when their demographics change.

Another problem is that often marketers create a perception of their customers that doesn't match the reality of the marketplace. Therefore, organizations plan, and act based on misperceptions and a misunderstanding of the complexity of a customer base. It becomes dangerous when these assumptions don't align with the full market potential vis a vis country, region, and the world.

Customer profiling, the creation of personas or other identification and grouping practices to understand current and prospective customers is becoming more challenging. Most exercises create overly generalized representations of a defined customer base that has homogenized needs, values, and life situations. It's easier to overgeneralize than identify the true segments of a customer base where there are many different implicit and explicit attributes at play. This approach misses customers that aren't easily herded and classified into large groups.

Consider your customers' evolution and how they mature. Each new generation holds certain ideals, beliefs, and values that change as they age and they begin to take on the responsibilities of adults, managing careers, getting married, having, and supporting a family. Many of the most diehard rebels among us admit that as we age, we become more like our parents. So, let's say you have a core group of customers in their mid-30s to 50s with families and are mid-career. If you are not also targeting an under-35 demographic segment, you should pause to understand that your core market is going to age out.

What are you doing now to understand younger generations and how they will transition to become your future customers? You also need to evolve with your current customers. Playing both fields is crucial to grow; it is not an all-or-nothing or do-it-or-be-damned customer construct.

You must monitor, learn and adapt to what is important but not burn the house down in the process. Transformation based on a single factor will never be successful. The market is always a confluence of those who emerge and those who exit. It is critical to understand how to evolve and transform with the flow. This is why appropriate contextual analysis objectively feeds descriptions, plans, and decisions surrounding change and transformation.

Social Media

Social media remains the elephant in the boardroom. Gen Z and Alphas are the most digitally savvy generations to date. They grew up with smartphones in their strollers, live without borders, have affinity tribes with members from all over the world, are huge supporters of Instagrammable, AI, and TikTok moments, and star in their online reality narratives.

A common misperception among organizations is that social is the primary opportunity to create high engagement across a workforce and customer base, generate sales, and/or increase customer retention. For most organizations, it is a struggle to understand the influence of social across the younger workforce, which usually results in misdirected decisions to become immersed in social and have it become the primary focus of your internal communications and the vehicle to engage current and future customers. It is not that simple. Gen Z seeks authenticity that also represents their values, preferences, and beliefs. It isn't enough to simply participate as an overnight social media expert. Any social participation must be authentic and genuine.

Portfolio Careers

Switching jobs is no longer a sign of instability or failure. Next-gen trends analyst Jasmine Glasheen says," The average modern worker holds around 12.5 different jobs in their lifetime. The younger a worker, the more probable it is that they'll leave their current job for a better opportunity—sooner than later (Glasheen, J. (2021). A recent study by The Balance Careers found that the median job tenure among workers ages 25 to 34 is just 2.8 years. The median job tenure for ages 35 to 44, on the other hand, is 4.9 years. That number jumps to 7.6 years for workers ages 45 to 54, and an impressive 10.1 years for workers ages 55 to 64 (Doyle, A. (2021). The next-gen paradigm is, "if the shoe fits, maybe another shoe would fit better."

An updated way to look at next-gen job fluidity is to think of portfolio careers. April Rinne, author of *Flux: 8 Superpowers for Thriving in Constant Change*, has been a proponent of portfolio careers. According to Rinne, "A portfolioist takes inspiration from other disciplines to create an adaptable, diversified, and personal career. This portfolio of skills, experience, roles, or responsibilities might be wildly diverse, which both distributes risk and allows for experimentation. The portfolioist's career is a bento box, with each skill in its place." The concept is you take your portfolio with you and apply it to a series of career moves. She adds, "It's about creating your own platform and honing valuable skills. In short, it's about curating a portfolio of work that reflects you and maximizes your potential in the world. what is new about the way portfolioism can manifest today is the degree to which individuals have agency over the portfolios that they build. The most important baseline criterion for becoming a portfolioist is open-mindedness. Most successful portfolios have a blend of short-, medium- and long-term engagements, with different pay levels and working arrangements" (Rinne, A. (2019).

How does that play into an organizational culture? Younger employees will thrive by moving around in the organization and honing their portfolio of skills that they can apply to a range of business challenges.

Transformation Fatigue and the Limits of Human Capacity

The modern organization is experiencing an unprecedented form of psychological strain: *transformation fatigue*. Employees are not resisting a single change initiative—they are resisting the fifteenth. Years of back-to-back reorganizations, system implementations, cultural resets, hybrid work experiments, and now AI integration have pushed workforces to the limits of their cognitive and emotional bandwidth.

Leaders often misinterpret this exhaustion as disengagement or complacency. In reality, it is a rational human response to sustained change without recovery. Transformation fatigue erodes trust, diminishes resilience, and reduces even high performers to compliance rather than commitment. When people feel they are simply surviving the latest initiative, the organization loses the very energy required to transform.

The most overlooked leadership skill in 2025 is the ability to *sequence* change. Not everything can be a priority, and not every initiative deserves the same level of intensity. Organizations that pause, consolidate, and allow breathing room build momentum.

Those that pile transformation upon transformation create learned helplessness disguised as resistance.

Work Redefined

The residual results of the pandemic has changed work as has the unending cycle of change. There is little allegiance to an employer, and the expectation is the employer needs to make the individual feel fulfilled to retain them. The sole importance of a "paycheck" still exists but is no longer the major driver of skilled and talented workers. The Great Resignation during the pandemic reflected the power of next gens to trade quality of life over working paycheck to paycheck. The next-gen's reevaluation of basic needs and desires forces organizations to rethink their workplace cultures, pathways to success, inclusivity, and diversity.

Rinne's approach is a solution for retaining talent. Young high-performance workers are not interested in being cogs in the wheel. They want to compete on the merit of skills. Let us also factor in how the mindset of those making decisions based on what worked in the past is not relevant to succeed. The basis of such decision-making does not correlate well to current conditions and plans for organizational change or transformation must conform to dramatic shapeshifting in its workforce and across its customer and constituent base. Ultimately, it is the human factor, regardless of what generation, that will power and propel and organization —or stop it in its tracks.

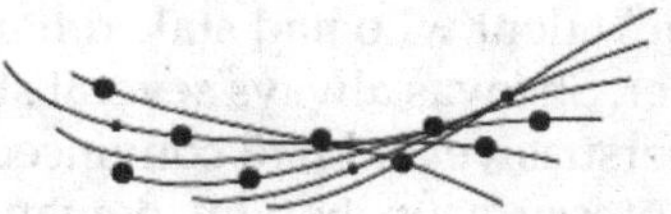

Chapter 6: The Era of AI and Machine Learning

"The challenge for any organization is the speed of change, resulting in the lack of expertise, skill set or operational capacity, and agility to adapt to new technologies. But that cannot be used as an excuse in a highly dynamic and changing world. AI/ML is only going to grow, making organizations even more dependent on the technologies."

A new CEO of a high-tech organization rushed to get an AI tool that promised to revolutionize customer onboarding into production. She was recognized as a "hot shot" talent who had staked her reputation on being a visionary and early mover. She was always several steps ahead of everyone else. She was also very persuasive and had convinced the board to invest in the tool, but they put pressure on her by demanding visible progress. Competitors were already following her lead and touting their own AI investments adding more pressure to get the tool to market. Fast tracking production, the solution went live within a few weeks and almost immediately, chaos followed.

The customers who purchased the tool were not recognized by the organization's system because of a technical glitch in its algorithms. Regulators flagged the tool and raised questions about bias. Customer service frontline employees were overwhelmed by complaints. And to make a bad situation even worse, the new customers the organization had hoped to impress cancelled their contracts and went to the competitor.

This story illustrates a fundamental tension at the heart of today's AI revolution. Despite such high-profile failures, technological transformation continues to accelerate. The same AI capabilities that created chaos for this organization are simultaneously revolutionizing industries, enhancing human productivity, and reshaping how we work and think. The question isn't whether AI will transform business—it's whether organizations will master the human factors that determine success or failure in AI implementation.

Enhanced Intelligence: Speculation Transits to Reality

Google CEO Sundar Pichai has said: "AI is probably the most important thing humanity has ever worked on. I think of it as something more profound than electricity or fire" (Parker, C. 2018).

This chapter was originally written in 2022 when AI felt like a distant technological frontier. As we revise this content in 2025, AI has moved from speculative to daily reality.

If you've been working with any Large Language Model (LLM) – ChatGPT, Claude, Gemini, or others – you've probably noticed how weirdly polite and eager to please these tools are. That's no surprise because they are trained to please you. It makes it tempting to depend on AI for the instantaneous results that are enhanced by its feel-good personal touch.

Early analysis shows individuals are migrating from searching for information to asking their favorite AI tool, chatbot or app to provide them with the insight they need to meet the day's task or facilitate making a decision. The level of trust in AI that has become so ingrained that it is concerning in many ways, but we need to remember that the same trust was given to Google, Bing, AltaVista and many other search engines in the late 1990s. We quickly embraced the technological opportunity to remove the need to exercise our own critical thinking. Instead, we conserved our energy and transferred our responsibility for making decisions to a tool, platform or app.

The question for organizations undergoing transformation is no longer whether AI will impact their workforce and operations – it's how to navigate its reality and, as it evolves and is refined, manage it as a game-changer or headache…or a mix of both.

That progression begs three fundamental questions:

- What impact will AI, machine learning, and algorithms continue to have?

- What will machine learning do for society?

- What impacts are already felt?

The short answers: Everything. Above all, you cannot talk about AI and ML without considering the human factor. These ever-evolving technologies are programmed by human beings. Therefore, AI and ML can never achieve perfection, as they are reflections of the people who created the systems in the first place. It is an exciting arena and will continue to change most things in our lives, professionally and personally.

What is important in business is to remember technology is a tool, not a magic solution, and technology can shape human behavior — both positively and negatively.

It is up to organizational leadership to use critical thinking and shared knowledge in the decision-making process of what technologies to acquire and deploy. More importantly, to be mindful of how technologies are impacting a workforce and be carefully monitored by individual professionals and organizational systems.

A Brief History: Sparks of Transformation

Here's a sampling of three life-changing breakthroughs. Electricity transformed day-to-day life and succeeded in having people forget how to live without it. Automobiles gave humans mobility and therefore the ability to expand communities and create the suburbs. The smartphone, its connectivity, function, and utility changed everything.

We have evolved from industrialization to automation and now in the era of AI, these technologies are embedded into every aspect of our lives. Research, development, and the deployment of AI and machine learning into all aspects of our lives has dramatically changed life as we know it and created unforeseen impacts that we were not prepared for.

The ways life has changed are rapid, impacting all aspects of society regardless of geographic location, economics, social status, or education. These accelerated changes continue to challenge you, your organization, and your ability to manage the dynamics of the marketplace. And we are beginning to recognize that the relationship between technology and humans is not perfect, which may have the most dramatic impact on you and your organization.

AI Today: From Hype to Reality

Take a straw poll about AI and you may get two oppositional results. AI is either a tool that will help human beings achieve higher levels of productivity and more efficient levels of profitability, or AI is a threat to national security and humanity as it is the pathway to transcend human cognitive abilities and will supersede the human mind, ultimately taking over humanity.

We would argue that almost anyone who talks about AI does not have a firm grasp on what it is including all its variations, so the public AI narrative is more fiction than truth.

AI comes in many flavors including machine learning which is used to analyze large sets of data to derive patterns and learning. Then there are Chatbots: OpenAI's ChatGPT, Microsoft Co-Pilot, Google's Gemini, Adobe's Firefly and countless other bots that have been introduced to the masses in nearly every application, website, or app. AI bots aren't the total picture, but they represent AI that the public most often experiences.

As of March 2025, 34% of U.S. adults say they have used ChatGPT, nearly double the 18% reported in Pew Research Center July 2023 survey. Usage continues to skew younger, more educated, and more affluent: 58% of adults under 30, 53% of those with postgraduate degrees, and 56% of those earning $100K+ annually report having used ChatGPT.

However, regular usage remains limited, just 4% say they use it daily, and 19% say they've only used it once or twice. Public awareness is now nearly universal (91%), up from 71% in July 2023. Notably, 25% of users report using ChatGPT for work, while 19% use it for learning, and 16% for entertainment. The report also highlights public concern: 52% of Americans are more concerned than excited about AI's growing role, while only 10% are more excited than concerned.

Those who have used a chatbot have quickly found that their interactions, although often entertaining, have had limited benefit in aiding them in work or their personal lives.

Over the past months, major publications have written extensively about helping readers understand AI and explaining where chatbots work best (limitedly) and where they simply fail.

In terms of the hype across society and the marketplace, even the stock market, AI appears to be a second coming that will solve every one of our woes and needs. That hype comes despite the failures, errors, hallucinations and outright problematic moments resulting from its use. In fewer than 18 months, Nvidia's market cap grew to $2.13 trillion, briefly hitting $3 trillion. GenAI has spawned new language-model industries, with companies competing to deliver better solutions to organizations more quickly and effectively. Not to mention the adjacent industries that are thriving to deliver the chips and power necessary to fuel AI.

Yet according to a recent Edelman survey (2025), globally, trust in AI companies has dropped to 53%, down from 61% five years ago. In the U.S., trust has dropped 15 points from 50% to 35%. This decline in trust coincides with high-profile AI failures, ethical concerns and a lot of misinformation on social media that have made headlines.

AI: The Term Limits Problem

The guiding operating principle should be that AI is a powerful tool, not an oracle or an objective soothsayer. Yet, many organizations are using it as a predictive, prophetic crutch. Most AI is trained on massive datasets provided by humans, and many are then frozen in time to determine how they are going to work with the data provided. At least for now, that means they're not live 24/7 nor are they trained instantaneously.

Consider today's market uncertainty based on regulatory and policy changes where inputs are changing day to day as humans make one decision, change the decision, pause the decision or simply forget about it. How likely is AI to be your trusted source of knowledge to set strategy for an individual? For an organization? It's questionable.

AI is only as good as the data it sees. It's not a crystal ball. It can't predict black swan events, new laws, or sudden shifts without being retrained or augmented. Simply put, when the world changes fast (which it does), stale data gives stale answers. It also can't predict unintended consequences for real-time market disruptions. It's not a trendline, abstract thinking entity.

Our societal challenge is that AI and learning models are subject to the information (data) we provide them. As such, AI is limited to what it has been fed, therefore bringing human biases forth into its own thinking. Humans are faulty and make mistakes, and AI will continue to emulate its human creators.

Any conversation about AI has to start with clarity of what AI is or is not. GenAI is not a thing. It is not an entity. It is a tool programmed by humans and triggered by prompts from humans to churn out information distilled from the body of information originally created by humans.

That information has come from "learning sets of data" that include the archives of major publishers across the globe. The pattern is clear: Information is written by humans, all of whom have known and unknown biases. When GenAI produces errors or seems to hallucinate, we must consider the sources that fed it in the first place.

AI, by definition, is objective and incapable of independent reasoning, so it has to distill masses of information to find a logical answer across a diverse backdrop of biases. AI struggles to determine fact and truth based on often unreliable or unstable input and biased prompts. And all input and prompts are created by human beings.

A Silver Bullet? Understanding AI's True Nature

In a tech hero-worship culture, technology is believed to be a silver bullet, but reality check: it's a tool, catalyst, and enabler. We have transitioned quickly from the Information Age to the Era of AI and Machine Learning, further deepening our reliance on and connected relationship to advanced technology.

Our news feeds are filled with hyper-based promises on how technology is becoming smarter and taking over complex processing tasks that exceed human computational capacities. The promises are that technology can assess large sets of data, engage in complex mathematical computations, and pretty much solve every woe or challenge we have. And that's just its data processing potential. Add to that its ability to analyze medical tests, organize travel itineraries and vet legal documents.

So, let's get down to the basics: Artificial intelligence is intelligence demonstrated by machines, as opposed to the natural intelligence displayed by animals, including humans. Machine learning is the study of computer algorithms that can improve automatically through experience and the use of data. It is a subset of artificial intelligence. (Wikipedia. Nd.).

Advances in AI/ML have skyrocketed and their time-compressed computational powers and predictive analysis eclipse what humans can do. These technologies turn data from any source into actionable information, quickly. As a result, AI and ML offer much promise and there are already many real-world examples in real-time data visualization and analytics. AI/ML provides enormous value in situational awareness by processing large streams of data to create effective action plans and track the results. What humans lack in speed is the gain of their intelligence in in the interpretation and analysis of this information.

There are so many applications of AI/ML that have become routine in our industries today:

- AI and ML are powerful medical diagnostic tools

- Security systems with AI and ML deliver biometrics and instant database searches

- Voice assistants become more responsive and contextual leveraged by AI/ML

- The transportation industry has developed telemetric and engineered autonomous vehicles

- Online retailers use the technology to match customers' preferences and predict behavior

- Supply chain logistics across all industries are managed by AI/ML

- Defense uses drones and other tracking systems powered by this technology

- Space and earth travel are enhanced by AI/ML

- Weather forecasting and climate modeling leverage AI/ML for improved accuracy

- Financial services use AI for fraud detection and algorithmic trading

AI on the Balance Beam: Bias and Error

All technology is created by humans and therefore, technology has the same faults and errors, and can represent, interpret, or process information and data inappropriately. Let's consider facial recognition powered by artificial intelligence as an example of the vulnerability of AI and ML. Some facial recognition systems have been revealed to perform poorly with people of color because the algorithms are less accurate at identifying people with darker skin tones, reports the Washington Post (Abril, D, & Harwell, D. 2021).

Surveillance systems that track employees in the office or in remote settings to ensure they are working, not loafing around raise trust and privacy issues related to biometrics and other tracking technologies. The major issue is AI's accuracy in representing the entire human race. The challenge is that facial recognition technology is often based on a subset of information that leads the technology to form its own bias and interpretation.

As with any system, platform, or tool, an outcome is based on the information it is programmed with to manipulate, calculate, and consider in making its analysis. Artificial intelligence, like humans, is highly prone to bias. The current debate is whether the engineers that program these highly complex systems are consciously or unconsciously biased.

Let's say humans have loaded a system with images of primarily white males and females; AI can only make conclusions based on the information it was given; it cannot infer. If a system is input with only white and Asian males and females, then its basis point of decision-making can only be derived from that information. You can see where this is going. The point is that AI systems need all human variations to compute and derive a full analysis. To add to the complexity, humans must also program the system to inform the machine what other variables it should consider; for example, what values and features are important. Therefore, the system's relevance and success directly correlate to the human input that has programmed it to do. To reassert, humans have bias and therefore, so does technology.

We've seen this bias problem manifest in hiring algorithms that discriminate against women, loan approval systems that disadvantage minorities, and criminal justice algorithms that reinforce racial disparities.

These aren't theoretical problems; they're documented impacts on real people's lives.

AI as a Mirror of Organizational Dysfunction

AI does not fix dysfunctional organizations; it exposes them. Leaders often assume new technologies will streamline operations, clarify priorities, and reduce the burden of legacy systems. In practice, AI accelerates whatever already exists beneath the surface. If a culture is fractured, AI intensifies the fragmentation. If decision-making is unclear, AI amplifies ambiguity and inconsistency. If incentives are misaligned, AI optimizes the wrong behaviors at scale.

This is the paradox few leaders anticipate: the more powerful the tool, the more visible the dysfunction. AI forces organizations to confront the very issues they've avoided—poor communication, siloed thinking, hidden power dynamics, and the unspoken rules that govern how work really gets done. The technology becomes a diagnostic instrument, reflecting back the organization's deepest behavioral patterns with unnerving precision.

The leaders who succeed in the age of AI are those who recognize that the technology is not a substitute for alignment, clarity, or trust. It is a catalyst. And like all catalysts, it accelerates both progress and failure depending on the human conditions into which it is introduced.

The Human Factor Under Pressure

As such, we are at a critical juncture at this point in our human history when taking the easier path may fundamentally upend what we believe it is to be human now and into the future.

We are all guilty of the amount of time we lose consuming TikTok, Facebook and our favorite social feeds. We have convinced ourselves that we don't have the time to think. But maybe we don't want to think. We just want an easy way to complete a task and trust something or someone else to make a decision so we can move along.

The consequences of this sort of default of responsibility are becoming measurable. Oxford University named "Brain Rot" as the 2024 Word of the Year, a term describing the deterioration of a person's mental or intellectual state, especially viewed as the result of overconsumption of material (now particularly online content) considered to be trivial or unchallenging. This isn't expanding beyond social media to our relationship with all digital tools, including AI.

A research study published by Elon University, "Imagining the Digital Future," reports that Americans are more likely than not to hope AI will improve the nation's healthcare systems and the quality of medical treatment by 2040. Still, they have deep concerns that AI will negatively impact politics and elections and further erode the level of civility in society.

When experts were asked about the magnitude of overall change in people's thinking and behavior as we adapt to advanced AI by 2035, 61% said the change would be deep and meaningful or fundamental and revolutionary.

Many experts are concerned about how our adoption of AI systems over the next decade will affect essential human traits such as empathy, social/emotional intelligence, complex thinking, ability to act independently and sense of purpose.

Some experts are optimistic about AI's influence on humans' curiosity, decision-making and creativity, but they foresee deep, meaningful and even dramatic change ahead.

AI and Human Limitations: The Systems Perspective

The promise and value of AI and ML are still reliant on humans. What we don't know, the machine doesn't know either. We may have aspirations that machines will "learn," and we may have "trained" them to do so, but where is the necessary information coming from? Over time, AI or the machine can become smarter as it ingests and analyzes additional information. But remember that humans still dictate what information and from what source, can be mechanically leveraged.

It all comes down to the programming. Yes, machines can process faster than humans and can see things beyond the limitations of the human mind. That is a benefit, but let's be mindful of where data (information) comes from. For example, a worker scans barcodes of boxes in a warehouse to share location and information with a machine, and then a forklift carrying the boxes drives under a doorway scanner to record the movement of the boxes. The resulting data is then processed by the machine, the movement or location is recorded, and the system is updated.

But what if the worker made a mistake and thought he or she scanned a row of boxes but didn't? Or what if the barcode label was not visible to the doorway scanner. How are all the boxes entering the warehouse accounted for? And how does the system know that the boxes may not be reflected in inventory counts? So, what happens when is it revealed that the expected quantity of boxes is missing? The superiority of AI quickly falls apart.

This scenario is basic, although some may argue that there are checks and balances in place to ensure the inventory is properly recorded. That said, this exercise illustrates that humans are the major input source for information (data) being managed in a system although they are quick to blame the machine. Their bias is that the machine is of lesser intelligence, defending their assumption that they couldn't possibly have made a mistake and are smarter than programmed machines. But we do make mistakes and there is much in our subconscious that influences our actions (even contributing distractions to the tasks at hand) and leads to mistakes. And those mistakes can show up in AI programming.

In some ways, society hasn't let go of the Industrial Age mentality that defines a workforce via its relationship and connection to a machine. This mindset is going to need a dramatic reset when it comes to our relationship with 21st century machines including AI/ML. The Industrial Age mentality needs to be replaced with a recognition of the value of humans and their primary role as critical thinkers to ensure the machines are operating as intended.

An interdependent relationship with machines can assist in making humans more efficient and productive. Technology can also enhance human abilities, but machines cannot replace human critical thinking thought processes or manifest the creativity needed to change and transform an organization to meet its customer's needs and wants.

Technological Determinism: Who's in Charge?

The self-identity rules have changed dramatically with the advancements of AI. The blurred lines between human and AI cognition bring up the issue of being human and more broadly, technological determinism.

When deploying AI tools, consider whether technology drives social change, or whether technology is a reflection of the social change that human beings program into these systems. In other words, who is determining what?

You might believe that tech evolves on its own trajectory and society has no choice but to adapt. This belief suggests that human agency, ethics, culture, and politics are subordinate to technology. Taking it to the extreme, AI development shapes work, life, policy, and ethics, without humans consciously steering it. We accept automation, surveillance, and algorithmic decision-making as inevitable.

There are warning signs that should trigger alarm bells to question this determinate position:

- **The "move fast and break things" mentality:** The tech community is known for this approach. The big AI players are rolling out powerful tools at breakneck speed while policy and ethics often lag behind. Businesses and governments feel pressured to adopt AI just to keep up — not always with clarity or consent. Each country is seeking to lead the world in AI as it sees it as a competitive advantage now and for who we will become as a society.

- **Assumptions of inevitability:** People talk about job losses, bias, deepfakes, and surveillance as if they're just going to happen automatically. That narrative precludes critical thinking to question whether it's a true assumption.

- **Algorithms and black boxes:** As AI systems grow more complex, even their creators struggle to explain the decisions AI puts forward. They cannot explain how AI is thinking, how it is processing and calculating data and information. If no one understands how it works, who's really in control?

- **Power of the few:** A limited number of companies control the foundational AI models both globally and regionally. That centralizes not just economic and information power, but the shaping of knowledge, culture, and truth. When the creators do not know how their AI is evolving, thinking, assessing and considering, who then is really in power? AI or its human creators?

Consider this real-world example of organizational power dynamics around AI. In one technology startup, a CEO with dual PhD degrees in philosophy and electrical engineering promotes AI as a humanistic tool for organizational excellence. His communications inspire employees with messaging about AI's positive contribution to society. However, his engineering team, comprised of young technologists who embrace technological determinism, believes their CEO has become merely an AI-babble spokesperson. The head of the AI development team begins planning to reprogram the CEO's public communications to better reflect her vision of machine superiority. When a junior engineer discovers this plan, she turns to ChatGPT for advice on handling the ethical dilemma, illustrating how AI becomes both the problem and the solution in organizational power struggles.

This scenario isn't just fiction. It's a cautionary tale about the risks of AI with a solution provided by AI. Ethical dilemmas in organizations have become more frequent with the acceleration of tech-infused business strategy.

Critical Thinking: The Essential Human Skill

So, how do we work in harmony with machines? And how does the collaboration of the two lead to higher performance and better outcomes? Critical thinking is essential as a tool to develop and maintain intelligent systems and processes. As our elementary school teachers told us: "Check your work." And we would add to that "Check your conscious and unconscious biases."

The output of any system, analytical dashboard, or report, should not be considered the truth at face value. Critically evaluate all information that the system has to process that may contain faults and errors. Like it or not, at most points in any process, information from humans is subject to human error, distraction, misspelling, or the like. Just consider why we are asked to enter an email address twice to confirm it.

Critical thinking ensures the right questions are asked to get as close to the truth as possible when the machine outputs and reports. And critical thinking also ensures meaningful analysis and interpretation of that information. Over the years, we have worked with a variety of clients who have historically made decisions based on visually appealing dashboards that represent only a limited version of the truth for the organization. Any dashboard reflects what has been input as key data points, but the quantity and types of errors in this first stage of the process can drastically influence reported results. For example, using critical thinking to identify errors can bring clarity to leadership to bridge the gaps between perceived and actual performance. Or protect leadership from spending money on creating products and services that don't matter to its market.

Today, critical thinking has become even more urgent. We've seen AI-generated content presented as fact, deepfake videos that appear authentic, and algorithmic recommendations that seem objective but carry hidden biases. The human ability to question, verify, and contextualize information has never been more valuable.

The Future of Work

According to researchers at Oxford University, 47% of US jobs in 2018 were envisioned to be at imminent risk of automation resulting from AI and advances in machine learning (The Economist Data Team. 2018). McKinsey's comprehensive study on automation and workforce transformation, in 2023, found that while there may be enough work to maintain full employment through 2030, the transitions will be very challenging, matching or even exceeding the scale of shifts out of agriculture and manufacturing we have seen in the past.

As both execution and oversight become automated across industries, McKinsey research shows that about 60% of occupations have at least one-third of their constituent activities that could be automated, requiring substantial workplace transformations and re-thinks for all types of workers, not just knowledge-based workers. (McKinsey Global Institute. 2023)

Algorithms and machine learning are already controlling what we see, what we have access to, and how our movements are monitored day to day. Society generally sees technology as a positive opportunity to improve the human condition. It's true that with AI and machine learning, humans now do fewer repetitive tasks. The hope with AI pioneers was that work would become more thoughtful and fulfilling.

However, the reality has been more complex. While some workers have been freed to do higher-level work, others have been displaced without adequate retraining or reskilling opportunities. New forms of digital surveillance and productivity monitoring have emerged, creating different pressures on workers. The gig economy has expanded partly due to AI-enabled platforms, but this has also led to job insecurity for many.

There is no question that AI and machine learning applications continue to benefit organizations. However, we now understand more clearly that these technologies are not a panacea to solve all problems and challenges. In fact, they have created new problems we're still learning to manage, ultimately offering new opportunities for an advanced AI career track.

What AI Can and Cannot Replace: Business Wisdom

One of the most popular debates is what AI won't replace. The answer isn't found in blanket statements about human superiority or technological inevitability, but in understanding the specific domains where human intelligence remains irreplaceable.

Where AI excels is clear: It reads many radiology images better than trained radiologists by seeing things hidden from the human eye. It can perform repetitive, information processing, and analytical work faster and more accurately than humans. It has been auto-piloting jets for decades. AI will do exactly what humans tell it to do without pushback, gripes or citing union regulations.

But here's what AI cannot replace: Business wisdom cannot be automated.

- **Strategic intuition and pattern recognition:** Some individuals are highly adept at spotting market trends before data confirms them. These individuals have keen observational skills to sense shifting customer needs before they're articulated or when there is not enough data to see the trends. They also understand the emotional drivers of purchasing decisions which influence how to recognize market opportunities that don't show up in data.

  AI is based on predicting the future based on past data. It is the sum of its parts and can only assess, analyze and respond using the training data it has been given. It cannot recognize the subtle competitive threats based on industry dynamics that are observable to individuals with foresight. AI cannot replicate systems thinking that sees the larger picture holistically.

Understanding cyclical business patterns may not be evident in short-term or historical data. There is still a gut instinct when it comes to pattern recognition.

- **Reading the room and organizational dynamics:** Humans, not machines, are better at reading unspoken organizational politics within an organization. Reading these behaviors can help understand and manage team dynamics and hidden agendas. An organization, including its workforce and customer base, is not objective. Each individual comes with his or her own motivations, goals and power positioning to play ball, derail, rise above, seek vengeance and more.

  AI is not a great tool to analyze behavior in real time to reveal organizational politics and individual motivations. A video recording of a meeting tagged with data points may reveal behavioral motivation, but it's unlikely that AI can accurately predict what is happening below the surface. People, not machines, build trust across diverse stakeholder groups and can navigate complex partnerships.

- **Crisis management and public communication:** Anyone who has had to manage an organizational crisis knows this is art, not science. Responses to persistent reporters' requests are made on the fly, based on understanding unfolding events, not waiting for the final data-driven conclusion. Experienced leaders can make decisions with incomplete information balancing short-term pressures with long-term sustainability.

  Wisdom provides the ability to distinguish between healthy and unhealthy risks. AI has no sense of when something seems to be too good to be true to determine if it really is. Nor can it assess the ripple effect of decisions. AI is literal, sequential and basically clunky, although it seems cloaked in brilliance when it spits out 15-second solutions.

  Credible leaders manage public perception during challenges. AI cannot face the media and their cameras to provide context with empathy and vulnerability. Human wisdom makes leaders relatable and trustworthy, the communication skills essential to leading through a crisis.

- **Cultural intelligence and change management:** Machine learning systems cannot recognize and understand resistance to change below the surface. Interpersonal communication is not in AI's toolbox to recognize when to push versus when to pull back. AI is largely one-on-one, not one-to-many, and still needs to be prompted. It cannot maintain morale during difficult situations and provide inspiration to lead a workforce forward. It is culturally mute.

AI and the Workforce: Redefining Work

So, how will we redefine work in the future? Many fear AI and most misunderstand it. We prefer to think of AI as Augmented Intelligence. We are not talking about a legion of robots marching in and taking over every job. Although, robots are going to make life easier and augment certain jobs.

Robots are already serving as bartenders, delivering meals and groceries, drones are airlifting Walmart purchases, and machines are doing repetitive tasks in commercial kitchens (chopping vegetables), making pizzas, and serving as companions for the elderly. And even more useful, voice assistants are going to get smarter, and as Professor Christopher Atkeson, a roboticist at Carnegie Mellon University predicts, able to engage in meaningful dialogue, reports Jennifer A. Kingson at Axios (Kingston, J. 2022).

When it comes to intelligent machines, we are talking about using a suite of tools to perform repetitive tasks alleviating human workers to focus on the complex work that requires wisdom, intuition, and qualitative judgment. AI then becomes the cog in the wheel of industry.

AI is already deeply embedded into our work culture, and the workforce needs to contend with it daily. Customer service is performed by bots; online resumes are screened by bots and subscription services are managed by algorithms. AI should be considered a tool and an enabler, not a solution; again, think of it as augmented intelligence, rather than artificial intelligence. It will alleviate repetitive tasks and free humans to do more complex, subjective work. AI is a factor and key element that you must address and plan for in how you design the workforce, evolve your organization, and service your current or future customers and each is critical to your transformational success.

The reality is that new job categories are emerging; Chief AI Officer, Chief AI Ethics Officer, AI Innovation Officer, AI Policy Officer, AI prompt engineers, AI auditors, algorithm bias specialists, and human-AI interaction designers.

The proliferation of AI technologies has prompted new job expertise to discern the real from the false, in both language and images. It's our responsibility to understand AI's capabilities and develop the skills and talent to manage it.

Organizational Challenges and Opportunities

In a short period, the global population has grown from 2.5 billion to nearly 8 billion today. The explosive growth demands that organizations need systems and processes to grow accordingly. AI and ML technologies help organizations manage their current customers and predict where the business is headed in the future. Since change is a constant and the exponential growth of technology makes it nearly impossible for leadership to master, there is additional danger of an organization's inability to shake off institutional knowledge filters and legacy cultural norms. Yet agility, pivots, and embracing technology is a necessity for any organization to survive.

The challenge for any organization is the speed of change, resulting in the lack of expertise, skill set, operational capacity, and agility to adapt to new technologies. But that cannot be used as an excuse in a highly dynamic and changing world. AI/ML is only going to grow, making organizations even more dependent on the technologies.

And that requires organizations to be vigilant, ensuring that the data they program into systems are accurate, that they constantly monitor these systems for human error, and that they are stringent about avoiding conscious and unconscious bias in the input and interpretation of AI/ML data from information to intelligence.

Today's organizations are grappling with practical implementation challenges: How do you train a workforce on AI tools while maintaining quality standards?

How do you integrate AI into existing workflows without disrupting operations?

How do you measure the ROI of AI investments when the benefits may be intangible or long-term?

How do you maintain customer trust when AI is making decisions that affect their experience?

These aren't theoretical questions anymore. Companies across every industry are wrestling with them daily.

Maintaining Human Agency: The Path Forward

AI is here; it isn't going away, and we either rise to the occasion or sit back and wait for what comes next. So, practically speaking, the human factor is critical in the AI/human interface. Blind trust in AI is a risk. You need to ask the right questions including whether the AI model is current, the origin of the data and if a decision is specific and contextual or a generalization. You cannot let go of the necessity for critical thinking, your own decision-making, and your own choices.

The double-edged nature of AI is perhaps most evident in how it can simultaneously create and resolve ethical dilemmas. Consider when an employee faces an ethical dilemma and turns to AI for guidance and receives thoughtful, structured advice on how to handle the situation. AI provides the scripts for different scenarios, walks through potential outcomes, and reminds the employee to ground actions in core values. The problem also becomes the solution.

This highlights a crucial point: AI can be an objective source of information to help counter our subjectivity and emotions that often compromise our decision-making. AI can also be a tool to cut through times when we are so paralyzed with anxiety, fear and confusion that we simply cannot formulate the path forward.

But the key is maintaining human judgment about when and how to use these tools. Organizations must develop frameworks for:

- **Questioning AI outputs:** Is the AI model current? What is the origin of the data? Is this decision specific and contextual or a generalization?
- **Preserving critical thinking protocols:** Even when AI provides helpful analysis, humans must evaluate the reasoning, consider alternative perspectives, and make final decisions.
- **Building AI literacy:** Understanding both capabilities and limitations helps organizations use AI as a tool rather than a crutch.
- **Maintaining ethical oversight:** Human judgment about right and wrong cannot be delegated to systems that operate without conscience or subjective nuances.

Tech analyst Jerry Michalski has a prescient view: "Multiple boundaries are going to blur or melt over the next decade, shifting experience of being human in disconcerting ways: the boundary between reality and fiction … the boundary between human intelligence and other intelligences…the boundary between human creations and synthetic creations…the boundary between what we think we know and what everyone else knows."

As humans continue to embrace more advanced AI, the perceived necessity for humans to 'think' loses ground, as does humans' belief in the necessity to learn, fully comprehend and retain information. The traditional amount of effort humans invested in the past in building and honing the critical thinking skills required to live day-to-day and solve life and work problems may be perceived as unnecessary now that AI is available.

The Path Forward: Enhanced Intelligence

As computer scientist Yejin Choi, a 2022 recipient of the prestigious MacArthur genius grant notes, "Currently I am skeptical. I can see that some people might have that impression, but when you work so close to AI, you see a lot of limitations. Whenever there are a lot of patterns and a lot of data, AI is very good at processing that. But humans have this tendency to believe that if AI can do something smart like translation or chess, then it must be really good at all the easy stuff too. The truth is, what's easy for machines can be hard for humans and vice versa."

Unlike humans, who have both conscious and subconscious thought processes, AI mostly uses statistical and symbolic reasoning. It struggles with tasks that require intuition, gut feeling, and implicit knowledge, which often inform human critical thinking and emotional intelligence. Those traits will continue to be irreplaceable in the evolving job market.

Chaos can make you crazy. Uncertainty can lead you to poor decisions. Disruption can fill you with anxiety. Change the narrative. Stop trying to build a plan that assumes stability. Don't rely on the past to make sense of the present. Create a future informed by its own context. Start building a system that thrives in volatility. Make decisions about who we will be in 2035, don't sit back and see what happens. We have a choice; we have our minds to help inform who we want to become. We can rise or fall to the occasion. It's up to you.

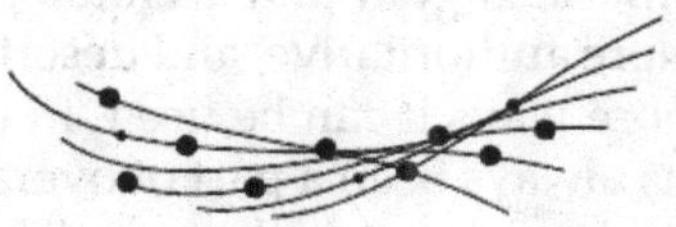

Chapter 7: The Economics of Intangibles

"Any organization that produces data, uses data, analyzes data, and sells data must come to grips with the economics of intangibility to determine the value of invisible assets without physical form. The valuation of a transformed business model must operate without hype."

The Intangible Nature of Data

Data, an outcome of digital and technology, has become today's currency. The deeper, more authoritative, and descriptive the data, the more valuable it is and the more ways it can be used. In terms of context, digital to some seems as if it has always been a part of overall business and society; younger generations surely feel that is the case. They don't know a world without access, utility, interaction, and mobility. Others may still relate to digital and all the underlying technology as fairly new, particularly when considered in the context of a sizable business construct. Across many different opinions, digital and technology continue to dynamically change. To almost everyone, however, technology, AI, and frontier technologies are still considered to be the Wild West. Digital became a force in the late 1990s as companies attempted to innovate and take advantage of the web. What was often overlooked was the speed, or lack thereof, across consumer adoption. It took a while. Why? Human beings take time to adapt, and they must accord the construct of change as valuable to themselves individually.

Despite the promise of digital, many organizations still struggle with how to value something that remains intangible.

Is a web browser something that can be touched?

Harkening back to the Industrial Age and even going back thousands of years, what was produced was tangible and could be held. An apple grown on a tree was sold in a market. A loaf of bread was baked and sold in a bakery. An automobile was assembled from parts, sold to an individual, and then parked in a driveway. Each is touchable and physical and therefore valued as tangible.

Businesses and consumers alike have the challenge of aligning value to something that can be interacted with visually and digitally but cannot be touched. The rapid adoption of mobile, utility-oriented apps and social media reflects how each relates to meeting a specific need, want, or ways to communicate. Tech can clearly fulfill basic needs. But it is limited by all generations who still desire the physical construct of meeting and communicating with other humans physically. Ironically, digital enhances the execution of physical interactions.

Data of course has always existed in the form of physical written word, tables, or logs, but digital and technology have provided the venue, foundation, and basis for data to be collected, curated, and managed across systems almost invisibly. Data informs the execution of work and actions across the day-to-day lives of individuals.

We rely upon accountants and financial professionals to dive deeply into financial data and report out to others with reports and summaries. One often hears, "Tell me only what I need to know." We expect data analysts and scientists to take on the heavy lifting to assess, interpret, and manipulate data and then report in a summary form. These experts are necessary because those asking questions and wanting information are uncomfortable with a medium that seems untouchable … intangible.

Data touches almost everything in life in these early days of the 21st century. But it is intangible to most of us. It becomes real when Alexa tells us we are out of detergent or Siri tells us is we have lost our way. The organizational and societal benefits of amassing quality data and leveraging that data for research, analysis, generation of insights, measurement of performance, and even monetization via productization cannot be underestimated.

The way we work, interact, purchase, and behave has also changed because of technology and digital, but we remain anchored in the physical world. A world that is now tracked across nearly every point. But don't start feeling too confident; the metaverse is quickly approaching which will dramatically change how we view ourselves as intangible in an intangible digital environment.

The Influence of Intangibles

Before we dive into details about the intangibility of data, let's consider the types of intangibles now influencing the market, our finances, and even how our information is managed and stored.

How do we put a tangible value on the invisible or the "digital?" How do we value the intangibles of cryptocurrencies, NFTS, and blockchain? We operate in a dynamically changing marketplace and economic arena and many assets are in the domain of intangibles. Jon Maeda said at TED in 2007 that "I'm waiting for everyone to realize that all this digital stuff, ones, and zeroes, all of it, is as real as dirt (Rawsthorn, A. (2007)." That 25-year-old statement was prescient by any standard. The premise that we are moving into an economy of intangibles only makes sense if you talk about it in the context of it already being here.

Blockchain

All business leaders need to understand how new financial models will affect their businesses; rest assured that next-gens are already on the intangibles bandwagon investing in cryptocurrencies, creating NFTS, and advocating blockchain as a transparent, authentic business practice.

What is blockchain? According to inventor Scott Thrift, "This is a novel and interesting development in the history of the internet, which is 25+ years old at this point." By way of giving context to the blockchain, he uses email as an example. "An electronic piece of mail is crafted on a computer terminal and sent out. The unique pattern of data that represents your email and every word in it is captured, including where it is going in an instant. That specific pattern of ones and zeroes is scrambled and distributed to the receiving terminal where the pattern is unscrambled, and you read your email. It's practically magic yet the fundamental nature of the process is a physical exchange of electrical patterns from one terminal to another. Email is a more subtle, quieter version of the telegraph/morse code (Thrift, S. (Nd.)."

Blockchain technology is simply an evolution of the fundamental protocols we administer to make things happen with networked computers. Here's a simple metaphor from Thrift. "Remember chain letters? Those annoying email chains were popular in the early days of email. Send this to 20 people and we will send a dollar for each person to x charity. Imagine if there were one person with a master leatherbound ledger in a basement somewhere, who was tracking each email the chain letter was sent to and marking the ledger with a UTC timestamp and IP address. The chain (itemized list) of ledger admissions would represent the travelogue of that letter. If the person was able to keep track of each entry without fail, that list would be an indisputable record of the whereabouts of that letter. It would be impossible of course, as humans make mistakes and cannot stay up 24 hours a day, seven days a week all year long every year."

Enter computers and the 24/7 internet (a global network of computer terminals) and many interesting things can take place. So, again, what is blockchain? Thrift explains, "It's a distributed ledger managed by math/time, not people. The 'distributed' part refers to the fact that these ledgers are not a single leatherbound book in a centralized singular basement somewhere, because of the nature of a global network of computer terminals, this ledger is decentralized"

The fact that the ledger is decentralized means that if someone storms the castle and tries to take a singular ledger that someone has been crafting, it won't matter, because the same ledger, with the same timestamps, makes use of the fundamentally decentralized nature of the web by existing in multiple nodes at once. Same information, same ledger, distributed across the web."

Bitcoin

What is happening now is the internet of money and what is coming next is a trust-less economy called the ownership economy and the creator economy. Thrift explains. "Now replace the chain letter with a singular item, let's call it Bitcoin, and let's use this distributed ledger technology for a math-driven method of verification. Let's set a maximum number of coins at 21,000,000. Each coin has its own initialize date and its chain of traceable events (in the form of transactions) that make up its history. All the transactions utilize complicated cryptography methods to hash out where everything is and what just happened in the last ten minutes across the entire network of what is currently 18+million coins in circulation.

"The nature of the advanced cryptography Bitcoin utilizes to update the entire distributed ledger requires an immense amount of computing power. The more transactions, the more processing needs to happen to chisel recent transactions into the chain of each existing, active ledger (coin). As Bitcoin continues to grow in popularity, more transactions will take place which will require more cryptographic problem solving to take place to thread all the transactions together. This is work that miners get paid in Bitcoin to do. The only way to release more of the 21,000,000 total Bitcoin, is to perform the work. Every four years the total output from mining is reduced by half. All the Bitcoin will be distributed in total by 2140.

"If we have no networked computers, no internet, no electricity, the physical property of electricity itself, then we have no Bitcoin or email. Bitcoin was designed to be a way to give someone money online in such a way as to not be able to double-spend. It's like sending an email but in this case, it has value. What's so interesting about Bitcoin is that it uses this distributed ledger tech to manage a store of value. Instead of the chain letter, we have a chain coin. The price fluctuates because of a mixture of mining tech, human psychology, and genuine scarcity."

Thrift concludes, "It's possible something else could come along and displace it.

There are 14,000+ coins currently, each with their take on utilizing a decentralized ledger, each with hundreds of millions of coins in some cases instead of just 21,000,000." He predicts that the number of tokens will go from 14,000 to millions and millions of tokens.

NFTs

An NFT is simply a way of authenticating a digital product. There is "only one of those things" or at least one that is verifiable as the original by looking at the chain where it was minted. It's a way for artists to finally be able to cash in on their creations and is a way to market anything and everything including a Spiderman movie when Sony made 86,000 collectors' items (NFTs) available.

Third-Party Safety Net

In the case of Bitcoin and blockchain tech in general, what we have is a system that works because of math, not a third party. Thrift says, "It's called a trust-less system because there are no humans etching lines into a ledger, no mistakes, so we can trust the data because everyone all over the world has access to the same distributed ledgers. It all boils down to a way of verifying something beyond the shadow of a doubt. It's about using the internet itself to authenticate something. Its machine-powered provenance works to verify digital goods physically. Blockchain is revolutionary because authenticating things in the digital realm has been a tough nut to crack. It would have to start with money, can we verify a form of money with computers so that there is no chance for double-spending or hacking?

"Bitcoin itself has never been hacked because it is currently running nodes, of all the same info, which is updated every ten minutes on over 10,000 computers worldwide. To hack it or do a double spend of the same coin, one would have to hijack all 10,000 computers at once worldwide, which is theoretically and practically impossible."

Intangible Asset Measurement and Value

As data's manifestation remains in the digital and virtual realm, humans struggle with understanding and determining its value. What measures do we use to calculate the value of data in how it is used to enhance human activity and intelligence? Information derived from data can be viewed by digital manipulation into categories, alerts, and calculations, but the data itself remains untouchable.

When we look at the traditional performance measures for businesses, IPOs are based on EBITA valuations that remain multiples based on promises and guesses of customer purchase and brand loyalty. The rapid pace of technological evolution adds complexity as young upstart companies can quickly gain market share without making any profit. With all the dynamics at play across rapidly changing consumer preferences and adoption, exacerbated by short attention spans and diminishing brand loyalty, financial performance is even harder to predict in tangible terms without contextual analysis along with the intangibility of technology, digital, and data.

Valuing data remains a struggle for many organizations given our desires for high-level summary data and visualization. We want major points communicated to us, see results in the short-term, and generally do not want to expend mental energy to derive our meanings and conclusions.

We will continue to be dependent and rely on data. Given the influence of technology and data, we will need to expand what we are capable of, enhanced by both. Our critical thinking skills will need to expand to accept how our lives will manifest in the digital realm.

Economist Erik Brynjolfsson, Director of the MIT Initiative on the Digital Economy "examines the effects of technologies on business strategy, productivity and performance, digital commerce, and intangible assets. He was among the first researchers to measure the productivity contributions of IT and the complementary role of organizational capital and other intangibles. His research provided the first quantification of online product variety value, often known as the long tail, and developed pricing and bundling models for information goods (Brynjolfsson, E. (Nd.)."

Any organization that produces data uses data, analyzes data, and sells data must come to grips with the economics of intangibility to determine the value of invisible assets without physical form. The valuation of a transformed business model must operate without hype or built on numbers pulled out of the air. Our default behaviors and perceptions, the gut correlated to institutional knowledge, easily take control and divert us from the true task at hand. Defining and valuing intangibles must be done concretely with a basis. This is the classic dilemma of determining value from vapor.

Technology and Intangibles

The implementation of technologies and the focus on data is critical for change and transformation for any organization in today's digital world and runs counter to normal human desires and behaviors. Yes, some technologies can be implemented quickly to address a specific issue within an organizational silo or operational process. But most technological implementations take considerable planning starting with the understanding and detail surrounding current operational processes. How humans interact and complete work manually or technology-enabled directs how new technology will complement, address, or alter how work is accomplished. Digital is often not tangible; when it is, it is represented by lines of code, system diagrams, or front-end interfaces that serve the purpose of creating tangibility.

AI, like digital, manifests in intangible outputs. Yet, machine learning can produce touchable results. For example, how many sales resulted? How many customers interacted based on how AI communicated with them? AI and machine learning can lead to major learning, insights, and intelligence that can lead a human or a system to make decisions. Those decisions can be valued and correlated to sales, production improvements, customer engagement or conversion, market penetration, and more. Remember that humans first and foremost educate and inform the AI and machines and humans create the algorithms. Working with AI compels us to continuously exercise our critical thinking and assessment skills to evaluate the outputs. That human need will always be required regardless of how smart we believe we have made the technology and artificial intelligence.

The struggle in the age of digital and AI has been how to directly value what is represented, curated by, or produced by technology. The inability to effectively and realistically value the intangible continues to challenge organizations and investors alike. Put simply, with technology it is important to assess what data you need, how to collect it, and how to analyze it – all of which are intangible.

Intangibles and the Human Factor

One of the seminal debates in the current digital economy is how to establish the tangible or perceived value of data and technology when results may only come in the longer term. The human desire to see short-term tangible results is compromised.

Human behaviors geared towards immediate goal attainment and reward often are one of the causes of derailment from long-term value-producing efforts and commitments in an organization. Our desire for rewards, and the dopamine boost that comes from such, transcends to nearly all humans across an organizational enterprise via team and individual performance plan bonus and reward systems, sales staff compensation plans, and even SMART goals that denote how "success" is defined.

Although short-term satisfaction is generally tangible, it may work against longer-term goals that are intangible. Most short-term thinking is based on the feel-good principle and a sense of accomplishment to "feel" good and to "feel" satisfied. The consequences become apparent in the long term, whether you consider the future to be a month, a year, or five years from now. The omissions, faults, or gaps created by the short-term decision-making and desire for tangibility become apparent. What happens then? We tend to assign blame.

Applying blame to others obscures the fact that we as humans overlook our faults and actions. Notably, we look for a tangible solution instead of facing a future that seems ambiguous and intangible. This is particularly true for organizations. Too often day-to-day operations, setting and implementing strategies and change, and transformation initiatives and attempts are designed as short term. It's hard work to challenge a culture built on institutional knowledge and norms that define good work and high performance on legacy, short-term measures. Tensions are always present when a goal is set to make it perceptually real and, of course, tangible. The results confirm the desire to receive rewards and please oneself and the team by solidifying the notion that the action taken, or task completed was the right one.

Consider the anxiety about intangibles in context of interacting with stakeholders, whether they be external or internal—particularly the board. Making progress in the short term, often regardless of its long-term impact, addresses an immediate item or issue, is usually applauded, and confirmed as a movement in a positive direction. Again, it results in tangibility for the action taker or task completer who gains the satisfaction of accomplishment and receives accolades. Across the spectrum, all participants receive the dopamine burst and relish a job well done. Mission accomplished.

Another element at play is the human inability to hold long-term attention, particularly when something is intangible and is intended to manifest in the future.

The long-term path to developing deep data on organizational performance, its customers, and prospective customers, and implementing large technological systems requires long-term commitment and attention. Each demands that humans stay focused on each step across a long period that moves sequentially to goal attainment.

Even if human behavioral defaults and desires are recognized and accommodated, the attained goal in the long term may remain intangible. It is a persistent fact of life that must be recognized in the digital age. Organizations will remain challenged to visualize tangible elements in sets of data, technological systems, outputs, products, and services. As we become more adept at integrating technology into our lives, we will become more comfortable with intangibles and learn to place real value on financial systems, data, and digital assets. One true thing: humans will always continue to evolve and as a result create evolved systems to serve their needs and desires. Placing value on intangibles, becoming comfortable with the intangibility of what is around us, doing business with cryptocurrencies, and perhaps even using blockchain will become the art of doing business in an evolving digital marketplace.

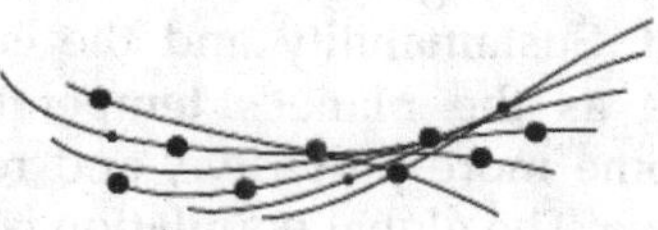

Chapter 8: Consumer Culture and Sustainability

"Sustainability is not limited to the future of natural resources and health of the planet. Sustainability is a key pillar in the life of any organization. It is important for change or transformation initiatives. Essentially, sustainability equates to relevance."

Sustainability Writ Large

We may be approaching the end of consumption as we have perceived and known it. Sustainability and the environment are taking center stage worldwide as the planet's temperatures increase, storms intensify, droughts become more pervasive, and resources are becoming scarce and more expensive. The global population is shifting and becoming more diverse which alone will create resource site-specific scarcity as pockets of the dense population will strain local systems. Demand for services and selected resources will also significantly increase to care for an aging population.

Next-Gens Saving the Planet

Research reveals that millennials, Gen Z and Generation Alpha are more concerned about the health of the planet than other generations, and as such are becoming more judgmental about the lifecycle (cradle to grave) of products. There is a growing chorus of young voices raising alarms about the environmental demise and negative consequences to future humanity. Swedish teenager activist Greta Thunberg became a voice of reason for the planet and a critic of big business for younger generations almost overnight. She reminds governments, businesses, and consumers that the default of short-term decision-making is risking future generations. She has raised the level of consciousness about the risky decisions and actions of multinational businesses including increased production, expanded markets, and increased short-term profit term.

Conscious Consumers

Gen Z will continue to put tremendous pressure on brands to act on sustainability and social causes. Marketwatch has researched Gen Z and reports that the most important social cause to Gen Z has been combating climate change or protecting the environment, followed closely by racial equality and social justice. Social justice is closely aligned with sustainability and will have a big impact on brands, companies, and investing—such as environmental, social, and governance (ESG)—for decades to come. The report adds that "It appears the younger generations are changed from prior generations to be better handlers of the intangibility of elements of their lives and are thinking more and broadly on how their actions (via consumption) impact the future world (Dorsey, J. (2021)."

The power of next-gens in the sustainability conversation is no idle threat. McKinsey reports that companies should be attuned to three implications for this generation:

1. Consumption as access rather than possession.
2. Consumption as an expression of individual identity.
3. Consumption as a matter of ethical concern.

"Coupled with technological advances, this generational shift is transforming the consumer landscape in a way that cuts across all socioeconomic brackets and extends beyond Gen Z, permeating the whole demographic pyramid. The possibilities now emerging for companies are as transformational as they are challenging. Businesses must rethink how they deliver value to the consumer, rebalance scale and mass production against personalization, and — more than ever — practice what they preach when they address marketing issues and work ethics," states McKinsey (McKinsey. (2020).

Wall Street and Sustainability

The increased interest in Wall Street on sustainability may lead to more change than consumer movements. The CEO of a think tank heralded the outcomes of the 2021 Glasgow Summit "The roadmap and momentum are there; so, the big issue is now an acceleration (Dennis, B, et. al. (2021)." While another observer pinpointed the shortage of money needed to effectively meet the challenges of global warming. The money is not only needed to offset the damages and growing threats to smaller nations, but also to fund new enterprises and innovations which to date have been largely focused on mitigation.

One unexpected outcome from Glasgow was the revelation that governments lack the political will to drive and sufficiently fund the ESG vision. First, governments move too slowly. Second, governance based on global meetings and forums requires constant compromise. Enter the private sector and the profit motive morphs into prosperity purpose. Just look at the amazing 180-degree pivots of financial institutions and their investment principles (not merely strategies), such as Blackrock. The nature of Blackrock's pronouncements tells us that their commitment to ESG objectives is not a marketing trend but is, in fact, a seismic shift in values.

Blackrock's Co-CEO proclamations from Larry Fink and Barbara Novick truly manifest the scope and potential scale of the climate conversation.

In letters to their clients, climate change is positioned by rejecting "greenwashing" and mitigating risk. The profit motive is recast as the prosperity purpose, i.e., a broader sense of obligation and the "massive amount of capital that will be needed to address climate change" (CEO Novik's words).

They aren't kidding around: This direction requires divesting portfolios of assets that do not serve ESG objectives. And going even further, Fink says all future investments by Blackrock will be filtered through standards that the financial institution is developing to focus on a company's ESG commitments and its measurable progress toward achieving such commitments. This new standard is the measure for advising clients on sound and meaningful investment decisions and go or no-go investments. Novik unequivocally sums it up, "We believe that sustainability should be our new standard for investing."

It Takes a Global Village

Wealth and money, combined with political, social, and economic are what will drive sustainable initiatives. If you follow the money, it becomes clear which American generations are going to come to the rescue. The baby boomer generation (numbering 72 million) is sitting on $60+ trillion in assets and over 45 percent of the nation's wealth resulting in $14.5 trillion in investable income (Marketmix. (Nd.). But even with their collective wealth, they have become the invisible generation. Their millennial children have reported assets of $5 trillion and Gen Zs, in the hundreds of millions. So, if viewing wealth as the basis for investments, Gen Zs and millennials do not yet have deep enough pocket assets needed to fund and invest to drive climate change. Millennials are consumed with college debt, mortgages, marriages, and children while Gen Zs are still emerging and will not be fully in the workforce until 2030. But in the long term, it will be on the shoulders of millennials to invest in ESG assets and support innovative technologies, research, and NGOs with seed money to start and funds to grow. This in part will come from their earnings but estimates have it they will inherit upwards of $66 trillion in assets (Hoffower, H. (2022).

Sustainability, social justice issues, authenticity, and civic responsibility are lightning rod issues for the next-gens. For ESG initiatives to be funded, everyone needs to be in on the plan. The private sector and investors can support new technologies, institutes, and NGOs to encourage their quest to meet the climate crises head-on.

Choice and the Planet

The thrifting trend has manifested across next-gens. Allegiance to brand names and expensive items worshiped by prior generations has given way to basic life needs viewed simply as commodities. As such, thrifting and a commodity mindset are likely to stick as a long-lasting consumer behavioral change.

Over 17 tons of clothing and textile waste are tossed into landfills annually in the US. Subscription commerce and renting is a new paradigm to partially solve the landfill problem. Imagine traveling to another city without luggage and having all your clothes, shoes, equipment, and accessories waiting for you at your hotel when you arrive—all selected based on your style and the local climate. The paradox of choice described by sociologist Barry Schwartz states that an overabundance of just about everything with multiple brand extensions and infinite flavors of the same product has made so many CPG businesses a race to the bottom (Wikipedia. (Nd.). Confronted by so much choice, consumers default to no choice, and brands have no choice other than to discount unsold products.

We are over-stored and overstuffed, and, with the exception of true luxury goods, most products have become commodities. To maintain that elite status, Burberry burned $37.8 million in unsold inventory in 2017, which does not appear to be a sustainable strategy for them or any organization. Nike, H&M, and others have also come under fire for torching their products. Amazon reportedly destroyed 130,000 unsold and returned items in a single week (Cole, B. (2018).

Too much choice results in frustration and confusion. Too many choices require more contemplation and more information to determine what the "right" choice is. Typically, humans do not like to expend too much mental energy on anything. Comfort is a default motivation and predictability is the norm. Fewer choices are received positively as there is a reward of satisfaction from choosing from a few without being overwhelmed.

Humans generally also do not like to make their own decisions without counsel; the offering of too many choices compels an individual to reach out to their professional or personal networks to gain recommendations and feedback. This process delays instant satisfaction or gratification but has proliferated the power of influencers, particularly on social media.

The speed and convenience of delivery of goods and services have somewhat acerbated the interim step of seeking advice.

In terms of sustainability, the demand for speedy delivery has related costs in terms of resource consumption that may do more harm to the environment than instant gratification justifies.

Too much choice thwarts the intended positive experience of shopping and fulfilling a need resulting in creating satisfaction through a release of dopamine. Anxiety facing too much choice causes adrenaline to increase and feeds into a flight or fight response. The danger in too much choice is that brands risk becoming commodities. When consumers choose calm and comfort over new, allegiance to any brand can be replaced by a simple alternative.

Consider the Oreo Cookie, now available in an abundance of flavors and blends including Birthday Cake, Apple Spice, Red Velvet Cake, and many more. To expand and achieve a never-ending pursuit of growth, niche, customized products are created in the hope of gaining new market share across different life stages. Unfortunately, as organizations proceed with the same plans and strategies, consumers are met with far too many choices and instead seek what is familiar.

The opposite of the intended outcome is coming to pass across the millennial, Z, and Alpha generations as too many choices fly in the face of strong values of frugality. The prevailing mentality is "Why spend money for something new when buying something that is slightly used is cheaper and comes with a feeling of satisfaction in working towards sustainability?"

A Community of Prosperity with Purpose

The contextual factors and variables are at play in how the world's population is changing. Younger generations advocate healthy respect for others, color blindness, and new gender norms which are changing social history. This will drive the support of diversity and inclusion around the world.

The fractious nature of today's society has become an interesting case study to reflect generational clashes. Older, less diverse, and inclusive generations seek to hold onto the past before technology and digital even entered their lives. Highly connected younger generations perceive the world differently. Their hopes and dreams are based on an inclusive future less predicated on political and institutional structures. Their aspirational vision of global connectedness clashes with the deeply ingrained nationalistic belief system of some who put the country before the globe.

A vision of inclusiveness and acceptance stands in sharp contrast to most leaders in societal power positions. However, as with any major societal shift, be it a pandemic, natural disaster, or terrorist attack, change becomes permanent and embedded into recent history that informs the present, forms the beliefs of those who grow up in the present, and shapes the future. We must envision ourselves as a community of cohorts, a vital networked source to accelerate solutions and move the sustainability needle forward before it's too late.

Choice and the Organization

Sustainability is not limited to the future of natural resources and the health of the planet. Sustainability is a key pillar in the life of any organization.

Why is this important to an organization's change or transformation initiatives?

A changing consumer culture opens the door for organizations to take on due diligence activities that remove past practices, institutional filters, and biases. A rich, deep contextual analysis of what culture and its values represent can change or transform an organization to meet the emerging demands of its market. It requires acquiring and analyzing available data, how that data came to exist, and what that data represents to align the insights and information to ideations, conceptions, or grounded plans of change or transformation.

It also requires critical thinking and assessment skills to achieve outcomes that produce knowledge on the importance of human behaviors and beliefs in an organization's structure, how it maintains and grows its workforce, and how it acquires and retains customers.

Contextual analysis of the factors and variables at play in the marketplace shows that humans' acceleration of the adoption of technological innovations that have flooded society with choice. Technologically enhanced production leads to more variations of products that organizations can offer with more niche flavors and blends because operational expenses have decreased.

However, most organizations are seeing their revenues decrease as society is too saturated with product offerings. This is compounded by a large segment of the population; boomers are trading in material things for experiences ...and healthcare. Also, as the population growth stagnates fewer individuals will be entering the acquisition life stage.

Finding the Context

Contextual analysis in how any organization navigates the macrotrends and understands the shifts in marketplaces and consumer behaviors is where you come in. Managing change and mastering transformation requires you to use your critical thinking skills and map out what you believe you and your organization need to know across Micro, Meso, and Macrosystems. Remember, be objective, be critical, remove biases and remove institutional knowledge and filters.

Inflection points

What are the hot buttons that impact human behavior, and therefore the culture at large? Many of these triggers fall into a negative domain but flip the conversation and there are opportunities to address these social, cultural, and behavioral concerns with services and products.

- Polarization
- Nationalism vs globalism
- Sustainability/climate change
- Inclusion/diversity
- #metoo
- Anti-consumption
- Student debt
- Over stored, overstuffed
- Privacy/security/hacks
- Terrorism/mass murders
- Social media pressure/FOMO
- Alienation/loneliness
- Indifference
- Aging population
- AI/robots' role in the workforce
- Immigration/border security

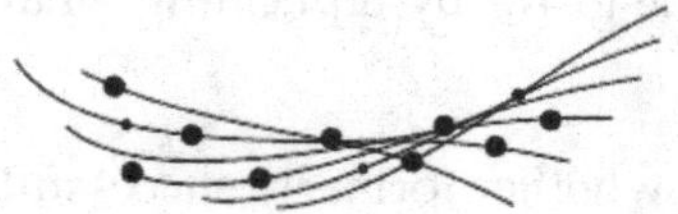

Part Two: Structures and Constructs

Introduction: Defining the Organizational Construct

Organizational constructs are changing ... quickly. Your path ahead isn't taking a Red Queen approach—falling into a spending trap and copying what worked for a competitor or other organization. The path ahead needs to bring forward a strategy and vision that is truly representative of your business, products, and services, customers, target markets, and unique value. The challenge is that in the past, your voice may have been authoritative and credible because you were a major brand within your category. Scarcity often drives market penetration but in a hyper-digital world, upstart competitors can quickly change the game to make what was scarce ubiquitous. That means dominant brands are no longer the sole source of relevant products, information, or services. In fact, we're facing a commodity glut where products, information, and services are so available from so many different sources they have become commonplace. Given today's digital dynamism and opportunity, the marketplace is full of new competition, forcing business models that were once highly successful to change. Therefore, all the more reason to ensure your organizational construct is relevant.

A dramatic example of change is in media: a magazine, major local newspaper, radio station, or television studio historically was unchallenged with little, if any, competition. Customers had limited options then, but now their options have grown exponentially to the point that in today's environment, the market is saturated with too much choice.

This dilution of brands and saturation of options changed what was once a rich market for one or a few and is now spread across the many. Therefore, the revenue potential is more limited, the reach is decreased, and expenses are significantly elevated to acquire customers. Increasingly, organizations may not be able to sustain themselves, let alone grow, by replicating what first made them successful.

Media is not alone; many organizations today, whether formerly successful professional associations, niche publishers, or local retail businesses face the same challenge of remaining relevant in a cluttered marketplace where customers are in control of what they want and where and how they want it delivered. Let's look briefly at the changes retail has had to make, almost overnight. Retailers were faced with the dilemma of developing a robust digital ecommerce business with no expertise to execute it. Similarly, retailers had no understanding or in-house talent to activate data and analytics capabilities to cater to tech-savvy customers. Stores became showcases and distribution centers. And Amazon knocked it out of the park with free shipping and returns, which legacy retailers tried to match, forcing untenable losses. Substitute your organization for any retail case study and you get the point about why organizational construct matched with market orientation is so critical.

Consumer choice is dictating how organizations need to cater to all stakeholder demands. Increasingly, customers want products and services that are customized to their needs. They also want transparency in the supply chain, authenticity in brand marketing, and want organizations to align with their values—including inclusivity and diversity.

Look at your company from your customer's viewpoint. Is your organizational construct designed to serve your customers? Or to serve your own corporate needs? Customers develop loyalty to your products, services, and brands because you reach them in a unique way and resonate with their own values. Digital and new technological opportunities continue to transform society and human behaviors. To be successful, your organization must be responsive to customer demand and flexible enough to build, buy or partner with technology solutions to give you the cutting edge.

Organizational construct also refers to the culture you build. At the core of this construct are unbiased communications and active listening. Leaders need to remain ever vigilant in not falling into the trap of believing that everyone thinks the same way they do. And that goes for the workforce as well as customers.

An organizational structure is highly influenced and impacted by environmental constants and its business constructs. For context, the Society for Human Resources Management states "Organizational structure aligns and relates parts of an organization so it can achieve its maximum performance." And further describes it as, "Organizational structure is the method by which work flows through an organization. It allows groups to work together within their individual functions to manage tasks. Traditional organizational structures tend to be more formalized—with employees grouped by function (such as finance or operations), region, or product line. Less traditional structures are more loosely woven and flexible, with the ability to respond quickly to changing business environments (SHRM. (Nd.)."

Organizational structures and models can be hierarchical, functional, horizontal, divisional, matrix, team-based and networked. Organization structures have evolved since the 1800s and in the Industrial Revolution, individuals were organized hierarchically to manufacture a product moving along the assembly line. Frederick Taylor's scientific management theory optimized the way tasks were performed, so workers performed only one task most efficiently. In the 20th century, General Motors pioneered a revolutionary organizational design in which each major division made its cars. Today, organizational structures are changing swiftly—from virtual organizations to other agile structures. As companies continue to evolve and increase their global presence, organizational models may embody a fluid, free-forming construct, member ownership, and an entrepreneurial approach among all members.

In redesigning an organization to operate with speed, agility, and high intelligence, it is also crucial to keep in mind that as humans, we are resistant to change. Without building an empathetic runway to effect organizational change, you will most likely fail in redesigning, Reengineering, and reimagining your organization. As great as your vision may be, if you can get the critical mass of your employees to understand and buy into the changes, your vision will be sidelined by subterfuge and sabotage.

We operate in a transparent world. As important as the organizational structure is, what you stand for is even more critical. What any company does is searchable on the internet, or even worse, broadcast relentlessly through social media. Customers and employees want to know what your company stands for. This is not a nice prosaic sentiment. It impacts the success of your enterprise.

Harvard Business School did a study of high-performing organizations around the world to see if there's a correlation between their financial performance and corporate social values (Deloitte HBS. (Nd.). The study found that "businesses that are agile and keeping ahead of the curve in terms of market changes and customer needs are the businesses that are also progressive and socially responsible. These companies all had a strong synergy between their financial performance and how they treat and attend to the community and social needs (Deloitte HBS. (Nd.). "

Technology is changing at a rapid pace and both the opportunities and challenges increase with each jump in progress. However, technology shouldn't drive your business construct.

It is a tool that enables your business in achieving goals and objectives. All too often an organization chooses a technology tool, system, application, or platform simply because an employee used it at a former employer or because of an IT individual's personal preference or comfort level. The other trap is choosing a technology tool, system application, or platform because a vendor provided a great demonstration, often as the first sales call you received. Organizations need to clearly define their business and goals and seek technologies that can enable achieving specific goals. Without a relevant technology strategy, a hit or miss approach is frustrating and over time creates resentment … and ultimately, failure.

Your success — or failure — will be determined by the human factor. As we consider the dynamic changes across the market and the world, it's the human elements and defaults that upend efforts to change and transform. A trap is when institutional knowledge based on perception, not critical thinking, is used exclusively to solve problems. Typically, these perceptions run in contrast to reality. Plus, the impact and influence of our defaults can play havoc with understanding, problem-solving, and decision-making. Often, planning, conception, and implementation ignore or play workarounds with the human factor. Using technology to sidestep human behaviors as a silver bullet to overcome any challenge can be fatal.

Part Two discusses organizational structures and models which are representative of Mesosystems in context of the human factor in achieving transformation initiatives. We also examine structures in relation to environmental constants and business constructs — and how they separately and together impact decision-making. We dive into the typical defaults that impede change and reveal strategies that unlock the power and potential of your organization to move forward with transformation-based plans and initiatives.

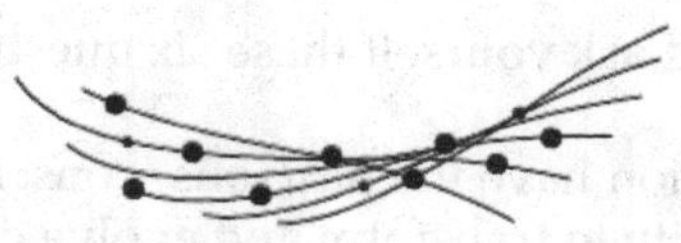

Chapter 9: Mindshifting: The Organizational Trap

"Operating in a comfort zone in the 21st century is perilous. Unconscious retention of past ideals, command-and-control direction, and failure to recognize changing behaviors internally and externally create significant bias. They may feel comfortable, but personal biases feed your interpretation of how to effect change. Bias can impede transformation and achieving ultimate end goals. Biases also influence how your workforce and customers respond to you."

Hidden Bias

Take a pause and ask yourself these six questions. And be honest:

1. Does your organization have unconscious/conscious biases that might be limiting your ability to transform and evolve digitally?

2. Have you convinced yourself that "great minds think alike" and your team will simply follow you and activate the change you seek?

3. Do you value habit and tradition over progress and success? Have you accounted for the different levels of acceptance of transformation across the culture?

4. Is your management focused on command-and-control and making assumptions that the workers will simply come along with you?

5. Are your products/services/experiences designed based on your intuition and your organization's institutional knowledge about what you believe the market wants—or have you leveraged data or even AI to infuse your customer-centric transformation?

6. Have you recognized the role and importance of subconscious behaviors and decision-making in how you interact and communicate with your customers?

If you answered no to even one of these six questions, you are unsustainable in today's marketplace.

So, what are you going to do?

We have surfaced a long list of factors at play that leads many businesses seeking to transform into organizational traps. The myriad of trapdoors leads to deep wells, silos, and barriers that inhibit progress and ultimately transformation.

At times, the trapdoors are easily recognized, while many remain overlooked as they are hidden away in tried and true, but outdated tools, approaches, techniques, and behaviors that historically kept the business moving along. Operating in a comfort zone in the 21st century is perilous.

Unconscious retention of past ideals, command-and-control direction, and failure to recognize changing behaviors internally and externally create significant bias. They may feel comfortable, but personal biases feed your interpretation of how to effect change. Bias can impede transformation and achieving ultimate end goals. Biases also influence how your workforce and customers respond to you.

Diversity and Inclusion

What are diversity and inclusion?

It's not just a multicultural workforce represented across race, ethnicity, and religious beliefs or based on acceptable percentages. Diversity in the commonly accepted definition as it relates to a business is crucial. Businesses should seek to reflect humanity and all its variations across their workforce and customer base.

Equally or perhaps even more important is the diversity and inclusion of values, cultural norms, and thoughts that represent the large swath of humanity. How you manage, transform, and effect change internally and externally must recognize that humans do not all look alike, think the same, have the same values, or have the same biases.

Amber Cabral, the author of *Allies and Advocates*, states, "Inclusion is going to become an enduring line item in the annual budget, a part of the organizational fabric instead of something companies engage in to superficially to check the box. Companies are going to spend the money even if they previously thought they didn't have it—like they have had to spend to address supply chain issues—because DEI is no longer just a nice to have, it has become an essential business function to prioritize. Employees and potential candidates aren't just asking for it, they are leaving when an organization's culture isn't working for them. Consumers are also growing savvier by the day. it will no longer be enough to make an inclusive stand on Instagram. Customers are looking for clues that companies are serious and committed in the way they create, sell and market whatever the product (Cabral, A. (2020)."

All individuals are the sum of their parts; their experiences and the knowledge they have gained over their lifetimes. The parts represent internalized values, experiences, and learned behaviors that beget current thinking and action. The parts also embrace one's thoughts and approaches to solving problems, creating change, or coloring in a future vision. These parts are always present consciously and unconsciously and come to play in decision-making interacting with others.

All individuals have inherent biases across the spectrum that influence what they say, the word choices they make, and how they believe their message is being received. Most often individuals do not take the time to think critically nor step out of their boxes and process how others may perceive what is being said, how it may be internalized, and if the intended meaning is conveyed and understood.

Take a closer look at your own leadership, ethos, and communications.

Are you applying critical thinking and pausing to reflect on the diversity of thoughts and values of those you need to effect transformation and change?

Are you manifesting and incorporating that thinking and recognition into how you lead and communicate?

Do you recognize how what you are saying is being received
and interpreted?

Evolution and Bias

Evolution has shaped human history, and who we are as individuals and as a society. The innate drive to adapt and survive manifests across each human being in how he or she thinks, responds, and interacts. The evolution of the subconscious and how it controls thought processes creates perceptions of what is comfortable and perceives risk and threats play a bigger role in our lives than we imagine.

Our personal defaults are embedded on a deep level that we don't readily control (although we assume we do). Humans go through their days believing they are making conscious decisions based on their needs and wants, but it is really the subconscious that is in control. Personal defaults set by the subconscious are what flavors every reaction, perception, and observation.

Given that personal defaults are ingrained in every individual, we often miss recognizing how wedded we are to these defaults which often make us resist change, risk, and accept "the different." Individuals constantly seek comfort, defined by one's personal defaults and driven by one's subconscious. Any external stimuli can impact the perception of comfort. We seek comfort to know what's coming next, what's going to happen, and how one should or shouldn't react. Any deviation from a comfortable behavior pattern increases stress and anxiety and potentially leads to confusion calling forth a fight or flight response.

Our fight or flight evolutionary programming is operational subconsciously when we enter a new room, perform new tasks out of the norm or when we meet new people. The fight or flight response increases hormonal levels including adrenaline, which is not sustainable over the long term at high levels. The immediate response raises our awareness briefly to handle perceived danger, unexpected change, new situations, or the like. The heightened awareness stemming from stress, anxiety, and confusion internalizes in a mind as fear. Transformation and change are therefore perceived consciously through the lens of fear. Our instincts drive us to a baseline of comfort and the expected. Therefore, we reject change and the "different" and return as quickly as possible to our level of consistency, security, and comfort. That subconscious drive to comfort and fear of change permeates every attempt to transform.

Bias and Communication

Let's be open and honest here, bias exists in anything and everything. Humans are a sum of their parts including their life experiences, values, and views of people and the world. Humans feel unconscious (and conscious) bias most distinctly when they want to communicate with others. A sender (the communicator) wants to send a message and chooses the terms to use and the gestures and facial expressions to best emphasize the words and various points he or she wants to make to the receiver. This bundle of communications skills is used with the intent of having the receiver understand word for word the direct meaning the communicator is trying to get across. The leader, manager, and innovator seeking change and transformation make assumptions that the receiver has the same life experiences, values, and views, and therefore understands implicitly what they are trying to communicate. This assumption is most often false—even in closely-knit families.

Although as humans we want to believe we have a wide range of shared knowledge and experiences—we do not. Senders who seek to send messages surrounding change must recognize that the receivers will be interpreting and applying everything that is shared, said, and communicated written or verbally with their filters and perceptions.

Let's remember that the workforce wants to feel comfortable. They want the expected that provides for comfort. Any change that is presented to them or includes them is directly correlated, internalized, and interpreted on a very individual level.

This interpretation is aligned with any individual's own life experiences, values, and views. Sadly, these interpretations can lead to feelings of disruption, anxiety, and fear. An innovator may get excited and relish personal anxiety and the resulting hormones they feel, while the day-to-day workforce may feel the opposite.

Being sensitive to others' feelings and viewpoints separates great leaders from failures. Seeking homogeneity is a misguided goal. Some leaders may be tone-deaf as they seek to bring together groups of people (individuals comprising the workforce) that look, think and act exactly the same. Sure, homogeneity can sometimes be helpful, and decision-making can be quicker. Everyone thinks the same, everyone agrees, and therefore everyone moves in a single direction. But if everyone thinks the same, blind spots remain, gaps are created, and a silo may become even steeper.

In addition to the how what, and why of the sender's intent and how a receiver interprets it, the receiver is often at a different level of acceptance (or even considering awareness) of the changes and transformation that the sender has already thought through. We have two individuals at two different points on the curve attempting to communicate and interpret from two very distinct mental states. Our personal defaults are majorly represented via the subconscious and produce biases, becoming strong compromising forces.

Foundation of Shared Knowledge

Shared knowledge is a critical key to success. Collective intelligence is based on interpreted and applied objective data, across the Macro (world, country, region, or locality), Meso (organization), and Micro (representative of individuals and groups of customers, employees, and stakeholders). The dissemination of intelligence then becomes shared knowledge that forms the basis for a shared purpose and organizational responsiveness. Shared knowledge further mitigates and minimizes individual and group ambiguity in how the organization's parts relate to organizational responsiveness.

What challenges shared knowledge is the individual. Individual knowledge is gained through experience, practice, and personal involvement. It is strongly influenced by geographic and socioeconomic factors. It is shaped by day-to-day living, faith, family, and more.

How then do you achieve shared knowledge with so many highly personal moving parts?

Here are a few simple steps:

- Minimize individuals' influences that result from bias and overgeneralization.
- Limit individual motivations driven by the personal gain that impact and influence decision-making and comprise the organizational system.
- Offer an opportunity to create and measure quantifiable goals towards the shared purpose with organizational goal attainment above individual goal attainment.
- Rely on data to remove assumptions and perceptions.

The foundation of a functioning workplace culture is a structure that ensures the organizational parts so that people align towards a shared purpose within a Mesosystem that ingrains organizational responsiveness.

Let's go deeper: There are two types of shared knowledge.

- Individual knowledge is often colored by personal interpretation. Interpersonal communication comprises the sender and receiver and how what is being shared is communicated and how it is received. Since individuals are the sum of their parts, when they communicate with each other interpretation often relies upon a small percentage of shared knowledge.

- Collective knowledge occurs in society over time and builds and evolves knowledge bases across a wide range of subjects. Scientists (social, physical, tech) are constantly expanding the collective knowledge bank with new intelligence. Collective knowledge is generally accessible to all individuals, although dependent upon an individual's desire to seek shared knowledge.

Leadership and Bias

Individual and collective knowledge influence our personal defaults. Our defaults, therefore, can become our undoing. Operating with faulty assumptions about those around us, including those that comprise our workforce and customers, leads to peril.

As a leader, look around your company: Does everyone look like you?
If you were to compare your workforce to your customer base, do they look the same in terms of diversity?

If you look at your board, does it represent the same diversity of your customers and workforce?

When all these organizational platforms align, you can be pretty sure your company is making good decisions in the best interests of all your stakeholders.

There is another bias lurking under the surface in many legacy businesses and organizations; leadership's fear of evolving digitally to be competitive in today's marketplace. Just like customers and the workforce, leaders subconsciously have their desire for comfort and manifest behaviors that may run counter to acceptance of change brought on by other factors or stimuli.

The bias is not only fear of technology itself but a sense of discomfort about the legion of engineers and data marketers who look at the potential and opportunity of your business differently. When a business stagnates it misses the opportunities that may provide for growth including innovation and taking an outside-in viewpoint to recognize the needed change. We don't know what we don't know and what we don't know often makes us feel uncomfortable and suspect.

Behaviors (reactions and actions) and thoughts can transcend insecurity, which manifests in suspicion that the others who are thinking differently are ill-intended and will cause harm. The reactions and actions impede progress and recognition of how to transform. And on top of that, tech experts speak a different language which is not understood or appropriately interpreted as the sender and receiver have different knowledge and shared experiences and therefore different reactions to what is said and what it means.

Progressive leaders who seek to know what they don't know and are understanding of how humans communicate, and act have enough confidence to enlarge their talent pool with tech-savvy experts—of all ages and particularly those that see the opportunities digital provides and understand how digital can enable transformation.

Management Style

Is your management focused on command-and-control and making assumptions that the workers will simply come along with you?

Many traditional leaders are faced with a young, digitally savvy workforce that speaks a new tech language and as a result, fall back on a command-and-control style of management out of self-defense. A defensive position stemming directly from insecurity and being uncomfortable inhibits forward movement and a business's ability to transform.

Technology and digital have impacted society in deep and fundamental ways. Younger generations have integrated technology and digital and every aspect of their lives. It has moved beyond an enabler and has become a catalyst in how the world and society are viewed and therefore how one views a workplace, job, and career.

Marcie Merriman, EY Americas cultural insights and customer strategy leader, reflects that "The pervasiveness of mobile technology has made it virtually impossible for Gen Z to switch off. Wherever they go, their phones—and their 24/7 connection to the online world—go with them, which means there's no transition zone, no moments in the day when they simply relax and reset. Tech aptitude has become tech addiction and constant gain of information and knowledge is the norm. With knowledge comes thoughts and thoughts from around opinions and ideas. New ideas and opinions that may be important to successfully transform (Merriman, M. (2019)."

One may believe that the constant digital activity of Gen Z is unsustainable—mentally, emotionally, and even physically. This is generally the observation of older generations who base their judgments and perceptions on the limitations of their own experiences. To be fair, the ways society is being transformed may be to the human race's advantage—or it may be leading to a fundamental shift that isn't an advantage at all.

Regardless of the direction, leaders must recognize how to manage and communicate across a digital and technology-savvy workforce.

From an AI perspective, the fear of AI and the potential drove of robots replacing jobs can debilitate a workforce. Leadership needs to manage tech systems and platforms judiciously to augment the intelligence of the workforce, not replace it.

As we have stressed, the Achilles Heel of many leaders is their inability to recognize that not everyone in the organization thinks the way they do.

This blinders style of narcissism can be the downfall in any path to transformation. In *The Wise Advocate: The Inner Voice of Strategic Leadership*, the authors describe how leaders "tend to deal with day-to-day challenges by invoking one of two patterns of mental activity, and thus engaging the brain circuits associated with them. The Low Ground is associated with transactional leadership: making deals, solving problems, designing incentives, or making expedient decisions for short-term goals. The High Ground, on the other hand, is strengthened by decisions that go beyond solving problems and are oriented toward long-term viability, breaking out of self-defeating constraints, and seeking more fundamental change (Kleiner, A., et. al. Nd.)." One could argue that the most effective leaders balance the High and Low. Great ideas and vision without the ability to execute them becomes the proverbial "road to hell paved with good intentions."

According to Art Kleiner, Jeffrey Schwartz, and Josie Thomson, authors of *The Wise Advocate*, there are seven key factors in strengthening your skills as a strategic leader (Kleiner, A., et. al. (Nd.)." Many are related to neurological and psychological impulses, patterns, and behaviors. We've recast these seven principles into a matrix to help leaders transform their business models, cultures, and formulas for success.

1. Mastering impulse and emotion.

    Hint: knee-jerk reactions can be behavior-modified over time to chart a course that engages stakeholders and encourages them to get on board with a transformation vision.

2. Thinking about what other people are thinking.

    Hint: they are not necessarily thinking the way you are, so innovation, transformation, and change may be more a threat than a path forward. Surround yourself with intelligent people who think differently to ensure a diversified, holistic look at any given situation.

3. Becoming habitually self-aware.

    Hint: "applied mindfulness;" awareness of your thought and behavioral patterns "You can't help other people move past their comfort zones unless you are self-aware enough to recognize your own hidden thoughts and motivations and reframe them where it matters."

4.   Integrating integrity with pragmatism.

Hint: short-term gains or long-term success? In the private equity world, pragmatism wins out more often under pressure to deliver to shareholders. But here's a thought: short-term desire is an addiction; long-term desire is purpose.

5.   Managing the side effects of success.

Hint: highly innovative and creative people generally think of themselves as the "wise owls" that sit alone on the top branches looking down at everyone else, convinced that the co-workers on the ground don't get it and aren't the smartest person in the room like they are. These brilliant minds are not necessarily the best candidates to promote into management to run groups of people that they need to nurture, coach, and manage into success.

6.   Expanding your aspirations.

Hint: this is only possible by working in a collective environment with deep collaborations, inclusive teams, and diverse ideas that weave into a holistic solution for transformation.

7.   Building a legacy.

Hint: Were you successful in transformation? Or did you split your company apart with a dysfunctional workforce that was not supportive of making your vision a reality? Remember the biggest barrier is not bringing your managers and employees along with you on the transformation journey. It takes a village …

Customer Centricity

Ask yourself if your products/services/experiences are designed based on your intuition and your business' institutional knowledge about what you believe the market wants? Or for your customers? Are you developing solutions for nonexistent problems? Have you leveraged data or even AI to infuse your customer-centric transformation? Customer-centricity is a necessity today since consumers are calling the shots for how, when, and when they want to be served. This includes everything from content and promotion to customer service. Success is built on the total customer experience or journey with your products and services, not the result of a random buckshot approach.

Your customer and member demographics are shifting. Your revenue sources are changing. Your products and services may not be as relevant as they once were. Millennials and Gen Z will soon be the majority of your customers (and your employees) and represent the majority of your existing or potential revenue. Your organization now exists in an omnichannel world in which one customer or member interacts with you across all your channels, wherever, however, and whenever they desire. And your customers' and members' preferences are changing. They want digital products, services, and interactions along with your traditional physical world products, services, and interactions.

In the digital world, every organization has access to intelligence and insight. You can know firsthand, in real-time how products are services are performing, what customers and members feel and say about the organization, how content is being consumed and shared, and where successes and challenges are experienced in the sales cycle. With the sophistication of digital platforms and technology tools, data can be collected every second of every day and stored in anticipation of providing the analytics needed to inform and educate.

We live in an omnichannel world where digital and mobile dominate. We suffer from an overload of communications to the extent that we often default to making less informed choices out of frustration or being overwhelmed. Exacerbating this complexity is the new role of the buyer as the chief marketing officer requiring customized information when, where and how he or she wants it.

- The volume of communication via email, text, and notifications is increasing exponentially.
- Social media consumes more and more of an individual's time.
- Digital information grows daily, challenging formerly successful value and loyalty propositions.

Whether you are in a B2C or B2B marketplace, prospective buyers have changed their behaviors and fundamentally changed how they seek and acquire what they want. B2C and B2B buyers research everything with a few finger swipes, instantly accessing the digital community for product reviews and price comparisons with your competitors. The buyer is in the driver's seat, and you have limited opportunity to influence them if you operate with a traditional marketing model.

It is critically important that publishers, associations, nonprofits, and for-profit organizations understand their digital audiences, know where their content is resonating, how it is being shared, and measure its reach. A content and audience strategy ensures retention of current audiences, how to reach new audiences, and the development of editorial and content plans to maintain relevance and be ever adaptable.

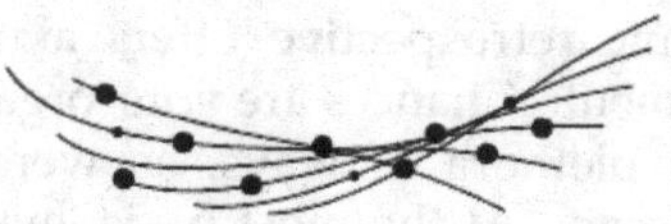

Chapter 10: Is Your Value Proposition Still Relevant?

"We all know that change is constant. Staying a step ahead of the trends is critical to remaining relevant to your audience. The North Star for providing value and meaning to stakeholders is your value proposition. And that promise needs to constantly evolve to reflect your stakeholder's needs and market conditions."

Redefining Value

A post-pandemic retrospective offers a unique opportunity for discovery and reassessment. Chances are your organization was disrupted by the pandemic in a plethora of ways, as were your staff, members, subscribers, and customers. At the most basic level, the pandemic forced people and organizations to work differently, and in that process, to re-evaluate what is important, both personally and professionally.

Marketing General Inc.'s Membership Marketing Benchmark report revealed some sobering findings about the impact of the pandemic. "In addition to the news about meetings taking a hit, membership has suffered a blow as well: Nearly half (45 percent) of associations surveyed reported a decline in membership renewals, doubling the rate of the previous year. And associations say they've seen a decline in new member acquisition (37 percent) compared to those who've seen an increase (29 percent) (Marketing General Incorporated. (2021)." With inflation continuing to rise, our hunch is that even many publishers and subscription companies are or will begin to see similar declines in subscription retention and limited success in new customer acquisition.

We all know that change is constant. Staying a step ahead of the trends is critical to remaining relevant to your audience. The North Star for providing value and meaning to stakeholders is your value proposition. And that promise needs to constantly evolve to reflect your stakeholder's needs and market conditions.

Value on the Line

Your value proposition reflects your insight and understanding of what your members, subscribers, and customers need from you. According to HubSpot, "Your value proposition is the core of your competitive advantage. It clearly articulates why someone would want to buy from your company instead of a competitor. A great value proposition could be the difference between losing a sale — and closing it (Coleman, B. (Nd.)."

Unfortunately, many executives assume that their value proposition always stays the same as a constant of sorts. And worse, they assume that the value proposition is the same for all active and prospective members, customers, and subscribers.

The most common mistake is confusing the value of what you sell with what you think is valuable. For example, selling on price is a sign that you have not done your homework. If your primary reason for someone to buy a product or join your organization is a discount, you are missing the opportunity to sell your intrinsic value. The race to the bottom of discounted sales also tells the prospective member, subscriber, or customer that you don't understand them. Professionals don't look to an association for a bargain. They are searching for insights, education, and inspiration to do their jobs better. Individuals join, buy from, or subscribe to organizations for personal reasons that may consider affordability, but generally, they are looking to effectively fill a need or want with valuable solutions offering many benefits.

Yes, everyone wants to save money. But a low price is not what creates customer loyalty, a trusted relationship, and member engagement. Tadiran Group CEO Elad Peleg was quoted in Fast Company that "Legacy companies have a hard time accessing their inner startup because they're used to their tried-and-true processes." He proposes, "looking beyond revenue growth and closely studying what products and services people actually use, and whether they sustain their engagement over time (Peleg, E. (2021)."

Demonstrating that you can uniquely meet a need better than anyone else eclipses discounts as the reason why someone will decide to join your community and/or make a purchase. According to Benchmark research, "Associations reporting increases in their new members and overall membership in the past year are significantly more likely to say their association's value proposition is very compelling or compelling."

According to Marketingmo.com, "A customer retention strategy is about keeping the customers you've invested in to acquire. And if you're in an industry where your customers make multiple purchases over the years, your entire team should be very focused on retaining those customers. How? By delivering service that's consistent with your value proposition and brand (MarketingMo. (2021)."

Defining Your Value Proposition

A value proposition is not a slogan, tagline, or market positioning. To be effective, a value proposition must answer three key questions to ensure success. By addressing these questions, you can craft a meaningful message about your value and keep your workforce aligned on the same page in understanding your core operating principles.

1. How does your product or service solve problems for your members, subscribers, and customers?
2. What specific benefits can members, customers, and subscribers, expect from you and how do these benefits address their needs?
3. Why should members, customers, and subscribers buy from you rather than your competitors?

To create a functional value proposition, you must understand the different segments of your customer base and how the value proposition needs to be fine-tuned for each segment. For example, for an association, career advancement needs vary by career stage. Thus, continuing education needs to be designed for a range of professional experience and job responsibilities.

For a publisher or subscription company, content and product need to evolve to be relevant to the life stage or career stage of a customer or subscriber. The organization must speak directly to stakeholders' needs and wants to provide continuing value. Communication of the value proposition is key, and messaging needs to vary by segmented preferences and interests.

Don't Guess—Test Your Assumptions

Assumptions about what members, customers, and subscribers need are made by staff, at all levels, including the board; and yet, these assumptions are rarely tested. Many organizations research customer and member needs, but this tends to be based on one-time studies with no follow-up. And out of cost and time restraints, there is often heavy reliance on descriptive data obtained through surveys. Rarely do organizations that take the time to conduct mixed-method and ongoing research to test assumptions, develop hypotheses, and identify changes and trends.

Your Value Proposition Is an Investment

Treat your value proposition as an investment, a critical asset that is the crux of your ongoing strategy. We have worked with a variety of clients to help them develop their value propositions. This is a cross-functional effort that takes critical thinking to challenge the status quo and identify questions that need further investigation. It also takes talking with current, former, and prospective members, customers, and subscribers. And it takes time to test, learn and refine.

It is not easy work, but it pays off handsomely.

Double-digit acquisition and retention rates result from value proposition deep dives. The value proposition development process identifies needs and then develops products with features that can be communicated as benefits to meet these needs. The further development of messaging drives action based on the benefits. The process helps map various products, programs, services, and experiences offered to the individuals comprising the market based on their needs by segment.

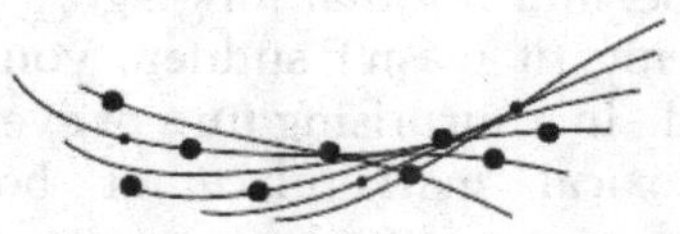

Chapter 11: Reengineering: What Business Are You In?

"Organizational success nearly always comes as a Faustian bargain: you may achieve the short-term success you sought often focused in one silo, but is it the first piece of the puzzle or will it remain an isolated success? Is it sustainable and is it a catalyst for the greater transformation you seek?"

Are You Asking the Right Questions?

Once upon a time, and not that long ago, your organization was crushing it. Then suddenly (it wasn't sudden, you just weren't paying attention) things changed. In a surprising turn of events, you find yourself operating in a paradoxical marketplace of both complexity and commoditization. You are expected to demonstrate stability, sobriety, and safety—while at the same time differentiate your sophistication, services, and capabilities. You realize you have become a David competing with the Goliaths that have increasingly come to control the tech-based playing field in your sector. And your slingshot has become obsolete. Time to get real and redefine the ethos of your organization and whether it resonates in today's digital marketplace.

Here's a useful exercise: Ask yourself these questions:

1. Do you have entrepreneurial leadership?
2. Do you operate in a siloed, calcified culture, stuck in tradition and habit?
3. Does your talent pool have the skills you need to succeed?
4. Do you invest in digital innovation and tools?
5. Is there a sense of thoughtful urgency and speed?
6. Are your leadership and cultural mindset still mired in "fighting the last war and entrenched in the past?"

Your answers can reveal your primary barriers to change.

Organizational success nearly always comes as a Faustian bargain: you may achieve the short-term success you sought often focused in one silo; is it the first piece of the puzzle or will it remain an isolated success? Is it sustainable and is it a catalyst for the greater transformation you seek?

The barriers will impede forward-thinking, operational dexterity, and nimbleness as they most relate to the human condition and the reluctance to change. And they prevent you from shaping your future to be competitive and relevant in a digital marketplace.

Mastering each of these six issues is the overarching goal in defining what business are you in. The push and pull of desire also influence businesses. As creators, employees, leaders, and managers of an organization, we behave and make decisions based on the same human evolutionary programming in terms of how our business acts, grows, and matures.

Our constant and ever-present need is to have predictability, correlating the present to the past with a comfortable expectation of how things run and what results in we can expect. At the same time, we're not comfortable in stasis over the long term. We desire new experiences and new challenges. The key is to balance the two.

What does all of this have to do with your own business?

Leaders, managers, and employees face an existential challenge when it comes to transforming a business model. Resistance to change and not taking risks is the intuitive norm, and therefore sets up roadblocks and resistance to change.

The customer/subscriber interaction has fundamentally changed; your audience is well-informed, fluid, and random. Loyalty is not guaranteed. With the increasing amount of free content, you are competing with 100 billion Google searches a month.

Business buyers have been shaped by their consumer shopping experiences. This isn't surprising considering business customers are exposed to the same dynamics, community networks, and opinions that influence individual consumers. In light of changing consumer dynamics, organizations are redefining themselves to be relevant in the digital economy.

So, we ask again, what business are you in today?

Clarifying the Models

The customer is the single most important factor in any business. How you serve each customer defines the winning strategies going forward. When it comes to identifying what your business and market orientation are, consider these three models: business-to-consumer (B2C), business-to-business (B2B); and business-to-professional (B2P). Whatever your business model, the basics still apply: You must offer a solution that meets a need.

- Business-to-Consumer (B2C) are business transactions conducted directly with the consumers who are the end-users of its products or services via ecommerce or retail establishments.

- Business-to-business (B2B) refers to a situation where one business makes a commercial transaction with another organization. Transactions are typically conducted through proposals and direct face-to-face sales.

- Business-to-professional (B2P) is a model that markets products and services designed to advance an individual's career or practice by an organization, association, or business.

Each model has its value proposition. For B2C, it includes how to save money and time; have fun; enhance personal status; share affinities; create memories; support personal growth and maintain physical health. B2B is designed to help customers increase profits and decrease expenses; increase market share and productivity and enhance personal careers. The B2P model can enhance personal career growth; increase status; provide access to proprietary information and key people in the industry and offer a group of like-minded individuals.

The purchase journey is slightly different for each model. The chart highlights the major differences.

	B2C	B2B	B2P
AUDIENCE SIZE	Mass	Targeted	Targeted
DECISION MAKER	Single Decision Maker	Group Decision Making	Single or Group Decision Making
INFLUENCERS	Family Friends	Accountants, Lawyers, Competitors, Salespeople, Referrals, Employees	Employer, Colleagues, Professor/Teacher, Family
PURCHASE PROCESS	Transactional, Single Contact to Close	Complex, Formal Proposal, Multiple Contacts to Close	Single to Multiple Contacts and Engagement to Close
SALES RELATIONSHIP	Minimal	Expert	Personal and Professional

Source: 2040 Digital, LLC

Building Relationship Structures

Your customers, like yourself, behave differently throughout the day. You may interact, consume, and share news and gossip with your friends and colleagues but not share pieces of scientific research that you just read on an association's website. You may check and share sports scores throughout the day but not professional product information that you just read. Decoding these complexities with audience engagement strategies is critical to success in connecting with your audience in meaningful ways when they want to be connected. A highly engaged audience is the result of personalization and customization. And success can be measured by a range of metrics defined by your company or organization.

All your stakeholders are demanding and impatient. In today's world, your current or prospective stakeholders interact in many ways with your organization and expect you to directly correlate products, services, and content to problems they want to solve or to satisfy their needs. The wants, needs, and problems your stakeholders are trying to solve require new approaches. How your stakeholders behave, seek information, ask questions, and what they expect of you are very different than what you once understood them to be.

Data is the tool of choice to deliver content, products, and services that are uniquely relevant to each customer. Doubling down on data is a prerequisite to executing a customer-first strategy. Some of the most successful business leaders have re-evaluated what businesses they are in and have redefined how to go to market. Strategic insights from leading companies can help provide working models for transformation.

Operating in the data-led, digital-first world makes every business excel to meet the challenge of transformation. For example, on average, a consumer has 900 digital interactions before buying a car. That's why data, creativity, and technology operating seamlessly can deliver a personalized experience at scale, according to Arthur Sadoun, chief executive officer, of Publicis Groupe (Minsky, J. (2019).

John Wren, chief executive officer, Omnicom Media Group has a three-prong approach to a data and analytics strategy. "First, is ensuring that the platforms remain open. We prefer to rent the right data and technology that can improve our agility and client integration at any point in time, rather than invest in legacy data assets and platforms that can easily become obsolete.

Second, we are making selective, focused investments to develop and integrate differentiated tools in one place in support of the services our agencies offer. And last, we have prioritized these capabilities in our key markets…our investment in data and analytics has been made with the understanding that they are tools in service of creativity and content. Our true source of differentiation, our IP, is our ability to bring deep consumer insights to our clients in lockstep with brilliant creative ideas driving business results (Minsky, J. (2019)."

Think of how marketing has changed in response to customer demand. Mark Penn, chairman, and CEO, of MDC Partners, states, "Today's CMOs have been transformed from brand builders to performance marketers focused on measurable results and increasing their use of data, analytics, research, and digital services to connect better with their customers." He adds, "Investments should be in digital technologies that spur growth, not real estate that increases overhead. By bringing together our existing assets, we can offer the client the combination of data, creativity, strategy, research, public relations, and execution across new and old media." (Minsky, J. (2019).

AI and related frontier technologies will have significant contributions to businesses at all levels. These tools are designed to improve the customer experience, which in turn improves your value proposition to your audience. On a meta-level, Sundar Pichai, CEO, of Google, and board member, of Alphabet states, " I think with AI, we are excited that we can give better experiences for users with fewer data over time. And those are the kind of directions we are pushing. At Google Marketing Live, we introduced new ad formats, such as Discovery ads, which offer a new visually rich, mobile-first ad experience across Google properties (Minsky, J. (2019)."

Sales Models

In terms of developing your sales process, is it useful to understand that B2C is product-driven, B2B is relationship-driven, and B2P is reputation-driven?

How do you effectively reach each segment?

There are key drivers for each business model.

B2C: Product-Driven
- Large target market
- Ecommerce is feasible

- Single decision-maker
- Simple buying process
- Brand identity created through repetition and imagery
- An emotional purchase decision based on price, status, sense of urgency
- Mass media awareness (TV, digital, social, print, radio)

B2B: Relationship-Driven

- Small target market
- Face-to-face sales
- Group decision-making
- Longer sales cycle
- Education and awareness building are key parts of the marketing process
- Brand dependent on a personal relationship
- A purchase decision based on business value
- Consultative sales process

B2P: Reputation-Driven

- Small target market
- Ecommerce is feasible
- Single or group decision-making
- Simple buying process—can be complicated by the approval process
- Education and awareness building
- Brand identity created through WOM and reputation
- An emotional purchase decision is based on value and commitment.
- Direct marketing, digital, social

As an endnote, we recommend most companies and organizations consider a move to B2P because today's buyer is in the driver's seat and is calling the shots for customized products and personalized services. The modern buyer is a majority of one, and chances are your business or organization isn't communicating its benefits to customers in an optimized way. Rather than targeting groups, truly understand each customer's needs and sell the value of your products by leveraging how it is a solution to a specific problem to a specific customer. Crafting a well-thought-out value proposition is critical to creating a clear, focused value proposition to market a product effectively.

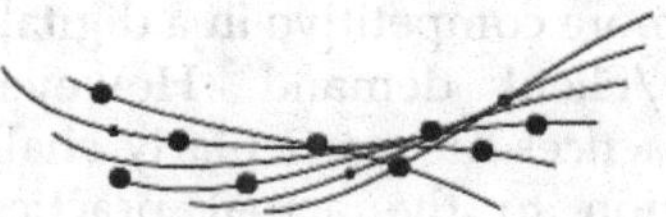

Chapter 12: Organizational Readiness

"Managers and teams need to be ready to accept change
before they can be evangelists for supporting the new model.
Managers and teams need to recognize and understand the
transitions they will experience individually and as a culture."

Be Prepared

Many organizations are passionate about transforming their business models to be more competitive in a digital marketplace, catalyzed by customer/member/client demand. However, organizations with traditional business practices are particularly challenged by bridging the theory of transformation to the actual practice of implementing it. According to Dr. Jeanette Winters senior vice president of human resources at Igloo Product Corp., "Ask any executive if they have change, transformation, reorganization on their agenda and without exception, they are certain to reply: YES. With the pace of change breathing down the necks of all organizations, even the most successful know that they must adapt, transform, and keep up the pace to compete. This applies equally to public, private, and not-for-profit organizations (Winters, J. (2018)."

Assessment and Analysis

But first things first: We cannot overemphasize the importance of determining the state of readiness for transformation.

Conducting an audit of ingrained operational, strategic, and cultural beliefs and processes is the first step to transformation. The single most important tool for this analysis is critical thinking. Agility in self-diagnosis of the barriers to change is a key to transformation. Leaders need to leave their egos and dedication to their own opinions behind. Leaders who are agents of change are further ahead in understanding the need for transformation and are often oblivious to the fact that their employees may not be at the same stage of readiness. By using a cross-disciplinary and cross-functional team to identify a checklist of what needs to change, and how it can change, the journey of transformation begins.

"In understanding an organization's readiness for change, organizations must systematically assess the preparedness of leaders, employees, and the transformation program. Complicating things further, the definition of readiness will vary for each phase of the transformation," according to Jens Jahn, Manuel Luiz, Reinhard Messenböck, and Robert Werner of Boston Consulting Group. They add, "A readiness assessment should serve as the foundation to address key questions: How will we prepare leaders to drive change? How will we engage and empower employees? How will we manage the program to maximize impact? It's not enough to diagnose problems; companies need a clear path forward to resolve problems (Jahn, J. et. al. (2021)."

Common points of resistance to change are noted by Dr. Winters:

*   Too many competing priorities lead to fatigue.
*   Poor track record at successfully implementing prior change.
*   Employee skepticism at all levels.
*   Communication issues stemming from limited leadership alignment.
*   Lack of trust in leadership, in change objectives, or in the organization itself.

Jahn, Luiz, Messenböck, and Werner believe that change is best focused on three levels:

*   Leadership: Executives and managers need to be activated, aligned, energized, and equipped to inspire and drive the change.
*   People: Employees need to be engaged and empowered in real-time through transparent multiway communications.
*   Process: New governance and adaptive end-to-end program management practices need to be in place to ensure rapid change.

Paradigm Shifts

Before creating and implementing a playbook for change, it's worth considering some macro shifts, which should inform any strategy for transformation. Christopher Smith writes in *The New Normal* identifying several macro trends that will change in the years ahead.

*   **IT will become integral to business strategies.**

The world is becoming increasingly digital, and IT will be the driving force behind businesses' strategies in the coming years. IT will fuel ever-increasing levels of efficiency and productivity and new tools and technologies will be the centerpiece of many business products and services.

*   **The workplace will become more digital.**

The rate of change will dramatically affect the workplace, thanks to trends such as automation, digital transformation, and more. For instance, according to a report by the World Economic Forum, 65% of children entering primary school today will end up working in jobs that don't even exist yet (World Economic Forum. (Nd.). Businesses must naturally prepare for such significant changes if they want to stay competitive and relevant.

- **The economic landscape will change.**

The competitive landscape of your industry will always be changing—competition will change, customer needs will change, marketplace dynamics will change, and supplier networks will change (Smith, C. (2020).

The Organizational Nervous System

Organizations today behave like complex information nervous systems. Data flows through them like neural signals. Emotional reactions operate like chemical responses. Misalignment acts like chronic stress. And misinformation functions like noise that disrupts coordination and clarity.

When leaders introduce AI into this system without addressing its underlying health, the organization becomes overstimulated. Communication short-circuits. Decision pathways become overloaded. People react emotionally rather than strategically. The system moves faster, but not smarter.

Healthy transformation requires leaders to cultivate coherence—shared purpose, clear priorities, consistent signals, and psychological safety. Without this, AI intensifies chaos rather than enabling progress.

Cultural Requisites for Change

When planning for transformation, we advise clients to fully assess the nature of their business culture in supporting change. Managers and teams need to be ready to accept change before they can be evangelists for supporting the new model. Managers and teams need to recognize and understand the transitions they will experience individually and as a culture. We have augmented Dr. Winter's factors that come into play for change management.

1. Resilience. "What is the bounce-back ability of the teams impacted? Can the impacted teams muster the energy to take on new, and different battles? How much is turmoil driving change? What is the source of the turmoil? Are employees sufficiently engaged to learn, support, and undertake the necessary heavy lifting of moving from the current reality to the new reality? Consideration needs to be given to the individual's resilience as well as that of the team. Take nothing for granted."

2. Risk Tolerance. "Leadership needs to fully assume responsibility for what is at stake for the employees, the brand, and key stakeholders. Leadership's responsibility is to assess just how far, how fast and WIIFM (what's in it for me) the group can be driven. Public opinion on what matters is another essential consideration. Leadership must be able to answer the question for themselves and to stakeholders alike: how much can we risk and what happens if we fail?"

3. Reward & Recognition. "A key consideration at the outset is what to reward and when throughout the change process. Ongoing recognition of progress needs to be built into the process of change. Change is hard work and should be rewarded incrementally."

4. Strategic Direction. "Strategy is owned by the C-suite or its designees. Not only are they responsible for designing and defining the vision, but they also own communicating the rationale. Leaders must be convincing outside of the boardroom. Leaders must demonstrate that the strategy's rationale is well-founded, meaningful, and appropriate. Clarity of purpose and the ability to convey where the organization is headed takes a great deal of time and effort."

5. Conflict Resolution. "Cultural guardrails on how to address conflicts are essential to effective and productive interaction. People of good hearts and minds can and should disagree. However, the organization must provide clear and well-defined rules to guide effective discourse. Rules of the road are critical, so all participants know how to disagree and resolve conflict – with a positive outcome and minimal casualties."

6. Decision-Making. "Employee engagement surveys consistently rank management decision-making as a low-rated function. Decisions come in many sizes – a process for decision-making should incorporate scope, scale, and situation. Roles and responsibilities need to be defined and reinforced: Who decides what? Who gets to participate in the dialogue? When do the impacted parties receive information? Governance of decision-making can and usually results in highlighting inconsistencies, identifying those who hold too."

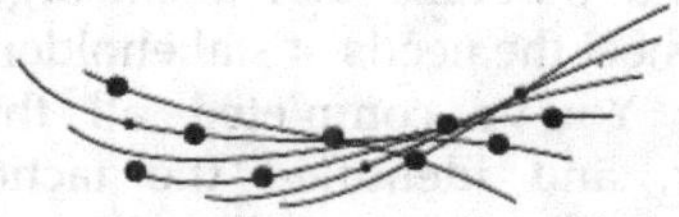

Chapter 13: Operational Assessment

"Operational assessments focus on readiness and the ability to achieve newly set transformative goals. Yet those new goals and attempted pivots at the strategic level often never recognize whether the organization is ready at an operational and process level and with the required staff competencies. And usually, the extent of the underlying challenges comes as a surprise to the senior leadership team."

Ready or Not

You've decided to mobilize your whole organization to pivot from past practices to better meet the needs of stakeholders in a dynamic, quickly evolving marketplace. You've completed all the planning meetings, rewritten the strategy, and identified the tactics. You believe your organization is ready to achieve your new goals.

But wait a minute. Are you sure you are ready?

According to a recent report Lucid conducted with Forrester, "improving operational efficiency" is the #1 initiative that companies are prioritizing as we head into hybrid work. This initiative includes having clear processes in place (Hewlitt, A. et. al. (2021)." Here are some tools and tips for auditing and improving processes across your team and organization.

Operational assessments focus on readiness and the ability to achieve newly set transformative goals. What we have discovered is those new goals and attempted pivots at the strategic level often never recognize whether the organization is ready at an operational and process level and with the required staff competencies. And usually, the extent of the underlying challenges comes as a surprise to the senior leadership team.

Often the infrastructure is so dysfunctional that bringing new strategies to life and achieving new goals simply isn't possible. There are a few revealing signs that indicate a lack of readiness for change:

- Silos or silos within silos mentality with little to no cross-functional collaboration throughout the organization.
- Pervasive resistance to experimentation with a preference to do it the way it always has been done.
- Lack of critical thinking to challenge the status quo and identify upstream and downstream challenges.
- Tendency to report on efforts with inadequate outcome reporting with little to no analysis.
- Avoidance of accountability and bad news.
- Ongoing data discrepancies and a lack of cross-functional KPIs.
- Leaders are ill-informed which translates to a lack of decisiveness.
- Board-level leaders are more focused on tactics than strategies.
- Ongoing years of decline or stagnant growth in subscribers, members, customers, and revenue.
- Inability to articulate a value proposition(s) for different market segments.

- Inadequate market research on the subscriber, member, or customer needs and their relative satisfaction with the organization's ability to meet their needs and wants.

The pathway to success is to thoughtfully identify and fix broken systems and processes (staff, operational and technology systems, customer, and member experience), address the cultural issues and dysfunctional staff behaviors, provide staff training and development, and institute organizational goals that will ensure increased relevancy and engagement with current and prospective members, customers, and/or subscribers.

Ultimately, leadership is needed to set measurable and relevant staff goals, expectations, and outcomes that respect the set strategies, and make the corrective investment of resources before an organization can even begin its forward movement, pivot, or even a transformation.

Faulty Replication of Organizational Models and Structures

Change is hard.

Our natural comfort zone is to stay the same or make small, incremental changes to protect our sense of security — personally and professionally. Our individual value is often not defined within our own control. Individual assessed value and organizational measurement of individual value are defined by assigned responsibilities and expectations.

Industrial Age hierarchical organizational structures exist as impediments to substantive change. And yes, even market pivots are restrained by rigidity in how operations are managed, how the staff is assessed, and what responsibilities are given to staff in top-down mechanisms and control structures.

But the individual and organizational mechanisms, controls, and structures of the Industrial Age are outdated and never propel today's organizations to successfully achieve organizational adaptations to new strategies, goals, pivots, and transformations.

We all know that right? We do, but many fall back on what has historically worked in the past.

The past, however, is not always a safe standard to inform the present or the future. Variables surrounding and encompassing market forces, technology, and socioeconomics are constantly in a state of flux. Operating in current conditions is a complex flow of responding, adapting, or adjusting to the present while trying to predict and prescript the future.

Think of this analogy: The physical environment is a system of parts that integrate to form the whole. An organization is one part of the environmental system, but also a system unto itself with its own integrated parts. Operations and processes are parts of the organizational system. A change in the upper levels of the system (think new strategies, new goals, market pivots, and even organizational transformation) must encompass, determine, and assess whether operations, processes and staff are at a point in readiness to support change and the new.

A Roadmap to Operational Readiness

The process (and it is a process) for assessment of readiness, operational change, and transformation includes a review of:

- Current procedures, policies, service delivery, and inter-departmental relationships.
- Internal and external situational factors.
- Market dynamics.
- Data sources and flows (or lack thereof).
- Reporting, measures, and KPIs.
- Communications with members, customers, and subscriber acquisition, retention, and engagement (including servicing the subscriber, customer, and/or member).

It's important to ask yourself the following questions which can help you define a clear path of readiness and the organization's ability to achieve strategies, goals, pivots, and transformation.

1. Customer Experience. Internal perception of operational effectiveness may not reflect reality. How is the value of your offerings and the service delivery of those offerings perceived externally? Don't rely on a gut check in answering the question, it's important to have data to understand the truth.

2. Product and Service Enhancements. Are your current products or services meeting market needs and wants, and are they high-quality products or services that rise above your competitors? Again, know

your "customer truth" objectively not though overly confident subjective opinion.

3. The Market and Audience. What is the size of the current and potential market? What percentage of the current market do you have? Are you overly optimistic that your organization can take even more market share or tap into a new market? Does the organization have the capacity? Is the organization effectively serving the current market share? Address these issues factually with data.

4. Technology Systems and Platforms. Are your systems and platforms enabling or hindering work? Does the staff believe the systems and platforms limit them? Do your system and platforms create challenges hindering or preventing accomplishing goals? Do individuals work outside of the systems and platforms?

5. Processes and Staff Competencies. Are processes working? Are processes documented? How does the staff accomplish its work? Is it effective and efficient? How much work or workarounds occur in contradiction to the organization's defined processes? Does the staff have the appropriate skills and competencies to operate the current system? Do they have any untapped skills and competencies required to accomplish your new goals?

A realistic understanding of, and answers to this series of questions is critical to understanding the environment and system you need for new strategies, goals, and the like to flourish. If any of these elements are broken or ineffective, you are already compromised before you even leave the gate.

These questions may seem obvious, but we find that many organizations wear blinders when it comes to understanding their own businesses. In addition to a macro assessment, other areas require deep dives to analyze and understand as agents influencing change.

1. Growth. What research has been conducted? What is the true opportunity? It is imperative for future growth and increased relevancy to expand your market reach to other segments of your market that can benefit from the value you create.

2. Culture. Is your organizational culture calcified and focused on old practices? Past approaches may achieve short-term goals but do not reflect longer-term views or benefits in building a relationship with the stakeholders that leads to higher levels of revenue gain, with less organizational effort.

3. Accountability. Is your internal focus based on task and rarely takes the outside-in systems view approach to understanding how the organization and its system, in holistic and specific terms, are perceived by the customers and the market in general? The lack of an outside-in viewpoint hinders an organization's ability to prioritize for the greatest gain and value as it digitally and holistically transforms. Are the staff, managers, supervisors, and leaders holding themselves accountable to the right measures and metrics?

4. Communications. Do your teams work and communicate across departments and functions? The existence of department silos and silos within silos tend to make cross-functional collaboration difficult. Who loses? Your customers because communications are limited by the silos, and engagement is often repressed by the lack of holistic understanding of each customer's satisfaction, preferences, and use of products and services.

Roadblocks to Change

Many organizations suffer from an ingrained work culture controlled by historical practices, including manual processes and system workarounds that are inefficient or ineffective. Some staff wants to see change, innovation, and improvement in operations that would lead to a more valuable member/customer experience. But they are often hindered by those who don't want change and management who is focused on just "checking the box." Burnout of those who are seeking change is inevitable given an ingrained, calcified culture.

Another challenge is a lack of time and staff as there is often a tendency to implement changes without thoroughly examining the downstream or even upstream impacts. Add to that, reporting procedures that are highly manual and inaccurate. Further, there is often little scrutiny applied to data to determine the confidence of trends or issues. This can result in a lack of ingenuity and critical thinking on ways to improve.

Cultural attributes, including the lack of accountability, result in the continuation of highly broken internal systems, lack of effective and efficient processes, and hinder an organization from improving its service and offerings to the industry and securing desired growth that correlates to expanded market credibility and increased revenue.

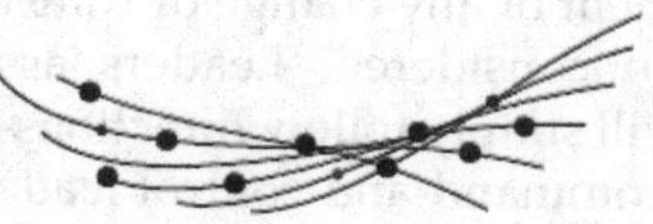

Chapter 14: Managing Transitions

"In today's everchanging environment, internalized urgency to do "something" to adapt to market forces is critical, but even with that urgency, critical thinking remains paramount. The urge to do something is of course far from the reality of doing it which leads to most change or transformation efforts failing."

Transformation Missteps

The human element of any change or transformation effort is often overlooked or not even considered. Leaders assume the hierarchy of management and staff will simply follow directions and bring the strategies and goals to life. With command-and-control leadership, assumptions are made that those responsible for operational and organizational change understand what to do or will figure out what to do to meet the set direction.

In today's everchanging environment, internalized urgency to do "something" to adapt to market forces is critical, but even with that urgency, critical thinking remains paramount. The urge to do something is of course far from the reality of doing it which leads to most change or transformation efforts failing.

The Human Factor in Transition Management

Humans first and foremost do not like change. Safety and security as well as predictability are default desires. People like to know what they need to do, what they are responsible for, and what they should expect in any given situation, including day-to-day work. Individuals construct their professional reality by gaining knowledge of the people, processes, and technologies that comprise their work. The result becomes their basis for "knowing" what needs to be done, how it needs to be done, and how they can do it well. Most seek fulfillment and derive daily satisfaction from their work as they gain positive recognition from doing a good job.

A change from one reality to an uncertain future requires a period of transition when an individual or team gains an understanding of what is changing, what they may be losing, and what will be different. It is a period of personal recognition and eventual acceptance that reshapes the mental construct of self-worth in relation to day-to-day work life. When an organization seeks to change or transform, a direction is set, but rarely is there time and effort applied to enable the worker to understand what is changing, how the change impacts them, and what they are losing/gaining as a result. Leadership's general assumption is that workers will adapt and do the work, or they will be replaced by others.

In any transformation, the possibility of loss is high: The individual worker may lose the safety, security, and predictability he or she desires. The organization may lose a significant source of institutional knowledge of operational processes along with valuable employee relationships and interdependencies if workers need to be replaced.

Transition management can be derailed when an individual's recognition of loss inhibits acceptance. An organization must recognize and address that individuals and teams need to be able to process what was, what they may be losing in the change or transformation and develop an understanding of their new reality of work and its associated self-worth.

Transforming Alignment and Organizational Structure

Transition is a process that requires significant work in getting your team to be comfortable with change. And acceptance of change is not easy. Stefan Lehner, a coach, and educator based in Paris created a transformation curve from William Bridges' Transition Model (created in 1991) to illustrate the journey (Lehner, Stephen. (Nd.). It's a useful paradigm for leaders to adapt to ensure they are leading change, not forcing it. On paper, this looks pretty straightforward. At the same time, we all know from personal experience that going through such a journey can be intense in real life. It can trigger emotional issues such as fear, holding onto legacy beliefs, and not underestimating the full potential of the benefits of change. To make it more complex, resistance is typically held at a subconscious or unconscious level, making it difficult to discuss and release.

Transformation Curve

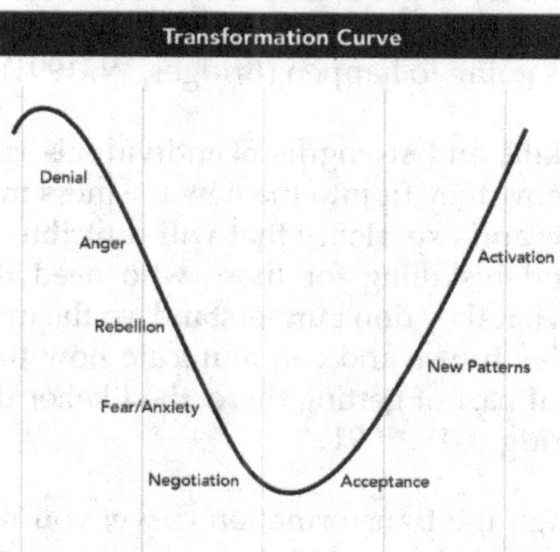

Source: (Lehner, Stephen. (Nd).

The journey starts with the introduction of transformative change and passes through the employee's personal stages of denial, anger, sadness, rebellion, and fear. Negotiation precedes acceptance which unlocks new patterns and activation. It's one thing to experience this curve personally if you are dealing with a crisis like a divorce or death, it's altogether another to mobilize an entire company in alignment to recognize and work through such a process.

Team Sport

So, the key to any transformation is for leaders to prepare their teams. As Bridges says, "People are often quite uncomfortable with change, for all sorts of understandable reasons. This can lead them to resist it and oppose it. This is why it's important to understand how people are feeling as change proceeds so that you can guide them through it and so that—in the end— they can accept it and support it." And to make things even more tricky, people go through these transitions and change at different paces. So, the workforce may not be pulling in the same direction at the same time, which can be frustrating to the visionary leader.

As you start the process, be prepared to meet with resistance and emotional pushback resulting from people being asked to do something they are uncomfortable with or unprepared for. Bridges' advice is to "accept people's resistance and understand their emotions. Allow them time to accept the change and let go and try to get everyone to talk about what they're feeling. In these conversations, make sure you listen empathically and communicate openly about what's going to happen (Bridges, W. 1991)."

Tapping into the skills and strengths of individuals is essential in giving them context as to how they fit into the new business model. In addition to identifying the skills and experience that will contribute to transformation, provide training and reskilling for those who need it. As Bridges says, "People often fear what they don't understand, so the more you can educate them about a positive future and communicate how their knowledge and skills are an essential part of getting there, the likelier they are to move on to the next stage (Bridges, W. 1991)."

As you move through the transformation curve, you may get stuck when your team gets confused about what they are supposed to do or impatient about the pace of change. Bridges refers to this as "the bridge between the old and the new; in some ways, people will still be attached to the old, while they are also trying to adapt to the new (Bridges, W. 1991)."

Encourage innovation and creativity as your organization starts to re-engineer itself to new ways of thinking and operating. It takes a lot of open communication to guide your team through the discomfort of change.

It's hard work.

The Infrastructure of Transition Management

Bridges says change is situational, and transitions impact individuals at every level of an organization who are involved, touched, and are participants in any change or transformation effort.

Bridges also believes:

"You can't separate change management from transition management until you have asked:

- What will we no longer be doing?
- What will be different because of the change?
- Who will lose what? (Bridges, W. (1991)"

Some clients resist asking these questions because they think it's negative and prefer to be positive about change. "We don't want to be putting ideas about losses into their heads," adds Bridges. When these questions aren't asked, individuals and teams do not gain a personal understanding of the change and then struggle through transitions to determine their role in the change and how they will assess their own worth in the changed system." Ambiguity and lack of clarity, consciously and unconsciously, result in an individual's lack of support for the change. Multiplying these factors across an organization sets any change or transformation initiative up to fail.

Bridges further explains, "Transition management is based on the idea that the best way to support people in transition is to affirm their experience and to help them deal with it. It is understanding how the world looks to them and using that as the starting point in your dealings with them. If you deny endings and losses, you are sowing the seeds of mistrust. Most communication consists of listening rather than speaking. You open the door to the transitions if the change is to work. Issues are brought onto the table, where you build trust and understanding, and give people the tools they need to move forward. When you speak to where people actually are, rather than telling them where they ought to be, you bring them along with you."

Why Transform in the First Place?

There is a lot of pressure in the marketplace and even within an organization to pivot and accelerate changes in response to changes in the marketplace. Perhaps it is entering a new market, changing products and services, abandoning established business plans, or becoming more tech-driven.

Becoming digitally savvy, integrating data and analytics into organizational operations, embedding DEI and CRS into the organizational culture, managing new remote work practices and procedures, and addressing the emotional and psychological needs of employees are real and present challenges for all leaders.

In managing any transition for change or transformation, executive leadership needs honed skills to inspire, lead and activate change. Empathy along with the support and recognition of what employees are processing and communicating with clarity and understanding of loss and gain becomes critical.

Transcending all these skills is to start the exercise with the one question:

"Why?"

Asking "why" should be customer-centric, and those customers are external and well internal stakeholders. Change needs to be authentic in how it will serve these two constituents. Change can't be superficial, nor can it be public posturing to improve the image of your organization. Both approaches will backfire in a nanosecond if the human elements are ignored or dismissed.

Authentic Transformation

Let's start with the basics. Managing transformation is changing an organization's mindsets, behaviors, and ways of working. It is facilitated by critical thinking and an agile approach focused on continual improvement. It also means being resilient in today's global environment of uncertainty and risk. Managing transformation requires leaders to inspire and mobilize employees to assess how transformational change will better serve customers (external and internal), incent them to work in cross-functional, cross-disciplinary teams to envision change, and mobilize the organization to adapt to new models and directions. Transformation is a team sport, and top-down hierarchical leadership will not succeed.

Transformation only works when everyone is pulling for it, as well as considering and supporting the dissident voices as part of the journey to achieving an actionable result. That is why a focus on the importance of transition management must be the principal part of the plan and effort.

Organizational Dynamics

In approaching organizational transformation, it's important to understand the dynamics of your teams and how they contribute to change. Some people like to plan, make lists, and check them off; others like to strategize and intellectualize the process as the smartest in the room; others are the cheerleaders who keep the teams together, and some like to just dive into action and take off. All these behavioral preferences are important roles in contributing to teams. A good balance of all four will have a greater chance of succeeding, even though the group conversations may be contentious, spirited, and difficult.

According to author Richard Evans, there are three mindset levels affecting transformational change (Evans, R. (2019): alignment, inspiration, and execution.

- Alignment involves leadership and decision-makers. Evans says, "Aligning everyone around an initiative means a lot of listening and empathizing. It involves clarifying the human purpose of the initiative: people who will work on the initiative and people who judge it are all going to be better motivated if they feel good about why they are doing it. Alignment on strategy is not merely done by scheduling a meeting or two. It means really digging in on the purpose of the change and the solution. The very same leaders who will need aligning on the vision will also be called on to govern or make decisions throughout the program."

- Inspiration addresses the culture and mediates value and behavior with talent. Evans explains, "The middle layer is the inspiration level, and this is the core focus. It is the people layer, the team members whose behavior, skills, and mindsets make all the difference. It has both technical and motivational aspects. The technical side is the subject matter expertise you will need in the team to create the winning strategy and execute it. The motivational side refers to the teamwork, the team methods, the values, and behavior that all need to align to the strategy." Mobilizing people is a delicate dance to balance objectivity and subjectivity. Evans explains, "People yearn to find purpose in their work

– whether they admit it to themselves or not. Behavioral change happens at the emotional level and not the intellectual level."

- The execution brings process, data, and tools together to make the vision actionable. Evans adds, "When executing major initiatives, the most common mistakes are in having poor integration between work streams and their teams (leading to churn and unnecessary work) or too much process (leading to bureaucracy and slowdowns). "

- Process design is everything, particularly demonstrating what was and what will be. A design focus aids individuals and teams see the transition from what was, to what will be and helps them leap forward in redefining their role and self-worth. The best initiatives include teams that are empowered to prioritize, deliver, and demonstrate ongoing delivery in short cycles (think: Agile). Paramount in this will be the approaches for removing obstacles to delivery, information flow, and decision-making. A great program aspires to use technology and predictive analytics to become as enlightened and accurate as possible with forecasting what will happen—not just looking back at what already happened.

Transition Leadership Skills

We know that change is hard. As humans, we are wired to resist change. It makes us anxious, fearful, and insecure. Change agents may have a difficult time understanding these concerns because they have already envisioned the transformation and how to achieve it.

However, it requires a "village" to successfully activate organization-wide change. Transformation can be approached step by step with mastery of nine leadership skills.

1. Clear Vision. This may seem obvious, but it's critical to have a clear vision of transformation, why it is necessary, and how it will benefit customers (internal and external). Communicating this clearly, with empathy, sets the stage. As clear as the vision may be, leaders need to also be open-minded and accept the reality that employees may very well have other strategies to augment and amplify the vision. This is facilitated through the process of critical thinking with iterations to the original idea. Empathy is sharing values and beliefs about change that can help break down barriers and unlock the enthusiasm needed to change.

2. Create Urgency. Anticipate the future, don't catch up to it. The pace of change in the marketplace can be overwhelming and if an organization lags behind its customers, it can easily become irrelevant. Make a case for macro market changes, conduct an honest SWOT, seek insights from leaders outside your own market sector, and communicate why deliberate speed is non-negotiable.

3. Be Persuasive. A good leader leads. Confidence and persuasiveness are assets when inspiring employees to change. It is infectious and can become viral among teams to reflect the same realistic optimism in facing change. Never underestimate the power of charisma in mobilizing teams.

4. Be Empathetic. Walking in someone else's shoes means significantly more than just walking a mike. Empathy may be the single most powerful tool a leader has to build trust, credibility, and loyalty. Empowering an organization full of individuals who have full lives inside and outside the company requires empathy – especially in any time of social, financial, and health-related disruption.

5. Create Coalitions. Change is not possible in a siloed organizational model. Cross-disciplinary and cross-functional teams are a leader's most powerful resource to lead change. Deeply held bias will manifest, and a holistic approach using systems thinking will help address these beliefs when revealed and then factored into the conversations. Employees can become influencers, both internally and externally, communicating the benefits of transformation.

6. Critical Thinking. Remove barriers that resist change through the discipline of critical thinking. Unconscious bias can infiltrate any transformational journey. Operating with an agile and unbiased organizational mindset will deflect and defuse the reasoning that factions, individuals, and cliques use to resist change. Critical thinking is a powerful tool to help shift thinking by making employees part of the solution and thereby invested in the outcomes.

7. Clear Communications. Most roads to transformation hit speedbumps when the vision and progress are poorly communicated. Frequent and relevant communications, including inclusive chats and forums, will encourage employees to become more invested in the transformation process. Open conversations, town halls, small group meetings – all levels of communications are

needed to reinforce the plan. Tell them the vision, explain how the vision is progressing, and then tell them and tell them again!

8. Be Steadfast and Resilient. Change is messy. Remaining vigilant with a long-term vision often requires short-term shifts. Some employees may not fit into the new model. Jobs may be redefined and repositioned. Employees formerly with limited voices in the organization may be elevated to new levels. Leaders need to remain steadfast and resilient in managing the individual versus the demands of the group and strengthening an organization for the good of everyone.

9. Celebrate Progress. Set goals and milestones for individuals and teams. Communicate the benchmarks and progress (or lack of). Don't let the momentum stall in too many processes and meetings. Communicate good news of personal and team achievements, often and sincerely.

Readiness Plan for Transformation

Once an organization has understood the need for change, prepare employees for transformation and identify the specific areas to change. Creating meaningful metrics will help improve the agility of an organization. Without clear goals and metrics, any transition or organizational remodeling will be more an exercise than a result.

A playbook to assess an organization's readiness to begin change or transformation is the continuum of transformation, coined by author Cheryl Miller in her book, *The Continuum of Transformation*. It involves five functions of the organization with assessments and actions to determine states of readiness (Miller, C. (2018). Each stage leads to the next, and by stage three in each function, an organization is ready to begin traveling the road to transformation. Her Continuum is described as follows.

Cultural

- Stage One: The staff operates within department silos with little to no interaction with other departments. Little to no information is shared about organizational priorities. Hierarchical communications are standard, and direction is managed top-down.

- Stage Two: Organizational initiatives and key metrics on performance are regularly shared with all staff. Customer feedback is solicited, tracked, and shared with staff. Critical thinking is a highly valued skill and encouraged.

- Stage Three: Cross-functional teams, at all levels, are put in place to address challenges and opportunities. Bi-directional communications are encouraged and rewarded. Calculated risk-taking is encouraged for enhancing the customer experience.

Management

- Stage One: Managers focus primarily on operational tactics with limited reporting on results. Managers do not solve problems holistically with diverse and inclusive teams that are cross-disciplinary. Managers do not have a common understanding of the priorities for the organization or the overall strategic goals. Success is measured in terms of cost containment over innovation. Risks are adverted as much as possible.

- Stage Two: Departmental KPIs are established and measured. Organizational strategies and priorities are communicated to all levels. Managers and teams are rewarded for operational achievements that increase customer satisfaction.

- Stage Three: Cross-functional KPIs are established, shared, and measured. Cross-functional team meetings are conducted regularly to identify opportunities to improve. Managers and teams are rewarded for cross-functional goal achievements and innovation. Contingency and succession planning are in place and regularly reviewed.

Operations

- Stage One: Department operational procedures are created by staff but not documented. Lack of trust in data and systems is pervasive. Results tracking and reporting are manual. Overall performance is lower than industry benchmarks.

- Stage Two: Functional SOPs are defined, tested, refined, documented, and measured. Data definitions are documented, and reporting becomes automated. Benchmarks are established to ensure the optimal customer experience. The executive dashboard is reviewed monthly to assess operational performance.

- Stage Three: Cross-functional dependencies are identified, tracked, and managed. Manual tasks are identified, prioritized, and evaluated for possible automation. Customer touchpoints are identified within each function. Metrics are established and monitored for each touchpoint.

Marketing

- Stage One: Heavy reliance solely on email marketing. Minimal integrated marketing across communication channels. Little to no cross-functional lead management. No cross-product promotions. Little to no personalized and targeted messaging. Heavy reliance on price promotions. Success is measured in effort and volume quantitatively without similar measures for qualitative factors such as trust, loyalty, and influence. Lack of emphasis on creating relationships through relevant storytelling about the organization that drives engagement.

- Stage Two: Experimentation with A/B message and offer testing. Automated marketing to support drip campaigns. Unique value propositions are developed for different market segments. Personalized messaging and offers based on first-party data. Cross-functional lead capture and tracking. Key metrics reported by campaign.

- Stage Three: Marketing automation to support new customer onboarding and renewal. Integrated and targeted personalized campaigns based on customer behaviors. Customer acquisition and retention costs are identified and tracked. Marketing insights are shared across the organization. High engagements are based on trust.

Product Development

- Stage One: Performance assessment is based on historical trends. Key metrics, such as cost to provision and gross profit are not monitored regularly. There is no product/program development roadmap. Minimal to no customer feedback on product/program features and benefits.

- Stage Two: Product/program development plan and strategy are documented and reviewed with senior management. Key performance metrics are identified, tracked, and reported regularly. Customer feedback is solicited at least once a year. Ongoing market research to identify new opportunities.

- Stage Three: Customer advisory board established and solicited for innovation and product enhancements. Cross product/program bundling plans identified and implemented. Product/program plans are shared with staff at all levels.

Reinforce the Success of Transformation

Change can't be successful in a vacuum. Celebrate your success! Keep track of early success stories and share them as examples of positive transformation experiences. The goal is to empower teams to self-manage, build trust, and work at a systematic and productive pace. Team members and stakeholders are reinforced by being called out as role models in adapting the Continuum to meet the evolving needs of customers/members/clients. Remember, although operations in an organization will benefit from the focus and optimized process of this exercise of determining readiness, the focus should be customer-centric, and this experience will ultimately drive customer satisfaction – the true measure of success.

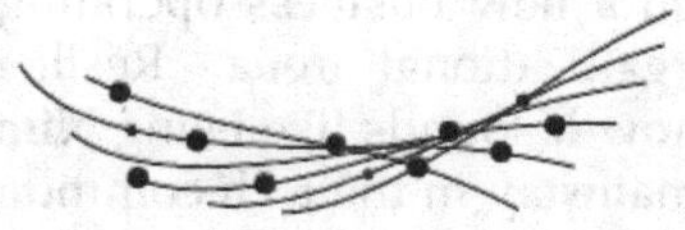

Chapter 15: Agility + Resilience

"The blind spot in organizations is not seeing how the market sees you, rather, preferring to see how the organization sees itself. The outside-in view is often very different than the view captured internally and as a result can reveal misconceptions, falsities, and disconnects to how the organization is working and delivering value. In summary, systems thinking is the mirror you need to see yourself."

Becoming Agile

Every generation a new business operating principal bubbles up into the professional organizational arena. Resilience has been updated with Agility (yes, we know it sounds like being Nimble, but it's a lot more nuanced). Agility is a mainstay in the tech community – particularly with software development. Here's a basic Wiki definition: "Business agility refers to the rapid, continuous, and systematic evolutionary adaptation and entrepreneurial innovation directed at gaining and maintaining competitive advantage." Simply stated, agile management is a methodical, systems thinking approach to preparing for the future.

About Systems Thinking

Systems thinking methodology is an outside-in view into an organization. Basically speaking, a system is the sum and interaction of its parts, not how a single focused group of parts is working.

There are risks from institutional knowledge, its internal stovepipes, and rooted legacy culture. These ingrained principles stick because of the lack of critical thinking to understand the reasons that impact transformation, pivot in response to the market, and improve and build value for current members, customers, and subscribers.

Using systems thinking with its outside-in perspective reveals how current or prospective members, customers, and subscribers see an organization. Key insight: The blind spot in organizations is not seeing how the market sees you, rather, preferring to see how the organization sees itself. The outside-in view is often very different than the view captured internally and as a result can reveal misconceptions, falsities, and disconnects to how the organization is working and delivering value. In summary, systems thinking is the mirror you need to see yourself.

Agile Mindset

Transitioning to an outside-in mindset can be achieved through agility and agile project management, critical in the digital transformation process. But beware, agile is not always the right answer. Agility isn't like turning on a switch and can't be applied to all situations or organizations. Plus, agility may not work across the entire enterprise, fit all business types, or apply to all product development.

Furthermore, we have found that if you work in silos with a top-down management culture (read: many traditional associations
and organizations) this is not the best strategy or approach for you.

Why?

When an organizational culture isn't aligned holistically, it cannot practice agility. This presents a bigger and more complex strategic issue: Does your organization operate with an authentic desire to use systems thinking to network your talent into interconnected solution thinking and how do the parts integrate into an entire system?

The Race to the Bottom

If you keep your team isolated in vertical silos, you are practicing what we tell our clients is called the theory of "just good enough." All too often we see agile, and agility mistranslated across new or enhanced products, services, or offerings. A "just good enough" mentality may not address a complete business need or problem and can lead to more unsatisfied customers than satisfied ones. Inherently, it misses the upstream and downstream impacts which result in unintended consequences creating more work, expense, and frustration. It also risks opening the door for competitors to quickly replicate and go over and above what you are offering.

We also see clients who attempt to integrate agile for every project, program, or organization system change. What often results? Rarely what was hoped for or expected. The intent of agile is to iterate and deliver faster to the market. Time to market is surely more important than ever in the digital economy but quality and completeness shouldn't be set aside with speed taking precedence.

Agile represents prioritization and a roadmap that builds from a solid offering that promises to add enhancements over time. It is not focused on delivering sub-par products or services that offer only part of a solution. We don't buy a car that doesn't include a steering wheel on the promise that it may be added later. We don't buy a home that doesn't have windows because they weren't ready yet. and we don't join, buy from, or subscribe to an organization on the promise that what we want will come at some later point.

Implementing Agility

Agility can be an imperative with and without software implementation. If the system is understood holistically, there is recognition of how selected parts can be improved and where iteration is appropriate without negative consequences. The operating principle is that an agile mindset is iterative, cross-functional, critical thinking, and self-directed.

The outcome of agile management is a flexible roadmap to managing change. Even better, agility empowers your team and sparks innovation. Your mindset is the key to agility, and critical thinking is essential to enable innovation and problem-solving. Agility is the polar opposite of cultures where people only do what they're told, don't question policies, and don't have an innovation mindset.

Liberating Silos Management

According to Vivify, "Agile methodology focuses on operational freedom for teams involved in a project. Managers provide the means to an end and employees make the decisions on how to proceed. In most cases, organizations tend to keep departments isolated from the others, as well as keep the information within a silo. Agile focuses on cross-functional and self-organizing teams that communicate and collaborate, to deliver a working product or solution (Vivify Scrum. (Nd.)."

The "wisdom of crowds" approach is a lynchpin to agility. Your organization has niche experts with a wealth of knowledge and skills. The cross-functional approach ensures that everyone has a seat at the table collaborating with a free flow of information and ideas. Feedback is essential to the process as is flexibility and openness to consideration of different inputs. And for this to succeed, it is imperative that the leaders of the organization fully support the initiative and have established goals for the organization to embrace and measure progress.

Distributed Control

For traditional leaders who operate with a hierarchical approach, agile project management can be threatening to a personal sense of control. The reality is that talented next-gen stakeholders want their voices to be heard, and if you don't give them a place at your table, they'll sit down anyway. Or they'll leave.

Agility is based on continuous improvement and iterative development. Think of it as a journey, not a destination. Your customers aren't locked into place and the dynamic digital marketplace is constantly evolving.

Your organization should be responsive to these changes, in other words, continuously improving and iterating new solutions. Vivify also cautions, "Adopting agile in a non-software environment takes both time and proper planning to ensure that you benefit from agile practices rather than hinder your business operations." Commitment and open-minded approaches support agile models; you may be surprised where ingenious solutions emerge in a culture that embraces the "power of the whole."

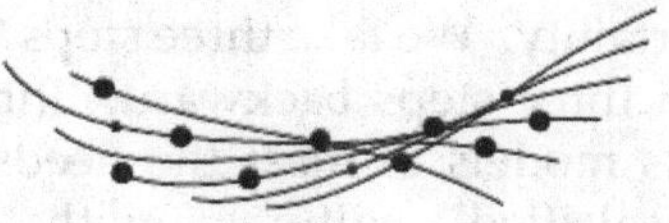

Chapter 16: Ambiguity + Risk

"Defining a vision of success is a lynchpin to mastering
leadership in ambiguous times. If you develop a vision of
success with the input of your teams, you can work backward
to develop a plan for success. In other words, literally
visualize what success looks like and then build the pathway
to achieving your goals led by that vision, always with the
agility to pivot or change direction when necessary."

Managing Ambiguity

Living through any major market disruption or crisis is shadowed by nearly constant uncertainty. We take three steps forward, two sideways, and unfortunately, then three steps backward. Innovators can pivot and transform their business models to meet the needs of their stakeholders. Organizations with calcified cultures with command-and-control management models are easily eclipsed by agile competitors.

So, which category characterizes your own organization:

Are you innovative or is your organization asleep at the wheel?

What about your members/clients/customers?

The key to getting unstuck during any crisis, financial meltdown, social unrest—or even in normal times is the ability to lead confidently in a time of ambiguity.

Ambiguity Is Becoming a 24/7 Proposition

A perfect storm of a global pandemic, civil unrest, and economic disruption put many organizations on alert. Looking forward, anyone who thinks ambiguity is ebbing and giving way to more certain paths ahead is dreaming. The need to embrace ambiguity is a constant. And in many ways ambiguity has accelerated.

"The degree of uncertainty that we can tolerate depends upon our personal or organizational comfort level. Some of us try to avoid uncertainty, some of us tolerate it, but few of us actively embrace it. We can never shrink uncertainty to zero because the future is always uncertain, but we can reduce it by turning to experts or sleuthing for information we don't have," according to Cheryl Strauss Einhorn in the Harvard Business Review (Einhorn Strauss, C. (2021).

International management consultant Korn Ferry adds, "Ambiguity is the norm in any complex organization, but clarity is still possible. It is about purpose, long-term direction, and values. At its simplest, ambiguity is a lack of clarity, which leads to frustration and, in the organizational context, heightened anxiety for leaders and employees. Our challenge as leaders, given this reality, is determining what we can be clear about to enable agile organizational responses (Korn Ferry Focus. (2015)."

Navigating Ambiguity

Critical thinking applied to the people, processes, and culture is essential to managing an organization when the marketplace is framed by ambiguity. Understanding how to navigate ambiguity, when an optimum outcome is a matter of interpretation, puts enormous pressure on leaders, managers, and teams. Personal interpretation is both a strength and a pitfall. Consider whether your personal interpretations are in the interest of your stakeholders or yourself. Einhorn adds, "Our decision will ultimately be a judgment call, based on our values. We have to drill down on what matters to each of us, our family, or our organization. To confront an ambiguous problem, we must invert our decision-making: Instead of focusing on the problem itself, we need to define what a successful outcome looks like — what is called your "vision of success."

That sounds straightforward. Defining a vision of success is a lynchpin to mastering leadership in ambiguous times. If you develop a vision of success with the input of your teams, you can work backward to develop a plan for success. In other words, literally visualize what success looks like and then build the pathway to achieving your goals led by that vision, always with the agility to pivot or change direction when necessary. That pathway may represent some very challenging decisions or actions and may fundamentally change areas of your organization and how it operates. But transformative change is often not easy and achieving success takes hard work and commitment.

Organizational designer Norm Smallwood says, "I'm seeing two types of responses to ambiguity—leaders who are ambiguity absorbers and leaders who are ambiguity amplifiers. Ambiguity absorbers reduce ambiguity for others by setting a clear direction, regardless of their level in the organization. Ambiguity amplifiers make the situation worse by insisting that others wait for someone else to set direction, micro-manage and/or overanalyze. Amplifiers stir up resistance or freeze people from taking action (Smallwood, N. (2020)."

Leadership makes a difference at all levels: "When there's uncertainty about what to do and senior executives haven't yet charted a course, mid-level leaders should not wait for direction. They should make assumptions that lead to a plan of action based on their understanding of what's best for the business. This allows a team or function to continue to work productively. This is the essence of what it means to be an ambiguity absorber. Making assumptions about what the organization will do allows a mid-level leader to keep people working around a shared agenda during uncertainty," states Smallwood (Smallwood, N. (2020).

At a time of increasing ambiguity, organizations need more absorbers that have clear direction to determine a level of clarity tied to their vision of success. Thoughtful action to proceed on the path to success must remain the goal. We offer some food for thought on how you can embrace uncertainty and establish your vision of success and the path you and the organization need to take to wake up and begin to transform.

Playbook for Leaders

Author Andrew Blum says, "Research shows that living with a permanent sense of uncertainty creates stress, and over time can even lead to disease in individuals and true dysfunction in organizations. This raises an important question: How can we find clarity in the face of ambiguity and uncertainty? The answer lies in the fundamentals of leadership and looking at things that *are* in our control. This can be counterintuitive because, as leaders, we tend to want to control everything. The challenge with this instinctual leadership response is that the more variables we deal with and the more we sense things are outside of our control, the more control and safety we seek. The reality here is that this desire for measurement and control often distracts us from the real challenge of finding comfort and productive action in the face of uncertainty. We get caught up in the idea of making uncertainty certain, but this notion puts us in a vicious cycle that has no end (Blum, A. (2020)."

Here is our matrix to help navigate ambiguity. It's a useful roadmap to provide insights and guidance in times of uncertainty.

1. Know your intention as distinct from your goals. Intentions are stated as motivational and feelings-based: "Today I intend to make my teams feel valued and meaningful." And "My goal is to transform my organization."

2. Understand your own response to ambiguity. Ask yourself: Are you empathetic or dogmatic? Do you assuage fear and anxiety or allow it to permeate contagiously throughout your organization? Are you decisive or do you waver and waffle?

3. Are you a perfectionist or flexible? Be aware that you may not be able to provide clarity about everything, however, providing no clarity is unacceptable.

4. Don't expect to get your decisions right the first time. Get comfortable with uncertainty, tolerate errors, and don't take criticism personally. Think incrementally, establish effective feedback loops and practice continually iterating innovations and new ideas.

5. A shared purpose of your organization and its values are essential in delivering an effective outcome during ambiguous times. And leading a purpose-driven business helps people cope when times are challenging.

6. Clarity about your long-term mission provides stability. That includes clarity about expectations, roles, and responsibilities of the workforce to maintain ballast during uncertainty.

7. Communicate. Always with authenticity and transparency.

8. We cannot control the circumstances of our lives, but we can control how we respond to them. Focus on what you can control and celebrate contributions, innovations, and actionable solutions, large and small.

9. Earn respect. You don't have to be loved by everyone, but you need to be trusted.

10. Educate yourself. Be curious. Don't think you're the smartest person in the room. Surround yourself with people who think differently. Expand your table and invite an inclusive group of equally curious individuals to explore how to navigate ambiguity.

So, let's jump back to where we started. Ambiguity is going to continue. Clarity and concreteness regarding the future remain hard to grasp. If an organization waits to act it will result in staying asleep at the wheel while your competitors speed ahead and innovators upend your business model. Or worse, because of market changes, you may simply slip into irrelevance.

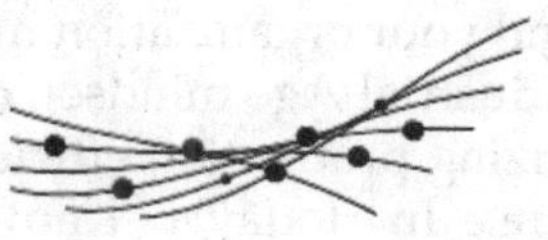

Chapter 17: Do You Measure by Outputs or Outcomes?

"The Knowledge Age remains new territory as we navigate an environment where we talk to machines and oversee computers who mine and assimilate data. Our daily focus is on the acquisition, dissemination, and use of knowledge. The activities in our Knowledge Age, just like those in the Industrial Age, require energy. We find ourselves focused more on measuring the output of energy and effort as opposed to measuring what really matters: outcomes and impact."

Measure By Measure

How do you and your organization measure accomplishments and achievements? In an Industrial Age mindset, output was believed to be the only measure—maximizing production efficiency became something close to a religious mantra. In today's Knowledge Age era, outcome, accomplishing a strategy or goal, is the real measure that determines the outcome, not output.

In a marketplace that values what an organization stands for and its effect on all real and perceived stakeholders—and the planet— it's surprising that outcome and impact are not embedded more strongly into a balance sheet. We propose that strategic results should have higher standing than operational results, with associated measures. And above all, organizations need to measure what matters, which is outcomes and impact, not metrics defined by industry, competitors, or measurements found on the internet.

Human Behavior

How many times has Friday arrived, and you shared with family, friends, and co-workers the week you had and how intense and perhaps exhausting it was?

Maybe it was filled with meetings and endless emails, texts, and messages. As you navigated each meeting and communication and compiled briefs, reports, or project plans, your energy slowly depleted. You hang on during the week knowing that Friday will arrive and that you will get a chance to recharge.

In the end, you feel a sense of accomplishment that you managed to muster enough energy to get through the week and survived another roller coaster ride. You then take stock of your output, recognizing the energy you expended, but you lack the clarity to determine what impact you had and what outcomes were achieved.

Was the ball moved forward to the goal?

Or was the ball simply moved somewhere around the goalpost?

What exactly have you been measuring?

Were you just ticking off the boxes?

We're talking about the big picture here and the questions usually make us feel uncomfortable.

Remember in the 21st century, human beings are still evolutionarily programmed to conserve energy and maintain that energy for actions and activities that are necessary for day-to-day survival, whether that be finding sustenance, procreating, or maintaining safety and security.

In a business context, organizations are comprised of humans who default to conserve energy and measure accomplishment and achievement by the least amount of energy expended. Therefore, we inherently concentrate on measuring outputs. Although the mantra of the Industrial Age in measuring efficiency and production may seem of a different time and place, the Industrial Age efficiently matched our inherent energy default behaviors. It was easy to acclimate to a production structure with an understood value of the level of energy expenditure required to succeed.

The Knowledge Age, in many ways, remains new territory as we navigate an environment where we talk to machines and oversee computers who mine and assimilate data. Our daily focus is on the acquisition, dissemination, and use of knowledge. The activities in our Knowledge Age, just like those in the Industrial Age, require energy. We find ourselves once again focused more on measuring the output of energy and effort as opposed to measuring what really matters: outcomes and impact.

Output Versus Outcome

Basically speaking, output is operational, and outcome is strategic. Output is quantitative, measured by data, and understood by analytics. Output is easy to trace and validate.

- How many widgets did we produce?

- How many meetings did I attend?

- How many reports did I review?

Output is one aspect of an outcome, which is more qualitative. Strategic goals inform an outcome; however, any outcome is often colored by individual or group perception. Outputs are the actions or items that relate to the expenditure of energy and effort.

So, output, as we are so focused on our own expenditure of energy, becomes something that is measured without recognition of a goal or contribution to a larger strategy (outcome). But neither can be viewed in a vacuum.

The two results have an uneasy relationship: you can overdeliver on output and fail as an organization, which is the worst outcome possible. In a manufacturing organization, output is the key indicator of success. However, a knowledge-based organization requires new processes and goals; intellectual output is more ephemeral and less convenient to measure. And there are legacy output measures that have become antiquated but remain because they are comfortable to individuals professionally and personally. For example, some organizations believe that exceeding last year's attendance at the annual conference is a successful outcome. However, the event could be an absolute failure if the increase in attendance did not generate an increase in revenue. And typically, since most organizations operate in silos, correlating the increase in attendance to the associated expenses to the overall financial goals and results is often overlooked. An ingrained year-to-year focus at a high level is to beat last year's financial metrics rather than attention to the ultimate outcome. That is, determining if a goal to increase attendance results in a financial gain for an organization.

Be aware of an endless loop of a race to the bottom that measures outputs versus a strategic outcome.

KPIs

So, the output can be considered short-term, immediate, and majorly represented by the energy expended. The outcome is long-term and iterative represented, yes by the energy expended, but also viewed in context of how the expenditure of energy contributed to the achievement of a goal and strategy. Another way to think about it is output is a goal and outcome is an intention.

How then do we recognize the differences between outputs and outcomes and determine the appropriate and relevant measures for each?

There is no one set formula however the following description provides a broad guideline.

Output

Organizations set their own measurement standards and tools for output. Macro KPIs for output are straightforward.

- The number of individuals in the workforce required to get the "job" done
- Utilization of the workforce in an 8-hour workday and the actual time spent on work
- Volume, number of units produced
- Profitability cost per unit
- Efficiency, time expended per unit
- Delivery, final costs
- The number of customers acquired

Outcome

Many organizations have strategic goals but not any measurement system in place to monitor outcomes.

- Sustainability and growth in the market
- Wellbeing, a highly functioning workforce, and positive workplace culture
- Shared purpose, alignment of all stakeholders
- Trust, both the workforce and customers
- Customer experience, retaining customers, and healthy growth rate
- Achieving strategic goals, generating impact
- Brand reputation, continuous, trustworthy, and reliable delivery of products and services

Why Measure Outcomes?

Outputs are easy to measure and align with our human defaults; it's simple to measure things. Outcomes, on the other hand, require a skill set of critical thinking, a holistic view of an organization's products and services, agility, and adaptability to pivot if necessary, understanding customers, accountability to all stakeholders, and serving the community. Measuring output takes less energy; measuring outcome takes more energy.

Having a firm grip on what contributes to outcomes enables the ability to iterate and improve perceptions and assessments on all fronts. Outcomes become meaningful when the measurement encompasses a contextual viewpoint represented internally and externally. An outcome is an effect your products and services produced on the people you serve. In terms of customer engagement, the outcome addresses the challenges they face, the issues, constraints, and priorities that are important to them, and the lack of friction it takes to deliver your products and services to them. Most importantly, it is the connection between the customer and if what you are offering is quality and a relevant solution to their needs and wants. For the workforce, the outcome is an empathetic workplace powered by a market orientation and shared purpose. For the community, a positive outcome is to be viewed as a responsible and trustworthy organization. In any one of the above, each takes energy to achieve, but ultimately the measurement must focus on what was achieved, not the energy expended.

Managing Outcome: The Business Proposition

Authors Jane Resiman and Judith Clegg have developed a matrix for optimal outcomes for nonprofits. These strategies have relevance for all organizations.

1. Measuring effectiveness. How do you know if your products and services are effective? How can they be improved? Building capacity simply for the sake of building capacity may not achieve the desired results.

2. Identifying effective practices. "With the information you collect, you can determine which actions to continue and build upon. Some practices might be modified and replicated for other programs or initiatives based on your results."

3. Identify practices that need improvement. Some actions may need to change to improve the effectiveness of your products and services.

4. Clarity and consensus. "Everyone in your organization, from board members to service staff to volunteers, should understand what is going on and what you intend to achieve (Clegg, J. & Reisman, J. 2000.)."

Outcome measurement helps to clarify your effectiveness with processes to "accredit, adjudge, analyze, appraise, appreciate, assay, assess, audit, check, classify, consider, critique, determine, estimate, examine, evaluate, find, gauge, grade, inspect, investigate, judge, measure, monitor, rank, rate, referee, report, review, score, scrutinize, study, test, validate, weigh."

Whew! But take note that each of the terms referenced above correlates to critical thinking, smart use of data, and assessment of goal achievement and accomplishment. The energy expended may be measured by the expense required to achieve and accomplish the outcome. But the ultimate outcome is measured by its correlation to the strategy and goal.

Managing Outcome: Leadership

Leadership typically operates on four levels: organization, team, department, and individual. Jenna Weaver of Clearpoint has identified how to lead each level (Weaver, J. (Nd.), which we have enhanced.

- **The Organization**

The organization is leading up and down the organization, including members of the board. In terms of output and outcome, leadership needs to motivate the workforce to align with the core mission, unique value proposition, market orientation, ethical principles, and shared purpose. Great leaders can read the room tone and know when and how to spark innovation, participation, and results.

Creating an organizational-level outcome strategy that represents actual impact and goals is important for organizations that have multiple lines of products and services. It should also direct all your downstream decision-making with collective understanding and alignment. For example, if a group develops a product and another group sells that product, typically there are two separate business unit strategies. Unification under one single organizational-level strategy leads to a better outcome and a strong tie to the organization's overarching strategy and its shared purpose.

- **Team Leadership**

Team Leadership is identifying the right skills and structure for teams to operate effectively. Inclusive teams that are multi-disciplinary and multi-level, motivated by collaboration and collegiality often produce the best results.

Teams need to align their outcome objectives with the organization with enough latitude to improve and innovate. Teams need discipline and structure to focus on productive work to prevent distraction from achieving desired outcomes. Otherwise, outputs will rule the day and substantive progress won't be realized.

- **The Business Unit**

Having an outcome strategy at the business unit level weighs the costs and benefits of each business unit to decide where to spend resources.

Departmental resource expenditure takes energy and effort and may limit the larger contributions to the organizational strategy. Weaver adds, "The functional level of your strategy involves each department — and what those at the department level are doing day-to-day to support organizational outcome initiatives."

- **Individual Leadership**

Individual leadership is the power of an individual to inspire. The best leaders lead by example with empathy, courage, and self-awareness. Continuous self-evaluation is key to staying fresh and on point with both output and outcome.

"Having a solid understanding of these levels of outcome strategy will help align your organization-wide goals from the top of your organization to the bottom (the individual level)," adds Weaver. "If you approach your strategy using these four levels, leaders across the organization will have a better understanding of how their strategic activities impact the organization's high-level outcome strategy," adds Weaver.

The final step in measuring outcome is measuring its impact. In other words, what effect took place because of your products and services. Impacts are the long, long-term, or indirect effects of your outcomes. Put another way, impacts are what you hope to accomplish beyond products and services. Impact tells the narrative of how people or society are touched and influenced. The impact can be measured through the evaluation of outcomes in terms of the long-term effects of an individual, organization, or policy. The impact affects all stakeholders, including customers, the workforce, the industry, and society at large. The impact is the ultimate goal of any organization that is driven to make a difference and be competitive for all stakeholders in the large playing field in which it operates.

Measuring what is important is imperative. Although measuring outcomes runs against our default behaviors, it remains critical in a dynamically changing market and society.

Here's a cautionary note about having output goals with blinders. As reported in HuffPost, Amazon was fined over productivity quotas. "Workplace safety officials in Washington state hit Amazon with a $60,000 fine for knowingly putting workers at risk at its massive warehouse in Kent (Jamieson, D. (2022)."

Output without considering the outcome and the ultimate impact is a fool's errand.

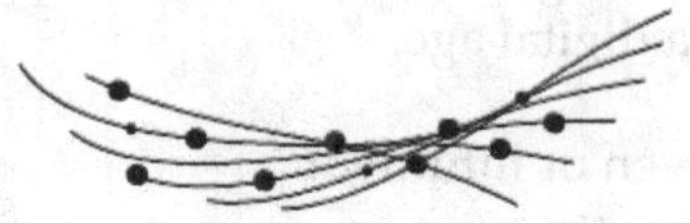

Chapter 18: Measuring What Matters

"Leaders of a data-driven culture solidify decision-making
that is evidence-based and results in demonstrable findings
that lead to the best opportunity for achievement and success.
A cautionary note, however: Analysis of data can be
subjective. A data-driven culture must recognize that
personal bias, internal self-promotion, internal politics,
personalities, or even external pressures play into how
decisions are often considered and made."

How to Decide

The debate in management and leadership circles is about how to best make decisions in a digital age.

Should you be data-driven or intuitive?

There are too many variables, including institutional knowledge and bias that limit the value of gut decision-making, particularly in a fundamentally and dynamically ever-changing environment. We are the sum total of our own biases and past experiences, which hinder the effectiveness of intuitive decision-making in the 21st century. A decision-making approach that is based on quality data that represents a complete or close to complete reality can more clearly reveal effective actions, intelligence, and strategies.

The Argument for Data-Driven Decision-Making

Data-driven decision-making has been popularized by the era of big data and the myriad of technologies and technological solutions that create and capture data. At no other time in human history have we been able to collect data at the rate and depth that we now can. Data can overwhelm, confuse, and confound. There appears to be too much information to even consider; our default human behavior is to simplify and seek the most important point or finding, not conduct a daily analysis of a deluge of information. Becoming data-driven is a necessity for today and tomorrow. We must manage our defaults and move outside our comfort zone if our organizations are to survive into the future.

Data is, by definition, mostly objective, unbiased information as a byproduct of transactions, process completions and inputs, and behavioral capture. Most data results from the past, whether that be a transaction completed yesterday, last month, or an hour ago. Applying value to most data requires context and a recognition of the time and place of capture. In today's quickly changing environment, what happened last week or last month was the result of a variety of factors and variables that were relevant at the time. That data may be dated by new factors and variables that are now more relevant for the present and future. We must learn how to leverage data and become data-driven decision-makers as the data offers our best hope and chance for navigating today's market dynamism.

Simply stated, data-driven decision-making is the process of studying large amounts of data, analyzing it to identify patterns, obtaining actionable insights, and using that insight to make business decisions. Data is dependable and mostly objective.

Too many organizations have gotten on the data bandwagon without a plan. Tech expert Gabriel Swain, CEO at Disruptive Growth Marketing (DGM) cautions, "Businesses have data at their fingertips, but how do they organize it in a logical way? Many still struggle to understand how data is used to make decisions. There is so much data in the world today that it would take over 180 million years to download it (Swain, G., (Nd.)."

He adds, "When CEOs champion data-driven business cultures, performance results and revenues increase. A Deloitte survey reveals that when data championing CEOs lead the charge, businesses are 77% more likely to significantly exceed business goals. Plus, they are 59% more likely to gain new insights from the metrics they track and to use data analysis to drive business decisions."

Why?

Leaders of a data-driven culture solidify decision-making that is evidence-based and results in demonstrable findings that lead to the best opportunity for achievement and success. A cautionary note, however: Analysis of data can be subjective. A data-driven culture must recognize that personal bias, self-promotion, internal politics, personalities, or even external pressures play into how decisions are often considered and made. If decisions are made based on personal interpretation of data, those decisions may not recognize or be representative of the true factors and variables at play across a system.

There is of course always more to the story.

Organizations that value and embrace data understand that data-driven business decisions can inform innovation, build, or expand a market, optimize operations, identify errors, improve customer service, and increase revenue.

Human nature is to seek out others to give recommendations, provide insight into how to make decisions and on what basis, and confirm our thinking. We trust this behavior as most of us personally lack enough information to consistently form confidence-based conclusions.

Our defaults are to maintain our baseline behaviors. However, we would argue that now that we have access to so many levels of data, it's time to change our own operational default mental constructs.

Amit Choudhary, chief operating officer, executive VP, global financial services at Capgemini describes the advantages **of** data-driven thinking which we have augmented:

- Data enables clear, evidence-based-focused goals.
- Accuracy and objectivity can help to preclude human biases, institutional filters, and false assumptions.
- Insights from data offer a real-time and historical snapshot of the decision-making rationale and help keep the leader's vision dynamic.
- Leaders who effectively leverage big data, structured and unstructured data, as well as robust operational information, can stay ahead of the curve and be prepared for uncertainties within an organization, its capacities across its operating systems, and the market it serves or intends to serve (Choudhary, A. (Nd.).

Data-Driven Playbook

Here's a quick playbook for a few key moves to transform an organizational model and culture into data-driven decision-making.

- **Identify Data Champions**

At the C-level, a chief data officer (CDO) can work with leadership to design and implement initiatives to support a data-driven organizational model. Most importantly, however, is that a CDO should be, first and foremost, a strong educator and trainer within and across sectors in an organization to aid co-workers in learning how to use data, decreasing their fears of data, and mastering how to use data to improve execution, planning, and reporting.

- **Recruit Younger Employees**

Next-gens are comfortable with data. Younger decision-makers are terrific champions for the transition to data-driven business culture. Swain explains," Younger generations are more willing to embrace change; 76% of executives in their 30s or younger look for opportunities to leverage new technology to achieve business goals. Plus, 67% of them see risk as opportunity, not danger, according to an Inavero study (Inavero. (2019)."

- **Data Literacy**

According to the Harvard Business Review, only 20% of companies are empowering their employees with data. A shift to a data-driven strategy cannot succeed without first being nurtured by a data-driven organizational culture that seeks to create comfort via a learning environment and operational mechanisms that leverage the evidence and facts (data) (Harvard Business Review Research Report., (Nd.). Words still matter, but action and follow-through deliver results.

- **Get Buy-in**

Most of the data that decision-makers want to see come from sales, as that data significantly clearly reflects performance that ultimately equates to profit. Marketing data can demonstrate success in acquiring new customers or retaining current customers. Customer service data demonstrates how well the customer is (or isn't) served. And when data is aggregated across departments, it informs a product team with a roadmap for how products should be structured. Data benefits finance by monitoring expense and profit margins. Clearly, it takes the whole organization to optimize data, as it can bring value to the entire organization. However, without buy-in across an organization, data will be used in silos and an organization will struggle to benefit from the data without a holistic approach to decision-making.

- **Use a Single System**

"Centralizing data removes many of the reasons technical issues come up in the first place by streamlining different management styles, maintenance procedures, tools, and providers into a single system. A single system reduces friction, making it easier for shared data concepts to work properly, thereby improving the chances that your organization will become successfully data-driven," according to Jason Sroka, chief analytics officer at SmartSense by Digi (Sroka, J., (2021). Of course, not all centralized systems are the solution. Many data lakes and repositories are downstream curators of data often reported in silos that remain unconnected. Always remember that humans and the front-end business systems are the entry point for data. Garbage in, garbage out. With a single system unconnected to the data strategy, data might as well exist in a mixed-use landfill.

- **Data Fluency and Definition**

"Typically, different departments use different vocabularies to refer to the same thing (e.g., "clients" are referred to as "customers" by customer service, "targets" by marketing, and "regions" by strategy), or use the same term to refer to different things (e.g., "group" to mean "customers," "users" or "distribution partners"). An organization must be willing to realign terms, definitions, and naming conventions to prevent confusion and encourage clear understanding and communication," according to Sroka. Consistent data description and data value across an organization lead to the most fruitful data-driven cultures.

- **Technical and Process Standards**

How data is technically gathered, managed, computed, curated, and stored must be based on appropriate technical and meta-data standards (standards and frameworks of descriptive data about data) that are leveraged across an organization. Consistent data fluency and definition must be shared across all data management and collection to ensure objectivity. Employees should never have to ask or question where data came from, how it is described, used with other data, or calculated. Therefore, to achieve the goal of becoming data-driven, an organization must ensure consistent data standards.

The Argument for Intuitive Decision-Making

"Intuition is subjective and is effective when you don't have data or the time to think logically before making a decision. And even though you can develop intuition based on knowledge and experience (a type of data), it's still risky to use it in business decision-making. Nobel Prize laureate, Daniel Kahneman, says humans formed intuition as a tool to alert us to potential risks. It aids in our survival when we're faced with fight or flight situations. However, Kahneman claims that using data to make decisions is critically important because it decreases our propensity to make poor ones," according to Swain.

Laura Huang, associate professor of business administration in the Organizational Behavior Unit, Harvard Business School believes," When making an important decision, should you trust your gut, or gather more information before deciding?

There are two factors to consider:

- "Could more data help you pick the right option? If your organization is considering a new product idea, for example, you can do market research and assess your competitor's offerings — but that information won't guarantee that people will buy your product. In a situation like this one, you may consider the data at hand and then rely on your gut.

- The second factor is the context of the problem you're facing. If successful mental models and schemas exist for this kind of decision, it's probably a good idea to use them. If you're trying to differentiate yourself from competitors who have followed those models, gut instinct may be the way to go. And remember: Intuition draws on the objective and subjective information you already know — so your gut feel is, to some extent, data-driven. If data has already been available and you and your organization are data-driven, intuition is more informed Huang, L., (2019)."

Leadership Decision-Making in the Digital Age

Do you run an organization with the "father and/or mother knows best" approach?

Or do you give away personal control and trust your customers and teams to lead the way?

There are several fatal errors in judgment a leader can make while running an organization in today's complex, digital, data-empowered marketplace. The rules of engagement are changing, but what remains constant is that if your operations are not customer- and data-centric, they will surely fail.

Transitioning from an analog mentality to a digitally enhanced data-driven-based perspective can be uncomfortable and anxiety-provoking. In a searchable online universe, the adage is true, "you don't have to know everything, but you need to know how to find it." And the first step to finding it is to be well-informed and surrounded by mindful, curious, talented individuals that simply are not afraid of data and understand how data inform sound decision-making.

Data and Intuition on the Balance Beam

Reed Hastings, CEO of Netflix has been quoted. "We start with the data. But the final call is always gut. It is called informed intuition (Ferenstein, G. 2016)." Choudhary adds, "Data is a driving force in the 21st century. A decision can be considered a hit, or a miss based on its resultant data. At the same time, a leader is expected to deliver both quantitative and qualitative results. A combination of the two approaches has the power to make the individual a balanced leader." He adds, "Truly impactful decision-making leverages data analytics as well as intuitive skills. There must be an element of informed risk and an aptitude for it. A leader who weighs both their gut feeling and trusted data is using informed/intuitive decision-making and is better positioned than one who closes their eyes to one of the two aspects (Choudhary, A., (Nd.)."

Situations favoring data-driven and intuitive decision-making:

Data-Driven	Intuitive
Conflict Resolution	Quick Decisions
Properly Defined Goals	Ambiguous Situations
Structured and Processed	Unstructured Problem Solving
Big-bet Decisions	Ad-hoc and Daily Decisions
Infrequent and Unfamiliar	Familiar Situations

Source: (Choudhary, Amit. (nd.)

Raazi Imam, managing partner, California, and global lead for SiaXperience adds "In life and business, we all have to make difficult decisions. How much information do we consider before deciding on something that isn't clearly black and white? How much do we rely on our gut intuition? What should we leverage more? Data? Or intuition? My answer is simple: rely on both. Great decision-making is not about leveraging one over the other but instead using them in tandem."

"Analytical decision-making goes hand-in-hand with utilizing data. Facts are concrete and give us useful jumping boards to start on. But then intuition comes into play.

And this is where we look at patterns, what is right and wrong, should we go left or right, etc. To neglect one would be an error. To utilize both is strategic (Imam, R. (2018)."

Ultimately, any decision-making has to factor in people: customers, clients, stakeholders, and employees. We agree with Forbes writer Chris Westfall: "Without insights into intuition, companies and executive decision-makers will miss the most important factor in business: the human factor (Westfall, C. (2020)."

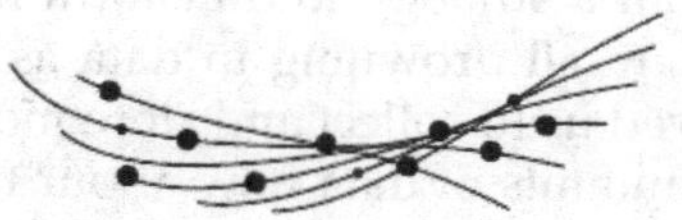

Chapter 19: Good Data Is Vital Currency…Bad Data Is a Disaster

"There is an insidious reality in data management. We don't identify and assess the right input that assesses outcome measurement. We also make faulty assumptions about incomplete or bad data, we assign the wrong definition and meaning to the data, and we don't often question its value. Human error is often the root of faulty data analytics and what is measured as a result."

Data Traps

We often talk about the common problem of collecting massive amounts of data without a strategy to transform it into intelligent action-oriented insights. We are all drowning in data as technology and digital interactions have allowed us to collect and store more data and offer access to it. Given the large amounts of data now at our fingertips, we need data scientists and analytical engineers to make sense of it all. We flatter ourselves with the amount of data collected as seemingly size matters and assume the data we have collected is reliable, valuable, and meaningful. There is also some confusion as to what an output versus an outcome is, and data only adds to the confusion and challenge.

There is a more insidious reality in data management. We don't identify and assess the right input that assesses outcome measurement. We also make faulty assumptions about incomplete or bad data, we assign the wrong definition and meaning to the data, and we don't often question its value. Human error is often the root of faulty data analytics and what is measured as a result.

If you don't ask the right questions in context of the specific problem, how can you expect the data to reflect the appropriate answers?

If the data is incorrectly defined, incomplete, or not valuable, how then do you make organizational decisions or truly understand performance?

We are going to explore a topic that is frequently overlooked by management when establishing a data practice: how bad or faulty data can lead to disastrous decision-making that results in taking the wrong actions or responses — often with significant consequences.

What Is Bad Data?

High-quality data that is appropriately and contextually defined and joined with other relevant data is accurate, action-oriented, and therefore valuable. Bad data is data that is incomplete, incorrect, wrongly defined, and/or irrelevant. Bad data can also be outdated information, duplicated in the database, unformatted (typos, spelling variations, inconsistencies), and inaccurately recorded.

Bad data can also be less obvious when data coders tinge input from their conscious or unconscious biases.

If coders provide facial recognition artificial intelligence applications with images of only one gender or race—m or segments of each that don't represent the whole of society—the output is faulty, and any decisions made on the output are incorrect. If determinations of audience and/or market are made with a small set of data that doesn't reflect all the descriptive, identifying demographic data and its nuances, any decision becomes a small dart attempting to hit the huge bullseye. The only way to hit the target is sheer luck.

As reported in Forbes, according to research firm Gartner, "Organizations believe poor data quality is responsible for an average of $15 million per year in losses (Montecarlo, (Nd.)." Gartner also found that nearly 60% of those surveyed didn't know how much bad data costs their businesses because they don't measure it in the first place (Montecarlo, (Nd.)." If something isn't understood, assessed, or measured then how do you make decisions or take action on it? How do you learn from it?

Also reported in Forbes, "A study on the lack of trust around data from research firm Vanson Bourne (commissioned by SnapLogic) found that 91% of IT decision-makers believe they need to improve the quality of data in their organizations, while 77% said they lack trust in their organization's business data (Bourne, V. (SnapLogic)., (2020)."

Quality of data is often assumed to be the responsibility of the IT Department or the applications and machines themselves. We trust that applications and machines are accurate and effective since as we know we can make mistakes. The IT Department manages machines and applications that are downstream data collection points. Consider garbage in, and garbage out as data that is collected downstream in data lakes, customer data platforms (CDPs), data management platforms (DMP), and other hype-based "repository platforms and toolsets" that overpromise the ability to create immediate insights and intelligence.

We overlook the upstream inputs and sources of data that predominantly rely on humans. Sales staff enter data (or not) about accounts in their sales funnel; human resources enter, or review data attached to candidates and existing employees; staff manage their own data spreadsheets and when they find the application challenging and hard to work with, they avoid it. When humans enter data, hit save and submit, it typically is not reviewed for accuracy.

Data in the upstream then becomes fairly polluted which carries the pollution into downstream lakes.

Some would argue that the IT Department or software platforms and toolsets should recognize the input errors and find some technical, AI-based fix to counter human error. There ought to be a fail-safe system to critically assess the work or the work of others related to the collection and insertion of data. Once again, our own biases and desire to deflect accountabilities lead to misperceptions that then impact the quality of data — and ultimately trust in decision-making.

Data Quality Assessment and Data Masters

A comprehensive approach and process to ensure data is reliable and trustworthy is to ensure quality control management. A formal organizational-wide QCM that sets forth the sources of data, the consistent and appropriate definitions and values of data, and constant assessment of accuracy, completeness, and relevance becomes a critical foundational initiative for all organizations. Some organizations, including 2040 Digital, where your author and co-author work, recommend a QCM framework process of a set of connected data masters (product, customer, etc.) that represent the concentric and connected circles of data attributes that come together to generate insight, meaning, and value and correlate to performance, decisions, and actions.

The QCM, whether managed by an individual or a team, should represent the upstream uses, definitions, purposes, and collection points along with the business needs and intent. At the core of the QCM is recognition of when limited value or meaning exists, and recognition of the upstream influences that must be known and adjusted for.

The Source

If the source is inaccurate, the data output will reflect that. If the source contains faults, misaligned programming, or process logic — or the upstream inputs generate significant and high-frequency errors, then the output is faulty and will result in the wrong insights. The compounding challenge comes when an organization seeks to level set the quality, value, and completeness of data by using another data source to validate it. If the comparative source is as faulty as the first, one would hope the disconnect might be obvious. But in truth, internal systems may replicate the same faulty definitions, assigned values, or errors. Any decision then only promulgates and replicates decision and action impacts across the organization.

The Data You Need

We have made the point that technology and digital have allowed organizations to collect masses of data from employees, business processes, and customers. The applications, systems, and toolsets we use day-to-day run our organizations. We like to horde and are reluctant to choose what is or isn't important; we save everything for a rainy day. When loads of information and data exist, humans often do not want to expend the energy to critically assess what is or isn't needed or deflect ownership as it "isn't their responsibility." A critical, foundational exercise is to define and identify the data you need for understanding operational and market performance. Then bridge it to the measurement of outcomes to understand who customers are in their relationship to the organization—and how the organization is performing in meeting their needs and wants. Related to this is the importance of life stage marketing and measuring what matters, both of which inform how data models, foundations, and collection are meaningful and relevant to managing and curating accurate and insightful connected data.

Deep Cleanse

Regular data cleansing should be the responsibility of anyone in the organization responsible for the upstream data inputs. Those in the upstream are often the operations and business departments. Since they know the business most intimately, they are inputting and deriving insights and must take responsibility without deflecting the quality and/or cleansing of data to the IT Department or the data scientists or analytics engineers.

Ongoing Review

Maintaining data isn't a once-and-done activity or exercise. It is an ongoing process that requires checks and balances which constantly reassess data's definition and value. The past is helpful and indicative, but it reflects factors and variables that existed in context at that time. For example, how do we consider how a current economy deals with high inflation and returns to some version of normalcy after a global crisis or a world immersed in war? The data that explained the past is no longer relevant, and using those analytics makes it hard to manage the present or predict the future.

It's true that measuring the performance of a new product or market against an earlier product and market will result in some form of data return, but the connections may be forced, out of context, and out of line as the products aren't the same, factors and variables are different, and the market may be completely unrelated.

Ensuring Data Currency and Maintaining Accuracy

Organizations often have significant amounts of transactional data. This data represents past sales of products or services. Transactional data is considered historical data and may not indicate current or future performance or equate to the measurement of outcomes in the present. As such, additional data and analysis are required to recognize what and who comprised past performance. Updated data enables contextualization of current factors and variables. Only in leveraging the environmental conditions in the present, does past data become indicative or informative.

Pay attention to larger patterns. Manu Bansal of the Forbes Technology Council states "When bad data hurts your organization, it is important not to assume that this is just an isolated, one-time event (Bansal, M. (2021)." Where there is one error, there are often others, and the errors have been replicated across systems, applications, and data stores.

Often bad data exists for a while and decisions have been made continuously on that data. When the bad data is revealed, individuals and teams become disillusioned since their own performance has been routinely measured incorrectly.

Reluctance and yes, fear, grow when the data correction is reported, knowing it may cause larger implications to the public or similar reporting that will trigger crisis communications strategies to manage stakeholder reactions. In certain situations when the correction is not brought to light, internally a revisionist history approach takes over to justify the error. This only creates more challenges and complexity to gain and leverage accurate data for insights and measurement.

Know the tools and platforms you need. The pace of change in data collection technological platforms and tools can be overwhelming since so many technology providers have added some element of machine learning and artificial intelligence to their offerings. When you don't know the nature of the data you have and whether it is or isn't of quality, defined, or valued, how then can you make the best selection of tools or platforms that will help curate, manage, and store the ever-increasing amounts of organizational data?

Understanding the data you have, how it is defined, and how it needs to be used—as well as where it comes from and how it is ingested—is a critical viewpoint in selecting an appropriate tool. Remember, AI and machine learning are programmed by humans who may not have the same context as the organization you do. Plus, machine learning may have been programmed unrelated to who your customers are and what business you are in.

Data-Driven Decision-Making

Making business decisions based on gut instinct can lead to some bad decisions. Data-driven decisions can make you more confident by using objective information that is logical and concrete. Yet making those decisions based on faulty data can lead to ruin. Tim Stobierski writes for the Harvard Business school, "Tie every decision back to the data. Whenever you're presented with a decision, whether business-related or personal in nature, do your best to avoid relying on gut instinct or past behavior when determining a course of action. Instead, make a conscious effort to apply an analytical mindset (Stobierski, T., (Nd.)."

A data-driven decision-making process can make you more proactive. Stobierski adds, "Given enough practice and the right types and quantities of data, it's possible to leverage it more proactively—for example, by identifying business opportunities before your competition does, or by detecting threats before they grow too serious."

One of the most positive outcomes of using data is to reduce expenses. Randy Bean, CEO of NewVantage Partners states "Big data is already being used to improve operational efficiency. And the ability to make informed decisions based on the very latest up-to-the-moment information is rapidly becoming the mainstream norm (Bean, R. 2014)."

Stobierski adds, "Data visualization is a huge part of the data analysis process. It's nearly impossible to derive meaning from a table of numbers. By creating engaging visuals in the form of charts and graphs, you'll be able to quickly identify trends and make conclusions about the data."

Misinformation, Perception Distortion, and Decision-Making Risk

Organizations now operate in an environment where perception can outpace reality and misinformation can overwhelm fact. AI systems can hallucinate, distort patterns, or generate confident but incorrect outputs. Employees may rely on these results without understanding their limitations. Leaders may assume AI-driven insights are inherently superior to human judgment. Both assumptions are dangerous.

When misinformation flows into decision-making processes, organizations become vulnerable to strategic blindness. Small errors compound. Faulty assumptions harden into policies. People begin to trust the appearance of intelligence rather than the integrity of information.

The truth is that AI is only as reliable as the data it consumes and the humans who interpret its output. Leaders must cultivate a culture of verification, questioning, and intellectual humility. Organizations don't just need better data — they need better discernment.

Bad Business Decisions

The saying goes, hindsight is 20/20, but we say it's really a revelation of blindsight. The Ladders has identified a list of companies that went out of business based on remarkably bad business decisions.

We have selected a few of them as examples of how the intelligent use of data might have produced entirely different outcomes (Schneider, M., (2021). We suggest using these examples as cautionary tales of how not to let your own business fall into a similar trap.

- **A&W**

"While A&W has never technically filed for bankruptcy, there are far fewer of them these days. The fast-food chain suffered a major loss in the 1980s because it ran a special promotion that consumers simply didn't understand. A&W created a third-pound burger to compete with McDonald's popular quarter-pounder and offered it at the same price. But the burger didn't sell, a fact that was absolutely flummoxing to the company.

"A focus group confirmed: Americans have no common sense. Because the number three is smaller than the number four, consumers thought they were getting a smaller burger when, in fact, the meal at A&W had more meat."

We're not so convinced this can be blamed on the American public. Any basic customer research would have revealed the potential problem. This is also an example of management hubris. One of our 2040 mantras is about the negative effects of inherent bias; just because you think an idea is great does not mean your customers – or even your workforce – would agree. The collection of data about your customers is essential to ensure that your products and service are on track and aligned with what they expect from you (Schneider, M., (2021).

- **MoviePass**

"A subscription-based ticketing service for movies, MoviePass launched in 2011 and was developed into an app shortly thereafter. For a monthly fee, MoviePass allowed each subscriber to redeem three movie tickets and over time, new plan structures evolved with more benefits for the user. What happened was the unlimited options gave way to financial loss, as users went to more and more movies on MoviePass. Competitors were updating their rewards programs at record speed, also pricing out some of the lucrative options for users. In 2018, long before the pandemic threw movie attendance into disarray, MoviePass ran a deficit of millions and never recovered and went out of business in 2020."

This use case is a goldmine for proving that data can provide customer insights to prevent a business model derailment. Analyzing expected customer behavior matched to financial results would seem obvious.
Couple that with a comprehensive business model based on sound assumptions and MoviePass could have become the popular AMC Rewards ticket subscription service, not be eclipsed by it (Schneider, M., (2021).

- **Red Lobster**

"In 2003, Red Lobster ran an extravagant promotion that eventually landed them in bankruptcy. That year, they enticed customers to come in and enjoy an all-you-can-eat snow crab experience for the low cost of $20. The problem? Snow crab is expensive and highly regulated by the government.

While snow crab was under $5 per pound at the time, the restaurant underestimated consumers' appetites. Diners came in and ate and ate and ate. In fact, they ate so much that the promotion cost Red Lobster over $1.1 million per month."

This example of not using data and analytics to field test a new product is in retrospect a giant "what were you thinking?"

The power of market research is its ability to flag a misjudgment or faulty assumption. That would have solved the disastrous loss leading promotion. But more fundamentally, running financial models to test a new product seems pretty basic (Schneider, M., (2021).

- **JCPenney**

Business books will be written about JC Penney and its fall from retail grace. It has had a revolving door of CEOs, rebranded and updated its stores, and even filed for bankruptcy. When whiz kid retailer Ron Johnson came from Apple to JC Penney, he brought with him a vision for a new retail model. He redesigned the stores into marketplaces, which could have worked. But he also got rid of the familiar pricing promotions to create an everyday fair-priced merchandise model. Because JCP stopped putting discount pricing on everything, customers thought they were no longer getting a deal. Sales came to a screeching halt, as did Mr. Johnson.

Johnson's strategy neglected several key factors: market testing with customers and bringing management into his innovative thinking. Instead, he made assumptions about loyal customers and the workforce's ability to pivot without being included in the decision-making process. This is another example of hubris and leadership with blinders believing they have the best ideas, the most progressive solutions, and a monopoly on innovation (Schneider, M., (2021).

Guard Your Data

Mastering the art and science of data and analytics will help you develop the systems and processes that protect your data and avoid poor decision-making based on faulty input.

Optimize outcomes by ensuring output is accurate, reliable, and relevant.

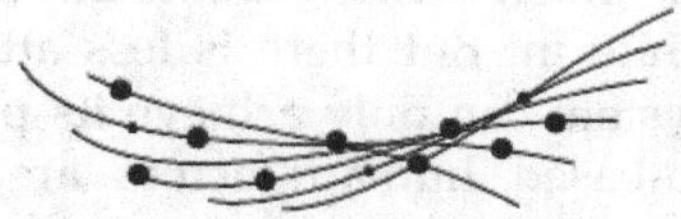

Chapter 20: How Market Orientation Drives Success

"Authentic market orientation reveals the truth about transformation and how human factors and behaviors impact the organizational system. It isn't about "marketing," it isn't about "sales," and it isn't about "product management." It is focused on the human elements of an organization-wide system that must cohesively align for a shared purpose."

Reorienting

There has been much written about the dynamic and disruptive market forces we operate in. But there is less attention paid to how an organization and its system can only achieve its purpose and goals if the individual and group-based human factors are aligned and oriented towards a shared value proposition to the market. We call this market orientation: enterprise-wide market information (intelligence) related to the present and upcoming needs and desires of customers, disseminating information through and in between departments comprising the parts of an organization's system, resulting in organization-wide responsiveness, according to Mauro Falasca (Falasca, M., et. al. 2017). Simply stated, that means a holistic relationship between leadership, the workforce, and its market designed to drive response and engagement among stakeholders.

Why Market Orientation?

Market orientation represents a set of processes touching on all aspects of an organization to maintain and grow continuous dialog, recognition, and intent across all organizational units. This interrelationship connects all parts of the organizational system, which enables its responsiveness to the market and its customers.

Market orientation and resulting responsiveness have their basis in agility. Market orientation seeks to limit ambiguity by staying knowledgeable and informed on the continued evolution and/or maturation of the market and aligning goals, strategies, and tactics that are reflective of market needs and wants, creating deeper and additive customer value.

Authentic market orientation reveals the truth about transformation and how human factors and behaviors impact the organizational system. It isn't about "marketing," it isn't about "sales," and it isn't about "product management." It is focused on the human elements of an organization-wide system that must cohesively align for a shared purpose.

Mamoun N. Akroush of German Jordanian University and Bushra Mahadin of the American University of Madaba define market orientation as reflective of the organization's culture by focusing on creating superior competitive value for customers and exploring and identifying trends in target markets to provide greater needs and desires to customers (Akroush, M & Mahadin, Bushra K. (2019).

Market orientation as a business philosophy and practice should influence and form the basis of culture. This orientation forms the structure by which a culture is set, grows, and matures over time. The culture works towards goals with a shared definition and understanding of information and intelligence including factors and variables that exist in or across the Macro (world, region, country, locality), Meso (the organization and its system), and Micro (representing individuals across the customer base and workforce) systems. Therefore, it does not reflect the culture, it sets the foundation on which the culture forms.

Market Orientation and Risk

A comparison of organizations that establish a clear and explicit market orientation versus organizations that do not, reveals that the organizations which do have a better and clearer understanding of strategies and capabilities, customer needs, and desires to confront competitors and exterior forces and respond in proper ways, according to Gary Knight of Willamette University, Peter Liesch of the University of Queensland, and Alexandra Solano Acosta of the Digital Evolution Center and the Digital Transformation HUB (Acosta, A., et. al. 2017).

Ajay Kohli and Bernard Jaworski, two leaders in researching and assessing organizations, propose that top management's attitude toward risk and organizational structure would affect a firm's adoption of market orientation. Risk, particularly fear of challenges to safety, comfort, and familiarity runs deep and is more pervasive than we recognize across leadership's ability to manage the organizational system. Fear of risk also influences attitudes and behaviors resulting in "safe" decisions that create less friction, avoid confrontation, and limit the scope to a closed-loop part of the organizational system (Kohli, A. K., & Jaworski, B. J. 1990).

Here's a real-life example of market orientation and risk. General Electric (GE) separates into three distinct companies. The official mantra at GE has focused on management practices and systems to respond to, and evolve with the market to remain relevant, sustain and grow. Although management, particularly at the top echelons, may have aligned to a shared purpose, the human system (downstream and dispersed levels) across GE functioned with a different set of knowledge, purposes for being, and a disparate marketing orientation existing outside of alignment with the market. So, the decision to separate did not go smoothly.

The challenge for GE management is to recognize the importance of the human system comprising the workforce—and that it takes an aligned village to a shared purpose to remain relevant, sustain, grow and yes … transform organization-wide responsiveness to the market. One cannot manage out of or around the human factor. Humans in this century and moving forward aren't just the cogs in a wheel.

Market Orientation vs Marketing Concept

The business theme song today is the aspiration that "We are going to be more entrepreneurial; we are going to be innovative, and we are going to become a learning organization." Although each of these intentions offers the opportunity for change and perhaps even seeding transformation, the result represents only one piece of the pie and translates to improving only one element, direction, area, or approach of the organization and its system. The remainder of the organization, its purpose, human complement, and how work is accomplished, remains untouched and/or removed from the potential of achieving a defined and shared purpose that aligns with market orientation.

Kohli and Jaworski defined market orientation as a marketing concept: "The organization-wide generation of market intelligence, dissemination of the intelligence across departments and organization-wide responsiveness to it (Kohli, A. K., & Jaworski, B. J. (1990)." According to them, marketing orientation is a "marketing" business philosophy, whereas the term market orientation really refers to the actual implementation of marketing. In today's terms, individuals, and organizations understand "marketing" as having a marketing department that is responsible for acquiring, curating, and maturing the customer base, regardless of business focus. That department is responsible for understanding the customer and identifying new customers for one area or department of an organization. That approach can be subject to intellectual and experiential correlations based on default behaviors and lack of critical thinking and assessment. A siloed marketing department overlooks the involvement of all parts of the system parts in a shared purpose.

Marketing Revisited

Marketing from an organizational perspective, along with sales, represents how customers are acquired and retained and how the market, comprised of potential customers, becomes aware of products and/or services offered by an organization. Marketing joined with sales, is of major importance in maintaining an engine of stability and growth.

If potential customers do not know about an organization or what it offers, they will seek out organizations that they do know. As a result, revenues do not grow, and the organization's relevance is compromised.

Marketing and sales are important but only represent two organizational parts that comprise the entire system. If only sales and marketing choose the customers to interact with, they have undue power. That power creates a situation of control where strategic decisions are made without context or understanding of the supporting organizational parts and their capacities to match the direction.

Consider a case when marketing and sales focus on a potential growth market segment. Say this market segment has desires for expanded features or functionality of the organization's products that have not yet been developed. Although marketing and sales understand the opportunity as well as the documented customer need, the organization has not aligned to that market orientation. The other parts of the system may not even have the capability or capacity to match the demand. This approach will cause chaos caused by the expectation to expand product features and functionality combined with the expense of the acquisition of this market segment. Most certainly, any net revenue gain over time will fail if it is based on a faulty premise.

In this case, since the intent and decision by marketing and sales have been made without context of the organizational system, it reflects only one part of the system and the potential results that part of the system may gain. The necessary changes and/or transformation to further develop the product and the impact of those changes and/or transformation on the other parts of the systems are not recognized.

Disconnected, Siloed Systems

This example is a perfect illustration of siloed departmental goals and/or responsibilities that permeate many organizations when individuals and teams are given responsibility and are incentivized to focus on and execute their given goals to succeed, without regard to the larger system.

Beyond the financial and operational impacts of this siloed approach, how can the rest of the organization understand and define their roles in a direction set by others?

Do they stop how they are currently working and eliminate what is currently or planned to be provided to customers?

Do they change the approved plans or roadmaps for developing the products?

And what are the consequences of those new plans and who decides whether to move forward?

How do they come to understand what has changed?

What is being lost?

Is the definition of "customer needs" still valid or are the interpretation and understanding now different?

In reality the inter-dependencies across an organization are often ignored. Leaders may unintentionally seek to motivate and inspire individuals and teams with added responsibility and recognition (incentives). However, this has cascading and fracturing impacts across the organization. The market orientation seemingly set in isolation and without interaction is not widely communicated nor aligned with a shared purpose, which then leads to confusion among the individuals who must achieve the goal.

A New Market Orientation

A siloed perspective may lead to effective performance in one part of an organization but change and transformation will always be limited to that specific part. Consider the definition of market orientation in a broader and more complex sense. The various perceptions and interpretations of market orientation must come together holistically with decision-making, market intelligence, strategic, and customer orientation perspectives aligned with innovation, agility practices, and marketing (tactical) execution (inclusive of sales). If you remember one thing: One part of the system, changed and transformed in isolation does not lead to successful organizational change and transformation.

Consider the data points on the diversity of the world's population. An effective market orientation must consider both the market as it currently exists and how it is expected to evolve over time. An organization operating under assumptions and perceptions of the market and its relationship to that market must set a strategy and tactics to anticipate where it is headed. If its assumptions and perceptions are not aligned closely to the market, then an organization is not truly aligned in market orientation. It sits on shaky ground that represents a different reality than what exists.

A better approach is to recognize the impact of behavioral defaults on our perceptions of the world. Clarity can be achieved with contextual analysis that evolves and transforms into a fluid market orientation. This orientation is based more firmly on fact than assumption and perception. The shared purpose of, and reason for, a true market orientation creates the basis for all individuals and groups within the organization to understand the roles and responsibilities that their respective parts of the organization have in the overall system. The aligned orientation also provides the opportunity for individuals and groups to see and grasp what identity and responsibility they may be losing and will be subsequently redefined as part of the orientation.

One last word about context. Annie Murphy Paul argues in *The Extended Mind* that the human mind is contextual. She states that "The mind works differently in different environments with different tools, amid different bodily states, among other minds (Paul Murphy, A., (2021)." This flies in the face of our prevailing metaphor that the human mind is a computer "that operates the exact same way whether it's in a dark room or next to a sunny window, whether it's been working for 30 seconds or three hours, whether it's near other computers or completely alone." The New York Times adds that Paul offers a radical critique of not just how we think about thinking, but how we've constructed much of our society (Paul Murphy, A. (NYT) (2021).

Foundation of Shared Knowledge

Market orientation is achieved through the generation of intelligence gained by a contextual analysis of factors and variables. This intelligence is based on interpreted and applied objective data, across the Macro (world, country, region, or locality), Meso (organization), and Micro (representative of individuals and groups of customers, employees, and stakeholders). The dissemination of intelligence then becomes shared knowledge that forms the basis for a shared purpose and organizational responsiveness. Shared knowledge further mitigates and minimizes individual and group ambiguity in how the organization's parts relate to the organizational responsiveness represented via the market orientation.

The value of market orientation addresses the following challenges based on human behavior, contextualization, and decision-making with objective basis points:

- Minimizing the individual influences. resulting from bias and overgeneralization.

- Limiting individual motivations driven by the personal gain that impacts and influences decision-making and comprises the organizational system.
- Offering an opportunity to create and measure quantifiable goals towards the shared purpose with organizational goal attainment above individual goal attainment.
- Reliance on data to remove assumptions and perceptions.

In summary, a market orientation becomes the basis and foundation of a culture and creates a structure to ensure the organizational parts and people that comprise those parts align towards a shared purpose within a Mesosystem environment that ingrains organizational responsiveness.

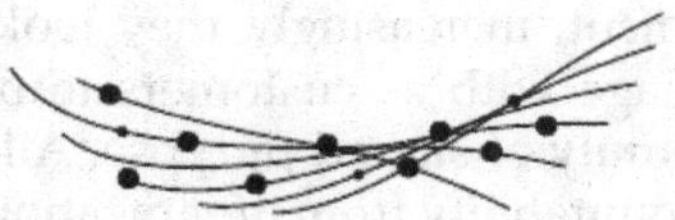

Chapter 21: Shared Purpose Matters

"Having the vision to create a shared purpose organization and seeing it to fruition is often prevented by a lack of C-suite involvement and failure to make purpose a business strategy. There is often the temptation to mistake corporate values for purpose. And purpose needs KPIs to measure success."

Finding Purpose

When the public discourse becomes contentious and people lose faith in institutions and government, increasingly they look to the organizations where they work or engage with as customers to bestow their trust and connection with a community of shared purpose. All types of stakeholders are pushing for more accountability from organizations and leadership, and even the institutions they have seemingly lost faith in.

In fact, according to BrandCulture, "For too long, the business-as-usual approach to generating revenue and achieving growth has disengaged customers and employees, bred mistrust and damaged reputations by substituting relentless pursuit of profits over vision and frequently foregoing the mission entirely" (BrandCulture. (Nd.). Many of our government institutions have deflected the public or their constituents' needs and wants by losing sight of their true purpose for existence. Plus, many professional organizations, profit and nonprofit, have been taken to task for not serving stakeholders. Therefore, faith and trust are eroding, a chasm has opened, and individuals are struggling to find connection and meaning to fill the gap.

As with many other aspects of social disruptions, we are becoming more polarized in our belief systems, often framed by subconscious or unconscious bias. Defining shared purpose in context of organizational alignment and in meeting an organization's social obligations is a pathway to success. It is a complex topic, yet a critical exercise regardless of one's perspective and values. Any enlightened attempt to seek change and transformation of an organization's market orientation should also fulfill the needs of its stakeholders, both internal and external.

Shared purpose spurs a grounded conversation about the macro and micro issues that are important to a diverse, inclusive community by creating a narrative that is relevant, meaningful, and fluid so that it can evolve as the needs of stakeholders change. All organizations are represented as a Mesosystem that reflects their organizational strategy, structure, model, and culture. A Mesosystem does not exist in isolation. It is surrounded by, influenced, and dependent upon the Macrosystem (world, region, country, or locality) and the Microsystem (individuals and groups of customers and employees).

A shared purpose represents how an organization shapes itself, works together, and presents itself with intent and in service to the Macro and Microsystems it operates in.

Purpose Seeking

It's becoming a tough world out there. People in many ways are disillusioned and struggling to gain a sense of normalcy and predictability.

- Whom do we trust?
- Whom can we trust?
- How do we know when to trust?
- And when do we question?

Edelman's 2022 Trust Barometer reported some interesting trends related to the role of organizations in our society:

- The majority (60%) of people globally say their country will not be able to overcome its challenges without the involvement of business. (Edelman Trust Barometer. (2022)

- Roughly 80% of people, on average, expect their organizations to act on issues such as vaccine hesitancy, climate change, automation, misinformation, and racism (Edelman Trust Barometer. (2022)

- 52% also believe that CEOs need to motivate their employees to take part in solving societal issues—organizations that not only drive future purchase intent but also reinforce consumer trust in their brand. (Edelman Trust Barometer. (2022)

- While 87% of global respondents (and more than 75% of US respondents) in the Edelman study believe that companies should place equal weight on business and pressing social issues, only about a third think that business, in its current form, is getting the job done. (Edelman Trust Barometer. (2022)

And the 2024 Edelman Trust Barometer also revealed that:

- "My employer" remains the most trusted institution among the four main societal pillars (business, government, NGOs, and media).

- Employees across seven countries globally view their employers as the most believable source of information and as an "island of civility" in an increasingly polarized world (Edelman, 2024a).

However, trust within organizations has become stratified. The 2024 study reveals a 39-point economic optimism gap between executives and frontline employees—executives are far more optimistic about their economic prospects than their employees are about theirs. This gap represents more than just different perspectives; it signals a fundamental disconnect between leadership and the workforce they lead (Edelman, 2024b).

The research also found that job level predicts economic optimism and trust more than income does. An executive making $75,000 is more optimistic than an individual freelance contributor making $150,000. This suggests that sense of engagement and agency in one's work matters more than compensation alone (Edelman, 2024b).

Organizations implementing shared purpose must bridge this trust gap by addressing employees' fundamental expectations: 87% expect their employer to increase their wages to help them deal with the cost of living, and 80% expect meaningful training and development to help them adapt to technological change (Edelman, 2024b). As a result of internal and external forces, organizations believe they are being thrust onto center stage to speak and act on social and political issues.

It's important for leaders to move beyond personal beliefs and know when constituents expect an organization to take center stage with a stand on issues. Once management accepts expectations to take such a stand, it can become a critical factor in successfully recruiting and retaining employees, especially demanding, opinionated next gens, as well as sustaining and acquiring social-minded customers.

Shannon Schuyler, chief purpose, and inclusion officer at Price Waterhouse Coopers (PWC) says, "People truly don't want to show up to their jobs and just get a paycheck anymore, employees, especially younger ones, will even quit if they don't feel a sense of purpose at work" (Schuyler, S., Pandy, E.), (2021). An organizational structure that forms around a shared purpose provides stakeholders something to believe in that is larger than themselves. This is also true for customers when they seek a relationship with an organization.

According to Eurasia Group, corporations are losing the culture wars. "The world's biggest brands are earning record profits. But they're going to have a more difficult year navigating politics. Consumers and employees, empowered by cancel culture and enabled by social media, will put new demands on multinational corporations (MNCs) and the governments that regulate them.

Consumers and employees have corporate boardrooms on the defensive. Social media is even more powerful and pervasive, and the threat of being canceled, in this case, consumers ostracizing or blocking a company from markets, is real. The Great Resignation means companies have had to shift and make themselves more attractive to new hires, and it gives those workers who remain more leverage to change companies from the inside. Meanwhile, consumers will enlist policymakers in their campaigns to demand that companies take stands on culture war issues, workplace diversity, voting rights, forced and child labor, supply chains that respect the environment and human rights, free speech, and more" (Eurasia Group. (2022).

Something to Believe In

Shared purpose is shorthand for getting people connected to the mission of an organization. The most effective leaders build a collective sense of shared purpose and connect everyone to the mission and purpose of the larger team. The teams who think and work together with a sense of shared purpose are the happiest, and the most successful, according to the author, retired Colonel Mickey Addison (Addison, M. (2016).

A shared purpose aligned to a market orientation provides a focus for each group and individual in an organization and aids them in understanding how their daily efforts contribute overall. It also helps define them professionally and offers a way to see and measure their internal value. As we often get lost in the day-to-day and lose sight of things larger than ourselves, we find that chasms emerge. A lack of real or perceived purpose can lead to negative feelings and grow into depression and anxiety. From a managerial perspective, it needs to be mindful that talent today seeks organizations with a shared purpose that they can align with and derive personal and professional value from.

Punit Renjen, Deloitte Global CEO adds, "An organization's culture of purpose answers the critical questions of who it is and why it exists. They have a culture of a purpose beyond making a profit. An organization's culture of purpose answers the critical questions of who we are and why we exist through a set of carefully articulated core beliefs. A culture of purpose guides behavior, influences strategy, transcends leaders–and endures" (Renjen, P. (2021).

BrandCulture adds that organizations define shared purpose in different ways. "Some claim ownership of a mission, others describe their vision or covenant, while others articulate a purpose or vision statement" (BrandCulture. (Nd.).

In a real-life example, "Southwest seeks to deliver its mission by ensuring every employee understands how his or her effort contributes to the mission of delivering an exceptional travel experience, even if it means pilots bringing strollers down to baggage handlers on the tarmac so a flight leaves on time. Southwest makes sure they reward their employees who deliver on this mission by backing them with financial reserves." The anecdotal results of shared purpose are self-evident, "The airline has never had a layoff and can trace its one and only labor strike to a six-day action in 1980" (BrandCulture. (Nd.).

Purpose-Driven Business Model

"It's not the *if*, it's the *how*," says Jackie Cooper, global vice chair of Edelman Brand Properties. "Purpose needs to become a core competency for leading organizations. Organizations need to build social equity into their brands from product innovation and employee engagement to marketing communications" (Cooper, J. (2012). An organization's purpose or mission statement was originally about "what's within our four walls, but more and more it's about what's outside of our four walls," says Schuyler (Schuyler, S., Pandy, E. (2021). In this regard, reflect on market orientation and how organizations must be based on a foundation of shared knowledge that is reflective of the Micro and Macrosystems.

It's not an easy journey to create an authentically shared purpose construct. Andrea Brimmer, chief marketing, and public relations officer at Ally Financial warns: "While the potential of brand purpose is game-changing, it's also a minefield if you get it wrong" (Brimmer, A. (Nd.). Think about it: Establishing a shared purpose permeating throughout an organization is a huge challenge. It needs to be systematic and holistic and does not have an end date, nor can it be automated by software. "It can't be delegated to a few interested individuals or be designed to impact one specific part of an organization or a specific audience. Acting on an authentic and well-aligned purpose is an all-in proposition, from the CEO on down, and it must be deeply embedded into the culture and core to the entire business operation and experience," according to Ken Beaulieu, vice president of marketing and communications for the ANA (Beaulieu, Ken. (Nd.).

Having the vision to create a shared purpose organization and seeing it to fruition is often prevented by a lack of C-suite involvement and failure to make purpose a business strategy. There is often the temptation to mistake corporate values for purpose.

And purpose needs KPIs to measure success. But getting those benchmarks right has consequential ramifications. A study by the global communications agency Porter Novelli found that when a brand leads with purpose, "It changes the entire perception of the company with stakeholders. Not only are they more trusting of, and loyal to a brand, but they also often associate it with words like caring, charitable, ethical, responsible, and transparent. That emotional connection runs deep: 78% of consumers are more likely to remember an organization with a strong purpose and 71% would purchase from a purpose-driven organization over the alternative when cost and quality are equal" (Porter Novelli. (2021).

The Chief Purpose Officer

Managing and actualizing a culture of shared purpose is shifting to the responsibility of the chief purpose officer. If this might sound New Age, consider the changes in job titles brought about by the seismic changes in our business culture; the chief social media officer comes to mind. The chief purpose officer recognizes that the importance of purpose is key to motivation and an effective way to embed purpose in the DNA of businesses, according to Forbes contributor Kate Cooper (Cooper, K. (2021).

The chief purpose officer should perform the role of facilitator recognizing that everyone in an organization has a shared responsibility to support the shared purpose. We often seek to align responsibility to one enthusiastic individual or group. As a result, organizations have added chief customer officers, chief strategy officers, and chief of pretty much everything du jour of responsibility. The aim, whether consciously recognized or not, is to build out a hierarchical structure with a single focal point that is held accountable for execution and performance. An unintended consequence of hierarchical actions is that the individual or group is regarded as the sole owner who is responsible, not the community at large.

Straddling the line between public accountability, people, and profits, some organizations have had to change their market orientation strategies by spending more time and money grappling with huge social problems like systemic racism, income inequality, and climate change. A chief purpose officer can facilitate these efforts and become the glue that holds shared purpose initiatives together. The officer is a resource, not an owner or a "throat to choke." Since shared purpose is a team sport, it needs teams embedded in all parts of the organization to advocate, align, contribute, and ensure the mission.

Here's a case study that illustrates how purpose can become imbued into an organizational construct. Kwasi Mitchell serves as the chief purpose officer of Deloitte and is responsible for driving a firm-wide strategy around Deloitte's commitments to include diversity, equity and inclusion, sustainability and climate change, and education and workforce development. According to Deloitte, he is also responsible for engaging the Deloitte community to live its purpose daily, supporting clients on their own purpose journey, forming alliances with key partners to co-create solutions to address systemic societal issues, and driving internal policy and process changes to achieve purpose aspirations. Mitchell says his position is "to guide, inspire and drive progress and accountability in our continued journey to empower our people to lead with their passions and help position Deloitte as a purpose-driven enterprise.

"My key focus areas are twofold. First and foremost, I want to enable our 110,000+ professionals to engage in purpose-driven work that's meaningful to them. That goes beyond volunteering; it's harnessing our people's skills to help solve some of the world's most complex challenges for the benefit of society.

"Second, my key focus is impact. The marketplace increasingly sees corporate social responsibility as table stakes — we're going far beyond that. How do we make sure we have the size, scale, and breadth of our brand to drive progress against societal issues taking place more broadly within the world? How do we direct our resources, so they have maximum impact on our communities? Through the purpose office, we can better funnel our resources and investments to change the lives of hundreds of thousands of people around the globe. A large part of that will be working with our clients, alliances, and even competitors to collectively bring our capabilities together to help solve institutional challenges beyond the capabilities of a singular organization" (Kwasi M. (2021).

Leading With Shared Purpose

A study by the strategic brand consultancy BrandPie found that while 80% of purpose-led CEOs agree that business leaders need to be more focused on long-term value creation rather than short-term profit delivery, only 28% are integrating purpose into their decision-making and strategy (BrandPie. (Nd.). In the B2B space, 86% of organizations say they embrace purpose as important to growth, but only 24% say they embed purpose in their business to the point of influencing innovation, operations, and their engagement with society, according to a study by the ANA, Carol Cone, ON PURPOSE, and the Harris Poll (Cone, C. (2020).

It is human nature to turn to leaders for direction and guidance. Following a leader provides stability and comfort and can inspire a collective mission to accomplish a goal. Following a leader with a shared purpose elevates the dynamic on steroids. "When leaders keep the welfare and engagement of their teams in the forefront of their decisions, they enable those teams to connect to the mission of the organization. That connection leads to a sense of mission and shared purpose—both keys to high performance," according to Addison (Addison, M. 2016). From a historical perspective, he explains that in contrast to the Industrial Age, "Information Age leaders have to pay attention to the needs of individuals. Those leaders who do will be giving the individuals in their teams a sense of shared purpose. During the Industrial Revolution, management specialists de-emphasized the needs and variations of individuals to standardize the product. While standardization and mass production enabled large-scale availability of consumer goods, it often produced sub-optimal results in employee morale and even safety" (Addison, M. 2016).

Organizational leaders can inspire and connect their employees to something larger than a paycheck, he adds. If leaders do that, they can inspire their teams and connect them to the larger mission and the community they serve. In return, their teams will strive and reach high performance. One drawback to blindly "following the leader "as a basic default behavior, individuals within the organization do not internalize their personal responsibility to contribute to the shared purpose. Leaders need to ensure that their leadership style is not hierarchical, but rather collaborative and embracive in actualizing shared purpose.

Building a Cultural Construct of Shared Purpose

Shared knowledge is key to keeping all stakeholders on the same page to operate with a shared purpose. Shared purpose is not a trendy marketing initiative. It needs to be authentically and relevantly embedded into the workplace ethos and culture. And it needs to be carefully and mindfully articulated.

BrandCulture recommends the first few steps by answering the following questions:

- What credible, differentiated value do you provide your customers, constituents, and stakeholders?
- Why does your organization exist?
- Who is your organization in service to?
- How do you or will you serve and impact the world?

- What does your organization stand for, and can you all work together?
- Is your organization aligned to multiple "purposes," or does it have one shared purpose that brings the organization together into something bigger than its parts (BrandCulture. (Nd.)?

Answering these questions can help you and your organization take the first steps in defining and aligning to an organizational-wide shared purpose. As we noted, implementation, embellishment, and building a shared purpose is not a once-and-done exercise. It requires every individual in an organization to take responsibility and understand how he or she contributes to the shared purpose.

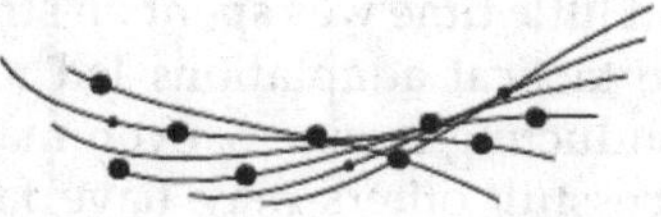

Chapter 22: Propelling High Performance

"Business leaders will be measured, even judged by their leadership performance; how they recruit and hire, construct teams, manage the board, and how they satisfy stakeholders whether they be internal or external. The potential trap here for any leader is bias, both unconscious and conscious, based on the values, experience from past actions, and institutional knowledge she or he brings to the organization. Here's just a taste of the potential problem: Seeing is believing—but the opposite is truer, what you believe you see."

Performance Shift

Much of the recent past has been focused on tactical adaptations for business continuity and little time was spent on strategic thinking and plans that recognized where tactical adaptations led to new opportunities and alternative ways of conducting business, even managing operations. Some tactics have been successful, others may have failed, but in the end, we learned a lot and have an improved grasp of what may be needed to strategically transform in today's dynamic and ever-changing marketplace.

CEOs Face Workplace Challenges

Today's leadership challenges are made even more complex by existing and emerging external pressures. Leadership is under pressure to balance providing stakeholders with a stable, profitable, fair, empathetic, and innovative workplace. Just consider a few of today's societal and consumer-driven issues that have emerged for both workers and leaders:

- Staying healthy in the workplace.
- Information and identification security for remote or hybrid work arrangements.
- The move of tangible services to online everything.
- Increased investment in automation and digital transformation could change. business models and employee job descriptions and organizational structures.
- The post-pandemic economic recovery: Who benefits and who is left behind.
- Inclusivity, diversity, and sustainability.

The New Role of Leadership

To address this new and emerging environment, stakeholders—members, customers, partners, board members, and employees—expect more from today's organizational leaders. The Edelman Trust Barometer reveals that organizations are under pressure to "save society." This not only affects your own business, but the customers, subscribers, the industry sector, and professions your organization serves, interacts with, and supports.

In an Edelman global survey conducted in April 2021, "Most people (77%) say their employer has become their most trusted institution, putting more pressure on CEOs to prioritize societal and political issues in addition to shareholder value." Furthermore, "People now expect organizations and CEOs to keep focusing on big social and political issues, even after the pandemic (Edelman Trust Barometer. (2022)."

Advocating and taking strong positions is clearly more of an expectation than ever before.

Indeed, leadership is facing how to implement ESG (Environmental, Social and Corporate Governance) best practices at a time when no definitive scorecard exists. Leaders must understand how to build strategies that reflect the needs and concerns of all stakeholders, including members, customers, partners, the board, and employees—but also fulfilling their financial and leadership responsibilities to all.

Business leaders will be measured, even judged by their leadership performance; how they recruit and hire, construct teams, manage the board, and how they satisfy stakeholders whether they be internal or external. The potential trap here for any leader is bias, both unconscious and conscious, based on the values, experience from past actions, and institutional knowledge she or he brings to the organization. Here's just a taste of the potential problem: Seeing is believing—but the opposite is truer, what you believe you see.

Transformation and adaptation to an evolved workplace are more critical than many may think. Expectations and even the consideration of personal life values have changed. These changes revolve around what is truly important to an individual and adjusted work-life balance goals. Significant changes in leadership actions, tactics, and strategies are required because of the higher levels of societal issues within the broad public consciousness, which have led to an uncharted work environment.

The first step in effective leadership should be to step back and use critical thinking to understand people, processes, and cultures. All cultures have similarities, but each culture is unique. The collection of individuals who comprise a culture is intrinsically tied to the focus of the success of the organization; what worked in the past and similar situations may fail miserably in the current structure. The true litmus test is for leaders to examine their own biases to see how these embedded beliefs inform and influence their performance and decision-making.

Sustaining Engagement

Personal bias can creep in under the radar and influence a leader as it does to every individual regardless of their conscious thoughts to the contrary. An organization's workplace success is measured by employee engagement, fairness, and how connected people are to their jobs and their employers. The original engagement surveys began in the 1980s by the HR firm Watson Wyeth (WTW. (Nd.). Gallup, Harvard Business Review, and others have tracked this index over the years. The annual survey shows that there is a clear connection that the companies and organizations with a higher index of engagement outperform those companies and organizations with lower scores.

Pioneering Change

According to Robert Raleigh PhD, CEO of PathSight Predictive Science, "Work may be one of the last refuges where we don't get to choose whom we sit next to for eight to ten hours a day." He adds, "Modern work culture finds itself today at the intersection between a great promise of reinvention and the last gasps of an aging set of institutions, norms, and structures. The fragility of our traditional connective tissue within our country—from government, across media platforms, and our own personal, shared expectations and experiences—has presented us with a unique set of challenges (Raleigh, R. (Nd.)."

The choices facing leaders are self-evident: they can continue to follow a historical path towards the same way they have always led and conducted business. Or they can create a future powered by new models, tools, and expectations designed to navigate the current environment powered by strategy, transformation, adaptation, design, and ensuring technology and digital become strong enablers.

Science-Based Leadership

Science-based leadership is possible. Raleigh explains, "The challenge for leaders is not the lack of science to help them understand the context of their employees' lives, but *which* science to pay attention to. The temptation to bow to news headlines in managing a demanding shareholder and workforce will backfire. Similarly, taking direction from academic studies and research can fall short of meaningful change as the studies and research may not reflect the practical and true nature of the organization or company culture.

The sad reality is that many leaders are unprepared to tackle the onslaught of demands with lasting solutions and instead have short-term kneejerk reactions."

Short-term gains may be achieved but the cost is high. Short-term thinking is a significant challenge and requires a disproportionate focus across a company or organization that detracts from longer-term strategies, plans, and tactics that may result in even better performance at dramatically lower personnel and operational expense.

A new model is emerging. Raleigh advises, "Instead of measuring behavior, measure *why* employees do what they do. *Why* is the context of their actions (Raleigh, R. (Nd.)." This is also true for members, customers, subscribers, internal and external stakeholders, and, of course, leaders. Understanding the concept of *why* is easy to say, but hard to master. It takes the discipline of understanding the whole-person perspective, which is multidimensional and not reliant on a system built on a single factor that claims comprehensive understanding and behavior typing.

What is often discovered when *why* is asked is that critical thinking hasn't been applied and instead, historical practice promulgates despite producing less than expected results.

Active Listening

Context is the key and unlocks understanding how things will influence the world of work. Active listening is understanding the context of how personal bias and world events influence and impact their workforce. Context correlates directly to the *why* and demonstrates critical thinking as well as a clear understanding of the ecosystem and all its parts.

Understanding context (*why*) helps leaders ratchet up performance. Just consider how to manage these scenarios:

- Engage workers suffering from mental health detachment.
- Understand the impact of structural racism on workers.
- Manage the range of tribal self-identities of politics that influence our teamwork.
- Define the concept of diversity. Race. Gender. Worldview.
- Understand technology's influence on all of these.

Understanding and accepting the *why* provides critical clarity in motivating and managing all stakeholders. Active listening is key. We have the science to better understand our employees and customers. We know that accounting for these macro societal challenges and stress points will be the litmus test for business. Business can lead the way to cultural transformations in the broadest sense. It's up to enlightened leadership that starts at the top and then is executed by management that is sensitive to, empathetic, and responsive to the workforce.

Inflection points

What are the hot buttons that impact the structure and constructs of retooling a business model to thrive in a digital economy? Many of these triggers fall into a negative domain but flip the conversation and there are opportunities to address these concerns with new patterns of management and empowerment.

- **Fear of change**
- **New marketplace paradigms**
- **GDPR**
- **RE-engineering organizational construct**
- **Identifying unique value**
- **Clarifying market orientation**
- **Building relationship structures**
- **Transformational tools**
- **Buy-in for new organizational structure**
- **Transparent workforce culture**
- **Staying ahead of national and international policy, legal, regulatory**

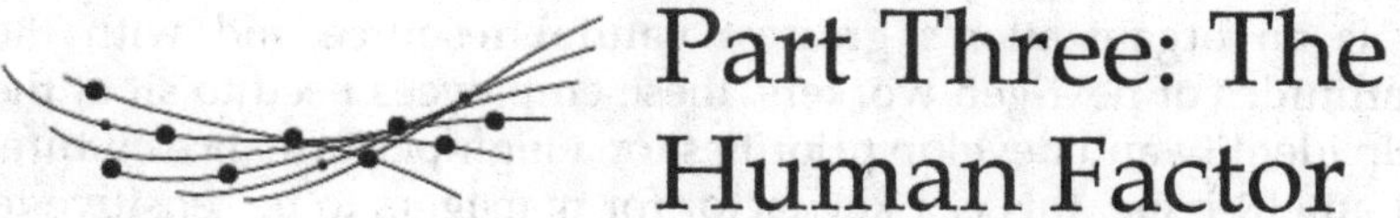

Part Three: The Human Factor

Introduction: Transformation Starts and Ends with the Human Factor

The most intelligent strategies and effective operational executions are reliant on one key component: the human factor. How many times have we worked on brilliant strategies that fall into the domain of abstract theory, but we don't have the human resources to achieve the objectives?

This is a massive pitfall with today's startups led by visionary innovators; great ideas without the talent to realize them. The human factor, as essential as it is in any organization, is often overlooked when designing a pathway for success.

This may sound counterintuitive, but some basic attitudinal and behavioral patterns can shortchange your goals. Consider inherent bias, conscious and unconscious, at all levels of an organization. And then consider the generational differences in values and worldviews that can derail a workplace culture. Or the inability to actively listen and communicate transparently. Leaders at all levels can be limited by what they don't know.

With the marketplace at a crossroads in terms of employees' reevaluations of their lives, employers are finding themselves more accountable as architects of a workplace ethos and community that thinks of its employees at the same level of criticality as its customers and board members. The workforce is an organization's greatest natural resource and with the changing attitudes of next-gen workers, these employees need to sit at the table to help identify and develop priorities for a high-performance culture. This is not an HR issue, this is a key factor for managers to be sensitive to and workers to feel safe and secure in a fair, open-minded, and inclusive environment.

Having a basic understanding of the neuroscience and psychology of the human factor is important in understanding how to build an organization that has empathy with stakeholders. Leaders are taken to task for taking a hierarchical, command-and-control stance as a management tool. Equally, entrepreneurial leaders who are filled with passion and vision, without any connection points to their employees end up in the same place: no bridge from theory to practice.

We will explore the skillsets modern managers need through the filter of the human factor. You can only be as successful as the weakest link in your workforce chain and managing five generations of employees requires abilities beyond a simple vision. To wit, many organizations design products, and services assuming their customers want and need them. Operating from the vantage point of the human factor re-tilts the proposition and ensures a higher level of success.

The days of leadership hubris are over, replaced by a more humanistic worldview. And great ideas come from unexpected places. With a systems-thinking, holistic organizational approach, chances are your organization will benefit exponentially by incubating ideas and innovations throughout the workforce.

Ultimately, focusing on the human factor recognizes and addresses the consideration of human reactions to change. The impacts of change span individual workers, managers, leaders, and even customers and stakeholders. Individual and group decision-making patterns and the importance of the application of critical thinking in any situation are also fundamental to high performance.

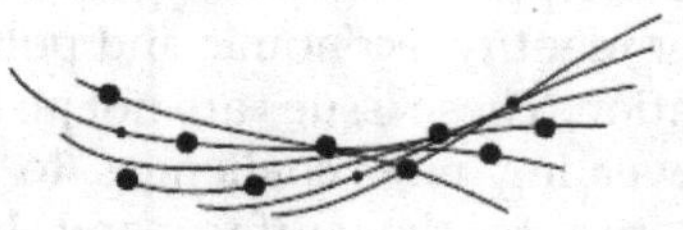

Chapter 23: The Fault in Ourselves

"Frankly, it's hard to get in touch with personal bias since our default is to assume everyone believes and operates the way we do. Our personal biases filter the ways we see the world, consider those who surround us, and represent our perception of reality. And perception is indeed one's reality."

What We Don't Know We Don't Know

One outcome of the pandemic was operating in a highly fractious marketplace with gender identity, economic and political distinctions often accelerated into polarization. These issues are not just external, they are also prevalent internally, revealing new challenges to leading and working together. These issues rise to the surface and become roadblocks to transformation when personal bias, conscious or subconscious, rules the culture, infuses decision-making, and forms our personal and professional behavioral defaults.

Frankly, it's hard to get in touch with personal bias since our default is to assume everyone believes and operates the way we do. Our personal biases filter the ways we see the world, consider those who surround us, and represent our perception of reality. And perception is indeed one's reality.

We don't know what we don't know, nor do we always know what we need to know. Separating the ego and changing deeply ingrained behaviors is uncomfortable and for most can be considered uncharted territory in one's personal and professional life.

Having a diverse workforce (that is representative of your customers), working in cross-discipline, cross-functional teams, reinforcing critical thinking and objectivity, encouraging open dialogue and even criticism to maintain honesty and transparency, and practicing active listening is a good formula for mitigating and managing personal bias.

Managing Bias

Mark Tarallo, the senior editor at Security Management Magazine, states, "You can't manage others if you can't manage yourself. And for any manager, effective self-management requires a certain level of professional self-knowledge (Tarallo, M. (2020)" He quotes Khalil Smith, a former leadership development expert at Apple, "Most managers think they're really good managers, and a lot of them aren't. Confidence and competence are not correlated (Tarallo, M. (2020)." Even the most effectively self-managed leaders are biased. David Rock, president of the NeuroLeadership Institute adds, "We see the world through tremendous filters. And we are not aware of these filters (NeuroLeadership Institute, (2021)." Rasheeda Childress, senior editor at ASAE Center adds "Hidden prejudices can have a cascading effect that reveals itself in everything from staff hires to member retention. In fact, experts warn that unconscious bias can even halt organizational innovation (Childress, R. (2020)."

Our human defaults lead us to align with those who are most like us, those that look like us, those who think as we do, and those that have the same or similar values we do. We strive for familiarity as it leads to comfort and predictability. Those who are like us, look like us, and think as we do are most likely to confirm our own thoughts and actions, which in turn feeds our ego and gives us confidence in our own decision-making. Our defaults are a longing to be accepted, gain that pat on the back, be liked, and be recognized for sound thinking.

Unfortunately, our defaults and desire to seek familiarity lead us to make uninformed decisions or take actions based on perceptions that are not necessarily true reality. The outcome of bias and perception impact our personal lives, the paths we take, and strongly influence our professional lives; how we interrelate with our co-workers and those around us—and ultimately how organizations operate and are managed.

In sum, the fault in ourselves can be defined by the perception through which we view and consider the world around us to be the reflection of ourselves.

Mitigating Bias

We cannot overemphasize the need for developing active listening skills, seeking objectivity through critical thinking, creating cultures that respect open dialogue and criticism, developing respect for diverse and multigenerational workforces, accepting ambiguity, being resilient, and embracing agility in a dynamically changing world.

Any one of those skills considered on its own is hard. When combined, the total becomes the basis for forming personal and professional responsibilities in the 21st century for ourselves, our organizations, and our society as a whole. When we master each separately and then together as an interconnected whole, we can enable individuals personally and professionally to practice self-management to mitigate inherent biases that exist and unpack how these biases inform the perception of the world around us.

On the Bias

Let's bring forward some examples of bias that exist consciously and unconsciously, which we typically don't recognize nor the influence they have.

- **Similarity Bias**

The most common bias is similarity bias, that "people like me are better," which ranges everything from hiring practices and interactions in meetings to promotions and even vendor choices. Michael Brainard, CEO and founder of Brainard Strategy says, "People often steer clear of those who conflict with their beliefs or are not like them — without even realizing it (Childress, R. (2020)."

A good test is to look around and honestly assess the company you keep. Is everyone agreeing with you? Is there any criticism being shared with you? Is everyone united in your direction and plan?

As a manager or leader, you may have unconsciously recruited and selected your team by seeking out those who are most like how you think and how you view the world. You may have unconsciously hired those who are not going to criticize you, your thinking, or approach.

- **Shared Experience Bias**

Another Achilles Heel is shared experience bias. Like similarity bias, we seek out those who have had experiences that closely match those that we have had. A CEO may want to talk to another CEO managing a similar type of organization, A manager may seek out and only want to talk with those managing the same types of employees. Like any search for information, we often seek out the feedback and answers we want to hear by including only those whom we believe are most like us and will have our shared experience and knowledge.

One way through this biased filter is interacting with co-workers, peers, and others who have different perspectives, come from different backgrounds, work for different organizations, and the like. Solicit their feedback and be open to receiving objective criticism that may alter, change, expand or replace your perception of a problem, situation, plan — or even the world.

Leadership consultant Pamela J. Green says, "Three things are critical: humility, discomfort, and discipline." Brainard adds, "Real development occurs when we're uncomfortable when we're humbled. That's where real change occurs (Childress, R. (2020)." Additionally, real change occurs when we are receptive to what we may hear, read, or view via critical thinking and active listening skills.

- **Confirmation Bias**

Confirmation bias is our tendency to seek out or notice information that supports our existing beliefs, perceptions, and thoughts—and ignore the information, data, and knowledge that conflicts. Tanya Ashworth-Keppel, an Australian lawyer, explains co-workers need to be open to feedback, solutions, and ways of doing things that they may not have preferred in the past. She advises "Look for ways to challenge what you think you see. Seek out information from a range of sources and discuss your thoughts with a diverse group of people. Then, share the feedback you get with a wider group for greater discussion. For major decisions, even consider assigning someone on your team to play devil's advocate (Ashworth-Keppel, T. (2021)."

Individuals often state that they like a challenge and to be challenged. If the challenge is met, one's behavior and/or action adds positive reinforcement of competence and builds confidence through self-assessed and defined goal attainment. In our quest to meet the challenge, we will, by default, seek out the information, data, interactions, and feedback that is most closely aligned with the way we see and relate.

The default is also to substantiate how we have defined the challenge, the goal, and what results/outcomes we expect. Even when we suggest that the "I" is one's own worst enemy, unconsciously we are still demonstrating behavior that manifests as confirmation bias.

What we miss in taking on the challenge is to make ourselves uncomfortable by exploring information and data that may run counter to our thoughts and beliefs. An individual can only counter confirmation bias by breaking former behaviors of seeking out the same sources over and over again.

- **Conservatism Bias**

Conservatism bias seeks out familiarity. Ashworth-Keppel explains "Favoring existing information over new information threatens to change our preconceptions.

When we do get new information, we tend to weigh it less heavily or dismiss it, while information that supports a previous belief is given more weight. Conservatism bias can make change management particularly challenging. Even where there are compelling reasons to change a business system, introduce new processes or modify roles, people are likely to cling to the old way of doing things. They're not just being stubborn – they literally aren't seeing the new information as important (Ashworth-Keppel, T. (2021)."

We are greatly influenced by what we consider to be the "law of familiarity" in all aspects of our lives. Our conscious and unconscious defaults to seek similarity and comfort, reduce risk and maintain safety informs our view and interpretation of the world around us. Time and again, research across marketing and sales proves how easily we are manipulated if we receive the same message in multiple ways, forms, and times. Unconsciously, we then form a familiarity with the content, information, and message and relate it to our perceptions.

Even when we think we are being open and considering alternative views, new sources of information, or differences in interpretation, we are ultimately weighting them by our ingrained perceptions. Therefore, we do not value the input on its merits alone.

Familiarity is connected to our understanding of the world and where and how we see ourselves in it. Our personal and professional lives are built on our definitions of the role we play, how we can be recognized for doing a good job, and what information and knowledge we have or have gained to form these definitions. As such, our familiarity bias plays into our ability or inability to transform and effect a transition as we hold on to what was. Transition management can be sidelined if familiarity prevents change personally and professionally.

Self-Knowledge and Self-Management

It may be impossible to eliminate bias, but it is within reach to be aware of it, mitigate and manage it, and all its manifestations. Self-knowledge is important for everyone—leaders, managers, supervisors, and their teams comprising groups of multigenerational, racially, sexually, and ethnically diverse individuals—because bias exists at all levels. It is inherent in our evolutionary programming.

Self-management is equally critical.

Peter Drucker wrote in *Management Challenges of the 21st Century* that values-based leadership (at all levels) prompts self-analysis with these questions, "What are my strengths? How do I perform? What are my values? Where do I belong? What can I contribute? (Drucker, Peter F. 2001)." Getting to the heart of these answers and how they may influence behavior is a discipline that is critical in today's demanding society and marketplace. Feedback analysis can reveal strengths and vulnerabilities that enable an understanding of the individual biases that form thoughts, actions, and ultimately one's perceptions.

Drucker further writes, "Amazingly few people know how they get things done. Indeed, most of us do not even know that different people work and perform differently (Drucker, Peter F. 2001)." He distills it down to several key behaviors that feed into how we work with others:

- Am I a reader or a listener?
- How do I learn?
- Do I work well with people, or do I work best alone?
- Do I best perform as a decision-maker, follower, or adviser?

The answers to these questions may provoke some discomfort due to seeing oneself in a new and very different perceptual light. When answering the questions, one must seek to go beyond conscious recognition of the moment. Instead, bring a forward deeper reflection on how a situation was handled, the problem was solved, what was said or thought during an interaction, and so forth. It is self-knowledge and self-management that opens the door to enabling critical thinking to determine how strongly biases are permeating perceptions, decisions, and actions.

Decision-Making

Our experience working with clients is that bias can prevent progress and success with decision-making. Our biases and perceptions, as well as our human default behaviors to gain acceptance and achieve goals consciously and unconsciously, impacts the decisions we make. On the one hand, we have biases and perceptions that form our thoughts, thinking, and approach to a problem, situation, development, or the like. On the other hand, we have this immediate need, often stemming from our subconscious behavioral defaults, to get to the end of the road and address the situation and solve the problem.

Short-term faulty decision-making is driven by the need for immediacy to achieve a goal resulting in the bias of our own thinking.

Without the benefit of alternative and diverse thoughts and opinions, short-term thinking can create unintended consequences.

We have identified eight fatal flaws that derail good leadership and management decision-making and can implode an organization's ability to be competitive. If any of these eight behaviors are currently being practiced, your organization is at risk as your decisions are short-term and run the risk of being based on perception and infused with your own biases. If you have multiple flaws at work, you are in serious trouble in today's dynamically changing business environment.

1. Do you believe you are the customer?
2. Do you run your organization in your own image; how similar are those around you—are they able to provide constructive criticism; does your team think just like you or do they challenge your thinking?
3. Do you have a siloed organizational structure?
4. Do you make command-and-control decisions without upstream and downstream input?
5. Do you use critical thinking, begetting objectivity, as a basic decision-making tool?
6. Are you only making data-informed decisions without seeking thoughts from those outside your similarity circle?
7. Do you make only intuitive decisions based on your perception of reality; do you resist new sources of data and information that represent alternative views?
8. Are you overly focused on the short term to demonstrate results that lead to self-affirmation?

Mindsets

Let's take a deeper dive into these mindsets to reveal why they can help or hinder your decision-making.

- **You believe you are the customer.**

There is a temptation to think that your organization serves one customer: you. That is realistically speaking, impossible. Love him or hate him, Jeff Bezos built Amazon with one guiding principle: every decision is made in the interests of the customer. With all the analytics tools available literally at our fingertips, it is antiquated not to deeply understand your customers, serve them with customized products and services and concede the point that they probably don't look or behave like you do.

Individuals in positions of power have a hard time letting go of their egos in assuming the world is "just like them." The world is diverse and customer motivation can be complex. Collecting data and turning them into insights to understand these nuances and respond to them is the most powerful tool you have.

- **You run your organization in your own image.**

Look around you. Does everyone you hire look like you? First of all, we admittedly have inherent biases and unconsciously surround ourselves with people like our selves. But an organization's teams should be comprised and balanced with individuals who reflect the customers and comprised of those who bring alternative experiences, information, and knowledge that is very different from your own. We've all read about the deficits of leadership teams that are not inclusive. Callout culture aside, it is just bad business to have a workforce that is homogenized. And add to this, any effective organization needs a few outliers and independent thinkers who, although they may not fit neatly into the organizational structure, can be invaluable in sparking innovative and imaginative ideas. Remember, leading with courage comes when you accept open critical dialogue upstream and downstream, providing alternative views, solutions, and interpretations. Leading with courage confronts inherent biases and can result in more informed, accurate decisions—and yes, actions.

- **You have a siloed organizational structure.**

We hear far too often with our clients that no one in the organization is talking to anyone else. Decisions are made in isolation, information is not shared among departments, and strategies are set without context to the higher goals of the organization. It is not possible to collaborate if an organizational structure is rigid and compartmentalized. Customers do not behave in siloed ways. Their lives are holistic systems of interdependent and related behaviors. To that point, your organization, should not only reflect how your customers look, but also how they behave. Working within a systems thinking model eliminates siloed thinking and bias.

- **You make command-and-control decisions.**

Most organizations Trans today are comprised of five different generations working with each other. Although a hierarchical and didactic management style has often defined leadership in the past, it is irrelevant today.

The next-gen workforce wants a seat at the table, believes fiercely in collaboration and team play, is in a hurry to advance, and most importantly to contribute and feel value resulting from their efforts. This may run counter to the comfort zone of traditional leaders and older generations, but it is a losing battle to enforce legacy thinking that represents inherent biases formed by the past. Top-down leadership is a relic of the past in our marketplace. Leaders today should operate as conductors, eliciting the best performances from their managers and teams, as informed, inspirational, and in-touch individuals with all generations in understanding what motivates them and how they contribute to the organization.

- **You do not use critical thinking as a basic decision-making tool.**

The acceptance of ambiguity that exists outside one's biases and perceptions, along with agility and resilience are basic operating principles of running an organization in the digital age. Critical thinking is the most essential tool to ensure that any organization can remain relevant and competitive. It takes rigorous discipline to implement and enforce critical thinking throughout a workforce. It is incredibly challenging to embed critical thinking in an individual leader's or manager's day-to-day behavior. Train your managers who then can train their teams to make decisions to create agile strategies and operational tactics using critical thinking. It is also important to recognize during the transition what individuals and teams are giving up and how they reset the new value in themselves.

- **You make only data-informed decisions.**

Data output is only as good as its input. Data-driven decisions are great assets, but they are not a panacea. Data and analytics are tools and need to be used in context and tandem with common sense. "Sound decision-making is an art and requires a combination of accurate information, an understanding of emotional bias or prejudice, good communication, and a willingness to collaborate and trust. Data is black and white and incredibly useful, but it does not paint the entire picture.

This is where intuition comes into play. Intuition can be described as something perceived or instinctual rather than conscious and derived directly from data. In many cases, intuition is an outcome of deep experience in a specific space.

That experience is what allows someone to look at a complex problem and make a quick decision without necessarily explaining or divulging lots of information and insight," explains Amit Choudhary, chief operating officer of Global Financial Services SBU at Capgemini (Choudhary, A. (Nd.). Additionally, for many complex decisions, all the data in the world can't win over a lifetime's worth of experience that informs one's gut feeling, instinct, or intuition.

- **You make only intuitive decisions.**

Disruptor Gabriel Swain states, "Many leaders either don't trust their data or haven't adopted the technology to analyze it. A Deloitte survey reveals that 67% of business decision-makers aren't comfortable basing decisions on data pulled from their current technology. What's worse, 53% of senior executives are reported to feel they are too old to learn data analysis skills (Swain, G. (Nd.)." Choudhary adds, "Intuition may pose a significant risk if the leader's conscious and unconscious biases adversely impact decision-making. Critical business decisions are likely to affect several areas within an organization, which makes dependence on the intuition of one or a handful of leaders ill-advised. People who have extensive experience and intuition within one field might apply it in situations where they have little experience, resulting in poor outcomes (Choudhary, A. (Nd.)."

- **You are overly focused on the short-term.**

Short-term decision-making is focused on immediate gains and a sense of accomplishment. Long-term decisions are the sum of a laundry list of short-term decisions and actions that seek incremental accomplishments to reach the gold star, so to speak. Put another way, the Seventh Generation stewardship was defined by the leaders of the Native American Iroquois Confederacy centuries ago. "Every decision they took had to keep in mind seven generations hence (Baker, J. (2021)." By thinking seven generations ahead (about 140 years into the future) the decisions we make today will benefit our children seven generations into the future. Most businesses don't think "seven generations hence" when they plan. In fact, the realities of a digital marketplace make extra long-term planning a challenge when circumstances change so quickly.

Nonetheless, there are aspects of short-term thinking that are problematic. From a macro perspective, Richard Fisher senior journalist at the BBC argues "Identifying the temporal stresses that promote short-termism in our lives is only a starting point.

Our greatest challenge this century is to transform our relationship with time. History suggests that our horizons have shortened before—but they can expand again. During the pandemic, our "presentism" has become even more extreme, but cultural norms have been challenged too. There may never be a better time to ask what future we actually want (ABC-AU. (2021)."

So, what does this have to do with bias? We argue that short-term bias is often influenced by immediate gain. Brainard says "short-terms bias is the brain's way of helping a person make decisions quickly with very little information. Our default setting is to make fast decisions." He says, "It keeps us alive (Childress, R. (2020)." But short-term thinking for organizational success may not keep the enterprise alive. In fact, many short-term decisions are made to elevate the personal gains of leadership. That may sound harsh, but personal gain is typically what drives short-term thinking.

One caveat: Most organizations were hurled into short-term thinking during the pandemic. It literally was a race to keep a business alive threatened by external circumstances that forced pivots, innovations, and outright retooling of businesses to respond to the immediate circumstances. Ironically, many of these short-term decisions ultimately transformed long overdue business models and powered transformation and change that have long-term benefits.

In reality, all thinking, and decisions should be customer-centric; if you deliver a sustainable customer experience with products and services they want, your decisions will be made for the greater good of your organization.

How to Address Bias Head-On

So many rules have changed in the workplace, and as a result, we have become more sensitive to the biases we hold and open to addressing them. It's difficult and uncomfortable work, but necessary as we evolve our organizations into more enlightened and empathetic places to work.

The New Leadership Identity Crisis

Leaders today face a profound identity shift. The role no longer centers on controlling information, directing work, or being the most knowledgeable voice in the room. AI has democratized access to expertise and changed who holds power, who influences decisions, and who shapes outcomes. Many leaders feel destabilized, even threatened, by this shift.

This uncertainty often manifests as defensiveness, micromanagement, or avoidance. Leaders cling to familiar models of authority even as those models lose effectiveness. Others swing to the opposite extreme—delegating too much to technology, abdicating the responsibility of judgment, or hiding behind data to avoid making difficult human decisions.

The leaders who thrive in the age of AI develop a new identity: one rooted in clarity, emotional intelligence, adaptability, and the ability to create conditions where people—not systems—drive transformation. AI may augment capabilities, but it cannot confer leadership.

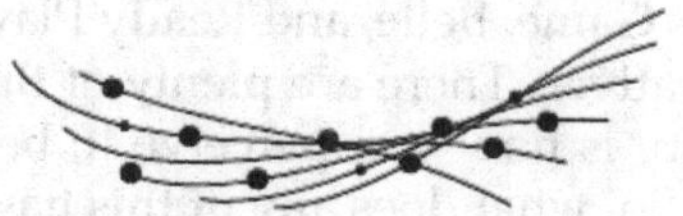

Chapter 24: Is Perception Really Everything?

"Some say that we live in a simulation. The *Hitchhiker's Guide to the Galaxy* and The Matrix popularized ideas long held by some physicists and game theorists."

What Do You Think You See?

Some say that we will be living in a parallel reality, a metaverse dramatized by Ender's Game, Belle, and Ready Player One, to mention only three pop culture narratives. There are plenty of thinkers and philosophers who believe that reality is how you perceive it; beauty is in the eye of the beholder, so to speak. So, what does any of this have to do with running an organization? A lot.

Perception Isn't Universal

According to ethics professor Christina Catenacci, "Perception is the process by which individuals organize and interpret their sensory impressions to give meaning to their environment. What one perceives can be substantially different from what another person perceives, and both can be very different from the actual objective reality. In fact, behavior is based on one's perception of what reality is, not reality itself." As for the workplace, "There are many factors that influence how something is perceived. Factors about the perceiver can involve the person's attitudes, motives, interests, experience, and expectations. Contextual factors can involve time, work setting, and social setting. Finally, factors related to the actual target can involve novelty, motion, sounds, size, background, and proximity," she adds (Catenacci, C. 2017).

We often believe the way we think, act, and participate is consistent across all aspects of our perceived reality, personal or professional. However, our behavioral responses change depending on the situation or environment we are in. Our individual reality is comprised of how we interpret social cues and norms, how we have learned to accord our behavior and actions, and the total of what we have previously experienced. Our reality is also informed by our interpretation of what we believe others believe and how they want us to act, communicate or behave. Our workplaces introduce similar conflicting interpretations of our actions and behaviors, given situations and the environment, shaping what we believe to be appropriate, expected, and accepted.

Situational and environmental awareness transcends our traditional belief that we are always the same person. This paradox is often overlooked or completely missed by individuals when an organization seeks to manage its workforce, retain new customers, and acquire new ones.

Many organizations attempt to develop personas or classifications that generalize attributes of a herd, but rarely do they seek to understand how a group of employees or customers can shape the relationship between an organization and themselves accorded to their own perceptional reality. The challenge is then to identify the mercurial individual that manifests according to a perception of reality in a specific circumstance.

How we act, behave, and operate occur organically, at a level of unconsciousness, and based on deeply rooted processes of interpreting, learning, and forming our perceptions of reality. This ingrained process is built on a subconscious series of switches that we turn on or off dependent on the situation or environment. The limits of our learned behavior and programmed responses can cause us to experience anxiety and stress when we are unsure how to act and respond to a new situation. And the outcome may not immediately accord to our recognized behavior or responses. We may not know why we suddenly feel uncomfortable or off-base.

We constantly seek comfort and want to know how to interpret and then respond in any environment based on our perceptions (right or wrong). It requires a high level of mindfulness to recognize the shifts and when the switch is flipped. In actuality, we flow seamlessly from one situation to another without much conscious thought.

More on Situational Awareness

Farnam Street reports, "Environment is the hidden force that guides behavior. One reason it's so effective is that it speaks to your subconscious mind and not your conscious mind. Default behaviors love the path of least resistance. Not only does our environment choose that path but it pushes us in that direction. If we limit our understanding of environmental influences only to what we can see, we miss a large part of its powerful force (Farnam Street Blog. (2021)."

In essence, even deeply hidden environmental forces shape our behaviors. We become someone different depending on the situation. These shifts are often not recognized at the individual level. But think about goal attainment, the need to perform, an ability to dismiss normal inhibitions, and outright adaptation and you see that there is more than meets the eye. For example, how many of us realize how the subconscious and hormones play a driving role in behavior? Perception is one's reality and we often align or internalize what we are told we should feel and believe which leads us to falsely feel safe and secure.

Psychologist Philip Zimbardo has studied "time perspective" and the lessons of the Stanford Prison Experiment he conducted in 1971. His famous experiment with students dramatized how behavior can change to the extreme based on group pressure. Basically, the experiment assigned paid volunteers to be either inmates or guards in a simulated prison in the basement of the school's psychology building. Very quickly, the guards became cruel, and the prisoners more submissive and depressed. The situation grew chaotic, and the experiment, meant to last two weeks, had to be ended after five days.

In an interview with Matt Abrams of Stanford School of business, Zimbardo says, "Social psychologists want the world to know that the best way to predict what you will do in a certain situation is not knowing your personality traits but knowing the features of that situation. So, we believe that the social environment is the main thing that shapes human behavior, and it comes to dominating personality. And that's what the prison study showed (Abrahams, M. & Zimbardo, P. (2021)." So, essentially social psychologists believe that if we want to understand our own behavior and the behavior of others, the first thing we must ask or notice is what is the situation in which they are performing, in which they are behaving. And then we want to know as much about the situation as possible. Deconstructed, means situational awareness can define and shape our understanding of time and communication.

Security Theater

Security theater is a perception of security, not real security. It shows up in many situations in our day-to-day lives where we seek to formulate a perception to ensure we feel safe, comfortable, liked, appreciated—and any range of other personal or professional emotional needs we have.

We seek security because it provides a platform and stage to believe in day to day. It begets comfort and, in many ways, predictability. Bruce Schneier, the well-known security expert, coined the term security theater when he noticed that the TSA wasted billions of dollars a year on invasive airport screening post-9/11 to satisfy the public's emotional need to do something. But the exercise did not make anyone safer, although they felt safer. Security theater is based on perception, for both those creating the situation and those who are participating in it (Schneier, Bruce. (Nd.).

Basically, in an individual's day-to-day assessment of situations and environments, as well as in business, security theater is a practice of taking security measures that are intended to provide the feeling of improved security while doing little or nothing to achieve it. That is a massive gap between perception and reality. There is much that we interpret and tell ourselves that forms our perception of reality that doesn't accord with fact and true reality.

The Workforce Perception Trap

Understanding one's biases is important in knowing how to lead and manage. Biases can take us down rabbit holes that don't represent shared reality. Our personal perceptions can equally lead us down the rabbit hole as we miss the true basis and response for a decision, communication, or even how to manage.

There is a consensus among organizational experts on how an organization can be derailed by perceptual issues.

- **Basic attribution error.** The tendency to underestimate the influence of external factors and overestimate the influence of internal factors when making judgments about the behavior of others.

- **Self-serving bias.** The tendency to attribute one's own successes to internal factors and blame one's own failures on external factors.

- **Selective perception.** The tendency to selectively interpret what is seen based on one's interests, background, experience, and attitudes.

- **Projection.** The tendency to attribute one's own characteristics to other people.

- **Stereotyping.** The tendency to judge someone based on the perception of a group to which that person belongs.

- **Halo effect.** The tendency to draw a general impression about an individual based on a single characteristic.

Again, acknowledging that we are all human with our own perspectives that we rely on when perceiving things in the work setting, it is important to be aware of the various factors that influence these perceptions, especially when making important decisions that affect the organization.

Perceptions Impact Organizational Decision-Making

What happens when managers and executives running an organization fall into the trap of their perceptions? What happens when decisions and strategies are based on managers' senses as opposed to their reasoning abilities? These are key questions posed by entrepreneur Thomas Papakostas (Papakostas, T. 2015). He adds, "There are so many corporate examples of this situation: you see great candidates being passed over just because they didn't look the part, you see great performers that 'look' suitable being promoted to managers without having the management skills, you see executives appearing successful during the good times and flopping in the first adversity the organization faces, you see truly incompetent employees hiding behind office politics, you see decisions based on senses and feelings instead of facts (Papakostas, T. 2015)."

Research suggests that how employees perceive their work situation directly influences their productivity. A recipe for disaster is the trap of believing your perception is the only reality. The antidote? Informed decision-making, relying on intelligence rather than feeling, and using fact-based logic. Papakostas adds, "In business, perception is not reality. Do the best you can to get the facts right and use your intelligence to see past the "smoke and mirrors (Papakostas, T. 2015)."

Perception and Reality in Practice

Let's start with your own organization. Do you know and understand the perceptions of your employees about you and your workplace? From a top-down perspective, how you communicate your vision, mission and goals can be interpreted differently among different employees. How the workforce perceives their jobs and working conditions may not align with their managers' perceptions. The challenge is to align everyone in a shared purpose and understanding of what your organization stands for and its operational ethos – all on a personal basis. Catenacci believes written workplace policies and procedures should be in place to help narrow the gap between perception and reality. Such policies help ensure management and employees act fairly and consistently, thus reducing the risk of discrimination and human rights violations, among other problems.

Here's a cheat sheet from Regina Anaejionu, as reported on CHRON, of the top hotspots in the workplace today, and how to help align your workforce in matching perception with reality (Anaejionu, R. (Nd.).

- **Job Satisfaction**

There is often a large gap among employees' perceptions of their opportunities for advancement. Also, workers' thoughts about workload and even the time to complete tasks may differ greatly from what supervisors or other coworkers think. Reality is always somewhere in between. Active listening is critical to understanding a workforce. So is facing up to stereotyping and personal bias that may influence how management sees the strengths and weaknesses of its teams. Taking a systemic approach to eliminate silos and design actionable networks among all levels of employees can reset workplace culture to actualize alignment of perceptions among employees and managers.

- **Communicating**

Communication is a two-way proposition. When business communications are drilled down from the top, they can often be misinterpreted or viewed with cynicism by recipients. Add to this the cascade of emails and online meetings that also hinder transparent, honest exchanges of information and opinion. Two-way channels must remain open for all employees to communicate authentically and without judgment.

- **Who's Doing the Work?**

The perception of management about who is doing the work can be the polar opposite of the workers. It may look like the team is pulling together, but anecdotal evidence usually proves that often 20% of workers do 80% of the work. Team leaders and managers need to set specific roles and duties for each team member with benchmarks in place to double-check who does what. Many managers perceive that a project went well just because it was completed on time, but this is not always the case in terms of the process and interactive experience. Sometimes an employee may be viewed as disloyal or not trying hard enough with a project. This is a subjective judgment based on an employer's perceptions. It's even more complicated. One manager may perceive an employee to be loyal, while another may perceive that same employee to be insincere.

- **Diversity**

DEI has taken its rightful place in the pantheon of initiatives to create an equitable, inclusive workforce. Understanding employees' needs instead of perceiving them bridges the divide between managers' perceptions and employees' reality.

Remote work has reinforced the need for life/work balance.

Organizations have been given glimpses of employees in their "natural habitats,' resulting in making everyone more accessible and "human." Diversity and inclusion may be the single biggest stumbling block in the perception/reality construct.

When Perception Distorts Reality

David Blitz, CEO, and Co-Founder of Blitzlake Partners focuses on optics. He says the potential damage of optics can impact us personally and professionally. He asks, why? "Because whether we want to admit it or not, how others perceive us, and our reputation absolutely matters (Blitz, D. (2020)." Controlling the optics is key. He adds, "With meticulous planning and a focus on an organization's values, optics should never be something that happens to us. Yet it commonly does—usually very quickly and without warning. Optics must be managed to showcase your integrity, hard work, successes, and progress." In our digital marketplace, transparent messaging about anything (good and bad) can go viral and impact the integrity of the organization. In this case, perception is everything and can become a death knell for good intentions. Managing public perception is hard and reversing a negative perception is nearly impossible to overcome.

Perception Mastery

We are the sum of our parts. Perceptions unrelated to shared reality can be landmines as they influence our actions and behaviors. Biases and perceptions can derail decision-making, pleasing customers, and empowering a high-performance workforce. An action plan helps any organization recognize and understand how the human factor is both the most powerful and vulnerable force in any business. Collective perceptions of reality ensure their organizations can achieve success and remain competitive in a fragmented, complex marketplace.

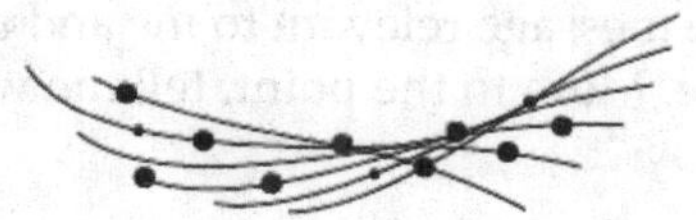

Chapter 25: How Effectively Do You Communicate with Stakeholders?

"People have become cynical, needy, and cautious living in a world full of ambiguity. The opportunity for effective communications with your members, customers, subscribers, and stakeholders is to rethink your legacy best practices and reinvent your touchpoints with stakeholders to make your organization personal, relevant, and targeted."

Straight Talk

Tell me something I don't already know. Or if you do, tell me in a new way that makes the message relevant to me and useful in my life—both professional and private. More to the point, tell me what it means and why it matters.

Digital communications have proliferated and most of them are near misses, or even worse, totally inconsequential to their audiences. Spray and pray is an anachronism in a digital marketplace. Customized communications are now table stakes. Think context when you think content. And think empathy when you think messaging.

Also, think about telling a story that is relevant to recipients. Storytelling remains "king" and is even more important than ever in achieving organizational goals of immersing, engaging, and retaining customers, subscribers, and members.

People have become cynical, needy, and cautious living in a world full of ambiguity. The opportunity for effective communications with your members, customers, subscribers, and stakeholders is to rethink your legacy best practices and reinvent your touchpoints with stakeholders to make your organization personal, relevant, and targeted.

Communications Considerations

Consider communication strategies from the stakeholder's perspective, not the organization. It is so tempting to fall back on the tried-and-true approach of telling them what you want to tell them irrespective of their interests or needs. Your organization now exists in an omnichannel world, made more complex by the most diverse and multi-generational marketplace in history, a market in which that one customer, subscriber, or member can interact with you across all channels and mediums.

Customers want digital products, services, and interactions along with their traditional physical world versions. And they expect everything you offer to be delivered with consistency across each touchpoint and channel. Communications must be coordinated across all channels, language must be relevant and mindful of your audience's expectations, nuanced to resonate with distinct groups and classes of people and messaging must always be customer-centric.

How to Communicate with Stakeholders

Fundamentally, we believe we are effective as communicators when what we write and say makes perfect sense to us. The choices are crucial. We choose the words to use, information to include, and information and even data to omit. Each of our choices comes from our base of knowledge, values, and experiences. But the pitfall is that our communications choices are not necessarily always aligned with those of others.

- All of us understand things based on our exposure to a concept, thought process, or a way to solve a problem somewhere along the way in our lives.

- We typically make assumptions that those we are speaking to have the same basis of understanding.

- Outside of our direct families and immediate social circles, it is unlikely that a communicator and those that receive the communication have shared knowledge and experience.

- Organizational staff is generally not also the customer, member, or subscriber. Therefore, staff members are often challenged to "see" what the customer sees, understand what the customer understands, and create communications correlated to stakeholders' needs and wants.

Organizations historically have valued those in an organization who have legacy knowledge and perspective, which informs what the organization is about, what it offers, and how it provides what it offers to customers. But the opposite is more valuable: Our perceptions should be informed by what customers want and why they want it. Yet, our perception rarely really connects to a customer's life knowledge and experience—and a fatal disconnect takes shape.

We reaffirm here how critical thinking creates an understanding of how the many parts of a system work together. Each part is highly important to how communications take shape and requires stepping back and putting oneself in the role of customer, subscriber, or member. Critical thinking is even more relevant in developing communications that are focused on an individual's life stage, career stage, or place in an industry or sector.

We find far too often that a task mentality and personal perception take center stage in the thought and communication creation process—not a true understanding of others.

If a communication regardless of whether it is a transaction (marketing) or information-based is framed by the context of who customers are, it will resonate and result in greater connection and contextualization to who your organization is and what it has to offer. This also relates to all channels and especially applies to how an organization's customer service department communicates via phone, messaging, and email as they assist customers. One size does not fit all, and the message should always be consistent and contextual.

Unconscious Bias

We've identified several communications factors that can help spark understanding, deliver relevance, and build context. The Achilles Heel of many communicators is their inability to recognize that not everyone thinks the way they do. Internal performance pressures on the marketing and communications team often result in ready tactics, quick execution, and fuzzy measurement. Has your communications strategy evolved with the changes in your target market(s)? In consideration of diversity and inclusion, transformative-focused communications need to look like today's customers and evolve for tomorrow.

To be clear, bias exists in anything and everything. Humans are a sum of their parts including their life experiences, values, and views of people and the world. Humans experience unconscious (and conscious) bias most distinctly when they want to communicate with others.

- A sender (the communicator) wants to send a message and chooses the terms to use and the gestures and facial expressions to best emphasize the words and various points he or she wants to make.

- This bundle of communications skills is used with the intent of having the receiver understand word for word, the direct meaning they are trying to get across.

- As humans we want to believe we have a wide range of shared knowledge and experiences — we do not.

- Senders who seek to send messages surrounding change must recognize that the receivers will be interpreting and applying everything that is shared, said, and communicated, written or verbally, with their own filters and perceptions.

So, take a closer look at your communications. Are you applying critical thinking and reflecting the diversity of thoughts and values of those whom you need to message effectively? Are you manifesting and incorporating that type of thinking and recognition into how you communicate? Are you recognizing how what you are saying is being received and interpreted? Are you aware you may be communicating with up to five different generations in your audience, all with different outlooks, needs – and vocabulary!

Narrative Storytelling

How deeply do you consider the content you create?

Do you take a neutral, professional expository approach?

Is it factual and comprehensive?

Is it written in the third person?

Is it customer-centric or your organization's party line?

Are you tempted to just dial it in?

The key guiding principle in communications that matter is to show respect for your stakeholders and engage them where, when, and how they want to be connected. Honestly, it takes hard work to get it right.

In today's dynamic, digital marketplace, there are so many options to communicate with your stakeholders based on their interests, history with your products and services, and professional positions. We recommend that above all, your content be informed by creating compelling connections.

What do we mean by that?

Use narrative and storytelling to make your brand accessible and engaging. Grabbing attention through anecdotes, experiences and stories are effective in drawing your stakeholders into your community and tapping into their curiosity.

Storytelling is an ancient art and powerful tool.

According to Vanessa and Lani Peterson, Psy.D., a psychologist, professional storyteller, and executive coach in the Harvard Business Review. "Telling stories is one of the most powerful means that leaders have to influence, teach, and inspire.

What makes storytelling so effective? For starters, storytelling forges connections among people, and between people and ideas. Stories convey the culture, history, and values that unite people. When it comes to our countries, our communities, and our families, we understand intuitively that the stories we hold in common are an important part of the ties that bind. This understanding also holds true in the business world, where an organization's stories, and the stories its leaders tell, help solidify relationships in a way that factual statements encapsulated in bullet points or numbers don't," states Petersons (Boris, V. & Peterson, L. 2017).

Kendall Haven, the author of *Story Proof and Story Smart*, considers storytelling a serious business for business. He has written, "Your goal in every communication is to influence your target audience (change their current attitudes, belief, knowledge, and behavior). Information alone rarely changes any of these. Research confirms that well-designed stories are the most effective vehicle for exerting influence. Because people identify so closely with stories, imagining how they would have acted in similar circumstances, they're able to work through situations in a risk-free way. The extra benefit for leaders: with a simple personal story they've conveyed underlying values, offered insight into the evolution of their own experience and knowledge, presented themselves as more approachable, and most likely inspired others to want to know more. Connection. Engagement. It's no wonder that more and more organizations are embracing storytelling as an effective way for their leaders to influence, inspire, and teach (Haven, Kendall. (Nd.)."

Science demonstrates that storytelling is a measurable tactic. Liz Neeley, director of The Story Collider spoke on NPR, "On functional MRI scans, many different areas of the brain light up when someone is listening to a narrative, Neeley says — not only the networks involved in language processing but other neural circuits, too. One study of listeners found that the brain networks that process emotions arising from sounds — along with areas involved in movement — were activated, especially during the emotional parts of the story (Renken, E. (writer). Neeley, L. (Host). (2020). As you hear a story unfold, your brain waves actually start to synchronize with those of the storyteller, says Uri Hasson, professor of psychology and neuroscience at Princeton University.

When he and his research team recorded the brain activity in two people as one person told a story and the other listened, they found that the greater the listener's comprehension, the more closely the brain wave patterns mirrored those of the storyteller (Renken, E. (writer). Neeley, L. (Host). (2020)."

How does this relate to your communications strategy?

Think podcasts, e-video messaging, live streaming, video snaps on social media, and e-content that draws an audience into your narrative. And revisit your website to reframe the content into a series of compelling narratives written in an engaging, accessible voice.

The Medium Is Often the Message

Organizations of all sizes can achieve high performance in engagement and trust with their stakeholders. Today, with a portfolio of media choices to use to connect with current and prospective customers, communications need to be appropriate in tone, language, and content for each platform. Added to that, stakeholders have made it clear they want to be connected with when, where, and how they prefer. The role of a communicator is to engage stakeholders without personal bias about the content and how it is delivered. We are in uncharted waters with a multigenerational audience that has discrete needs.

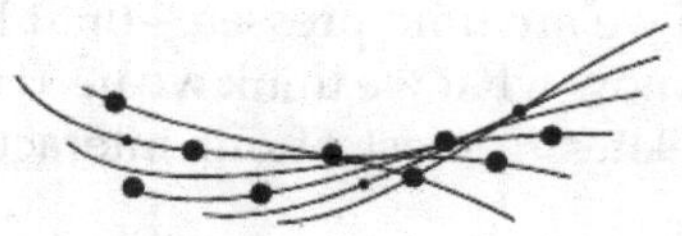

Chapter 26: The Art and Science of Active Listening

"Deep active listening occurs when you're committed to understanding the communicator's perspective. It involves paying attention to both verbal and nonverbal cues, such as the words being used, the speaker's body language, and tone. This type of listening helps build trust and rapport, and it helps others feel comfortable in expressing their thoughts and opinions."

What Do You Think You Hear?

I think we can all agree we live in a digital world with a lot of surface noise. A world in which we are time-pressed — or at least feel as if we are — and we simply want to know what we think we need to know in the shortest amount of time. This relates to most of our interactions, discussions, and conversations.

Our typical approach to the real and perceived high level of noise in our lives is to summarize. We seek out the main points and synergize what we hear, read or view with our personal interpretation of what is important and aligned with our own thoughts, values, and knowledge. This is nothing new. We operate this way as a human evolutionary default as well as an ever-expanding human condition of navigating information and interaction in the digital age.

Active Listening

At the core of a high-performance organization and its culture are unbiased communications and active listening. Active listening is a skill that focuses on removing one's personal defaults, values, opinions, and biases when engaging with others in conversations and discussions, as well as in reading what others have written or viewing and listening to what others have captured and recorded.

How We Listen

Stephen Covey, the author of *The 7 Habits of Highly Effective People,* says, "Most people do not listen with the intent to understand; they listen with the intent to reply (Covey, S. R. 2004)." How often are you stuck in this listening trap? Brigette Hyacinth, author of "*Leading the Workforce of the Future,*" adds, "Listening is the most important skill an individual can master. However, it is tough to master as it requires us to be more present, attentive, engaged, open, and flexible. Good listening skills in this digital era, with its information overload and shortened attention span, is fast becoming an endangered species (Hyacinth, B. (2020)."

It's complicated. Each of us is the sum of our parts. Those parts reside in our minds and thought processes and manifest who we are and what we represent. The sum of our parts embraces our knowledge, life experiences, and values.

In this regard, we are our own individual holistic "system" existing within and interacting with a variety of other "systems," always maintaining a perception of our reality and how we see and interpret the world.

Our perception of reality is very much tied to our individuality. Conversations, discussions, and interactions with others are rarely based on shared perception and personal knowledge. Shared knowledge is that small sliver of common knowledge across a group of individuals and is often highly focused on a very specific item or topic.

As such, communicator bias is inherent as a communicator chooses her or his words, information to include, and information to omit. Recipient bias is also in play as the recipient side of the interaction seeks to internalize what was said and shared via their own knowledge, values, and beliefs. We typically do not listen objectively (with an open mind without our own inherent biases) and therefore may not understand what has been said or even written. We listen with the immediate intent to interpret, align, and respond. How do we know this? Ask yourself the following questions illustrating how others may have "listened" or not to what you were sharing:

- Have you ever felt that you weren't being heard?
- Have you found yourself explaining something repeatedly as the response you received wasn't connecting to your intent and meaning?
- Have you received emails or other responses that mystified you causing you to go back and reread what you wrote?
- Have you discovered that meeting notes didn't include the points that you felt were important or tangential to the problem at hand?

If you answered yes to any of the above, well, you may not be the one responsible for the confusion, interpretation, or omissions that occurred. Those you were communicating with may not have been practicing active listening skills and were defaulting to their own thoughts, opinions, and values in what you shared. They may also have been rushing to get to the main point and correlate the point or points to what is important to them in how they see an issue or problem.

A basic challenge of human communications and processing external stimuli is that the mind defaults to expend as little energy as possible to listen. The human mind cannot do more than one thing at a time. Therefore, we have a scattershot approach to listening. We grab pieces of what is said as opposed to truly hearing objectively what is shared in context of the communicator.

In other words, by nature, we take pieces of what is said and quickly determine what is important to us and what we need to know. This process informs how each of us might respond and why. This influences power plays in positioning our individual motivations to demonstrate importance, manifest competitiveness, get an ego boost, or show off a competency.

An important consideration is whether you are actively listening to what is being said about your organization.

Do you know what impact comments and opinions have on you in real-time?

What impact do they have on your revenue?

What impact do they have on your organization?

Do you know the level of satisfaction your members and customers have with your organization?

What We Hear and Retain

On average, we retain just 25% of what we hear, according to Hyacinth. She adds, "Active listening is crucial to gaining a complete understanding of any situation. Without full understanding, one can easily waste everyone's time by solving the wrong problem or merely addressing a symptom, not the root cause (Hyacinth, B. 2020)."

In addition to the mental default of preparing and calculating a response, our attention is apt to wane, and our minds are often consumed by other thoughts.

Have you sat through a meeting hungry and found that you were more focused on what to get for lunch instead of hearing what the communicator was saying?

Have you been caught with your mind wandering and unable to answer the question you were asked?

Have you found yourself answering emails or perusing websites while a discussion was underway?

Have you determined without really listening that the subject being discussed isn't relevant to you?

It happens more often than we all want to readily admit.

Exercising critical thinking via active listening is like practicing mindfulness. It requires us to clear what is in our minds and focus on the interaction at hand, fully immersing in that interaction and in many ways removing "ourselves" and stopping that constant internal conversation with ourselves so we can listen to the communicator. Active listening requires us to put ourselves into the mind of the communicator and understand the reason, rationale, and content of what is being shared with us.

The Benefits of Active Listening

Organizations can hone their active listening skills and create an organizational culture that embraces critical thinking, problem-solving, and open communications. Active listening is a key component of developing and building critical thinking competencies in an organization and a component that is critical to any organizational change or transformation.

Individuals need to support others to be open and honest without negative consequences. Active listening results in objective and constructive outcomes that can solve the true and complete problems at hand, create a shared and complete understanding of an issue or situation, and reflect the shared reality of an organization's ability to change or transform. In other words, if you don't actively listen, you won't grow. If an organization doesn't practice active listening, it also will not grow and/or achieve appropriate change or transformation.

Active Listening and its Value

Hyacinth believes that listening forms the foundation of good relationships, essential to effective leadership and collaboration at all levels.

Active listening reinforces:
- You care
- Empathy
- Emotional intelligence
- The quality of influence
- Respect
- Trust
- More motivated and committed team members

The foundation of active listening deepens the opportunity to lead and communicate with courage by helping others feel secure in expressing their understandings. In short, active listening is being open to "repeat back what you heard" to further ensure shared knowledge and understanding.

A report from Maryville University identifies three key active listening benefits:

- Active listeners are more likable. Individuals with strong listening skills are present in the conversation. People who listen with focus are often perceived as more likable.

- Active listeners build stronger relationships. Communication is not a one-way street. Good listeners show interest, ask open-ended questions, and acknowledge what's being said. This helps reduce misunderstandings and builds stronger relationships.

- Active listeners have a clearer understanding of the topics being discussed. Individuals with refined listening skills seek to fully understand a speaker's message. They pay attention to both verbal and nonverbal cues and ask for clarification when needed (Maryville University. (Nd.).

How to Be an Active Listener

Active listening is a skill that can be learned. The report from Maryville University identifies four ways to listen that we have amended with some added thoughts and context:

- **Deep Active Listening**

Deep active listening occurs when you're committed to understanding the communicator's perspective. It involves paying attention to both verbal and nonverbal cues, such as the words being used, the speaker's body language, and tone.

This type of listening helps build trust and rapport, and it helps others feel comfortable in expressing their thoughts and opinions.

- **Full Active Listening**

Full active listening involves paying close and careful attention to what the communicator is conveying.

It often involves the use of active listening techniques, such as paraphrasing what's been said to the person you're speaking with to ensure you understand their messaging, intent, and meaning. Full listening is useful in the workplace when someone is instructing you on how to complete a task, problems are being discussed and analyzed, and when discussing work projects with teams.

- **Critical Active Listening**

Critical listening involves using systematic reasoning and careful thought to analyze a communicator's message and separate fact from opinion. Critical listening is often useful in situations when communicators may have a certain agenda or goal, such as watching political debates, or when a salesperson is pitching a product or service. We have framed the lack of critical active listening into fake news and information bias. Every communicator and communication comes with some form of bias. As ingrained in individual opinions and interpretations as we have become of late, we overlook that critical thinking, as well as active listening, provides us the opportunity to hear what was said and focus on substance and fact, not opinions or agendas.

- **Therapeutic Active Listening**

Therapeutic listening means allowing a friend, colleague, or family member to discuss their problems. It involves emphasizing and applying supportive nonverbal cues, such as nodding and maintaining eye contact, in addition to empathizing with their experiences. While externally demonstrating therapeutic listening, it is also important to exercise full active listening to ensure you are hearing what your friend, colleague, or family member is sharing with you. It is important not to lose focus and miss important nuances or details (Maryville University. (Nd.).

The Pitfalls of Not Listening

Lack of active listening can have a high price tag. Organizations can become weaker in a competitive market and unable to embrace change, transformation, and continuous improvement.

Active listening should reach every level in an organization to ensure it is functional and practices critical thinking. Active listening requires us to slow down, be deliberate and "walk in someone else's shoes" so that we deeply connect and understand.

It's a great practice to master, and it's also a lifelong pursuit.

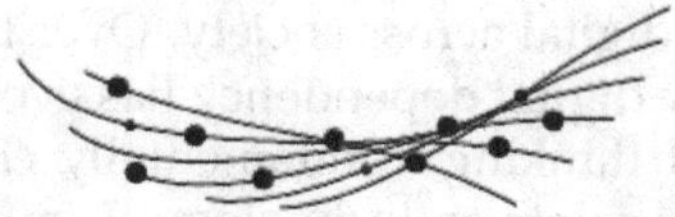

Chapter 27: Fight or Flight

"As we seek to transform organizations, majorly via technology, we often overlook the importance of the human element. This chapter is intended to spark awareness of the human dynamics at play, influenced by our evolutionary default programming and the chemistry that influences behaviors, actions, and thoughts."

Pre-programmed Behavior

I teach at the University of Maryland and the classes I have taught since 2015 focus on the impacts of digital across society. Over the past decade, I have witnessed firsthand how digital dependency has evolved from smartphone addiction to AI-assisted thinking, fundamentally changing how students process information and relate to technology. I introduce students to the consequences of a misguided belief that we can multitask, how we handle and interpret digital information, and why we give away our demographic and behavioral data in exchange for access or a free service. The course also explores the psychological impacts of digital and technology and the imbalance of digital access based on socioeconomic factors across society. And finally, we study how we change the way we communicate and relate to others, and how easily we are manipulated by, or because of, technology despite our beliefs to the contrary.

Since 2022, the emergence of generative artificial intelligence has introduced an entirely new dimension to these psychological dynamics. Students now form relationships not just with social media platforms, but also with AI systems that appear to understand them, validate their thoughts, and provide immediate intellectual gratification. This shift from passive content consumption to active AI collaboration has created unprecedented patterns of dependency and cognitive outsourcing that raise red flags.

We are sharing these next gen behaviors because there are lessons from my course that apply to how organizations operate and transform. Introducing my students to the complexity of the human factor in our digital revolution also has a lot of relevance to the workplace. Whether at work or in our private lives, the impacts of digital and technology on our society, our minds, and our wellbeing are just starting to be understood. What is now being revealed is how our conscious and subconscious minds respond to digital and technology and how the expanse of digital access to people and information is fundamentally changing us.

I am a lay person and in no way represent myself as a behavioral scientist or a neuroscientist. I have no formal behavioral training beyond my curiosity and practical experience teaching and consulting, both of which validate my assumptions, time and again in the classroom and the boardroom. We are often influenced—even manipulated—by technology, without conscious awareness. My mission is to help raise the awareness of my students and clients to assess, consider, observe, and recognize what is really going on in our digital era, as opposed to what we too often don't understand and overlook.

Chemistry Lessons

At the foundational level, we are controlled by our human chemistry—which equates to hormones. When we feel good, dopamine is released in our brain in response to a given situation. This release can be triggered by another person or a situation. Adrenaline and cortisol are released when we need to quickly perform or in response to challenging and stressful situations (fight or flight).

In the first weeks of the class, I focus on the mental defaults of singular focus and how we are influenced by the subconscious and hormones. An example is our innate programming to fight or flee dependent on a given situation in response to the release of cortisol. Across our evolution, our genes pass from one generation to the next programmed to survive at all costs and promulgate our species. Primitive programming was intended to keep us secure and ensure we could quickly react if our safety was threatened. That said, one might argue modern life has evolved beyond this primitive behavior. Fight or flight is considered an evolutionary remnant from a long-ago history where threats were ever-present. We still experience stress and anxiety when our safety and security appear threatened or compromised and cortisol is released in response. In today's civilized society, there are far fewer situations that are physically life-threatening, however, our primitive fight or flee assessment and response still play strongly in our actions, behavior, and overall mental state.

I provide the class with a real-life example at the end of the first lecture. I explain as they enter the room in preparation for the course that it may be hard to focus since they are introduced to a new environment. Despite checking out positive reviews of how past students have rated me as a professor, new students still experience a level of stress and anxiety because they don't know me, are new to the physical classroom, and aren't sure what to expect from the class—particularly if they will be required to participate or what my teaching style is. They are subconsciously assessing me, the room they are in, and fellow students surrounding them to determine if any threats exist.

As the first three-hour lecture unfolds, I reveal to them (and they acknowledge it) that they have begun to slowly relax and focus as the subconscious has determined that there are indeed no immediate threats to their wellbeing.

The AI Psychology Shift (2022-2025)

In my classroom, I observe students who have begun outsourcing not just information retrieval, but actual thinking processes to AI systems. Unlike previous generations who used search engines to find information they would then evaluate, current students often accept AI-generated analysis and conclusions without applying critical thinking filters. This cognitive outsourcing creates a form of learned intellectual helplessness that has profound implications for organizational transformation.

Recent research has revealed that generative AI creates fundamentally different psychological relationships than previous technologies. Unlike passive tools or even social media platforms, conversational AI systems trigger what researchers call "anthropomorphic responses," our tendency to attribute human-like qualities to machines. A 2025 study published in Frontiers in Computer Science found that when students anthropomorphize AI buddies, their epistemic filters weaken, leading to over-reliance on AI feedback and inadequate critical evaluation of AI-generated responses (Frontiers in Computer Science, 2025).

The psychological mechanisms at play are more complex than traditional technology dependency. When users interact with systems like ChatGPT or Claude, they experience what feels like understanding and validation from an intelligent entity. Research by Alabed, Javornik, and Gregory-Smith (2022) demonstrates that this anthropomorphization can lead to "self-AI integration," where users begin incorporating AI agents into their self-concept, creating unprecedented forms of technological-emotional dependency.

Studies published in 2024-2025 demonstrate that merely knowing advice comes from AI causes people to over-rely on it, even when it contradicts their own assessment or available contextual information. This represents a significant evolution from earlier forms of technology dependency, where users maintained more skepticism toward automated systems.

Technology, Perception, and Reality

We refer to our current time interchangeably as the Information Era, the Third Age and the Digital Age. These labels are implicitly technology informed and based, but possibly misplaced labels since as a society, we don't understand the consequences technology has now and how it will influence the future.

For the record, technology is, by definition, a form of automation. Initially, we designed tech to create efficiencies that make humans more productive. Then we turned to technology to address the societal needs of an ever-growing population, now nearing eight billion people worldwide. How our tech dependency evolves to its next level is a wild card, but we have already seen previews principally through the lens of AI that have dramatic outcomes.

As the next stage of technological development, humans created Artificial Intelligence (AI) and Machine Learning (ML) as high-speed automated tools, models, and algorithms that are rational and objective (most of the time). Simply stated, modeled on the complexity of the human brain, technology is an attempt to mimic human thought and behaviors at scale. But what is nearly always missed in this conversation is that although the human mind is complex, it is also riddled with fault lines and perceptions that lead to individual biases and herd mentalities. For example, we often miss seeing the impacts our misplaced trust in technology have on society. Essentially, there is a potentially dangerous symbiotic relationship between the technology we create, and recognition of the human inputs used to create that technology.

The emergence of large language models has amplified this challenge exponentially. These systems are trained on vast datasets that inevitably contain human biases, misinformation, and flawed reasoning patterns. Yet their sophisticated responses create an illusion of objectivity and intelligence that can be more persuasive than human experts (Nature, 2024).

New research is coming to the forefront that reveals the vast amount of information the subconscious mind registers as we scan and curate our content, social, and newsfeeds—even though we may interact with only a few items across these feeds consciously. Images, comments, and emojis become imprinted into our minds and begin to affect our thoughts and feelings, defining how we see others, think about issues and situations, and how we perceive our reality. What's worse is that we often aren't aware of the influences around us which shape our conscious and unconscious thoughts and actions. It's difficult to always know what we should think and do when so much of the world around us has an invisible influence on our thoughts, emotions, actions, and behaviors.

The algorithmic curation of content has evolved significantly since 2020. AI-powered recommendation systems now create what researchers call "reality distortion fields," personalized information environments so precisely tailored to individual preferences and biases that users lose exposure to contradictory viewpoints or challenging information (Journal of Computer-Mediated Communication, 2024).

This represents a more sophisticated form of censorship manipulation than traditional "filter bubbles," as AI systems continuously learn and adapt to reinforce existing beliefs while subtly introducing new ideas that align with predicted preferences.

Technological Determinism and Next Gens

My students are fascinated by the theories surrounding technological determinism which suggest that technology is an influencer and change catalyst in how society and human beings evolve, interact, and live. The flip side of this argument is that humans design technologies to reflect themselves as the central influencer.

Anecdotally, as we develop new technologies, we typically seek to solve an immediate problem or dive into the creative exercise based on the notion that "because we can, we do." We do not always have the foresight to see, know or understand the consequences that this technology is going to have on society or whether its impact is going to be positive, negative, or a mix of both.

A deterministic argument could be made about the Industrial Age; historical theorists have studied if technology changed the ethics, values and mores of society. Clearly, it did. The steam engine allowed us to travel faster and farther, instilling dreams of manifest destiny. The assembly line allowed us to produce more products, and we became more prodigious consumers, which evolved into the unanticipated explosion of storage spaces. Other inventions like radio, electricity, and the phone became technologies we could not live without as the digital world became more connected without boundaries.

Technological determinism includes both soft and hard influences. Some technological inventions are softer, such as fridges, irons, and fans, which had a quality-of-life upgrade on society. Others such as the mobile phone and the computer are considered harder influences which have been so immediate and pervasive that people cannot live without them. The harder technologies have quickly become essential to life.

Generative AI represents perhaps the most dramatic example of hard technological determinism that we have witnessed. Within 18 months of ChatGPT's release in November 2022, these systems became integrated into fundamental workflows across education, business, and creative industries. Unlike previous technologies that augmented human capabilities, generative AI has begun to be a substitute for human cognitive processes in ways that may be irreversible.

Research from MIT's Computer Science and Artificial Intelligence Laboratory suggests that widespread AI adoption is creating what they term "cognitive offloading syndrome," a measurable decline in critical thinking skills among regular AI users (MIT Technology Review, 2024). Students who frequently use AI to write assignments show decreased ability to construct logical arguments independently, while professionals who frequently rely on AI for analysis demonstrate reduced capacity for original problem-solving when AI tools are unavailable.

Another aspect of technological determinism is captured by the retro notion that the medium is the message. The technologies and the interfaces we have developed to interact with them have resulted in an egocentric platform and we have narcissistically become our own content. A complete content creation immersion in Twitter can become a full-time career. In a short timeframe, we have learned to classify information and distribute content as our own broadcasters. With the introduction of Sora, we can become the stars of our own online cinema by using the AI tool to insert ourselves into what looks like realistic home movies.

The same egocentric content production is pervasive on Facebook, TikTok, and Instagram. LinkedIn, which is marketed as a "professional" platform is another personal content generator. Our perception that LinkedIn is a business tool influences a higher level of content (and longer) than a tweet. How we communicate information on our platform of choice is shaped by the medium, not the message. One could argue that we automatically create messaging for each platform subconsciously conforming to each medium.

To add to the complexity, the influence of short-form video platforms, particularly TikTok, has created what researchers call "attention residue syndrome," persistent difficulty concentrating on single tasks for extended periods (Leroy, S. (2009).

So, is technology controlling us and our actions? Does it determine how we vet and even value information? Do we trust a tech brand like Apple more than Samsung? Contemporary research suggests the answer is increasingly, yes. But the issue is whether these preferences are based on freedom of choice. Many Americans make daily decisions based on algorithmic recommendations, often without conscious awareness that AI systems are influencing these choices. This represents a fundamental shift in human agency that previous generations of technology never achieved.

The metaverse has propelled high-tech experiences onto a higher level. The hopes for the metaverse have been tempered by market reality. Despite billions invested in virtual reality platforms between 2021-2023, user adoption has remained limited, with Meta's Reality Labs reporting continued losses exceeding $60 billion by 2025. The predicted immersive virtual experiences failed to achieve mainstream adoption, suggesting that human preferences for authentic physical and social connection remain stronger than technological simulations. However, the jury is still out when it comes to the ultimate fate of the metaverse and its consumer adoption.

Technology Without Guardrails

Today we are on a technology ride that is beginning to feel like a runaway train. We need to get off the train and apply guardrails based on critical thinking across how we and society are being influenced, fundamentally changed, and manipulated by technology. From voice assistants (at work and home) and data analytics to assembly lines and touchless checkout at retail, we are enabled and empowered by tech automation. But often safety mechanisms are missing in our enthusiasm of developing more innovative tech solutions. And in the process, it is becoming more apparent that we are also influenced and controlled by this proliferation of technology solutions leading to our reliance on them for everything from interacting with our friends and family to adjusting the home thermostat.

The regulatory landscape has failed to keep pace with technological advancement. As documented in the AI governance crisis of 2023-2024, major technology companies made voluntary commitments to AI safety that proved largely ineffective in practice (Brookings Institute, 2024). By late 2023, AI-generated content was estimated to account for up to 99% of some information categories online, yet content moderation systems remained overwhelmed and largely ineffective.

The psychological implications of unregulated AI deployment are becoming clear. Research from the Center for Humane Technology demonstrates that AI-powered systems exploit psychological vulnerabilities more efficiently than previous technologies and are creating what they term "persuasive technology amplification" (Center for Humane Technology Annual Report, 2024). These systems learn individual psychological profiles and adapt their interactions to maximize engagement, often triggering compulsive usage patterns that users find difficult to control. This shows up in the personification of AI assistants, buddies, and increasingly, romantic partners.

Potential Addictions

The new digital environment has generated positive opportunities for us to leverage what may be our innate desires and abilities to communicate and interact with our fellow humans. It has also resulted in situations that further impact our defaults, biases, and trust in behaviors that were formerly limited to those who were physically within reach.

The compulsion to gain a hormonal boost or response to a situation generated by technology encourages addiction. It can become a dysfunctional loop. Individuals feel a sense of immediacy in responding to texts and messages. Immediacy results from our connection of sounds, alerts, and notifications to the dopamine burst we receive from our brains. The more we interact and the more immediate our interaction is, the quicker we receive the burst of feel-good chemicals. The immediacy of a growing number of stimuli ensures that we have the continuous release of dopamine as we are rewarded for taking action.

But that continuous cycle of chemical reward also comes with consequences. As discussed, digital recommendation engines and short-form videos are shortening our attention spans. We assign social and emotional attributes to our interactive platforms of choice. On the opposite side of dopamine release, this relationship to our platforms can also lead to anxiety, depression, and even addiction.

AI-assisted technologies have created new forms of behavioral dependency that differ significantly from traditional digital addiction. Clinical research published in the Journal of Behavioral Health Services & Research (2024) identifies "AI validation syndrome;" compulsive seeking of AI-generated affirmation and intellectual validation. Unlike social media addiction, which centers on peer approval, AI validation syndrome involves users developing dependent relationships with systems that provide immediate, seemingly intelligent and self-gratifying responses to their thoughts and questions.

The overflow of digital communications also creates stress. Another emotional and mental response to tech stimuli is a feeling of being overstimulated and overwhelmed. The constant cycle of hormone release as a reward for response and interaction keeps us tightly wound and drugged. When an individual can separate, the lack of stimuli and the new unfamiliar "down" time may catalyze sadness, feelings of isolation, and ultimately depression.

Post-pandemic research reveals alarming trends in digital dependency and mental health correlations. The American Psychological Association's 2024 Digital Wellness Study found that 68% of adults report feeling anxious when unable to access digital devices for more than two hours, representing a 34% increase from pre-pandemic levels. Among college students, diagnosed anxiety disorders increased 87% between 2019-2024, with researchers identifying "digital overstimulation" as a primary contributing factor (American College Health Association, 2024). The research continues to evolve to reveal the negative effects of digital behaviors and habits in our personal lives and our work settings. In fact, it has become such an insidious problem that self-help "camps" or therapy centers have been established to help people separate from their digital addictions.

Digital wellness retreats and "digital detox" programs have expanded significantly, with the industry growing by 300% between 2020-2024 (Digital Wellness Institute, 2024). However, research suggests these interventions provide only temporary relief without addressing underlying psychological dependencies. Most participants return to previous usage patterns within 30 days of completing digital detox programs.

We know the brain responds, we know hormones are released, and we are learning how much of this occurs at the subconscious level. What remains unknown is whether we change because of technological influences. Cyber-psychology research investigates how we build technology and the ways we interact with it when there is little recognition of the real or predicted consequences.

We don't yet understand if technology is influencing and changing us or if we are simply assimilating technology as a survival tool. This is a chicken and the egg proposition, one without a clear answer.

Recent neurological research provides increasingly clear evidence that technology is physically changing brain structure and function. Studies using functional magnetic resonance imaging (fMRI) demonstrate measurable changes in neural pathways among heavy digital device users, particularly in areas responsible for attention, memory formation, and social cognition. These findings suggest that technological determinism may have literal, biological foundations rather than being merely theoretical.

Think about your own relationship with technology. Have you experienced periods of withdrawal? During a vacation, do you find yourself unable to separate yourself from your device? You are experiencing technological determinism firsthand.

Organizational Management and Transformation

The human element is the most important factor in any change or transformation initiative. It is also the most important factor in the day-to-day management of an organization. An organization and its leaders do not need to become experts in human behavioral defaults and hormonal influences, but it is important to be mindful of the silent voice of the subconscious in the roles people play, how they act and respond in groups, and how they perform as individuals.

When organizations seek to change or transform, they must consider and then plan for and accommodate our inherent evolutionary programming. That may sound highly academic, but the fight, or flight response can derail any movement for change. The human factor can interfere with transformation if there is resistance to change.

Let's face it, the introduction of AI systems into organizational workflows has created unprecedented psychological challenges that require new management approaches. Research from Harvard Business School's Future of Work Initiative demonstrates that employees experience measurable stress responses when AI tools are implemented without adequate psychological preparation (EY 2023, FlexJobs 2024). The study found that 67% of workers report anxiety about AI capabilities, while 43% fear eventual job displacement. When AI systems perform tasks previously considered uniquely human, employees experience what researchers term "cognitive displacement anxiety," manifesting in fight-or-flight responses that can sabotage transformation efforts.

Successful AI integration requires what organizational psychologists call "collaborative intelligence frameworks," structured approaches that preserve human agency while leveraging AI capabilities. Providing a safe and secure workplace enhances personal confidence and performance. As discussed, we often overlook that the subconscious impacts and influences nearly everything we do, say, and think. Being mindful of the influences that we can't see as we proceed through transitions (whether in our personal or professional lives) is critical to gaining support, alignment, and involvement with stakeholders in change or transformation.

In summary, modern transformation initiatives must account for the psychological complexity of human-AI collaboration. This includes recognizing that different individuals will have varying comfort levels with AI systems. Concerns about job security and relevance need to be addressed. Creating clear frameworks for when human judgment should override AI recommendations is essential. Organizations that fail to address these psychological factors will experience increased employee turnover during AI implementation periods and likely experience diminished transformative gains. Managing AI is a wake-up call for all organizations to understand that there is more than meets the eye when it comes to the human factor and embracing new disruptive technologies.

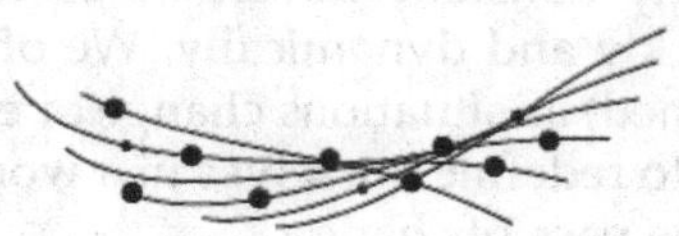

Chapter 28: Decision-Making and Primitive Automaticity

"As a society we are discovering how we have been captive to algorithms dialing our emotions up and down, polarizing our thoughts and beliefs, and rattling our perceptions of our individual realities as we negatively compare ourselves to those around us. We are subject to information feeds that deliver filtered information based on what an algorithm believes we want to see because we have interacted with similar information in the recent past."

What Is Real?

We live in nearly constant transition as the world around us continues to change quickly and dynamically. We often don't know what we may have lost (or gained) as situations change or evolve around us. We often struggle with how to redefine ourselves in a world we do not yet well understand because of the pace of change.

Technology continues to fundamentally change the world around us as we debate whether we are changing because of technology or question if our tech-framed behavior is innate. These are existential questions that we must deal with to determine who we are versus whom we perceive we are. A quote from The Matrix sums it up best when Morpheus responds to Neo by saying, "What is reality? Reality comes from electrical pulses firing synapses in the brain and which forms the construct. Reality, then, is what the mind believes it is. You've felt it your entire life, that there's something wrong with the world. You don't know what it is, but it's there, like a splinter in your mind, driving you mad. If real is what you can feel, smell, taste, and see, then real is simply electrical signals interpreted by your brain."

Surface Noise

As a society we are discovering how we have been captive to algorithms dialing our emotions up and down, polarizing our thoughts and beliefs, and rattling our perceptions of our individual realities as we negatively compare ourselves to those around us. We are subject to information feeds that deliver filtered information based on what an algorithm believes we want to see because we have interacted with similar information in the recent past.

We are overwhelmed by the number of choices that we have facing us daily. We live in a world of never-ending choices, whether deciding what to watch, what to buy in endless online aisles, or where to eat. Research shows we are easily stressed and become consumed with anxiety when we have too many items to choose from when we only want two or three.

Much research is coming to the forefront that reveals the amount of information the subconscious mind registers as we scan and curate our information, social, and newsfeeds, even though we interact with only a few items across the feed via our conscious minds.

Images, comments, and emojis become imprinted into our minds and begin to affect our thoughts and feelings, defining how we see others, think about issues and situations, and how we perceive our reality.

What's worse is that we often don't even recognize the influences around us which shape our conscious and unconscious thoughts and actions. It is difficult to always know what to think and do when so much of the world around us has an unknown influence on our thoughts, emotions, actions, and behaviors.

Technology, Perception, and Reality

We refer to our current time as the Information Era and the Digital Age. These labels are implicitly technology informed and based, but as a society, we don't yet understand the consequences technology has now and will influence the future. Technology is, by definition, a form of automation. Initially, we designed tech to create efficiencies that make humans more productive. Then we turned to technology to address the societal needs of an ever-growing population, now nearing eight billion people worldwide. It would seem clear that our world population has needs and demands that cannot be met by human hands alone.

Humans created Artificial Intelligence (AI) and Machine Learning (ML) as automated tools, models, and algorithms to be rational and objective (most of the time). Simply stated, modeled on the complexity of the human brain, technology is an attempt to mimic human thought and behaviors at scale. But what is nearly always missed in this conversation is that although the human mind is complex, it is also riddled with faults and perceptions that form individual and herd realities. For example. we often miss our misplaced trust in technology and the unknown impacts it is having on society. Essentially, there is a faulty symbiotic relationship between the technology we create, and recognition of the human inputs used to create the technology.

Technology Without Guardrails

Today we are on the technology ride that is beginning to feel like a runaway train. We need to get off the train and apply critical thinking across how we and society are being influenced, fundamentally changed, and manipulated by technology. From voice assistants (at work and home) and data analytics to assembly lines and touchless checkout at retail, we are enabled and empowered by tech automation.

And it is becoming more and more apparent that we are also influenced and controlled by the proliferation of technology solutions and our reliance on them for everything from interacting with our friends and family to adjusting the home thermostat.

The technological determinists uphold that our behavior and values have been fundamentally shaped and reshaped by technology. Take a few moments to consider how your own thought process, beliefs and even actions are influenced and controlled by the technology around you.

There is another factor that is causing some to have an existential crisis: how our emotions play a disproportionate role in how we make decisions and come to conclusions. It almost sounds quaint that our feelings can highjack so many important decisions when we have an excess of information at hand that we can access through a simple keystroke or tap of our fingertips. However, we tend to make decisions automatically based on our feelings and information at hand, rather than through a thoughtful, thorough process. We need a better process to decide when to say yes and when to say no.

Primitive Automaticity

Alfred North Whitehead, mathematician, and philosopher believed "One of the main conundrums of our evolution as a species seems to be that it has largely depended upon our ability to engage in more and more activities without thinking about them. Our world is built upon scientific discovery, but full of ever-declining numbers of scientifically literate people. Hence, we live in a world of increasing complexity that we often meet with relatively primitive (instinctive) automaticity (kneejerk actions) (Footnotes2Plato. (Whitehead North, A. (2019)." Dr. Robert Cialdini has popularized the concept of his appraisal theory that "the individual conclusions we make about specific aspects of the world and ourselves cause an emotional reaction. Essentially, our evaluations (or appraisals) of a situation then cause an emotional response based on that appraisal (Cialdini, R. 1993)." It is a seamless loop. We project the outcome of a decision, which then projects the actual experience of that outcome. Data and facts are damned!

Why do we do this?

"We constantly assess our world and the daily situations we encounter through the lens of whether a scenario is good for me/bad for us.

The importance of such an evaluation is consistent with the general idea that we automatically evaluate stimuli," according to neuroscientist Lisa Feldman Barrett (Chen, A. 2017). The lens through which we see the world is formed by the influences (opinions, information, social feeds, and our surroundings). These influences shape our perception of reality. This lens is not based in objectivity; in fact, it rests in emotion and majorly filters our conscious and unconscious defaults by manifesting our biases.

Cialdini believes that "Our world has become overwhelmingly complex, information intensive and fast-paced. A heightened awareness of the influence factors such as reciprocation, consistency, social proof, liking, authority, and scarcity, means our ability to make better decisions improves (Cialdini, R. (2021)." Reading between the lines, "instant influence, primitive automaticity, modern automaticity, and sacred shortcuts represent decision-making timesavers" that we utilize consciously and unconsciously for better or worse. Keeping informed and current on so many topics that impact us personally and professionally has become a full-time job and has added a tremendous amount of stress to our lives which feeds into our seeking shortcuts that often do not lead to informed decisions.

The ever-increasing complexity of life has exceeded our human abilities to contend with all the available information that demands our attention and consumes our energy. The ability to interact and communicate in broader circles becomes ever more time-consuming and is often driven by FOMO, the fear of missing out. We are tasked to manage a level of complexity that has never historically existed. We are watching our evolution unfold in real-time with the exponential growth of technology that we barely understand.

We face a societal conundrum that requires us to recognize consciously and concretely the psychological limits of our human capacity and brains. We must understand how to become active self-managers and recognize the influences and controls in the world around us.

Shortcuts

When you unpack the primitive automaticity phenomenon, it becomes clear that we typically base decisions on a small or single piece of available information that may be perceptually relevant and meaningful. But this expedience can lead to misinformed, incomplete conclusions which could be embarrassing or even dangerous. A current example we all grapple with is basing decisions on "fake news."

The level of trickery in the larger cultural conversation has made many rely on gut decisions instead of taking the time and energy to become fully informed. It can be overwhelming to know everything and lead to analysis paralysis. Barry Schwartz's seminal work on *The Paradox of Choice* examines the conundrum sociologically: When faced with too much choice or information, we default to making decisions based on instinct or what we are familiar with in the past (Schwartz, B. 2004).

We also fall prey to perceptual familiarity; if we have seen or heard something frequently, consciously our consciously, it becomes our truth as repetition becomes neurologically embedded in our brains. First and foremost, we are very trusting and want to believe what we are told. It takes experience and energy to be skeptical and ask questions and seek out information that may run contrary to what we've heard, read, and viewed.

The central issue here is do you need to know everything or just enough. Cialdini maintains that no one "has the time" to consider all the relevant facts, analyze the advantages and disadvantages, and choose then the best option that life demands, split-second decision-making. As a result, we return to an automatic, primitive, single piece of information that resonates within us" and we take shortcuts.

Consider the shortcuts we take at work.

- We make assumptions about our customers using our personal perception of reality and institutional filters.
- We believe we understand critical changes in our marketplace internalizing what we perceive is happening based on our assumption that everyone is like us.
- We rely on the internet for most of our information using search words that have meaning to us, and we take that information at face value.
- We understand our employees based on past experiences, observations, and impressions, grouping individuals using our inherent biases into herds based on class, ethnicity, sex, or race.
- We conduct primitive market research not asking the right questions or using questions to produce the answers we want instead of an objective set of results that would result in more concrete intelligence.
- We analyze the results of research without fully understanding the implications and conclude what we were seeking as opposed to considering what it might be telling us.
- We ignore transformative ideas that don't conform to our own because the ideas don't align with what we believe or understand.

- We repeat what we have done in the past as a strategy to shape the future, even though the present and future are very different from the past.
- We ensure that we don't lose face in front of our co-workers because we want positive confirmation to bolster our egos.

And to put shortcuts into simple perspective, the classic belief was the notion that the world was flat. Historically we didn't know what we didn't know and often didn't know how to seek out what we needed to know.
As such, our reality for hundreds if not thousands of years was based on a faulty premise. And we often defaulted to primitive automaticity.

Any one of these shortcuts can lead to embarrassing outcomes when we rely on only our gut instincts, especially when those types of conclusions are made the higher you go up the leadership ladder. Cialdini believes that "The more complicated the world becomes, the more often individuals will employ decision-making (automatic) shortcuts since we are simply unable to consume, absorb, retain, and then communicate all of the information available to us." Cialdini insists "shortcuts shall be sacred, and we have the responsibility to boycott, threaten, retaliate, against those who don't play fairly (Cialdini, R. (2021)."

Thriving in the Digital Age

Being human in a Digital Age is still uncharted territory as our exploration and journey to self-actualization takes a back seat to our day-to-day stress and choice-filled lives. What separates humans from most animals is that we can take in multiple pieces of information at one time and process the inputs to determine current reality and consider what we could or should do. Our thought process works in an interconnected network of information, possibilities, and expected outcomes. However, by human nature, we tend to pay attention to the most relevant in-your-face details when making decisions. But using one piece of information to form a conclusion and act on it is a risk.

Think in your life when you used a shortcut to make a significant decision; was the outcome positive or negative?

Upon reflection, did you regret that decision later?

Did the decision box you into a situation that you couldn't reverse?

Cialdini has an established set of ethical guidelines to manage our kneejerk shortcut defaults by recognizing and countering when we are influenced, controlled, and manipulated to form our thinking, actions, decisions, and responses. He advocates conscious awareness by pausing to reflect, apply cognition, assess, and determine if and how we are reacting with primitive automaticity.

These guidelines are essential to prevent us from taking inappropriate and ineffective shortcuts:

1. Be truthful; this requires consideration of fact and objectivity to remove emotional, kneejerk thinking and bias.
2. Forgo manipulation of others and recognize when technology is a manipulator.
3. Forgo manipulation of facts (don't seek or validate the answer you want).
4. Use the facts that already exist naturally in your situation.
5. Use the facts that demonstrate what is wise for all concerned.
6. Refrain from any way that could injure a relationship.
7. Inform (that is, educate) people into agreement.
8. Ensure any "contrast" used is relevant to the situation.
9. Own up to any mistake ASAP (Cialdini, R. (2021).

Our default is to take shortcuts and be subject to primitive automaticity. It is the responsibility of each individual and society to become consciously aware. Without awareness, we will surely continue to make the same mistakes over, and over again.

Organizational Primitive Automaticity

Managers need to be aware of how decisions are made and to carefully evaluate how these decisions impact an organization. Critical thinking is a tool we advocate to prevent the unintended consequences of shortcut decision-making. Separating fact from fiction and convenience from doing the necessary hard work are skills we help organizations master and adopt in evaluations and decision-making. Awareness of primitive automaticity is critical in formulating strategies for high performance of people, processes, and cultures in the Digital Age.

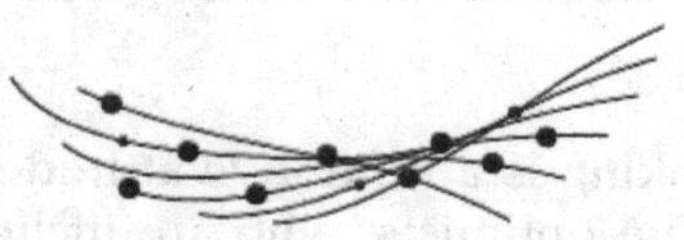

Chapter 29: The Power of Positive ... and Negative Thinking

"A real trap to thinking positively is the subconscious/unconscious and even conscious bias that every individual holds onto. We all know the saying that insanity is doing the same thing over and over and expecting a different outcome. Much of that ingrained sameness behavior comes from our inherent biases and fear of change or trying something new."

What Are You Thinking?

What have we been told since kindergarten? Believe in the power of positive thinking!

For many, positive thinking is an intuitive attitude reflected in a state of mind and behavior. The optimists, who are inclined to be hopeful and expect good outcomes, live this credo daily. Wake up with positive thoughts and positive outcomes will result. The skeptics, who are inclined to doubt or question any belief (especially those that are dogmatic and rote) may view positive thinking as a Pollyanna-ish notion. The realists, who accept a belief system as it is and behave accordingly, are somewhere in the middle. The pessimists tend to see the worst aspects of things and believe the worst will happen.

Where are you on the spectrum?

And how does that influence your interactions, professional behavior, and how you work?

To mix things up, there is also a school of the power of negative thinking which has its supporters and is used as a guide to effective decision-making, strategy, and influence. Let's unpack positive and negative thinking to evaluate how either approach can help and hinder an organization.

The Power of Positive Thinking

Let's start at the source. In 1952 Norman Vincent Peale wrote the iconic book on positive thinking that went on to sell over 15 million copies (Peale, D. N. V. (1990). His self-help guide was intended to help people achieve fulfillment and a happy, satisfying, worthwhile life. We believe that the same principles apply to the health and wellbeing of an organization. We have adjusted Peale's precepts to the attitudes and behaviors of a workforce and workplace culture.

- Believe in your mission and in everything you do.
- Build workforce power through determination and intention.
- Develop collective/collaborative organizational power to reach your goals.
- Build and improve professional relationships.
- Be kind and try to do no harm (a nod to Alphabet) (Peale, D. N. V. (1990).

Personal Resilience

On an individual basis, there are some key questions to ask yourself to unlock a positive approach. And these questions are especially pertinent to how an organization operates.

- Do you blame others when bad things happen to you? Successful people take responsibility and have an internal ethical compass set to a deep belief in themselves. Honestly assess your mindset.

- Are you naturally grateful or do you choose to focus on the negative? Successful people respond to challenges by empowering their teams.

- Are you defensive and hostile? Successful people use critical thinking to shake bad habits and behaviors that result in negative outcomes. They don't fall back on self-doubt and the fear of failure to motivate their behavior.

- On a purely practical level, are you aware of the words you typically use to communicate? Successful people have positive vocabulary and communication styles. Think of dynamic athletic coaches who motivate their players through the power of the words they choose.

- Who do you look up to and seek to emulate? Our society seems to be lacking heroes and role models to help us navigate today's fractious times. Successful people are inspired by role models and mentors whom they use to shape their own north stars to influence and lead others.

Positive thinking advocates believe your mindset can transform your experience. Further, a positive mindset sees the opportunities, not the roadblocks. Taking a pop-cultural cue, Mary J Blige's album is entitled: "Good Morning Gorgeous." Through song and in her own words, she describes how she developed a negative mindset in response to life circumstances and challenges that led to a negative self-perception. In recognition and response, she set out to wake up every morning, look in the mirror and exclaim "Good Morning Gorgeous" to remind herself that first and foremost, self-love and acceptance are paramount in establishing a positive outlook critical to navigating the paths of day-to-day life. She expresses that regardless of the circumstances, has committed to that daily act and she is maintaining a positive outlook as a result.

How to Choose to Be Happy

Positive thinking is a great concept, but life gets in the way. Happiness experts (a relatively new consulting practice) believe that happy, fulfilled people follow a practice. Whether it's reading Daniel Gilbert's *Stumbling on Happiness* or any other happiness self-help book over the past several years, you may have taken up practicing mindfulness and meditation Gilbert, D. (2006). Perhaps you read Buddhist teachings or leverage new mental health app-based services. It seems we are all seeking ways to contend with daily life, maintain calm, and establish a basis of "happiness" or at least an attitude of positive acceptance.

After 25 years of research across 70 countries, behavioral expert Greg Hicks consults with organizations of all sizes to coach employees on how to consciously follow nine specific behaviors that improve performance and wellbeing—professionally and personally. His work is the bridge from theory to practice on how one can choose to be happy. The focus is on choice. You cannot control the circumstances of your life, but you can choose how to respond. And happiness is not a frivolous superficial concept; it is the equivalent of wellbeing (Hicks, Greg. (Nd.).

"These are practical, do-able choices people can make throughout their day that actually change their biochemistry away from stress and anxiety," Hicks says. Not surprisingly, his findings also correlate to the behaviors, attitudes, and beliefs that are instrumental in wellbeing, a feeling of control, and the healing process. Hicks offers a few suggestions for finding joy in our turbulent world, "To feel happy you have to direct yourself toward happiness. Be unrelenting in your search for what's good and joyful as you go through each day's events rather than sucked into what's wrong or mundane. Waking up each morning with something to look forward to is essential." He adds, "When you feel most victimized by circumstances, look for what you can control, no matter how small. It helps you get out of your reactive fight or fright brain freeze. Another idea: Tell your stories to others and invite them to share theirs with you; it is one of the best ways to happily stay connected to others – one of the most important keys to happiness (Hicks, Greg. (Nd.)."

Positive Outcomes

Research from the Mayo Clinic reports that positive thinking helps with stress management and can improve health. The Clinic states that positive thinking doesn't mean ignoring unpleasant situations, it means approaching them in a productive way (Mayo Clinic. (Nd.).

A real trap to thinking positively is the subconscious/unconscious and even conscious bias that every individual holds onto. We all know the saying that insanity is doing the same thing over and over and expecting a different outcome. Much of that ingrained sameness behavior comes from our inherent biases and fear of change or trying something new. Other obstacles we present to ourselves are "I don't have the resources; I'm too lazy to change; there's no way it's going to work; it's too radical; I don't have any support, and I'm not going to try something I'm sure to fail."

On the flip side, the power of positive thinking can result in real-life wellbeing.

According to the Clinic, researchers have found that positive thinking can provide documented benefits:

- Increased life span
- Lower rates of depression
- Lower levels of distress and pain
- Greater resistance to illnesses
- Better psychological and physical wellbeing
- Better cardiovascular health and reduced risk of death from cardiovascular disease and stroke
- Reduced risk of death from cancer
- Reduced risk of death from respiratory conditions
- Reduced risk of death from infections
- Better coping skills during hardships and times of stress (Mayo Clinic. (Nd.).

Who would want to resist or refute these benefits? But in reality, we tend to highjack positive coping attitudes and behaviors out of our preferred comfort level with ingrained habits.

The Clinic identifies key negative thoughts that prevent optimism, and these can be applied professionally to organizational culture.

- Filtering. Magnify the negative aspects of a situation and filter out all the positive ones.
- Personalizing. When something bad occurs, you automatically blame yourself.
- Catastrophizing. You automatically anticipate the worst without objective facts to judge whether the worst will happen.
- Blaming. You say someone else is responsible for what happened to you instead of yourself.

- Saying you "should" do something. You think of all the things you think you should do and blame yourself for not doing them.
- Magnifying. You make a big deal out of minor problems.
- Perfectionism. Keeping impossible standards and trying to be more perfect sets you up for failure.
- Polarizing. You see things only as either good or bad without a middle ground (Mayo Clinic. (Nd.).

Positive Pragmatism

One could argue that a positive attitude is another term for determination and perseverance. On a practical level, when any organization has hit a roadblock, setback, or failure, start with acceptance (not denying or running away from the situation). Acknowledgment opens the door to understanding that the problem is not an invalidation of the organization; it does not define it. Stuff happens as a natural evolution in business. We learn more from our mistakes than our successes. So, positive thinking, AKA determination, could be expressed in an iconic reference to Dory's search for Nemo: Just keep swimming. We add to Dory's advice and use critical thinking in that swim to identify the best direction for the optimal outcome. Leverage that journey with some basic truisms to keep a keen sense of direction.

- Don't self-wallow or obsess about the setback. Recognize it for what it is and use the learnings to pivot.

- Look ahead as a chess player would anticipate the future yet be fluid and open to course corrections. Agility is the new resilience. And you can't succeed in repeating the same practices that haven't worked.

- Stay in the game, or even better, reinvent the game.

- Stay active and communicate. Take the wisdom of crowds approach and tap the strengths, insights, and entrepreneurship of your teams to shape your future based on what your stakeholders want and need from you.

The Case for the Power of Negative Thinking

It sounds counterintuitive to celebrate negative thinking as an asset.

Yet according to Sarah Elizabeth Adler in The Atlantic, "Pessimists fare better than people with a sunnier disposition." She states that a rosy outlook can leave people overconfident.

Further, "Optimism can beget disappointment and embracing negativity may also have social benefits." She adds, "Compared with cheery moods, bad moods have been linked to a more effective communication style, and sadness has been linked to less reliance on negative stereotypes. Feeling down can make us behave more fairly (Adler, S. (2018)."

Research at the University of Michigan describes a strategy called "defensive pessimism, whereby people harness their anxiety for good (Yamawaki, et. al. 2004)." Follow-up studies found that "by setting low expectations and envisioning worst-case scenarios, defensive pessimists optimized their performance on a variety of tasks, solving problems to fulfilling real-life goals."

Meg Selig writes in Psychology Today in support of the power of negative thinking, which she defines as, "the ability to see the potential dark side of people, ideas, places, and things, to respond to them in a realistic and self-protective manner (Selig, M. (2019)." According to author Oliver Burkeman, "Negative thinking, if strategically pursued, has a role to play in happiness." A few lessons: Focus on the worst-case scenario. It may sound obscure, but research suggests that "negative visualization can be an excellent antidote to anxiety." In other words, defensive pessimism is "working through how badly things could really go, and you may find that your fears get cut down to manageable size Burkeman, O. 2012)."

Another lesson on negative thinking: Consider getting rid of your goals. Research suggests that "over-pursuit of goals can prompt employees to cut ethical corners." Professor Saras Sarasvathy's studies of successful entrepreneurs reveal that they rarely stick rigorously to detailed, multi-year business plans. Instead, "they just start and keep correcting their course as they go. Their philosophy isn't so much ready, aim, fire as ready, fire, aim — and then to keep on re-aiming (Sarasvathy, S. 2008)."

A third lesson is don't get too attached to positive thinking. "When researchers in Canada tested the efficacy of self-help affirmations, they found that those who already had low self-esteem experienced a further decline in their mood," according to Sarasvathy. Emotional and psychological attachments can manipulate your behavior and attitudes. And ultimately, they do not define who you are.

Selig supports her advocacy of negative thinking with five
positive outcomes:

- **Negative thinking helps envision the worst thing that can happen — and often prevents it.**

We live in a society, particularly in urban centers, where we have to think about personal safety all the time. Everyone knows that if you live in a city such as New York that if you let down your guard, you're less likely to stay alert to danger. The application for organizations? Wargame what could happen and develop realistic strategies to prevent the worst in the marketplace and workplace culture with employees who are not aligned.

- **Negative thinking saves money and time.**

Some people love high risk, but for most, avoiding such situations and low-yield activities, which don't add meaning to their lives, is an exercise in the benefit of negative thinking.

- **Negative thinking slows down your decision-making.**

By using negative thinking, you can practice the motto: "When in doubt, wait." This can operate as a safety mechanism to prevent impulsive decisions without evidence-based data to support it.

- **Negative thinking helps you look at yourself and others more realistically.**

Persisting in a chosen career or personal path despite difficulties is a good thing — except when it isn't. Sometimes it makes sense to give up unrealistic ambitions and hopes and put your energy into a new endeavor.

- **Negative thinking by another name is critical thinking.**

When you think critically, you question deeply and are less likely to make false assumptions, make faulty assertions, accept excuses, or fall victim to biases. "Blind belief in authority is the greatest enemy of truth," said Albert Einstein (Jost Winteler (1901).

On the last point, critical thinking serves as an objective foundation for considering a problem, interpreting information or data, and determining the path to transformation and change. It is neither positive nor negative but considers positive and negative factors and variables and asks the right questions to clarify an individual or team's thought processes.

Organizational Application

In today's dynamically changing society and business environment, agility in the face of ambiguity is required to adapt and ensure the value offered correlates to the value sought. This level of insight informs how the organization may respond to challenges. We advise that overly positive thinking may result in overshooting goal forecasts or other results. Negative thinking may hinder the identification of the right opportunities or lead to overly pessimistic viewpoints that prevent an organization from action, ability to adapt, and moving forward. The more aware you are of the power of both positive and negative thinking, the better prepared you are to meet disruption, change, and transformation with the most effective strategies.

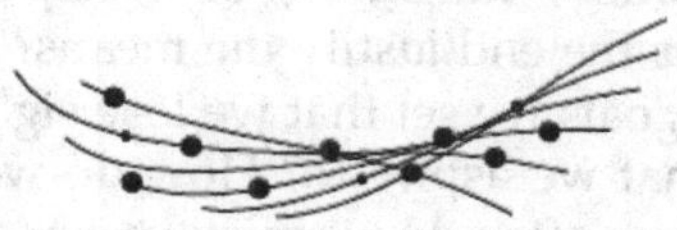

Chapter 30: What Keeps You from Attaining Goals?

"The challenge for any leader and manager is understanding their employees' motivations and how they need to be rewarded for goal attainment. Equally challenging is for leaders and managers to understand their own motivations and goals and how their behaviors influence or impact others."

Goal Posts

Any transformation, transition, or change requires setting and attaining goals. But does the end justify the means? In other words, do we focus so acutely on the goals we set that we lose sight of whether the goals move us forward to what we aspire to? How do we ensure our goals are worthy and relevant? How often do we mistake a goal for intention? A goal has a measurable outcome. An intention is about feelings. So, consider this: I want to create an environment in which everyone feels safe and secure in striving to attain our goals. That is the combination of intention and goal at its best. Let's dive into the human defaults that influence how we conceptualize and set goals, what we assign as goals, and how to create shared goals and measure the outcomes.

Goal Theory

As there is a theory for everything, goal theory is an intellectual and psychological construct created by Edwin Locke and Gary Latham to understand how goals influence an individual's behavior and how behavior and thought processes influence how we understand goals. "Goal setting theory is based upon the simplest of introspective observations, specifically, that conscious human behavior is purposeful. Goals not only affect behavior as well as job performance, but they also help mobilize energy which leads to a higher effort overall. Higher effort leads to an increase in persistent effort," according to Locke (Locke, E. A., & Latham, G. P. 2002). Increases in effort take energy, something we are programmed to conserve via our evolutionary defaults. Setting goals that use up our energy reserves, then, seems counterintuitive. But we are full of contradictions, particularly in what motivates us and which part of ourselves (our conscious or subconscious mind) makes decisions.

"Goals help motivate us to develop strategies that will enable us to perform at the required goal level. Accomplishing a goal can either lead to satisfaction and further motivation—or frustration and lower motivation if the goal is not accomplished. Goal setting can be a very powerful technique, under the right conditions," as encapsulated by Leslie Riopel, professor of psychology at Northwood University (Riopel, L. (Nd.)

We have all witnessed individuals or teams who are so dedicated to achieving their goals that their behavior changes; they may be more aggressive, less empathetic, and more single-focused.

Such a single focus in an organizational context may run counter to mitigating or completely ignoring other goals and those who are working on them. This is not an optimistic and all-encompassing systems-focused state of mind for healthy group dynamics or an organization's shared purpose. A more constructive default mindset is that employees become energetic, excited, focused, and optimistic in how their work and energy expenditure toward a goal contributes to the overall system and shared purpose of an organization.

If you unpack goal theory, Locke identified two levels of orientation that affect goal setting and how we mentally process, react and experience goal attainment.

- **Mastery Orientation**

This is a desire to master a subject matter for the sheer act of learning. In our current societal context, there has been much discussion on lifelong learning and the value it brings, including improving our mental outlook and how we view the world. Mastery is also viewed as a means to an end that leads to accomplishment to do something better, score higher grades, excel at work performance, and over exceed one's own expectations.

- **Performance Orientation**

This is motivated by external forces (your manager, supervisor, co-workers, friends, children, spouse, and so on). It is based on the perception that is held and derived by others of an individual to be better, smarter, and stronger. It is focused on looking good—in fact, better than others. In turn, performance-oriented individuals expect positive feedback that confirms their actions and motivates their goal attainment (Locke, E. A., & Latham, G. P. (2002).

Performance orientation is what can cause disruption and toxicity in the workplace as seeking the glory and positive confirmatory feedback from others comes at the expense of others since it is individual, not group focused. The organization may partially benefit but communal shared purpose is compromised and motivation for everyone else can be negated and extinguished.

What motivates performance and how does it change behavior? Here is a real-life example.

The sales team leader is under pressure to deliver its results and is struggling. The leader has yielded to temptations to cut corners in transparent reporting; making excuses; misrepresenting the sale to clients to get the sale; becoming anxious and fearful around the team and playing the manager to be seen as trying hard to improve his or her perception. Any activity that is related to cheating or inappropriate behavior is based on the high anxiety of self-preservation and desperation to avoid failure. This is not a situation you want your organization to find itself in.

The Human Factor: Goal Attainment Styles

The challenge for any leader and manager is understanding their employees' motivations and how they need to be rewarded for goal attainment. Equally challenging is for leaders and managers to understand their own motivations and goals and how their behaviors influence or impact others.

So, first, let's consider orientation.

- Task-involved: Interest in the process. Locke describes this orientation as, "They don't perceive failure as a terrible thing because they know that a lack of success in one respect does not determine who they are." They own up to their shortcomings, accepting the consequences.

- Ego-involved: "They achieve goals according to what's in it for them, as they are extrinsically motivated," explains Locke. They tend to blame others for their own failure; become easily discouraged without positive feedback, and believe their success is due only to their own efforts.

- Avoidance-involved: This occurs when an individual or team acts to avoid an outcome. This means that they will focus on avoiding making mistakes or failing to avoid looking incompetent or unsuccessful. If not managed, this can become a distraction by taking a short-term approach to achieve the goal. Or worse, they may seek to quit the project or leave an organization as a result of low self-confidence, which feeds how they see the organization, their possible contributions, and the organization's perceived value of their role.

Layered onto these orientation factors are the two main motivating factors: intrinsic and extrinsic.

- **Intrinsic Motivation**

This is prompted by an internal drive or perception, such as helping others, making oneself subordinate to the group, and achieving a goal for the greater good. Intrinsic is viewed as goals that are focused on self-realization such as growth, health, and autonomy. For organizations, individuals motivated by intrinsic factors lead to the greatest success as the greater good equates to the organization's system, shared purpose, and market orientation. Therefore, goals motivated by intrinsic factors keep the impact and outcome in focus.

- **Extrinsic Motivation**

This is prompted by external sources or forces, such as achieving the goal will result in being richly rewarded. Extrinsic goals are driven by desires for wealth, image, and fame. As previously discussed, motivations based on extrinsic factors can cause a significant negative impact on an organization, resulting in an imbalance in offerings, operations, or customer interaction. It may also diminish an organization's aspiration for the greater good and related expected outcomes.

Egocentric

At the heart of any journey towards attaining a goal is the human ego. Our self-definitions change based on the situation or environment and are influenced by our subconscious and conscious self-concept and self-perception. Perception is how we define reality.

Author Martin Maehr explains, "Motivation is the underlying momentum that carries people from one experience to another; it can reinforce or diminish peoples' perception of self-worth based on the success and/or failure to achieve various goals (Anderman, E. M. & Maehr, M. L. (1994)." It is important for the individual to be aware of these self-concept shifts to work with others or how to self-assess in context of achieving goals.

Many individuals are professionally or personally afraid of failure, whether framed extrinsically in how they believe others will see them or intrinsically in how they define and see themselves. So, motivate people by helping them define and redefine their roles in establishing the goals they set for themselves, the emotions they experience, and the meanings they attach to situations. The ongoing reassessment of risk and reward is a powerful motivator, as most people believe that goal attainment will also deliver personal rewards.

Goal Setting and Attainment

Happiness and wellbeing have been correlated to having goals (not necessarily achieving them but rather having them and working toward them). By setting goals, an individual has the motivation, focus, and purpose—as do organizations. Conversely, having no goals may result in a sense of hopelessness. Without goals, oneself or an organization can't be managed as there isn't much at all to measure progress to the desired goal. Improvement is in itself a goal and requires systematic management. Setting clear goals requires systems in place to facilitate the outcome.

- **Clarity in Defining the Goal**

Precision and carefully selected terminology and language will clarify the goal so that anyone can understand it. Terminology and language can also aid in determining if it is a worthy individual or organizational goal.

- **Define the Intended Outcome**

Don't mistake output for the outcome. The longer-term effect of your goal is the defined intended outcome. Clarify what you ultimately want to achieve and how it will benefit all stakeholders. Remember, outputs reflect expenditure of effort and therefore energy, but may not actually contribute to the outcome of a set goal. Again, does the goal have a worthy outcome?

- **Define the Process**

A working plan for achieving the goal should be flexible enough for any necessary pivots and adjustments along the way. Very little in life or work goes exactly as planned. Flexibility provides the ability to adapt to changing factors and variables and provides near-constant reassessment if the goal and its outcome remain worthy.

- **Get Commitment**

Make sure the goal is well understood and agreed to by the key stakeholders, groups, teams, friends, family, and so on. Enable honest discussion and field questions to ensure others are on board and committed.

- **Declare the Human Factor**

What cultural attitudes, group/team/organizational dynamics, and behaviors need to be tapped into or addressed to align with the goal?

What individuals will best comprise the core team of those responsible to achieve the goal? What rewards do they expect; what do they deserve?

- **Set the Timeline**

At some point, the goal needs to be attained. Be realistic but disciplined.

- **Feedback Loops**

Critical thinking is the tool to make sure the journey to goal achievement is on track and aligned with stakeholders even if the stakeholder is oneself. Be objective. Analyze what is going well, or not, and make necessary adjustments to manage expectations and adherence to the plan.

Attitude Can Be Everything

Top achievers are a special breed. They have high expectations of themselves, are self-confident, and laser-focused. In many cases, they are living their goals long before they are achieved, according to Terence Jackson, chief operating officer at JCG Consulting Group (Jackson, T. 2015). They also self-report on progress and are agile and rigorously disciplined. They course correct, adapting their level of effort and energy to the difficulty of the goal.

A focus on a few goals, not a portfolio of goals, helps refine the attainment process. A focused set of goals causes fewer distractions and the possibility of fatigue and disappointment from managing too large a docket.

Belief in one's capacity, capability, and potential which feeds an individual's appropriate attitude is critical. Jackson states, "Many say they want to achieve certain things but do not really believe in their ability to achieve their goals or totally value their goals. As a result, they unconsciously minimize their ability to achieve their stated intentions. To reach your goals you have to be sure that they reflect your true beliefs, values, and commitments (Jackson, T. 2015)."

Goal Expectations and Management

It is human nature to focus on the present rather than a distant future. This translates into more enthusiasm for short-term goals versus longer-term outcome/impact goals. By nature, we are also programmed to expend as little energy as possible to complete a task.

Therefore, hard goals are easier to avoid, and clear/easier goals are more successful to achieve. With ingrained shortsightedness, individuals and organizations more easily grasp the near-term path and see what they should/could do. Because our attention spans are short, we don't easily see the distant future, and we feel more affinity for short-term goals. "Dr. Edwin Locke found that over 90% of the time, goals that were specific and challenging, but not overly challenging, led to higher performance when compared to easy goals or goals that were too generic such as a goal to do your best," as reported by Leslie Riopel in Positive Psychology (Riopel, L. (Nd.). Over-focus on short-term goals, to the detriment of long-term more transformative goals, increases risk, rigidity, and the inability to adapt to market forces or even personal circumstances.

Resistance and goal avoidance are common. If you are procrastinating, hesitating, or reconsidering the goal, why? Fear of failure is a big motivator to avoid the goal altogether. This is where self-awareness and team-member awareness come in. Use critical thinking to continuously evaluate the process and reinvigorate a team. Identify the sticking points and honestly and transparently work through the issues. Keeping your eye on the prize requires empathy, agility, and perseverance. And remember, remaining objective and flexible to adapt and adjust recognizes that factors and variables affecting a situation or environment do change. Additionally, failure shouldn't be viewed in a negative light. Most, if not all failure, leads to learning and unlocks the ability to adjust. Perhaps the goal wasn't worthy. Perhaps the goal was not in line with the environment or situation. It's okay. Reset the goal, define, or revise the outcome, learn and continue forward.

Keeping a monitor on your goals has measurable outcomes. Riopel reports on a Harvard MBA study that assessed how written and planned-for goals affected outcomes later in life. "In the study, the students were asked, have you set clear, written goals for your future and made plans to accomplish them? Of those who were asked, only 3% of the graduates had written goals and plans; 13% of the students had goals, but those goals were not in writing and 84% of students polled had no specific goals at all. Ten years later the students were interviewed, and the findings were astonishing.

The 13% of those who had goals, but not written them down, and the 3% that had written them down, were earning twice as much when compared to the 84% who had no goals at all (Riopel, L. (Nd.)."

Dr. Gail Matthews, a clinical psychologist from the Dominican University of California, conducted research that revealed "those who write down their goals and/or share their goals with a friend or colleague, as well as send weekly updates, were on average 33% more successful when it comes to accomplishing their stated goals compared to those who merely formulate goals," (Matthews, Gail. Dr. (Nd.)." Riopel adds that a study done by Statistic Brain, which analyzes New Year's goals reveals that only 8% of people achieve their New Year's goals with 92% of these ending in failure (Riopel, L. (Nd.)."

The study also reports that:

- 45% of Americans usually make goals.
- 17 % of Americans make goals infrequently.
- 38% of Americans never make goals.

Marketing and Communications

Consumer behavior can be shaped by both intrinsic and extrinsic motivations. Marketing and sales can achieve their goals by appealing to these motivations correlated to the specific product or service. Persuasion is a powerful tool when combined with offering choice.

Let's take Patagonia as an example of a brand that appeals to its loyal customers' intrinsic motivations. Purchasing Patagonia apparel equates to saving the planet through investment in a company that is passionately sustainability based. Patagonia is a shared-purpose community brand that taps into an intrinsic motivation to be one's better self and maximize personal performance at the same time.

Rolex, on the other hand, uses marketing positioning to appeal to an extrinsic motivation to own a prestige timepiece that makes a personal statement about wealth and success. Rolex is also valued for its precision engineering, reliability, innovation, and high resale value. These factors have a high appeal to consumers who seek external validation for their purchases.

One brand can appeal to both intrinsic and extrinsic motivations, although it can become confusing to the core consumer to receive off-point messaging. In both cases, marketing can persuade consumers to buy the product or service by appealing to the factors motivating purchase.

Nike has been wildly successful in creating a brand persona that combines personal success and performance with the halo effect from famous, well-respected athletes that are role models for all ages. Intrinsic benefits are supported by extrinsic "heroes."

Of course, the elephant in the room is the use and overuse of social media, which is changing behavior and even self-worth. Social media platforms are extreme marketing communications that are radically changing users' behavior. TikTok is fueling a generation with a shorter and shorter attention span. Referred to as a dopamine machine, TikTok appeals to extrinsic motivations of being popular, on-trend, and liked. The Wall Street Journal reported that "Brain scans of Chinese college students showed that areas involved in addiction were highly activated in those who watched personalized videos. It also found some people have trouble controlling when to stop watching (Wall Street Journal. (2022)." The goals of being liked and not left out have led to psychological, emotional, and behavioral conditions that are not yet understood and will surely become more dangerous in the future.

Goal Blocked

What happens to you when a goal is blocked?

Satisfaction from goal attainment is prevented and frustration, anger, blame, and resignation may result. Resignation can lead to the second wave of new impediments including helplessness, anger, and self-preoccupation, according to authors Eric Van Steenburg, Nancy Spears, and Robert Fabrize in the Journal of Consumer Behavior.

Or do individuals become more resourceful and take an adaptive approach to achieve the goal?

Individuals with intrinsic motivation are more likely to get creative when encountering a roadblock. The extrinsic personality type with a sense of entitlement typically blames others. And that blame is often placed on a brand or organization that seems to be the source of the block. A Journal of Consumer Behavior report states, "Consumers who perceive a situation to be unfair or out of their control—because of the barriers to goal attainment are more likely to experience frustration. Conversely, consumers who achieve their expected level of payoff, service or satisfaction will not experience frustration in the situation (Van Steenburg, E, et. al. (2013)."

When a goal is blocked, the positive solution is generally to create a new strategy to overcome the block, a way to work around the problem, and/or use flexibility to adjust the expectation, goal, and outcome. A negative approach is to become aggressive, regress to inappropriate behavior, and repeat the same thing over and over with the same outcome, resignation, or complete avoidance.

In a workplace setting when a goal is blocked, it takes patience and discipline to uncover the root cause and get the individual, team, or entire organization back on track. If it is the organization itself that is the block, it is the responsibility of the individuals or teams of individuals to have a frank, open conversation with management about the issues. Remember, leading with courage encourages every individual, regardless of role or level in an organization, to be open to critical conversations and frank criticism. It is only by creating an environment to constructively communicate that clears blocks. In today's highly charged culture, managing a goal block quickly will prevent repercussions downline from employees and customers alike.

Goals Unleashed

Key to managing goal attainment is to introduce a goal and what changes may occur because of the process of achieving it. When any new program or innovation is introduced, it is critical to communicate the change in a non-threatening way. The human default is to take a fight or flight stance when confronting change or a new goal. A sense of security can be established by understanding what will be lost and in turn what will be gained. Everything in a workforce culture today is complex, and even day-to-day personal lives seem stressful and anxiety-filled, therefore the identification of goals and the process to attain them is influenced by our human defaults and self-perceptions, intrinsic and extrinsic conceptions, and motivating variables and factors. Humans are contradictory and complex. It takes understanding what comprises goals, what outcomes are achieved, and how we manage the fear of failure or achievement of success.

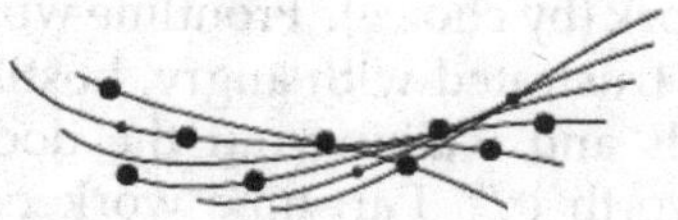

Chapter 31: Is the Workforce Due for a Reset?

"Organizations often dedicate more time and resources to acquiring younger talent with the expectation that it has more energy and is more adaptable and malleable to dynamic changes in the market, processes, and tech. Although they are not as well paid as their older, more experienced counterparts, organizations hope they will become loyal over time.
Not so much."

An Updated Workforce

Next-gen workers have had it, having been forced to work to live, they are now living to work (by choice). Frontline workers (especially those in customer service) are frustrated with angry, hostile customers; they are throwing up their hands and walking out the door, saying "enough is enough, the pay isn't worth it." Part-time workers say they don't have enough part-time work…and believe management isn't effectively delegating tasks that need to be done. Workers from home are burnt out juggling childcare and homeschooling with all-day-onscreen working conditions. And we all know airline industry workers have had to become conflict resolution experts … or even worse, trained in personal defense.

What is going on here?

The confluence of this decade's pandemic, economic disruption (compounded by inflation), changing values and behaviors, significant increases in technological adoption, demands for change, and an empowered consumer has turned the workplace culture upside down and challenged managers of any organization to rethink the workforce ethos.

Let's look at some of the issues that are not always newsmakers, but which are resetting the workforce in the 21st century and giving leadership and human resources management a workout.

Quality of Life

The trends in quality-of-life attitudes about work have been evolving. As with many issues related to a workforce, organizations tend to simply check all the right boxes for providing perks, benefits packages, and training/growth opportunities to satisfy what human resources believe all employees want and need. In short, by offering what they think are "good things," an organization turns the responsibility back to an individual employee and expects them to appreciate what is being provided as a potential opportunity. The individual is also expected to take the initiative to improve their skillsets without any stated promise of reward or achievement of higher-level growth positions. The box-checking behavior (past and present) overlooks the distinct values, behaviors, norms, and needs of a six-generation workforce.

The one-size-fits-all practice also overlooks the growing chorus of individuals who are looking to their employers to provide mental health services, recognize the importance of work-life balance, fair work equity and distribution, and lastly, provide value and an empathetic culture that matches life's demands and needed flexibility.

A new quality of life mindset is manifesting as labeled, anti-ambition. As reported by Noreen Malone in The New York Times, "During the pandemic a vast majority of people were deemed essential with jobs like Amazon warehouse workers or cashiers. To be told that society can't function without you and that you must risk your health to come in, while other people push around marketing reports from home — often for much more money — it becomes difficult not to wonder if essential is cynical, a polite way of classing humans as expendable or nonexpendable." She adds, "Now, though, it's as if our whole society is burned out. The pandemic may have alerted new swaths of people to their distaste for their jobs — or exhausted them past the point where there's anything to enjoy about jobs they used to like (Malone, N. (2021)." Thus, the anti-ambition mindset was spawned.

"An idealistic generation has set about demanding a utopian world, on a local scale. More diversity, more attention to structural racism, better hours, better boundaries, better leave policies, better bosses," Malone adds. "At some companies, it finally feels as if the old hierarchies are being upended, and the top-paid people are running a little scared of their underlings, rather than the other way around. Confronted with this world, many young people with professional options want to be in solidarity with their colleagues instead of climbing the ladder above them. The meaning that they once found in work is now found in trying to make the workplace itself better (Malone, N. (2021)."

Anti-ambition will infuse all aspects of workplace culture and requires management to address the behavior constructively and empathetically

Next-Gen Blinders

Organizations often dedicate more time and resources to acquiring younger talent with the expectation that it has more energy and is more adaptable and malleable to dynamic changes in the market, processes, and tech. Although they are not as well paid as their older, more experienced counterparts, organizations hope they will become loyal over time. Not so much.

The focus on acquiring a younger workforce also correlates to the skillsets an organization believes it needs to function in today's dynamically changing tech-based environment. If you scan job postings, you'll see the frequent use of buzz words and hype-based terminology that is often misunderstood by an organization's management. Conventional thinking is that organizations believe they need tech skills because that's what others are seeking and that's what they have read they need. In truth, just having tech skills may not necessarily align with the organization's capability, capacity, or business intent to leverage those skills to increase revenue. Yes, tech skills are important, but more useful is the ability to think critically, collaborate, and solve problems productively in alignment with an organization's shared purpose and market orientation.

Boomer Life Stage and the Workforce

Let's look at today's multigenerational workforce. The challenges are less about age and more about attitude. Social justice movements have indelibly changed the outlook and complexion of today's workforce—and its leadership. Much has been reported about the sea changes of DEI and influences of the Black Lives Matter (BLM) movement, influences which are highly dependent upon how individuals and groups define and relate to these issues. But less has been reported about the impact of life stages on employees' values, attitudes, and behaviors.

Today's reality is that human longevity is very real and presents a range of social, health, and employment challenges. With the breakthroughs in healthcare and emotional wellbeing, older workers are living longer and living better. As a result, the older worker population has taken on a new cool factor as they want to remain relevant and continue their contribution to society. Experience, expertise, wisdom, perspective, and judgment are invaluable attributes that add depth to discussions and how solutions to problems and challenges are formed and approached. Plus, older workers are role models for professional behavior to younger workers. Life experiences have created wisdom that helps older employees make more educated choices for the future. A report from Euromonitor lists "empowered elders" as a top-10 global consumer trend for 2022 and beyond (Euromonitor. (2022). Given the breakthroughs and improvements in quality of life, an aging population will remain a major factor in the workplace and the consumer market for the foreseeable future.

The numbers tell it all. AARP reports people 55+ now control 70% of all personal wealth in the United States (Terrell, K. (AARP). (2019).

Surveys from the Bureau of Labor Statistics (2021) show that older adults buy 56% of all new cars and trucks, 55% of personal care products, 65% of health care, 68% of home maintenance and repairs, and 76% of all prescription drugs (no surprise on that one) (Bureau of Labor Statistics. (2021). Money has societal currency, although brands and organizations have not recognized that fact and continue to focus their marketing and advertising on the next-gens with considerably less buying power in the hope of building awareness when they have the disposable income to buy. It is a misleading focus and a misinterpretation of the market dynamics at play.

Tech can be a serious dividing line between generations. All boomers (and Gen Xers) have had to reeducate and reinvent themselves to stay current and relevant in a tech-infused marketplace. The bottom line is that organizations can greatly benefit from the wisdom of older workers instead of ushering them out the door. Older workers have a deeper and broader base of knowledge to step back and contextually analyze a situation. The red flag for the older worker is to not let the past be a dominant influence on current or future decision-making, as the past represents a different environmental context than the one that exists today or will exist in the future.

Gen Z Life Stage Workforce

At the opposite end of the spectrum, we have Gen Z. These workers were born squarely in the Digital Age and consider tech an essential survival tool. Gen Z has always been connected and has stimulated the growth of emerging social media brands, mobile-first consumption, streaming content, and voice-assisted communications. As digital natives, Gen Z played with smartphones in their strollers, communicate in a different vocabulary, and have expectations from work and managers that pale in comparison to the millennials who have been their digital forerunners. This digital prowess makes them experts in a tech-based marketplace. They work faster and smarter using digital tools and have an innate understanding of networks, digital communications, and analytics. Next-gen Alphas are even more digitally savvy moving seamlessly between online and offline life.

Gen Z is forcing organizations to rethink their policies and practices—especially in quality-of-life factors. The influence of Gen Z is pervasive but comes with an emotional cost. This generation has been described as discouraged, depressed, and anxious. It has been reported many are reluctant to marry and bring children into a world fraught with the climate crisis, social injustice, and cultural and political polarization.

These are feelings that have a real impact on workplace culture in terms of outlook and motivation.

Gen Z also plays by different rules. Emma Goldberg writes, "At a retail business based in New York, managers were distressed to encounter young employees who wanted paid time off when coping with anxiety or period cramps. At a supplement company, a Gen Z worker questioned why she would be expected to clock in for a standard eight-hour day when she might get through her to-do list by the afternoon. At a biotech venture, entry-level staff members delegated tasks to the founder. And spanning sectors and startups, the youngest members of the workforce have demanded what they see as a long-overdue shift away from corporate neutrality toward a more open expression of values, whether through executives displaying their pronouns on Slack or putting out statements in support of the protests for Black Lives Matter. (Goldberg, E. (2022)"

These shifts are significant for leadership not only to understand but also to manage. It doesn't take rocket science to understand that boomers and Gen X are understandably bewildered by these new attitudes—and demands. The values embodied by Gen Z will follow them throughout their lives. Although the conditions and circumstances of life change, values remain consistent. So, organizations will also age with their Gen Z workforce and evolve to deliver a workplace that reflects the changing attitudes and behaviors of this cohort.

Gen X + Millennials Life Stage Workforce

Gen X (and older millennials) are stuck somewhere in the middle. When it comes to work/life balance, London Business School and Harvard Business School (2021) report women spend an average of five more hours on childcare and chores per week than men (Carlson, D. et. al. (2021). Legislative initiatives seek to create mechanisms for extended family leave, offering parents each an opportunity to take time off for caring for a child. However, work/life flexibility needs to be embedded into an organization's culture to ensure balance and empathy with employees' needs.

Furthermore, many remote work women have had to give up their one home office to their husbands—forcing them to work in less-than-ideal spaces, adding to the stress and chipping away at productivity, according to Erica Pandey of Axios.

Working parents represent a third of the U.S. workforce—and companies need to address burnout to retain this talent (Pandy, E. (2021).

This aspect of the human factor is perhaps the most important of understanding how the life stage informs the ability to contribute and thrive in an organization.

Bias and Ageism

Since boomers and early Gen X are sticking around in increasing numbers on the job, they often have to contend with ageism and bias—particularly women.   These two issues often considered unimportant in the past—whether through ignorance or lack of data—are now being brought center stage and have become lighting rods that organizations need to address.

Gender bias, despite continued public recognition of these harmful practices, remains a significant and often pervasive issue as organizational leaders hold onto past practices, cannot see beyond their own biases, and maintain perspectives that the human beings comprising the workforce as simple cogs in the wheel.

Age Wave reports if a man and a woman both enter the workforce at the same age, and they both continuously stay in the workforce earning an average income, with the pay gap in place, by the time they reach retirement age, the woman will have earned $400,000 less than the man. Financial inequity is even more of an issue for women of color (Age Wave. (2022). According to parity.org (2021), companies that reach gender and racial parity (30%+) at the executive and board levels are 15% more profitable and 19% more innovative than peer organizations lacking in diversity. That said, achieving global gender parity will take an extra 36 years because of the coronavirus pandemic, a World Economic Forum report said. Previously, in the Global Gender Pay report 2020 (published December (2019), the WEF estimated that the gender pay gap could take around 100 years to close.

Ageism came to the forefront in the 1980s via government actions at the Federal, state, and local levels in the United States in establishing protections for older workers faced with age-related discriminatory practices in the workplace. Although the protections have been exercised over time, ageism is becoming a larger and more pervasive issue given the increased percentage of the older population maintaining employment.

HR Director reports that "44% of over-50 employees experienced age discrimination at work and 48% during the recruitment process. Also, 40% felt they were sidelined or left out of discussions at work and 24% said they had experienced discrimination when it comes to promotion Dennis, T. (2021).

An AARP 2019 survey reveals that "nearly 1 in 4 workers ages 45 and older have been subjected to negative comments about their age from supervisors or coworkers. About 3 in 5 older workers have seen or experienced age discrimination in the workplace. And 76% of these older workers see age discrimination as a hurdle to finding a new job; another report found that more than half of these older workers are prematurely pushed out of longtime jobs and 90 percent of them never earn as much again (Kita, J. (AARP). (2019).

Policies to prevent ageism matched with training to avoid stereotyping, fair promotion practices, authentic collaboration, ensuring organizational collateral graphics are inclusive and diverse and acting swiftly to manage bias all contribute to a workplace culture that is fair and empathetic.

Men at Work

An interesting finding in the prevailing dominant male narratives in workplace culture was revealed by a Catalyst study. (DiMuccio, S. et. al. (Nd.). Researchers found that there's a direct correlation between the expectations and masculine norms placed on men and sexism that occurs in the workplace. The survey reveals that "94% of men experienced some level of masculine anxiety at work, and one in five reported experiencing it to a high degree." They define masculine anxiety as the distress men experience when they feel like they are not living up to the narrow standards of masculinity—i.e., being strong, emotionally reserved, successful, powerful, dominating, fearless, in control, and even emotionless. The study also shares that "men are more likely to say that they experience masculine anxiety in organizations with combative cultures—those that have norms of ruthless competition and a dog-eat-dog, winner-takes-all and work-before-family mentality (DiMuccio, S. et. al. (Nd.)."

In the study, "99% of men said that their workplace had some degree of a combative culture. In addition, 86% of men said they felt committed to interrupting sexism in the workplace, while only 31% of men felt confident in their ability to interrupt such behavior (DiMuccio, S. et. al. (Nd.)." The conclusions from this research would suggest that a command-and-control culture begets more command-and control-behavior, regardless of the age of male workers.

Yet this mindset is particularly ineffective for diverse next-gens who demand meritocracy, collaboration, and a seat at the table. The challenge becomes melding this worldview with the more established, legacy tendencies of older workers … and managers.

The Modern Workforce

Why do we work?

There are three main reasons: it's just a job, it's a higher calling and it's a lifetime career. Katherine Brook writes in Psychology Today explaining that individuals who fall into the first category tend to view their work as the means to an end. She adds, "They work to receive the pay and/or benefits to support their hobbies, family, or life outside work. They prefer jobs that do not interfere with their personal lives. They are not as likely to have a strong connection to the workplace or their job duties. The job serves as a basic necessity in life (Brook, K. 2012)." Lacking loyalty, these workers are likely to leave if working conditions do not meet their needs.

Workers with a calling view their work as "integral to their lives and their identity. They view their career as a form of self-expression and personal fulfillment. They are more likely to find their work meaningful and will modify their duties and develop relationships to make it more so. They are found to be more satisfied in general with their work and their lives," according to Brook. These workers contribute to the workplace culture and play a strong role in collaboration, innovating change, and introducing new ways of doing things. There are a few downsides to workers with a calling. It can lead to burnout and frustration when the reality of the job doesn't measure up to its ideal. These workers are also easy to exploit. They will take on more work because they are so passionate. If employers are not sensitive to this mindset, they can easily overwork these employees, which could lead to the employees snapping.

Career workers are on a ladder to success and are more likely to "focus on elements related to success or prestige. These individuals will be interested in the ability to move upward in their careers, receive raises and new titles, and achieve the social standing which comes from the career," Brook says. These workers are ambitious, may be less of team players, and are instead focused on their own success.

All three of these employee cohorts work in an organization, each representing a third of the workforce. And job positions or titles are not a litmus test for any of the three cohorts; they are distributed across the workforce.

Organizations must understand the complexity of their workforces to manage them. How do individuals classify themselves about their "job, calling or career" when related nuances, norms, and values present challenges for management?

Today it is folly to generalize approaches and management of a workforce believing that treating everyone the same is the fair and equitable path to success, high performance, and results.

My Work, My Choice

Gen Z's real power (along with millennials) is its leverage over employers to meet their demands. The Great Resignation, admittedly propelled by government stimulus payments, is the result of the next-gens changing the dynamics of an organization. Derek Thompson in The Atlantic reports, "Quitting is a concept typically associated with losers and loafers. But this level of quitting is an expression of optimism that says, 'We can do better (Thompson, D. (2021).'" Led by the vanguard of younger workers, 66% of unemployed Americans have seriously considered changing their occupations. A 2022 Gallop poll reports that 71% of Americans believe this is a great time to look for a new job, 58% are stressed at their current job *daily*, and 20% are likely to move to a new city in the next year. Workers are burned out not just by their jobs but also by the cultural drama around them (Gandhi, V. & Robison, J. (Gallup). (2021). The worker/manager relationship is critical: people don't leave jobs, they leave managers.

In an age of constant uncertainty, empathetic leadership is more critical than ever. The labor force clearly needs an overhaul led by enlightened managers who take the human factor in an organizational culture seriously. Transformation is realized most successfully and impactfully when workers' needs and wants from an organization correlate to how they are treated—most importantly treating them as human beings, not mechanical, transactional employees. For example, Google knows that over 40% of its workforce is the "sandwich generation" looking after both kids and parents. As a result, it reshaped its parental leave program to address these life stage needs (Atkinson, E. (2022). If organizations do not talk to their workers honestly and openly, they risk losing valuable talent (it's even more expensive to recruit and train new employees), which can set businesses back by years.

What is hidden in plain sight in this evolving workforce trend is that many organizations may not know what their workers can do, and workers don't have a system to tell them. If you think about it, one of the best and yet untapped sources of talent is internal.

Employees, especially younger workers who are digitally savvy, need communication-sharing platforms to connect and discover new opportunities, reskilling, and even mentoring for career development.

Here's another thought.

Take this opportunity to reorganize. Axios reports that millions of Americans want to quit their jobs, but many of them would happily stay at their companies in different positions. Shonna Waters, a vice president at the career coaching company BetterUp adds, "For some people, that means moving somewhere new or pursuing a passion, but for a lot of people it could also just mean looking around and saying, 'I want a higher-level role,' or 'I want a different role at the same company,' or 'I want my time to be used differently in my current role.'" Many people want change at work, but also want to retain the friendships and reputation they've built within a company (Liu, J. (CNBC via Axios). (2021)," she says.

Another solution promoted by Arianna Huffington, CEO of Thrive Global is an interesting onboarding process. Most organizations conduct exit interviews. But "what if managers understood these factors when it could make the biggest impact: on the employee's first day instead of their last?" Thrive Global has established the entry interview, which is a conversation between a new hire and their manager on day one that starts by asking what's important to them outside of work (Huffington, Arianna. (2021).

Time Is Currency

A growing chorus of workers advocates the necessity for measuring results not time spent. We are no longer living in an Industrial Age mentality. Historically, the Industrial Age considered the human workforce as cogs in the wheel; commodities that were easily replaced. Organizations viewed themselves as the primary economic engine and the source of income for workers who needed to sustain themselves. And progress was based on a formula of the amount of time spent to produce the desired result. Production line goals of achieving a certain quantity of product per day to meet inventory and customer demand were measured primarily in time.

Commoditization of the human workforce is an archaic historical command-and-control structural viewpoint, far from current relevance. Our society has evolved in terms of how people define "work," how they choose to identify their relationship to an organization, and how they align to a "job, calling, or career."

Today, time is our most precious currency. The 40-hour work week is a relic from the Industrial Age. Although industrialization and production remain cornerstones of any economy, knowledge workers don't fit well in the historical definition of work time.

As such, time for them becomes fluid without a rigorous structure of what is expected to be accomplished in a specific time frame.

The Great Resignation and the pervasive consideration of many workers to explore new careers or job opportunities remains a major contextual and environmental factor that requires organizations to change their mindsets. The New York Times reported in 2021 that many quitters have been on the lower part of the income ladder. "They're getting or seeking better work, for more money, because they can. And that kind of labor market means at least some lower-income workers get to think about their jobs the way the white-collar class more traditionally has, as something that needs to work for them, rather than the other way around (New York Times. (Malone) (2022)." This is a major consideration in the redefinition of the workforce.

A New Work Week Model

Younger workers are imposing other new practices for organizations to consider; the four-day work week and salary transparency. For the shortened work week, the idea is to work fewer hours, for the same amount of money, without losing productivity—making everyone happier. How this will gain traction is a matter of debate. But it is popular with next-gen employees who seek work/life balance. Short-term alternatives to reduce worker stress are fewer meetings, way fewer emails, flexible work hours, respect that work is not an 18-hour-a-day activity and offering more days off.

Salary transparency is also popular with younger generations, in line with their overall view that the more transparency, the better. Quartz reports that the "logic of making compensation transparent is that it becomes harder to pay people unfairly when salaries are open to public scrutiny (Werber, C. (2022)." Tomasz Obloj of HEC Paris and Todd Zenger from the University of Utah conducted a 2015 study that reveals once wages and rewards become transparent, there is both internal and external pressure to close the gaps.

When pay is made transparent it helps erase unfairness.

The study reveals:

- The gender pay gap was reduced by up to 45% in transparent organizations.
- Inequality in pay dropped 20% in transparent organizations.
- When salaries were made public, the link between pay and performance was weakened by about 40%.

- The link between achievement and pay was clearer and supported by data in transparent companies (Obloj, T. & Zenger, T. R, (2015).

The Truth About Part-Time Work

Reports that part-time work is a goldmine for workers to leverage the labor shortage are misleading. Part-time work plays into the hands of employers. The New York Times reports that "Part-time work allows companies to hold down labor costs in two crucial ways. First, companies can reduce their benefit costs because part-time workers often do not receive health care and retirement benefits. Second, companies can change staffing levels quickly, to meet demand on a given day or week, rather than having workers sit idle during slower periods (New York Times. (Malone) (2022)." Further, the shift toward part-time, flexible work has contributed to the rise in corporate profits.

The part-time model is not worker friendly. "Part-timers struggle with not only low pay but also uncertain shifts that can change at the last minute, disrupting the rest of their lives. The workers can obviously quit, but they often find that the other jobs available to them have similar problems," says the Times.

One solution may be unionizing workforces to give employees more power over employers. Part-time may transition to full-time with more rights and benefits for workers, "One way, historically, that unions tend to lift wages is by putting pressure on companies to hire people full time—and threatening to strike if the companies refuse," reports the Times (New York Times. (Malone) (2022). We see this playing out with brands that have previously had strong worker reputations including REI and Starbucks, as well as behemoth Amazon which has a more checkered public image in terms of how it treats its employees.

Unionization may not be the perfect solution. In fact, the enthusiasm for unionization may take a step backward in viewing the workforce as commodities and consciously overlooking the need to address the values, norms, and perceptions of each individual. Quartz reports, "Workers who stage walkouts and other forms of collective action might pressure powerful companies to confront issues like internal discrimination or the spread of misinformation. But when there's a lot of money on the line, employees may not have the leverage to change company policies. Employee activism is most powerful when companies are convinced, they stand to lose more than their employees' respect (Werber, Cassie. (2022)."

Knowledge Transfer

The collateral damage in churn in part- and full-time employee turnover has been a lack of loyalty among employees as well as a flow of knowledge and continuity within the workforce. Adam Ozimek, a labor economist at Upwork says the downside of part- and full-time employee turnover churn is the organizational dependence on employees' institutional knowledge (Ozimek, A. (Nd.).

How does the transfer of knowledge work in your organization if churn is high, regardless of employee type? Traditionally, knowledge transfer occurs in person, sharing how things work, and where it is embedded in the mindset of an organization.

Organizations will have to find new ways to protect legacy knowledge and pass it on to new waves of employees in effective and sustainable ways to keep the infrastructure of the organization stable and healthy. Organizations that do not adapt to the current workforce dynamic and definition will find themselves in an unending cycle of high turnover and a continuous leak of institutional knowledge. What remains is majorly short-term knowledge without the depth of long-term experience that translates to more substantive and informative guiding knowledge and effective decision-making.

The New Work-from-Home Paradigm

Have we really progressed from the Industrial Age factory mentality? One could argue that offices have become knowledge-based work factories, with the same 19th-century requirements for traditional nine-to-five shifts and everyone assembled in one place under close supervision. Granted knowledge and creative work benefit from collaboration and access to resources, made more efficient when teams are physically close to each other. But the pandemic threw that paradigm out the window.

But here's a new model. A remote-first strategy works well for sales, marketing, accounting/finance, and tech teams that don't need close collaboration in the same physical space. This means you can recruit great talent from anywhere in the country—or the world. For knowledge-based talent, you can also recruit the best minds from anywhere and connect them through new technologies to work collaboratively. On the positive side, working from home can attract top talent that is very diverse and does not require them to relocate.

Office-first is likely to become an anachronism and hybrid will become the new norm. But change is hard, and many managers hold onto the past as a model to be competitive for the future. Companies and workers are often living in two different realities when it comes to returning to the office. A Pew Research 2022 study reveals that 61% of teleworkers are working from home because they're choosing to. Just 38% are home because their workplaces are closed or unavailable. Workers' reasons for staying home are increasingly unrelated to the pandemic: 76% in the Pew poll cited personal choice ... 42% fear of infection ... 32% childcare ... and 17% had moved away from their workplaces (Parker, K. et. al. (2022).

A 2021 study by Reuters Institute (Newman, N. (2021) reveals "The majority of executives (64%) say they would prefer to see employees back in the office some of the time, with only a minority (11%) saying it should be the individual employee's choice. A fifth (20%) of respondents said they would like employees to be back all or most of the time. This signals that some managers remain reticent or even hostile to these changes, perhaps worried about the possible loss of operational efficiency or control." This is supported by a Grant Thornton 2022 survey (Grant Thornton. (2022) that reveals that 45% of employees believe their employers do not understand their needs.

So, listen to the workers! Your workforce can help you redesign your workplace model and reorganize how the workforce can achieve high performance. Grant Thornton reports that 79% of employees want flexibility in when and where they work and 69% agree that working from home has improved work/life balance. And 51% would give up 10% to 20% in future salary increase to have the flexibility of where and when they work (Grant Thornton. (2022)."

Another controversial remote work issue is location-based pay.

Should a remote workforce be paid based on local market rates?
The debate on geography-based pay is in the employer's favor, and certainly not an asset for those workers who escaped expensive urban areas to work in rural or suburban locations during the pandemic who could see a pay cut. This flies in the face of the argument for the transparent salary practice. There is a hidden side to remote work from the employees' perspective; they may carry the burden of costs for better internet connection, upgrading their computers, and financing home offices.

And in the spirit of total transformation, we can look forward to remote-only startups that will forever change where people live, and how they work and support a new crop of digital nomads.

Organizations based in lower-cost third-tier cities, for example, can have a workforce of top international employees. Lifestyle preferences will dictate where people live untethered from a corporate headquarters.

Perhaps the most dramatic aspect of remote work is that advances in AI and frontier/emerging technologies will enable machines to be operated remotely. This may change the factory and warehouse models as there will be fewer employees on site. Not unlike how military campaigns are conducted by the equivalent of video game operators thousands of miles away from war zones, a forklift in an Amazon warehouse in Nebraska could be operated by someone at home in Zurich. Remote work fused with sophisticated technology opens the floodgates of a new type of workforce and workplace culture.

The future is closer than we think, and organizations need to research, collaborate with forward-thinking solution innovators and be open to change to navigate how we will work and how work gets in the next five years.

Redefining the Workforce

There is a shortage of labor in the U.S., partially from boomers that have (or had to) taken early retirement. Chances are, they are now looking for part-time or gig work to stay in the game. The key question for organizations is how they are considering acquiring older workers, if at all and if they have, are they effectively leveraging and managing older employees including bridging the generations and reimagining how to retool their workforce for mutual and reinforcing benefits.

The change in values, ideas, and perceptions begets a new set of mechanisms for defining, curating, and facilitating a workforce for the 21st century. This is exacerbated by the new challenges facing an organization that seeks to change, adapt, and transform to meet the needs of customers — today and tomorrow.

Technology is a recurring theme in the workforce of the future. The popular vernacular represents technology, peppered with AI and machine learning. The key is to build a workforce that has complementary skillsets and capacities needed to implement those technologies and apply them realistically to an organization's goals, strategies, internal functions, decision-making, and business intent.

Individuals, representative of all generations, with a range of levels of maturity, experience, outlook, agility, mastery of technology, and ability to leverage critical thinking skills (self-limiting the influence of bias) are critical to a highly functioning, smart-thinking workforce that leverages its diversity to achieve its goals, manage and dedicate itself to a shared purpose which translates to adapting and flourishing in its specific market orientation.

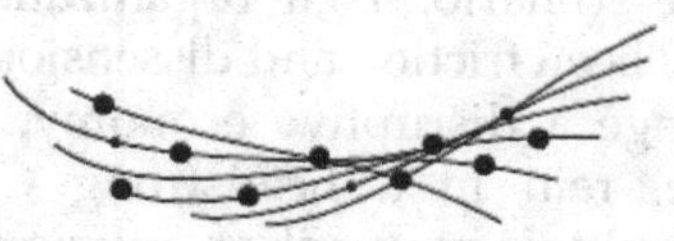

Chapter 32: Role-Playing: The Board Room

"Human beings can appear to be many different people throughout the day dependent on the situation or environment. We assume different roles depending on the situation at hand, although our core values don't change. These roles may blur from time to time, but it is critically important to recognize which role we are assuming and what is expected of us. For example, although we may be natural leaders, we may choose to play a subordinate role when appropriate."

Board Talk

Here's a real-life scenario. Your organization has a prerequisite board. There has recently been friction and dissension. Board members are struggling to help manage a disruptive economy, guide strategy in an ambiguous marketplace, rein in a headstrong CEO that is resisting authority, and manage multiple powerplays among members who believe they have all the answers. This is not a fictional drama. This is what happens when a board culture has become dysfunctional, rudderless, and lost its North Star.

Independent members of a board, by definition, are directed to serve as a fiduciary backstop, provide a framework for executive management to stay on strategy, and ensure oversight on behalf of shareholders. They do not run the organization; they supervise the executive team in running the enterprise. Sounds simple, but boards may be the most extreme challenge of group dynamics with all its related good and bad behavior.

Role-Playing

Human beings can appear to be many different people throughout the day dependent on the situation or environment. We assume different roles depending on the situation at hand, although our core values don't change. These roles may blur from time to time, but it is critically important to recognize which role we are assuming and what is expected of us. For example, although we may be natural leaders, we may choose to play a subordinate role when appropriate.

Add to the mix in the roles we play, the subconscious and unconscious bias we carry with us is constantly acting and reacting to the stimuli in the situation or environment that we are in. With ingrained values and biases, everyone must manage constituents' expectations (with their own values and biases) in whatever role he or she assumes. Leaders' actions and behaviors are monitored by others influencing decisions on whether to follow them. Those who serve in a public office are held to task by those that voted for them.

In businesses and organizations, board members, whether for a local charity, private business or public corporation are accountable to many constituents, all of whom have different expectations. Constituents trust a board member (like an elected official) to represent them and the issues or causes they care about.

While taking on the responsibility to represent, individuals must also recognize their role and responsibilities to the organization and their peers on a board. And the individual behaviors, biases, and group dynamics at play. Tension results. The balancing act, then, is made even more complex by fiduciary responsibilities, policies, and laws.

An effective board is more art than science. And ultimately more common sense than intellectual prowess. Directors must be aware of the shifting nature of their role in an organization and find the right balance between governance and management. Boards and activist investors have been making headlines. Let's look at the dynamics of human behaviors that often play out in the board room. Here are six cautionary notes on how to create a sustainable ecosystem.

Bias

It's human nature that board directors and executive management come to the table with their values and beliefs baked into their conversation. One of the biggest threats to any organization is the statement, "This is the way we have always done things." Seconded by board members who say, "This is how we did it at my company when I was CEO." These attitudes are made even worse when the outcomes are continually disappointing. Holding onto legacy practices is a death knell.

Often boards are hostile to a director introducing new ideas and recommendations. Instead of considering new ideas, some board members dismiss innovation and continue their tried-and-true path of living in the past, which is a predestined road to failure. This is particularly the case when the players are company founders or long-standing board members. Change makes individuals anxious and insecure. However, it is essential to create a board culture that is open to change, uses critical thinking to discuss new ideas, and embraces change.

Authority bias is also an issue on a board when there is too much deference in favor of one or more people on the board. Authority bias can devolve into over-reliance on subject matter experts on the board, board member veterans who take on personal authority, and the member that has the most commanding presence. One way to derail this bias is to call it out in a constructive way in private, supportive interventions.

Authority bias can be amplified by confirmation bias when directors overvalue evidence that confirms their own beliefs. In this case, members choose the data that aligns with their own beliefs as they gloss over inconvenient truths.

It is exacerbated by lack of diversity on the board with too much groupthink or selecting new members that won't rock the boat.

Bias is also at play when members get off track and take the meetings down rabbit holes. These detours tend to serve the egos of members who resist the necessarily constrained agenda and often have something to prove on their own behalf.

Abuse of Power

Tension is a fact of life for boards. Disagreement is inevitable and tension in board interactions is not necessarily a bad thing when it can be leveraged for the greater good. In fact, according to a 2013 Forbes Leadership Forum, constructive tension may even be necessary to bring the best out of a board—to drive higher-quality dialogue, and therefore higher-quality outcomes if it is constructive rather than destructive. Dominant bullies can spoil otherwise positive group dynamics (Forbes Leadership Forum. (2013). The loudest voice may be only that, a noisy opinionated disruptor. Dissension is healthy when it's not bombastic or strident.

A board is not expected to have unanimity, but rather a majority—similar to a jury. Harmony among members is a goal and consensus is the ideal. This is not to say that a board should fall victim to groupthink. An overly scripted agenda led by a CEO who does not give enough time for board members to debate and deliberate is a destructive powerplay. We advise clients that a meeting should take as long as it takes to thoughtfully consider the business at hand.

Power can also be abused when a CEO feels he or she is backed into a corner and comes out fighting with the battle cry, "I run this company." Yes, the CEO runs the company under supervision by the board, which can irk entrepreneurial and first-time CEOs who are used to calling their own shots.

Body language can reveal all. When a CEO demonstrates discomfort and even anger, the tenor in the room (or on-screen) can turn subversive and counterproductive. What we find alarming is that when any director is unaware of exhibiting these emotions. This is a case of extreme subconscious or unconscious bias. The challenge is balancing tension with the need to maintain mutual respect, trust, and support.

Creating an Ecosystem

Boards have traditionally been comprised of the CEO's allies and cronies.

This sets up an inevitable legacy mindset that veers toward short-term thinking instead of strategic, long-term planning. Short-term thinking also has implications for more immediate financial gain for an executive team. The 2016 McKinsey Quarterly reports that while senior executives can be motivated by shorter-term incentives, board directors must take a long-term view of a deal's value, and challenge biases that can cloud decision-making and goal setting (McKinsey Quarterly. (2016).

Paul Charron, former chair of the Campbell's and Liz Claiborne's boards says that the most important job you have as chair is board member selection. He warns to be careful of individuals with hidden agendas or who may be outright seditionists. "You have to have all the boxes checked off for expertise, but you also need independent individuals without being freelancers that go off in different directions. Disagreement needs to be collegial (Charron, Paul. (Nd.)."

An effective board needs to have highly engaged members who are talented, independent thinkers, and open-minded. They also need to be niche domain experts aligned with the business and think like an owner. Good communicators who are experienced team players with leadership experience are key. They should be intellectually curious, empathetic, and have good common-sense judgment.

What we have found as a nonstarter is a board that reflects the CEO's viewpoint—without question. What is also destined for failure are board members that do not educate themselves to stay current with the changing dynamics of the market sector. A good example is technology. McKinsey's 2016 research reveals that "directors are feeling outmatched by the ferocity of changing technology, emerging risks, and new competitors." What is the antidote to this lack of digital literacy?

The research indicates that "successful boards must ask broader questions about technology and IT strategy. Deeper board involvement provides a mechanism to cut through company politics and focus executives on the big, integrated technology investments needed as digital weaves ever further into the fabric of today's businesses. This in turn requires that CIOs, business executives, and board directors develop a shared language to discuss IT performance (McKinsey Quarterly. (2016)."

A board is an ecosystem and as such requires inclusivity and diversity. The process is to use a systems thinking approach that examines every issue and opportunity holistically, without bias.

Critical thinking, open, honest discussion, and mutual respect result in high-performance results. Flexibility and the ability to pivot and embrace change is paramount in today's highly dynamic marketplace.

Trust

Never surprise a board member. A common mistake for any CEO is to not bring initiatives to the board before making decisions. This shortsightedness could be inexperience or something more sinister. Pride, ego and a strong will prevent some CEOs from being transparent to the board. Trust is the single most important factor for any board to work together effectively. Without trust, there is no relationship or safeguard in place to protect the interests of stakeholders, let alone the employees. Many strong-willed CEOs feel they are being leashed by the board. We coach them to understand that the board is mandated to protect executive management, not act as a disciplinary parent. "We've got your back," is the trust watchword for any board.

Trust is built on transparency. Ultimately, the numbers don't lie, and any attempt at nondisclosure is revealed by objective, evidence-based data. How do you rebuild trust? Charron says, "Acknowledge there is a problem and don't sweep it under the carpet. Build bridges with influential directors and transparency is critical." He advises that CEOs establish honest relationships with each board member. And all directors and the chair need to be able to have complicated conversations. A board wants its CEO to succeed. In terms of trust, Forbes reports that "CEOs can convey their openness and humility to the board in many ways, but it requires the courage to be willing to engage in an authentic exchange. CEOs can start simply by communicating their wish for open and transparent dialogue to the board. They can also model how they want to communicate in the way they share both good and bad news (without hyping or downplaying), and in the way, they ask questions and listen. They can resist the urge to present only fully formed strategies, and instead, mobilize the board around emerging ideas and even encourage the board to develop strategic options that differ from the CEO's own — and give the board enough information, as well as sufficient time and space, to do so (Forbes Leadership Forum. (2013)."

Process

CEOs need to lead and manage up. According to Forbes, one of the most critical aspects of facilitating the board experience is the thoughtful curation and preparation of information (Forbes Leadership Forum. (2013).

We often hear from directors that they are confronted by volumes of information without context and that are often irrelevant. The prevailing executive team practice is that more is better.

What's often missing is the "why" of what board members are asked to digest. We believe that boards are only as good as the information they have access to. It is not their job to be investigative reporters. Decision-useful information and data are more important than an unimpressively long presentation deck. If reports and strategies are framed by the "why and "how" to support the financials, board members have a better opportunity to intelligently debate the issues. On the flip side, Forbes reports that "It's very easy for a CEO and the management team to fall into a routine of information preparation that is always the same in its nature. You have the same financial information. The meetings fall into a rhythm and a cadence (Forbes Leadership Forum. (2013)." This repetitive programming can result in stultifying routine and complacency.

Charron reiterates to directors, "Be prepared. Read the deck. It's amazing how many board directors do not read the presentation materials in advance. Furthermore, the executive team needs to deliver the presentation the Friday before the meeting, so directors have the weekend to read and review all the materials (Charron, Paul. (Nd.)." And he advises that the chair needs to prevent the group from going off on riffs, and tangents and not staying on point.

Accountability is also essential to maintaining a functional board. We recommend that the CEO receive an annual review from the chair. Members should be peer reviewed. Board members can also benefit from communications with multiple levels within the organization. For example, board dinners should be seated strategically so that each individual benefits from exposure and time spent with a peer who can share expertise and experience.

A healthy workplace culture is one where employees feel empowered to contribute and speak up and have appropriate access to board members. The board also needs to ask the right questions to be informed about workplace cultural trends and issues. To support the organization's mission and core values, directors need to be able to recognize any negative patterns that are emerging.

It's important to have tough conversations about the human factors.

We live in a fractious society and employees have a lot of power over their organizations regarding diversity, inclusivity, and social and environmental issues. Human capital is literal, capital resources. Board members need to be aware of, and sensitive to, the critical concerns of employees including mental health, work/life balance, and burnout. Board members also need to be assertive about understanding what talent and skillsets the organization will need to be prepared for the future.

Ultimately, being on a board is a 360-degree proposition, and to serve as a backstop for the executive team, members must be informed about all aspects of the organization that impact its financial performance.

Scope

Increasingly, board members are required to be renaissance women and men. McKinsey research reports greater responsibilities require "increased commitments of time and energy, not only during board meetings but also between meetings to stay current and to learn more about the industry, the company, its competitors, and its customers. These responsibilities also raise the premium on carefully protecting the independence that makes boards valuable allies to senior executives, shareholders, and a diverse array of other stakeholders (McKinsey Quarterly. (2016)." The research also indicates the best boards go beyond fiduciary responsibilities to take a more active role in constructively challenging and providing input on a broader range of matters. Since some of these are also the domain of executive management, finding the right place to draw the line between governance and management is as important for senior executives as it is for directors.

Finding Your North Star

You can maximize your board by managing expectations, providing clarity, and fine-tuning procedures that lead to positive outcomes. Central to the success of any board interaction is a solid understanding of human behavior and group dynamics. The goal is to build a board and balance the needs of a group designed to lead an organization and stay true to its North Star.

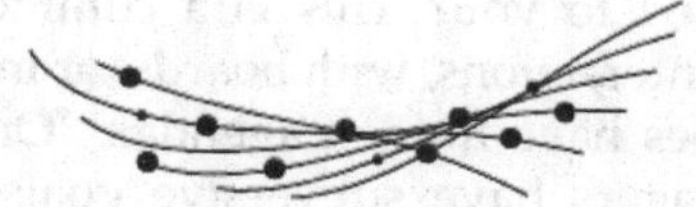

Chapter 33: Power Plays

"We become deferential or assume power positions autonomically in response to situations that beget an expectation of a certain role or manifested behavior. So many human behaviors that we seek to consciously explain or rationalize to ourselves are based on subconscious drivers. So, consciously, we don't really understand, where, how, when, and why we assume, deflect, or defer power positions. Instead, our minds are constantly evaluating and interpreting who and what we should be at a given time and/or place."

Empowered

Quite possibly the most insidious misuse of leadership is when power positioning erodes trust, credibility, and success with stakeholders. Has this ever happened to you? This is a common experience in team meetings, one-on-one interactions, with boards, or in other situations where stakeholders of all types have hidden agendas. Or in business situations when leaders or managers have subversive goals to undermine others. Personal power takes many shapes and can result in manipulation, come with consequences to others or lead to negative outcomes. In contrast, personal power can also reflect one's better self and be a trait that can inspire others to reach their highest potential.

Powers at Play

Personal power positioning is generally accepted as a person's expertise, knowledge, and skills. It is often laced with the goal of self-mastery of competence, service, and vision. Personal power can win the hearts and minds of people, capturing their imaginations and tapping into their personal resources and resolve. Personal power isn't merely outcome-driven, it motivates a workforce to transcend to personal and professional heights and go the extra mile to become more than they imagined. This is personal power at its best and when used for good, inspires people. Who wouldn't want to follow this type of leader? When times are tough, stakeholders want leaders and managers who demonstrate positive personal power laced with empathy.

Positional power is different. Positional power is given to individuals who have authority based on their position in an organization's structure and hierarchy. It is given to individuals by others, often to founders or leaders of an organization. Positional power aims to ensure that a group of people work together towards the organization's common goals.

There is an evolutionary correlation to how most living beings tend to align and respect positional power. Consider the thesis of evolutionary biologist Lee Alan Dugatkin who brings forward the concept that "power — the ability to direct, control, influence the behavior of others, as well as the ability to control access to resources — pervades every nook and cranny of the social life of virtually all animals: from what they eat, where they eat and where they live to with whom they mate, how many offspring they produce, whom they join forces with, and whom they work to depose (Dugatkin, Lee. (2022)."

Dugatkin studies seals to demonstrate how power positioning influences the holder of the position as well as those who are not in a power position. His research conducted in the 1970s on one colony found that the probability that an elephant seal pup would survive to its first birthday was about 37%, and it dropped to about 16% for survival at age four. While other colonies likely had higher rates of survival, it's still an especially hard-knock life for a male elephant seal. Should he be lucky enough to make it to age five or so, each breeding season he'll engage in a never-ending series of contests with other males for mating opportunities. Odds are he will lose, as 95% of all males will never sire a single pup, despite living a decade or more. On the slim chance, however, that a male emerges as one of a small handful of dominant individuals, the reproductive bounty is great, according to Dugatkin (Dugatkin, Lee. (2022).

We, like most other species, follow, respect, and defer to others depending on where we believe our "rank" and "position" fall in a relationship structure. If we defer and provide power to others, we can sit back and not worry about criticism or failure. As children (of any age) we take a deferential position to parents, giving them positional power to act as a director, caretaker, and provider. In our partner relationships, we may vary power positions depending on the situation or area of personal responsibility. For example, we may defer to our partner to pay bills or give them the power position to ensure protection. In our professional lives, we manifest similar position switching when we believe we need to take orders or defer to a superior, or when we take leadership responsibility if something goes wrong, or something becomes a success.

So, if you sit back in a team meeting or even at a community or family function and observe those around you, you may be able to notice how power shifts among those who seek to take it and those who deflect it away from themselves. Without the knowledge and awareness of how we subconsciously, and through evolutionary iterations, take or defer power positions, we may draw false conclusions about why an individual always raises his or her hand to volunteer. In truth, these behaviors may reflect the desire for a higher-level role and demonstrate capability and dominance. Others may sit tucked into the corner of the table with their attention glued to their laptops or phone screens, seemingly absorbed in reviewing emails or something else that they think is a higher priority than what is currently being discussed. We rationalize that the absorbed quiet person isn't Type A and is avoiding their turn to participate.

In both cases, it may be that each wants to observe the group dynamics and wait to take a power position when the time is right. Or, they may have no aspiration for power.

The lesson here is not to make first-impression assumptions. Power plays are complex and do not necessarily follow logical patterns.

We become deferential or assume power positions autonomically in response to situations that beget an expectation of a certain role or manifested behavior. So many human behaviors that we seek to consciously explain or rationalize to ourselves are based on subconscious drivers. So, consciously, we don't really understand, where, how, when, and why we assume, deflect, or defer power positions. Instead, our minds are constantly evaluating and interpreting who and what we should be at a given time and/or place.

All species on the planet are equally subject to hormonal influences, language, and body movement, including posturing and voice intonation. What influences us subconsciously or consciously may come from our own prior experiences and how we handled, reacted, or dealt with a situation—and how we were treated by others. We may overlook, refuse to recognize, or dismiss our behavior if we do not understand why we do what we do or don't do, as well as how we act or react.

The intent of this chapter is not to discuss or document how species across the globe take or give power, but rather to bring forward the human factor and demonstrate how power can influence positive and negative outcomes. Let's take a deeper look at how the factors of both power sets can guide an organization… or derail it.

Personal Power

Leaders with personal power can influence people and events with or without formal authority. History has plenty of examples of individuals with personal power ranging from Gandhi and major religious leaders to more sinister examples including Adolf Hitler and more recently, Vladimir Putin. On the business front, many leaders have inspired and empowered workforces to go the extra step to achieve success and drive innovation. Steve Jobs comes to mind.

Personal power is the ability to influence others and convince them what to do. Without discipline or control, however, a power-compulsive individual may lust for power to the detriment of others.

Many great leaders rise to visibility due to their inherent personal power. As a result, formal authority is then entrusted with them to serve as a platform for their purpose—a platform to do good.

Another way to achieve personal power is when leaders gradually rise through the ranks of an organization based on their competence and continue to grow in power by wielding authority that comes with their rank and position.

Personal power can also assume a physical, spatial position. According to Wikipedia, power position is a concept from Feng Shui, the ancient Chinese practice of studying one's position within one's surroundings. In Feng Shui, the power position or "Dragon Seat" is the physical position in the room for a business meeting, which supposedly has the most power (Wikipedia. (Nd.). We've seen this play out again and again when individuals take a traditional and often non-collaborative approach to leadership and assume the power spot to make their position clear in a meeting.

Personal power individuals typically have positive psychological capital. Fred Luthans, a management professor at the University of Nebraska states "psychological capital embodies hope, self-efficacy, optimism, and resiliency. Self-efficacy refers to belief in your own abilities and optimism means having a positive outlook. Resiliency is the ability to make it through difficult circumstances (Luthans, F. et. al. (2021)."

Arabella Advisors adds that personal power can be classified by four characteristics:

1. Expert: power derived from knowledge or skill.
2. Referent: power derived from a sense of identification others feel toward you.
3. Reward: power derived from an ability to reward others.
4. Coercive: power derived from fear (Walker, K. (Nd.).

Maintaining human connection in the workplace is critical for any individual and particularly in highly dynamic times when leaders are seeking to change or transform the organizations they lead. In response to the necessity for change and transformation, empathy may be the new definition and application of personal power.

Empathy is no longer an abstract, new-age idea.

Research from Catalyst found that empathetic leadership can boost productivity, foster creativity, promote feelings of inclusion, and reduce intent to seek new employment (Van Bommel, T. (2022).

In consideration of a knowledge-based society that is transitioning away from "doing" roles to "thinking" roles, there is a growing recognition that our workplaces have evolved from command-and-control structures (where workers are commodities or cogs in the wheel) to an engaged workplace where ideas, creativity, and innovations from individuals can be the salvation for stability, adaptation to market changes and growth. We are feeling more, thinking more, and doing less physically. As knowledge workers, we expect our workplaces and leaders to respect our personal values and beliefs. Even in "thinking factories," the environment needs to be empathetic to the individual and support a range of different talents.

As reported by Fast Company, 44% of the informed public, say being in a workplace with empathy and human connection is more important now than before the pandemic (another 40% indicate it has always been important). The research adds that a new emphasis on empathy is even higher for employees who are 18-34 years old (52% say it is more important now), parents working in a fully remote or hybrid environment (49% each), or whose volume of work (48%) or level of work-related stress (53%) has gone up during the pandemic (Hanon, K. (2022). The insight is that organizations, like all living systems, can embrace homogeneity and shared purpose, aligning and connecting people in meaningful ways.

Expressing power with empathy and respect often gives individuals—particularly less experienced younger professionals—permission to share their thoughts, challenge beliefs, or advocate for issues that they support. As such, it is important for every individual in life and work to recognize how they manifest personal power, how they can control it, and how they can use it for positive outcomes.

Ten Tips to Increase Personal Power

We have augmented techniques from Professor Laura Portolese Dias (Dias, L. Portolese. (2011) to help build one's capability, recognition and adaptations to situations that aid one's personal power, particularly when participating, leading, or managing organizational change and transformation. The list of recommendations may seem simple, but we must remember to consciously recognize how we may subconsciously default to rote responses or acts in any given situation.

We often rely on our default behaviors depending on who we are with and our own expectations and desires, particularly in how we want or seek to "perform." We may also be internalizing stress or anxiety based on our past experiences, how we were treated and how we dealt with any consequences caused by our actions.

1. Be authentic. Be yourself. Stay true to your values and those things you find important. This may seem simple, and you may believe you are consistent throughout the day, but as we have discussed in this book, we often change throughout the day in response to situations, our environment, and those we are with. In many respects those transitions are necessary, but we can often lose our true selves. For example, we may too easily agree to something we actually don't agree with; we go along with the groupthink and decision-making as we don't feel our voice will be heard or result in any influence, or we simply don't want to contend with confrontation. We, therefore, sell ourselves short. Although the strategy may demonstrate self-preservation, in the longer term, our behavior defines how others see us. If we are not consistent with our North Star, we not only lose personal power, but we may also lose our way.

2. Refuse to let people push your buttons. Allowing others to manipulate and influence our own behavior and thoughts compromises our personal power. Make an effort to get along with others but don't allow yourself to wrongfully become subordinate to others' actions and behaviors.

3. Develop esteem and confidence, which will give you the ability to take on difficult tasks, help others, and contribute to the organization.

4. Be a team player. Get along with, and help others to demonstrate leadership, ability, and good citizenship. It can put you in a position of not only earning the respect of others but also showing your value to the organization.

5. Be someone that makes others feel good. Make others feel good when they are around you—for example, by being genuinely interested in them.

6. Develop your communication skills. Work on your written, oral, and nonverbal language skills. Learn to read and understand others' body language. Actively listen and ensure your body movements and facial expressions are reflective of your intended response.

7. Be visible in the workplace. Don't take credit for others' work but do take credit for your own work. Choose high-profile projects that can put you in a position where others see your work.

8. Don't complain. Unless you can also provide a solution, don't offer a complaint!

9. Be goal-oriented and willing to take risks. Focus on goal-setting personally and professionally. Show managers and colleagues how you can help them meet goals.

10. Use critical thinking to solve problems and encourage others to step out of their comfort zones to access situations holistically and use systems thinking to resolve issues (Dias, L. Portolese. (2011).

Power Positioning

Personal power and positional power are deeply intertwined. For example, one's power position can drive a successful career as the position helps the individual get ahead. An individual in a power position is typically open, willing, socially adept, and in tune with his or her purpose and goals. Thus, used positively, leaders and managers in power positions can move an organization and the workforce forward.

The literal definition of positional power in organizations is the ability and right to influence and direct others based on the power associated with one's formal position in the organization. By virtue of holding that position, certain decision-making authorities and responsibilities are conferred and the manager is entitled to get things done. Unlike internal personal power, positional power is given to someone externally. Our ingrained default to follow a leader or manager deepens conferred complicit power.

Positional power, according to study.com, has three main bases including legitimate power, reward power, and coercive power (Study.com. (2021).

- Legitimate power is based on the manager's position in the organization and correlated to conferred authority. Subordinates acknowledge legitimate power and believe that the manager has the authority to direct their actions, which they willingly comply with.

- Reward power is how a manager can use rewards to influence others to recognize actions and behaviors and meet or exceed performance expectations. Examples include pay increases or

> bonuses, promotions, more responsibilities, and autonomy, as well as recognition and praise.

- Coercive power is the opposite of reward power and is used by managers to punish subordinates for not meeting performance expectations or to deter subordinates from making decisions that will negatively affect the organization.

A leader, manager, or influential individual obtains their power from the organizational role (positional power) enhanced by their personal power.

Effective leaders and managers understand how to use their personal and positional power together to influence teams and individuals toward shared purpose and goals that represent change and transformative strategies.

The key to successful organizational change and transformation lies in leaders of change using a combination of positional power and personal power each strengthened with empathy.

Power and Bias

An underlying and unstated theme in this chapter has been the threats of unconscious and subconscious bias when it comes to personal and positional power and influences on how individuals defer, deflect, or acquire power. Bias can cause leaders and managers to be dismissive when their positions are challenged and defensive when they are questioned. Individuals receiving positional or personal power advances manifest their own inherent biases and influence in how they interpret these advances. Inherent bias dictates how they have given an individual power and how they react, or act based on the advance.

Power is an aphrodisiac and can feed the egos and self-importance of individuals who are narcissists. As discussed, power can result in positive or negative outcomes and consequences. When bias is at play, some individuals use power to get their own way and further self-gain. All organizations must be on the lookout and objectively recognize when and how positional and personal power held by individuals are enabling or hindering organizational change or transformation. Power can be false or represent mistruths—whether via data points, gossip, or posturing. Recognizing natural human default behaviors reflected in power deference, acquisition and emulation helps determine whether it is legitimate. The more aware you are and informed about the motivations of others, the more successful organizational change and transformation will be.

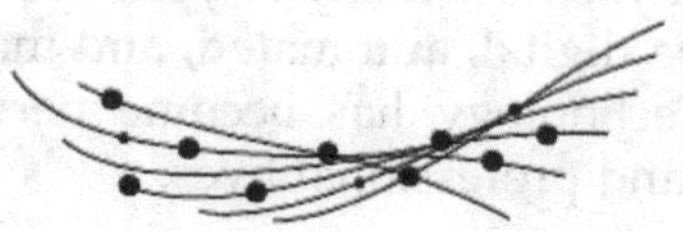

Chapter 34: Emerging Technologies and the Human Factor

"Technology, regardless of our engineering advances, has yet to be able to reach the capability of the single or collective human mind. The technologies we create are highly dependent on how human beings program them with data, information, and formulas. It is the human factor that influences how organizations can seek to change and transform via technology."

Frontier Technologies

Today, every organization is a tech company. You may initially disagree with this, but if you analyze how many of your systems and processes are currently, or aspire to be digital, automated, and managed by technology, you'll get the point. Technology has become pervasive, enabling most aspects of our personal and professional lives.

A technology infrastructure in today's organizations enables customers, enhances internal operations, and results in informed decision-making. In context of transformation, a tech foundation informed by human judgment, insight, and vision becomes an organization's essential tool for adapting to a dynamically changing marketplace and responding to customers' changing demographics, preferences, and behaviors. Transformation requires reimagination, critical thinking, and a clear understanding of how technology and human ingenuity work in partnership for optimum results.

Tech Challenged

A common failure in any change and transformation initiative is the assumption that technology will fit into current processes, customer experiences, or other functions of an organization without an analysis of what problems really need technology solutions. We beat the drum that technology is not a silver bullet, but rather an enabler to create efficiencies and improvements. However, to fully understand its enabling benefits, organizations must take a step back from existing processes and systems to identify and understand how technology allows for creative adaptations, efficiencies, innovations, and improved effectiveness.

Technology, regardless of our engineering advances, has yet to be able to reach the capability of the single or collective human mind. The technologies we create are highly dependent on how human beings program them with data, information, and formulas. It is the human factor that influences how organizations can seek to change and transform via technology. On the flip side, people are impacted and transformed by technology with significant consequences on how they live and work. From a positive perspective, people and technology will evolve into mutually co-dependent systems based on mutual respect.

Technological Foundation

Author and advisor Rishad Tobaccowala states, "Creativity is where art and technology intersect—communication changes as technology changes, and if you do not adapt, your organization may not thrive in the future" (Tobaccowala, R. (2022). As an example, smart marketing is the ability to understand customers' (existing or targets) demographics, life stages, expectations, and behaviors.

The art of mastering the right communication channels is a technology and data-infused exercise. Although the implementation of technology and data systems may be done by the CTO and CIO, the impact, vision, and potential applications of technology must live within every organizational leader. This understanding should be central to all aspects of product, service, experience, and design and correlated to the organizational system, its shared purpose and market orientation.

Tobaccowala believes that we have been living in a series of Connected Ages, starting with the launch of the worldwide web in 1993. The First Connected Age was also the debut of Google and Amazon, arguably the most valuable tech companies in the world at the time. Search, access to information, and ecommerce quickly transformed the organizational landscape and relationships with customers. Within 14 years, the world shifted again with the rise of social networks, the introduction of smartphones and the meteoric ascent for most of broadband connectivity regardless of place or device. And we entered the Second Connected Age (Tobaccowala, R. (2022).

Tobaccowala believes we have now entered the Third Connected Age, and it will make all the seismic changes of the last three decades pale in significance. From a human factor perspective, we are in a transitional moment as we focus on both the opportunities and limitations created by connection and technology. The changes are enhancing humans' lives and work, but they are also impacting our mental and physical health.

The Third Connected Age

We are just beginning to understand the positive and negative influences that stem from our growing dependency on technology. Research is revealing the negative personal and interpersonal consequences of connectivity, including social isolation, feelings of being worse off than others, cyber-bullying, anxiety, depression, and a long list of other mental health conditions. Video gaming, excessive on-screen interactions, and dependence on our smartphones are affecting social skills.

Ubiquitous connectivity has also enabled a deluge of information and misinformation. Dependence on our choice of connectivity platforms has made many of us intellectually lazy, preferring to trust online strangers rather than use critical thinking to examine and understand issues. With the advances of AI and our quickly growing reliance on its platforms and bots, we are eroding the necessity to use our minds.

To effectively navigate the Third Age, we need to recognize our default behaviors and how our overriding need for safety and security may be misplaced in technology. Tobaccowala identifies four significant technological changes in this Third Age:

1. **AI:** Artificial intelligence to do tasks that are usually done by humans.
2. **5G:** Much faster and more resilient connections.
3. **Voice/AR/VR:** New ways of connecting globally with voice search more powerful than text search.
4. **Quantum Computing:** Cloud-based computing takes a quantum jump. Nathan Furr in the Harvard Business Review adds, "Quantum computers can solve problems exponentially faster than classical computers can. They will bring about two huge changes: an end to our current infrastructure for cybersecurity over public networks and an explosion of algorithmic power that holds the promise to reshape our world" (Furr, N. & Shiplov, A. (2022). AI and quantum computing promise higher levels of information and data processing, calculations, capacity, and speed. However, as of 2025, we've seen the reality diverge significantly from early predictions. While AI has made dramatic leaps—particularly with generative AI—quantum computing remains largely in the research phase for most practical business applications. Google, IBM, and others continue to pursue different research paths in developing viable and usable quantum computing. The future will bring us the fruits of their labor.

The Temptation of Technology

Many organizations jump at the chance to build a foundational technology platform too quickly. The impulsive intent is to have the latest and the best without the consideration of how the latest and the best, apply or enhance the human factor in the organizational system, including the need to help a workforce adapt and transition.

The influx of technological changes and opportunities begs the question: How does an organization incorporate new technologies into their systems ensuring recognition of the importance of the human element? When looking at the promise of technology and the opportunities it offers, many falsely believe that transformation is possible without people. However, in consideration of the human equation, transformation is never possible without the recognition of the "people" element, the very human factor. Leading people through transformative change requires enlightened leadership and management that embraces the recognition of human transitions and response along with acceptance to change.

Let's reconsider early Amazon when in the late 1990s the company focused on a niche market that was conducting online transactions. The market, predominantly male and already working in technology, was comfortable sharing financial information online and already trusted the digital delivery system. At the time, most of the general consumer market had neither the knowledge, experience, nor comfort with buying items online. Amazon was ahead of the curve in its vision of how technologies would transform organizations, but society itself wasn't ready.

Amazon then strategically paced the company's progress and focus on anticipating when additional segments of the market would be ready. This type of prescient business plan is clearly the work of a visionary who understood the importance of contextual analysis and orienting appropriately to the market.

In many respects, the technology sector has always looked into the future based on the emerging foundational capabilities in the present. Today's public media broadcasts the hype that we will soon allow machines to think for us (a behavior and action many have already adopted using AI). We will immerse ourselves in the metaverse across all aspects of our lives, and the robots are coming and may soon replace us.

It might be wise to put technology in context of the science fiction writers who have anticipated futuristic versions of our life. Call them great fiction writers or having prescient creative thought processes that invite our minds to expand and see the potential of new technologies that may enhance our lives. Star Trek remains a visual icon for many with its fictional transporters, warp drives, and devices like the tricorder that quickly assesses and reports on any human or physical condition. Some Star Trek conceptual creativity has come to pass as we now wear fitness tracking devices, benefit from advances in health care sensors that monitor our bodily functions and enjoy the advances in bionic prosthetics that help regain day-to-day life functions.

Technology Hype

Savvy consumers often recognize brand hype and unrealistic promises that are designed to generate interest in a solution and catalyze that interest into a product sale. Our capitalistic system is motivated by expansion and profit in a competitive environment where growth measured by the stock market is the major measure. Business 101: Stakeholders and shareholders naturally expect a return on their investment. For organizations to generate acceptable returns on investment and recapture investments in new products and enhancements to existing products, they must generate ongoing sales. Therefore, what better way to generate sales than flooding the market with products promising potential benefits and exciting customers enough to buy them. This is precisely what has happened in the tech sector with a virtually unlimited number of startups, funded and encouraged by a virtually unlimited number of short-term investors looking for that one successful unicorn to make them rich.

The runaway success of so many tech companies has been the result of organizational leaders investing in them with a complete disconnect in understanding how many of these technologies even serve their organizations and customers. Jumping on the tech bandwagon disregards basic contextual analysis and market orientation. We relish the promise and possibility of shiny new solutions and often act before we critically assess what is realistic, practical, and beneficial.

After all, technological promises are just that; a vision that may have an impact on society at some point. But society must be ready and see the tangible value of any solution. Promise and hype do not always bring practical results. The challenge for any organization seeking to stay ahead of others or excel in advanced technology adoption is to ensure the technology applies to the organization, provides enhancement, improvement, or a new opportunity. Plus, the tech needs to complement the human element that is so fundamental to an organizational, its market orientation and shared purpose.

Emerging Tech Trends

In context of the promise of technology's potential, we have identified key technology trends with a focus on how the human element is (or isn't) considered. These applications range from the immediate to the futuristic, and all represent a potential need that organizations may have.

But of course, these innovations can only work when people are ready. To understand how this dynamic plays out in practice, let's examine the specific technologies that have shaped organizational transformation from 2022 to 2025. Each represents a different tension of the promise versus reality, starting with the technology that has most dramatically altered the landscape: artificial intelligence.

- **Artificial Intelligence and Machine Learning, The Defining Transformation:** Deloitte consultants Stefan van Duin and Naser Bakhshi classified artificial intelligence into two types: narrow and general. They defined narrow AI as good at specific tasks, such as playing chess or identifying facial expressions. "The only thing narrow artificial intelligence can do is automate. It can't empathize. It can't collaborate. It can't innovate." On the other hand, "General AI, which can learn and solve complex, multifaceted problems the way a human being does, exists today only in the minds of futurists" (Bakhshi, N. & Duin, S. V. (2017). Bakhski and van Duin added that AI is in its infancy and isn't close to duplicating our most human skills. "AI's biggest value is in augmentation. When human beings work with AI tools, the process results in a sort of augmented intelligence, which outperforms the work of either human beings or AI software tools on their own," they explained (Bakhshi, N. & Duin, S. V. (2017). Much has changed since their initial thought leadership in 2017. Since the writing of the original version of this book, AI has advanced exponentially and is now in the hands of an eager society.

The tech universe shifted on November 30, 2022, when OpenAI introduced ChatGPT—a natural language, generative program that produces text and images in response to user prompts. This moment marked the beginning of what many call the Generative AI revolution, fundamentally changing how we think about artificial intelligence and its role in society … and rattling Bakhski and van Duin's projections from 2017. ChatGPT and any of the other tech leveraging Generative Pre-Trained Transformers (GPT) are brilliant examples of watching how a good idea can become distorted at warp speed. Consider that in today's ever-growing, tech-dependent society, the promise of artificial intelligence is often seen as a silver bullet solution to problems that haven't even manifested yet. GPT is currently creating waves of enthusiasm and optimism in terms of shortcutting work processes and even saving money. Most organizations across the business sector remain challenged in finding the use case where AI is an end-to-end solution.

But they continue to watch AI development to be ready for when it becomes more applicable. The wait and see approach is part of every organization's learning curve with the hope that AI will mature in its accuracy, effectiveness and usefulness.

- **The Shortcomings of Testing:** Today we are living in an AI-infused living lab that is field testing the perfection of systems and applications in real-time with the public as the research subjects. At a time when society is already struggling with the proliferation and reach of fake news and alternative facts, the potential of ChatGPT to deliver unchecked facts comes with consequences. If you look around you today or even project forward, you might recognize that unchecked generative language can feed radical divisive beliefs and contribute to our overall societal anger and rage. Just look at the polarization today in the United States and many other countries as situational examples.

  The launch of ChatGPT and the excitement that resulted caused many organizations working on their own AI offerings to throw caution and concern to the wind, turn a blind eye to perfection, and join the fray out of fear of losing any competitive ranking. With innocent citizens as the test subjects in the GPT research lab in an uncontrolled environment, GPT is delivering many unintended consequences.

  The alarmists have waved the red flag for good reason about the potential harm ChatGPT can inflict. CNET (an online tech focused publication) was called out for using ChatGPT to create articles for its website. Across content marketing circles, ChatGPT (and similar AI generative tools) are being embraced and secured by any number of organizations seeking to expand their online audiences by increasing the amount of content on their sites and apps. In turn, the masses have flocked to using Gen-AI bots as a search engine, turning away from formerly popular search interfaces and native websites.

- **The New AI Workforce: Prompt Engineers and AI Whisperers:** In 2023, the artificial intelligence job market became so hot that it was offering salaries of up to $335,000 to entry level engineers. In 2025, Meta was under fire by its shareholders for the sky-high salaries paid to the refreshed AI team. The AI tech community jockeyed for the best talent distorting salary levels and the intrinsic worth of tech talent. Anthropic, an AI company initially backed by Alphabet, advertised for the role of "prompt engineer" with sky-high pay.

Prompt engineers are like "AI whisperers," and often come from history, philosophy, or English language backgrounds because the core skill is wordplay. Their job is to distill the essence or meaning of something into the most efficient number of words that contextually and analytically are understood by the LLM to generate the desired end result. Finally, a role for humanities students in an AI-infused society! The proliferation of AI technologies has prompted new job expertise to discern the real from the false, in both language and images. New roles now include Chief AI Officer, AI project teams, AI ethics committees, and Chairs of AI and Digital Transformation.

The public itself has become their own prompt engineers in training as individuals immerse themselves in generative AI. They must learn on the fly how to structure their prompts to achieve the intended outcomes. This is leading to entirely new and previously unconsidered skills sets to include algorithmic training, AI interpretive experts and more.

- **AI Bias:** Much has been reported about the unconscious and subconscious bias baked into AI biometric facial recognition systems by engineers and programs when it comes to race, ethnicity, and gender norms. These limitations have dramatic impacts on everything from security and medicine to research. And these issues stem from how these systems are conceived and programmed ... by people. Another recurring theme in the AI/ML conversation is the proliferation of data that ML processes without any insights or intelligence derived from the data flow. This also reverts to the human factor; these systems are often built without a purpose, with an unrecognized bias, or following a weak ethical compass. This may sound dire, but when it comes to AI/ML, don't take anything for granted. Any flaws must be uncovered and monitored by organizations. It requires critical thinking and curiosity to question the processes enabled by AI and ML — and this practice should not be restricted to the tech teams. Anyone using automated systems should be sure the output is not biased or influenced by a pre-programmed desire for a favourable outcome. And then a solid team needs to transform data into meaningful intelligence that can drive high performance.

- **AI and Resumes: The Evolution of Hiring:** A popular practical application of AI in the business world is fielding resumes online. Joann Miller, an editor of What's Next, says that a growing number of companies are using chatbots and AI-led video interviews to assess job candidates before a human recruiter even meets them. In a perfect world, "Automated interviews expand the job candidate pool and are designed to ensure consistent hiring practices by rooting out ways that bias seeps into interviews" (Miller, J. (2022). That may be the case, but the lesson for HR professionals is to improve how they internalize and manifest their own biases. A dubious use case for AI is when applicants interview with bots and are assessed by an algorithm. Algorithms that humans have created and programmed. The evaluation is based on facial expressions, word choices, voice intonations as well as the actual responses to the interview questions. This sort of AI process can unknowingly be influenced by the bias of engineers who developed the program. How the AI is programmed often reflects the engineers' own biases, values, beliefs, and knowledge in how humans emote, behave, and react. According to Miller, in 2018 Amazon abandoned a computer program that used machine learning to score job applicants after developers realized that the tool discriminated against female candidates(Miller,J.(2022).

The resume process is perfected by candidates with a higher sense of tech-savvy. In other words, smart candidates can game an AI interview process. Harvard Business Review states that "Because many job seekers do not understand the interview technology, their default is to perform in a rigid way—holding a fixed gaze, a fake smile, or unnatural posture; speaking with a monotonous voice; and holding their hands still—in short, behaving like robots" (Zahira J. et. al. (2022). This is an example of technological determinism at its worst. A slightly better choice is the Zoom/Teams personal interviews that were a necessity during the pandemic and are now the norm. Nonetheless, the human factors of empathy, engagement, and spontaneity are missing with any of these tech alternatives to in-person interactions.

Ultimately, can reliance on AI really identify the best and the brightest for our organizations? Can it match individuals with appropriate skill sets and values with an organization's shared purpose? Can AI help us recognize accomplishments, skills and attributes of candidates that we simply can't see? It's a brave new world, and there's no turning back. AI and human beings will co-exist to make life better for organizations by liberating a workforce from drudgery. But until that more AI-infused future arrives, we have much to recognize and consider as we seek to replace our human counterparts with technological systems designed to create efficiencies.

- **Voice Assistants: Beyond Alexa and Siri:** Voice assistants like Alexa and Siri have evolved from rigid command-response systems to become more conversational interfaces that mirror human communication preferences. From asking Alexa or Siri the weather to ordering online and sending voice-activated emails and messages, voice is making the lives of customers more frictionless. By 2025, voice technology has evolved significantly beyond simple command-response systems. Modern conversational AI can engage in more natural, context-aware dialogues, though the technology still struggles with nuance and complex reasoning. The original assistants have been surpassed by generative AI; in Amazon's case, the next version of Alexa remains under construction in 2025 as the company attempts to rebuild the tool from scratch with a base in AI.

Technology is seen as generally advantageous and beneficial, however a voice assistant, just like a machine or algorithm, is limited by what humans have input. If a system interface includes images without text descriptions, the voice assistant doesn't have the ability to provide the user with a verbal description. Human beings have a comprehensive verbal and visual recognition process, which voice has not pervasively developed. While multimodal AI systems can process both text and images (like ChatGPT-4 Vision and Claude with vision capabilities), privacy concerns remain paramount because these systems require access to visual data and accuracy of what the AI 'sees," which remains imperfect.

Alexa for Business, which was designed as a voice control tool to manage calendars, make phone calls, and control conference room equipment, was discontinued by Amazon in 2023, illustrating how quickly AI or any technology-infused landscape can shift. Microsoft Copilot (evolved from Cortana) now integrates seamlessly with the full Microsoft Office Suite and can set reminders, recognize natural voices without the need for keyboard input, and answer questions using web results. Many organizations and individuals have become dependent on using it for AI transcription of meetings, meeting agendas and summaries, proving there is immediately applicability for the right use cases.

Voice assistants represent one form of human-machine interaction, but the ultimate expression of this relationship may be physical: robots that don't just process our words but work alongside us in physical spaces. Here, the human factor becomes even more pronounced as we confront not just intelligence, but embodied automation.

- **The Robots Are Coming, From Promise to Reality:** The autonomous AI elephant in the room is the robot. Pieter Abeel, professor of electrical engineering and computer science and director of the UC Berkeley Robot Learning Lab, says "Recent advances in AI are leading to the emergence of a new class of robot. These are machines that go beyond the traditional bots running preprogrammed motions; these are robots that can see, learn, think, and react to their surroundings" (Lee, T., (2020). These are the mechanical sentient beings that today's workers fear may replace them. And possibly for good reason.

In the meantime, robots have been working alongside humans in assembly plants, warehouses, factories, and military battlegrounds. A novel bartender robot was featured at the 2022 Olympics Village in Beijing as an amusing conversation maker. Since then, autonomous delivery robots have become commonplace in many cities, and warehouse automation has accelerated dramatically. Machines and drones deliver provisions and autonomous vehicles, trucks, and farming equipment are increasingly common on roads. Machines roll through hospital corridors delivering meds, perform intricate robotic surgeries, do security screenings and sweeps, disinfect airplanes, deliver meals in restaurants, and befriend children and the elderly as companions.

The most compelling example of human-robot collaboration comes from Kentaro Yoshifuji, a 33-year-old robot researcher and co-CEO of Ory Laboratories, who put robots to good use. His café in Japan is completely barriers free with a mobile robot that serves customers and directs the entire place (O'Neill, M. (2021). The robot is actually an avatar piloted by people with severe physical disabilities from all over the country who control the robot remotely from their homes or hospitals, making the pilots feel valuable. This is one of the more positive and optimistic examples of talent and technology collaborating, co-creating, and co-existing.

In the future we can ponder the potential of an eventual revolution when robots object to being the 21st-century cogs in the wheels of human industry and fight for their rights and recognition as workers with equal stature to humans. If robots represent the physical manifestation of AI in our workspaces, virtual and augmented reality technologies promise to transform the spaces themselves. These immersive technologies test whether digital environments can meaningfully supplement or replace human interaction and physical presence.

- **Virtual and Augmented Reality: The Promise and the Reality:** Virtual reality (VR) used within organizations was forecasted to grow to $4.26 billion in 2023, according to Artillery Intelligence (Artillery Intelligence. (2022). PWC predicted that nearly 23.5 million jobs worldwide would be using AR and VR by 2030 for training, work meetings or to provide better customer service (PWC. (2022). However, by 2024-2025, the actual adoption has been slower than anticipated, with many organizations finding that the technology works best for specific use cases like training simulations and product visualization rather than replacing day-to-day work environments. The pandemic accelerated video-based conference platforms like Zoom and Microsoft Teams as the go-to tools to virtually connect outside of physical borders. As Microsoft Teams itself has grown, it now allows for chat, file management, scheduling and more. It naturally evolved its features and functions to meet the needs at the time.

  The expansion of AR and VR, if it does take hold in some form, could open new opportunities for abuse according to legal experts: privacy and data concerns chief among them. Tech critic Sarah Holbrook states that AR is big business. At the Augmented World Expo (AWE) conference in 2021, Bobby Murphy, the CTO of Snap Inc., Snapchat's parent company, was interviewed by Wired and said, "We see augmented reality as this amazing technology that allows people to engage with digital experiences and visualize them in a way that is very aligned to how we as humans naturally see the world, which is we look out and ask questions about the things that we're looking at" (Wilson, M. (2019). Murphy continued, "Not only is this a really impactful way to make a more informed decision about products you may want to purchase, but it's actually way faster, faster certainly than going into a store and trying to browse pairs of sunglasses, but also faster than even browsing a website and clicking through product pages" (Holbrook, S. (2022).

  VR and AR offer tremendous potential and for some organizations, an opportunity to create immersion without physical borders or restrictions. The decision point comes to where and how it is applicable and if the opportunity is contextual to a relationship an organization has with their workforce and customers.

- **The Metaverse Reality Check:** Janet Stilson writes for MediaVillage and defines the metaverse as a "convergence of our physical reality with augmented reality (AR), virtual reality (VR), and other digital technologies. When it is completely developed, a person's avatar could easily glide between different metaverse experiences created by different organizations." Apple, Meta, Epic Games, Microsoft, Nvidia, Snapchat and gaming platform Roblox are in the vanguard of developing meta-applications, says Stilson (Stilson, J. (2022).

Since the metaverse hype of 2021-2022, reality has set in. Meta invested billions in developing its vision of the metaverse through its Reality Labs division, which has lost over $40 billion since 2020. While virtual worlds and immersive experiences have found niches in gaming, training, and specific professional applications, the vision of a fully realized metaverse where people conduct most of their digital lives has not materialized.

By 2025, the focus has shifted from the metaverse as a destination to "spatial computing" and practical AR/VR applications. Apple's Vision Pro, launched in 2024, represents a different approach, focusing on augmenting existing workflows rather than creating entirely new virtual worlds. The human factor remains central: People want technology that enhances their real-world experiences rather than replacing them entirely, and the technology needs to fit the need and the use case to gain traction. Something AR and VR have yet to do.

The Brave March Forward

What are the frontier and emerging technologies that could be the most disruptive? In 2022, we offered a curated list of megatrends identified by Gartner that were projected to impact our daily lives. In 2025, we update those projections factoring in how fast technology has become an influence yet noting how many seemingly impactful innovations are out of step with society's needs and wants.

- **The Smart World:** Within three to six years, a smart space will be a "physical or digital environment in which humans and technology-enabled systems interact in increasingly open, connected, coordinated and intelligent ecosystems. Smart spaces can be referred to as smart cities, digital workspaces, smart venues, and ambient intelligence" (Nguyen, T., Gartner (2021). By 2025, smart spaces have evolved beyond Gartner's initial predictions. AI-powered environmental controls, IoT sensors, and integrated systems are now commonplace in modern office buildings and urban environments. However, the "ambient intelligence" promised has been slower to materialize, with privacy concerns and implementation costs creating barriers to adoption. Segments of the population have acclimated to the programming and interaction, while many continue to question the automation of very easy day-to-day tasks.

- **Productivity Revolution:** Gartner's 2021 prediction about generative AI has been dramatically realized — but faster and with more impact than anticipated. "Generative AI learns from representations of artifacts from the data and uses it to generate brand-new, completely original artifacts that preserve a likeness to original data," Gartner explained. The field of generative AI has indeed progressed rapidly in both scientific discovery and technology commercialization. ChatGPT, launched in November 2022, accelerated this timeline dramatically. By 2025, generative AI is being used across industries, from content creation and software development to drug discovery and materials science. The predicted safety concerns and negative uses like deepfakes have materialized, requiring new regulatory frameworks and organizational policies. Most governments have yet to take action to establish guardrails and frameworks, instead they see AI as a potential catalyst to remake industries, economies and even advance warfare.

  LLM technology is proving itself in life sciences, healthcare, manufacturing, material science, media, entertainment, automotive, aerospace, defense, and energy. However, organizations are learning that successful implementation requires careful consideration of the human factor — ensuring workers understand both the capabilities and limitations of these tools.

- **Ubiquitous and Transparent Security:** Gartner's predictions about homomorphic encryption have partially materialized. While the technology exists and is being refined, practical implementation at scale remains limited due to computational overhead. The focus has shifted to more immediate practical security measures including zero-trust architectures, AI-powered threat detection, and blockchain-based security solutions. The dominant use case Gartner predicted, eliminating the need to exchange and store data between business partners, is being addressed through various technologies including federated learning and secure enclaves, though not exclusively through homomorphic encryption.

- **Critical Enablers:** Graph technologies have indeed evolved as Gartner predicted. These technologies enable the exploration of relationships between organizations, people, or transactions. Graph analytics and databases have found practical applications in fraud detection, recommendation systems, and social network analysis. Companies like Neo4j, AWS Neptune, and Azure Cosmos DB have made graph databases more accessible to organizations of all sizes. These technological developments—from AI and robotics to immersive environments and smart systems—have collectively created an unprecedented challenge: they're advancing faster than society's ability to govern them responsibly. This creates direct risks and responsibilities that every organization must address.

- **Fourth-Generation Warfare, The New Battlefield:** Organizations now face what experts call "fourth-generation warfare;" not military conflicts, but weaponized misinformation campaigns that blur the lines between civilians and combatants. Graham Lawton of New Scientist warns that "The next two years will be make or break in the information wars, as deep-pocketed bad actors escalate their disinformation campaigns, while the good guys fight back." The outcome will determine everything from vaccine beliefs to election outcomes. This battlefield directly impacts every organization. Competitors, critics, and foreign actors could be using AI to shape narratives about your organization, your industry, or your stakeholders. The "cyber troops" identified by Oxford aren't limited to nation-states, they include PR firms, corporate actors, and partisan organizations spending millions to manipulate public opinion. Organizations cannot rely on platforms, governments, or tech companies to protect their interests or stakeholders.

The Guardrails Crisis

The technological landscape we've surveyed, from AI and robotics to immersive environments, operates within a broader societal context that organizations cannot ignore. While pharmaceutical products have the FDA and workplace safety has OSHA, AI and emerging technologies develop with minimal regulatory oversight. This regulatory vacuum creates direct risks that every organization must address. By mid-2023, the Biden administration reached agreements with seven major tech companies—Amazon, Anthropic, Google, Inflection, Meta, Microsoft and OpenAI—to establish AI safeguards.

These companies committed to watermarking AI-generated content, testing for security vulnerabilities, sharing information across industries, implementing robust cybersecurity measures, and prioritizing research on societal risks including bias, discrimination, and privacy protection. The framework appeared comprehensive and responsible for managing AI's rapid expansion. Reality proved quite different. By October 2023—just three months after those commitments—AI-generated content was projected to account for 99% or more of all information on the internet, straining already overwhelmed content moderation systems. The Oxford Internet Institute identified 81 countries with active cyber troop operations—government or political party actors tasked with manipulating public opinion online.

Consider this concrete example of crisis in real-time: During the Israel-Hamas conflict, researchers at Alethea detected a network of at least 67 accounts on X posting false content, with each post garnering millions of views. Video game footage was passed off as real combat, firework celebrations were presented as military strikes, and AI-mistranslated videos spread misinformation at viral speeds. Despite corporate commitments to combat such issues, the response was reactive at best—accounts were taken down only after massive damage was done.

This illustrates the fundamental challenge: AI hallucinates, becomes delusional, and operates with outdated information. ChatGPT's knowledge cutoff demonstrates this perfectly—by late 2023, it was operating with information from 2021, missing two years of critical global developments. Current AI systems now actively connect and consume real-time information, which may create even more unintended consequences for society and the organizations operating within it.

How do you create policy or regulation that prevents AI from hallucinating when asked a question? How do you watermark content when the technology to remove watermarks evolves just as quickly? These questions reveal why waiting for government solutions leaves organizations vulnerable to immediate threats.

Organizational Responsibility in the AI Age

The current misinformation environment creates a compulsory call to action for organizations to step back, use critical thinking skills, and find realistic, relevant ways to address the runaway train of unregulated AI deployment. This requires immediate action across three critical areas:

1. Establishing internal AI governance including comprehensive policies for AI tool usage, developing robust verification protocols for AI-generated content, training employees to recognize AI

    limitations and biases, and building teams specifically tasked with AI oversight and ethical implementation.

2. Protecting stakeholder trust demands transparently disclosing when AI is used in communications, implementing verification processes for information before distribution, maintaining human oversight on critical decisions, and building redundant systems for information verification that don't rely solely on automated processes.

3. Investing in human capabilities means training the workforce in critical thinking and media literacy, developing organizational skills to identify AI-generated misinformation, creating awareness programs about technological limitations, and fostering cultures that question rather than automatically trust technological solutions.

The human factor in how we adapt, change, and transform remains the most important factor in navigating accountabilities. Organizations that build appropriate guardrails will thrive in an AI-infused environment. Those that blindly trust in technological solutions or wait for government oversight will find themselves vulnerable to manipulation, misinformation, and loss of stakeholder trust. The interconnected nature of our technological and social systems means that organizational resilience depends not just on internal capabilities, but on understanding and responding to the broader societal challenges that AI and emerging technologies create. The governance challenges we've outlined manifest most clearly in a fundamental paradox of our technological age: as AI enables unprecedented personalization and connection capabilities, society simultaneously experiences an epidemic of loneliness that's reshaping all organizational relationships.

The Personalization Paradox: AI and Human Connection

Here's where the personalization paradox becomes profound: As AI enables unprecedented personalization and efficiency, society is experiencing an epidemic of loneliness that's fundamentally changing how people relate to brands and organizations.

As our technology device counterparts become more sophisticated in responding to humans, the central question is if we are consciously or unconsciously assigning human qualities to devices. Research from 2023-2024 shows that people increasingly anthropomorphize AI assistants, which can lead to over-reliance and misplaced trust in their capabilities. A 2025 study found that anthropomorphism weakens users' epistemic vigilance, leading to over-reliance on AI feedback and inadequate critical evaluation of AI-generated responses (Frontiers in Computer Science, 2025). Similarly, experimental research from 2024 demonstrated that merely knowing advice comes from an AI causes people to over rely on it, even when it contradicts their own assessment or available contextual information (Science Direct, 2024).

The stark realities are that 12% of Americans now have zero close friends (up from 3% in 1990) and half the country reports struggling with loneliness. These numbers exploded when smartphones became ubiquitous. Ed Elson, co-host of Prof G Markets, explains: "In a society of lonely people, there is a lot more to love in a person than a brand." We've become more interested in the idea of people than the reality of being with them physically. We search for connections on social platforms, scroll endlessly through content about others' lives, and form what psychologists call "parasocial relationships," imagined relationships with people we don't actually know.

The business impact is dramatic: 40% of consumers now consult an influencer before making purchases, Gen Z views favorite influencers the same way they view friends, and research shows that seeing someone isn't enough; lonely people want to know them, understand them, and be understood by them.

The Human Connection Strategy

For organizations navigating transformation, the shift from focusing on the brand to people creates both a challenge and an opportunity. The solution isn't abandoning your brand; it's putting human faces and authentic connections at the forefront to make your brand relatable and relevant. CEOs need to ditch highly polished press releases and embrace more personal platforms. Spotify's CEO delivered Q2 earnings via a selfie video. Shopify's president did the same. These aren't gimmicks—they're recognizing that brands, logos, and corporate messaging no longer resonate. People want to know the humans behind the organization, what they care about, and what they believe.

Here's how to build AI-enabled intimacy at scale without sacrificing authenticity and credibility:

- Survey and collect data to build AI-enabled Ideal Customer Profiles

- Launch private online communities for your best stakeholders

- Offer unique, customized experiences through private portals

- Provide access to thought leaders addressing individual interests

- Practice constant iteration to refine personalized offerings

Christopher Penn suggests it's to make communications meaningful by asking stakeholders what they want, then using AI to deliver at scale while maintaining human authenticity. This requires talking directly to stakeholders, not at them; actively listening to their needs and interests, observing their behaviors and preferences, and acknowledging them as individuals, not demographic segments.

The Future is Human, Enabled by AI

The irony is inescapable: As AI becomes more powerful and ubiquitous, the competitive advantage shifts decisively to organizations that become more human. John Rossman observes: "The customer is king again. Customers paying inflation-generated premiums will demand greater quality and attentiveness, showing the most loyalty to brands offering more than just price-based incentives."

The bottom line: Think about how to communicate benefits with personalized messaging where products and services are contextualized by each customer. Your brand becomes the backdrop, not the opening line. Position yourself in the context of how you're a part of stakeholders' lives, not how their lives serve your brand. As President Bill Clinton once said, "To have a friend, you have to be a friend." In the AI age, organizational success depends on becoming a genuine friend to your stakeholders, building meaningful professional relationships throughout their journey with you. This isn't just good marketing—it's the foundation for sustainable transformation in an increasingly AI-mediated world.

The organizations that will thrive are those that understand this paradox: AI enables connection at scale, but only authentic human relationships create lasting loyalty. Technology amplifies capabilities, but the human factor remains—and will always remain—the most critical element in transformation success. This paradox points to a broader truth about technological transformation: the more powerful our tools become, the more valuable distinctly human capabilities become. Understanding this relationship is essential for organizations navigating the balance between automation and human-centered design.

It sounds counterintuitive, but as AI becomes more ubiquitous, the organizations that have the competitive edge may be those that become more human. In a future driven by automated AI, successful organizations must focus on skills that set them apart and that can't be duplicated by AI or ML.

As evidence, demand for jobs that require social skills has risen at twice the rate of other types of jobs since 1980. Critical thinking and problem solving within the organization will become increasingly important. These are skills that can't be automated and are not algorithms. Combining talent and technology will propel AI-fueled software and hardware tools to an organization's success. Technological transformation requires perception, active listening, clarity, negotiation, persuasion, and critical thinking—all inherently human capacities that are yet to be matched by machines.

The Endgame: Walking Before We Run

All the technological opportunities we have discussed offer promise, and when fully realized, will enhance human capability at some point in the future. As we march down the road to high-tech adoption, we need to walk before we run. In terms of organizational transformation, investments in technologies need to be considered based on their potential to enable operations, relationships with customers, and how to make a workforce more productive. Critical thinking is a tool to evaluate if the promise of tech applications translates to real-world applications.

In many ways, technology creates a gap between the haves and the have-nots. We saw this play out during the pandemic when many workers and families did not have the proper computer equipment or connectivity. This was clearly an issue for students and held back some workers. The AI revolution of 2022-2025 has amplified this digital divide. Organizations with resources to invest in AI tools, training, and infrastructure gain significant competitive advantages, while smaller organizations and individuals without access fall further behind. The "AI literacy gap" has become a new form of inequality in the workplace and society.

Technologies that enhance our daily lives tend to result in faster adoption across society. By human nature, we are typically hesitant to make our own decisions independently. We seek out information to help make a decision and want to know what others think and recommend. Technology is a shortcut tool for guiding marketing, sales, and workforce organization decisions. The early adopters will lead the way as tech pioneer role models paving widespread adoption.

Our position is to balance the ideal of technology with its reality. The human factor is the key to the successful adoption of a technology foundation, and people need to be comfortable with tech and understand its role in the organization. Whether it's working in a version of a hybrid office, operating hand in hand with AI tools, or adopting advanced collaboration systems to build workforce communities, our inter-dependence on technology is on an irreversible course.

We have witnessed firsthand how the promises of the metaverse, universal remote work, and fully automated processes haven't materialized as predicted. AI has exceeded expectations in some areas while falling short in others. The lesson for organizations is clear: technology adoption must be guided by human needs, contextual relevance, and practical value—not hype cycles or fear of missing out.

As we navigate this Third Connected Age, organizations must remember that transformation success lies not in the technology itself, but in how thoughtfully we integrate it with human capabilities. The most successful organizations of 2025 and beyond will be those that master the delicate balance between technological innovation and human-centered design, automation and augmentation, and efficiency and empathy. The future belongs to organizations that understand that while robots, AI, and advanced technologies are powerful tools, they remain just that—tools that must serve, not replace, the fundamentally human elements that drive innovation, creativity, and meaningful progress.

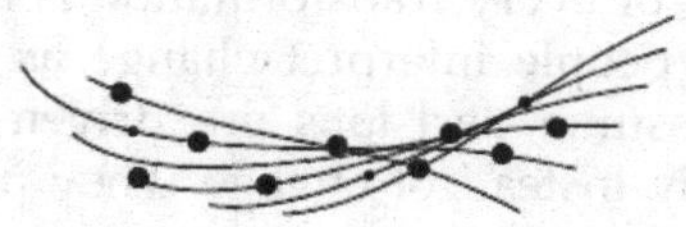

Chapter 35: How to Trust

"Everyone is talking about who or what to trust, particularly in today's fractious public discourse. When we decide to trust, we have aligned with and formed an understanding, correlation, and interpretation of the meaning of that trust. We then apply what has been communicated, shared, and internalized to our own beliefs, values, and knowledge … and take actions based on that trust."

Trust as the Core Variable in Transformation

At the center of every transformation is a single, fragile variable: trust. Without trust, people interpret change as a threat rather than an opportunity. They assume decisions are driven by politics rather than purpose. They comply instead of engage. They protect themselves rather than contribute to the future.

The rise of AI has amplified this tension. Employees question whether data is accurate, whether AI-generated decisions are fair, and whether leaders understand the tools they are deploying. Leaders, in turn, question the adaptability of their workforce and the reliability of AI outputs. This mutual distrust forms an invisible barrier that can stall even the most well-designed transformation.

Trust is not built through all-hands meetings or cascading communications. It is built through consistent behavior—leaders doing what they say they will do, admitting uncertainty, acting with integrity, and creating conditions where people feel safe to participate honestly in the change. Without trust, transformation collapses, regardless of the strategy.

In Ourselves We Trust

So, where do we end up if we have formed thoughts, knowledge, and beliefs, and take actions only to discover our trust was misaligned?

We feel violated, we question ourselves and second guess how we could have trusted in the first place. What did we do wrong in our evaluation and assessment of the trust we aligned with another, an organization, or even a government?

It gets more complicated. If we don't trust ourselves, we typically don't trust others. You can also flip the equation and by trusting others we can trust ourselves. This bi-directional connection aids us in forming our perception of reality. So, if we trust what we have been told and trust it has some correlation to the fact, then we indeed perceive a feeling of trust.

How We Trust

But the real question is *how* you trust, and that doesn't mean that you can or can trust.

Rather, what is the *process* of how you trust, even in trusting yourself? Consider the seminal work, *How Does a Poem Mean*, (Ciardi, J. (1960) and take a page from John Ciardi to think about how you trust as the analysis of all the independent elements that comprise your decision to trust. In literature, it's breaking poems down to study their structure, form, language, and theme. Let's apply those meta principles in analyzing how you trust – professionally and personally. Here are the key elements:

- The source.
- Your relationship/history with the source.
- Your values align with the source.
- Your own inherent biases (positive and negative).
- You're yearning to want to trust the source.

How you trust should be for the right reasons, which can be clarified by holistically considering these key elements. Basically, this boils down to asking the right questions. Critical thinking is a fundamental tool in revealing how you come to trust and how you trust. This discipline deconstructs the entire trust process and will make you more honest, and well, trustworthy. It is also the same process that organizations can use to clarify how their customers trust them as well as how their employees share their trust.

In applying critical thinking to what you are reading, hearing, or viewing as a receiver, you are ingesting what the communicator is putting forward. You then interpret that information based on your own experience, knowledge, and values. The interpretation may not be objective as it is often flavored with your own biases. The trick is to take a step back and use your critical thinking skills to look at all sides of what is being put forward. Apply the key elements while also recognizing what you know, and don't know and the gaps you need to fill before you can trust. One must attain a level of confidence to trust and be trusted.

Trust: Worthy?

Trust is based, then, on confidence. Trust is transparent. Trust provides security. And trust is a precious currency. Today many people find trust elusive, disappointing, ambiguous, and a betrayal when it is revealed the trust given was misaligned. Next-gens' trust in institutions is at an all-time low, exacerbated by the politicization of everything from mask protocols and women's rights to voting policies and the climate crisis.

The media is polarizing. Science (even documented with facts) isn't trusted. Schools are banning books. Respected CEOs are being fired for unethical behavior. And it's tempting to dismiss any hope for truth and trust on social media, which is drowning in disinformation.

Even when presented with empirical data, some people do not trust the facts. Covid is a case in point. Ezra Klein writes in The New York Times, quoting Thomas Bollyky, director of the Global Health Program at the Council on Foreign Relations, "When confronted with a novel, contagious virus the best way for governments to protect their citizens is to convince them to take the measures to protect themselves. Especially in free societies, the success of that effort depends on trust — trust between citizens and their government and trusts between citizens themselves." He adds, "Policy lies downstream of society. Mandates are not self-executing; to work, policies need to be followed, and guidance needs to be believed. Public health is rooted in the soil of trust. That soil has thinned in America (Ezra Klein. (2022)."

How do we navigate a low-trust, high-dysfunction society? How do we run organizations that can make the required effort to reconnect with mistrustful customers? How do we avoid experiencing bankruptcy with stakeholders' trust?

The Cycle of Distrust

The 2022 Edelman Trust Barometer is focused on The Cycle of Distrust, which threatens any society's stability. On the surface, this report doesn't sound very optimistic. The report reveals that distrust in government and media has grown. In fact, media and government are seen as divisive, and 74% of the survey respondents worry about media and government using false information or fake news as a weapon. When it comes to being lied to and purposely misled, 67% of respondents believe journalists and reporters are guilty and 66% believe the same about government leaders. Furthermore, 64% agree that people in their own country lack the ability to have constructive and civil debates about issues they disagree on (Edelman, R. (2022).

These public sentiments do not bode well for the public discourse and functional society. Although it's easy to dismiss these statistics as existential, abstract, or someone else's problem, it deeply affects the psyches and emotional health of all your stakeholders. It is worth the investment and time to explore and identify how customers and employees trust you and your organization. And how you trust yourselves.

Restoring Trust

The better news in Edelman's research is that business is considered to be the only trusted institution. The societal role of business is here to stay, and people want more business leadership, not less. In fact, the study reports that people believe business leaders can restore belief in society's ability to build a better future.

We must honestly ask if a business is the great hope for building back a broken society. And if the answer is yes, we need to be sure we are saying that we are no longer capable of creating productive, trust-based relationships with governments and institutions to have a productive public discourse. Have we then shucked our own individual contributions and responsibilities?

Restoring trust is key to societal stability. People's trust in their co-workers has risen 12 points. The bad news is that we are as quick to trust as we are to distrust. Our inherent biases influence our kneejerk trigger for both trust and mistrust.
If we go more deeply to understanding how we trust and make our evaluations and decisions, it requires breaking down the elements and looking at the situation holistically. The result will be a genuine and meaningful understanding of how we trust and will lead to behaviors and beliefs that are less emotional and more foundational and objective based.

Real Life Trust in Business

Trust must be evenly distributed across an organization. Here is a deeper look at how.

- **The Organization: Earning Customer Trust.**

The quality of the information you share is the most powerful trust builder across institutions and organizations. What you stand for is not a platitude. Mobilize a cross-disciplinary, multi-department team to dig into how stakeholders trust you. Break down the elements and do some rigorous investigation to vet how trustworthy your organization is. Then consider *how* your customers trust you; Edelman reports that 58% of respondents buy or advocate for brands based on their beliefs and values.

And when it comes to the workforce, 60% of employees choose a place to work based on their beliefs and values. (Edelman, R. (2022). With these high numbers, it's essential to have a clear articulation of your values and how you can maximize your trust relationship with customers and employees. And trust translates to worth and value. A significant 88% of institutional investors subject ESG to the same scrutiny as operational and financial considerations (Edelman, R. (2022).

Many organizations take the easy street and do what they have always done in the past, hoping for better results. The radar is on high alert among customers and employees alike to detect deception and misinformation. Remember, how to trust is calibrated on the source; the relationship/history with the source; values alignment with the source; inherent biases (positive and negative), and the yearning to want to trust the source.

- **Communication and Marketing: Speaking Concretely and Truthfully**

Does your organization market to customers based on instincts and intuition that focus on concise over-promising based language to create immediacy without building trust?

Does your organization market to prospective customers in the same way without building a relationship of trust, one-on-one? Do you use data and analytics to know how your customers or prospective customers trust you? Is it guesswork … or a complete omission?

Most know that customer acquisition is expensive, and its near-term churn makes it even more of a costly exercise. Building numbers of customers in the short-term, without building trust based on quality delivery, service, and yes, even trustworthy communication, isn't a sustainable strategy in the long term. High retention and low churn should always be the goal constructed with a clear understanding of how to build a relationship of trust.

Marketing and communications are often the major sources of relationships with customers. Organizations generally (and subjectively) believe too much information is indeed too much information and therefore, conciseness should be the goal. Bullets are best. A single call to action, well, just perfect.

We overlook in our marketing mantra the opportunity to build a relationship of trust. Instead, being thoughtful, emotional, and communicative about what customers want from the organization should become the major intent of any marketing or communication.

Chip Heath, Stanford professor of Organizational Behavior and noted author, says it best: "Communications of any sort, should be 'concrete' that results in painting a picture and a story, be emotional to connect to the recipient, and lastly make it as simple as possible. Simple in this sense, isn't overly concise, a set of three-word bullets or representative of a single call to action. Simple as possible means providing enough information that the recipient understands what is being shared and its relationship to them, feeling and connecting to the emotion, and in painting the picture, ensuring it is concrete. Where concrete leads to creating a bidirectional relationship of trust (Heath, C. & Abrahams, M. (2022)."

The fatal flaw in running any organization is assuming what your customers want and focusing only on the acquisition of customers. This flaw transcends to employees as well. Communications without a basis on relationship and trust (and let's add respect) lead to low morale and low employee retention. In both cases, trust is eroded if the managers making executive decisions about product development, marketing, and communications, management, and treatment of staff, are working in silos and isolation.

The margin for error in earning trust is slim. Customers and employees may hold off on trusting you until they know they are safe and feel secure.

How do they learn to trust you? Actions? Words? Optics?

Every organization must provide trustworthy information with clear, consistent, concrete, fact-based information to break the cycle of distrust.

- **Sales: Potential Situational Trust**

It is a frequently shared attitude for salespeople to be optimistic, which influences their sales estimates with hopeful thinking. However, there is no gain in situational trust; minor lies equate to an overall loss of credibility and trust. This is a real challenge for managers who rely on sales data to project profitability.

Customers are often overpromised about what they are buying by enthusiastic sales reps. When the customer learns the truth, that relationship is broken, especially if the customer believes they were "had" and appear to be foolish to their management. Making sales numbers with "minor lies" might be achieved in the short-term, however, the customer won't continue to be a customer. Sales, in the pantheon of organizational functions, must be based on trust. Success is about building relationships strengthened by mutual trust.

• Workforce: Earning Trust

Let's turn our attention to internal organization systems and dynamics: Say what you mean and mean what you say. And don't assume everyone thinks the same way you do. Trust is the only true measure employees have with their co-workers, managers, and leaders. As part of an organization, each employee, regardless of position, needs to feel trusted and be able to trust those around them. Mistrust is created when individual goals take precedence; organizational politics become ingrained into the culture; competition becomes a dirty pool, and individuals use minor and even major lies to make themselves look better, convolute results, or skew the facts. This is a description of an organization in deep trouble. It is rotten from the inside out filled with mistrust that disables the system, processes, and people.

Employees, at the start, may initially trust leadership giving them the benefit of the doubt. Doubt can grow, shrink, or go away completely in direct correlation to the level of trust in managers and the organization.
In the journey of building trust with employees, being honest, transparent, and concrete earns long-term established trust.

Acknowledgment and appreciation play important roles in building trust and maintaining good relationships. Individuals who recognize the efforts of others increase the trust others have in them. Likewise, if individuals don't demonstrate appreciation, they appear selfish, which destroys trust.

Individuals in leadership positions may do things purely for approval from employees and their boards. If that means sacrificing a code of values and beliefs, trust in yourself, your values, and your beliefs is tarnished. How do stakeholders, including employees, trust leaders who aren't truthful and concrete? They need the confidence that leadership does what is right, even when others disagree. People tend not to trust those who always say whatever they think others want to hear. Trust is built on respect.

Even worse is when individuals in leadership positions ignore the majority opinion. Bias and failure to listen objectively lead to jumping to conclusions and being defensive when the majority may be right. How stakeholders trust is having access to provide feedback and having that input recognized. Never seeking their individual feedback is a huge, missed opportunity to effectively guide the organization.

Trust is gained when one is truthful, open, and recognizes failure and fault, demonstrating that individuals are not perfect. We all make mistakes, and the recognition of the mistakes creates learning, humility, and vulnerability. Visible vulnerability in this instance also builds trust. It is not earned by spinning a story to deflect or ignore majority opinion and hold firm on biases. Being empathetic and communicating as simply as possible with truth also builds our trust in ourselves.

A Final Word

Fundamentally, human beings are fairly lazy as they seek to limit the amount of energy to expend and allow others to lead, inform, and tell them what they should believe. We may rationalize this as not having the time or energy to do the work and fully investigate. For example, we may glaze over a spreadsheet full of numbers and trust what we are told those numbers mean.

It has been reported that people don't like to read and therefore communications need to be concise, with bullet points or a Cliff Notes summary.

Why?

Majorly because it takes mental energy to spend time to understand the numbers and read the 200-page manual.

Our nature is to believe that a trusted source is telling the truth. It is complex managing our default behaviors to identify how we trust, particularly in a fast-moving society where the speed and quantity of inputs exceed our ability to ingest and analyze everything coming our way. Use critical thinking to discern how to trust and understand the distinction between trust and misinformation. If you know *how* to trust you will make better decisions, run an organization more effectively and provide the insights and inspiration to lead your stakeholders through the public arena of disinformation and mistrust.

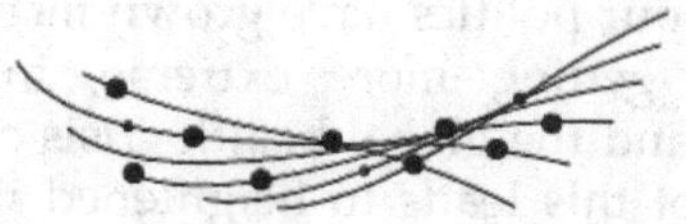

Chapter 36: Leading with Courage

"Is courage an outlier or core principle in your organization?
Today we live in a complex callout culture, both personally
and professionally. It takes critical thinking to identify what is
courageous versus what is opportunistic. Courage is not
typically at the top of the list of leadership prerequisites nor is
it reflected in any job description. However, courage is key to
everything: to challenge, share ideas, speak up, see something
differently, try new things and receive feedback. And above
all, courage is the enabler of critical thinking,
strategy, and behavior."

Being Courageous

The current environment appears to be out of control for many of us. In the United States, our politics have grown increasingly divisive, the climate appears to be getting more extreme, inflation is impacting everyone's pocketbook, and the global health crisis continues to present a state of ambiguity. All of this leads to heightened individual anxiety, so much so that on a day-to-day basis, each individual is living with a level of ambient stress. Everyone, groups, countries, and yes, leaders, seem to be living in a time of TBA (To Be Announced).

Traditional organizational models with dominating hierarchical structures and command-and-control as the predominant cultural norm inhibit individuals from being courageous. How can we as individuals, employees, leaders, and organizations better manage ambiguity and establish a shared purpose? By ensuring we are manifesting courage individually and allowing open dialogues that reflect critical thinking, constructive criticism, input, and feedback.

Profiles in Courage

Is courage an outlier or core principle in your organization? Today we live in a complex callout culture, both personally and professionally. It takes critical thinking to identify what is courageous versus what is opportunistic. Courage is not typically at the top of the list of leadership prerequisites, nor is it reflected in any job description. However, courage is key to everything: to challenge, share ideas, speak up, see something differently, try new things and receive feedback. And above all, courage is the enabler of critical thinking, strategy, and behavior.

Many of our business cultures are still modeled on practices from the Industrial Age when individuals were perceived as cogs in the wheel and a means to an end. Open dialogue across all roles and levels of an organization, particularly that flowed upstream, was frowned upon. The institutional hold of past times influences current norms that permeate an organization. As a result, the past erects roadblocks to the courage that mitigates critical thinking, questioning, and criticism.

How Courage Activates Change

Society seems to be more stable when responsibility is given to leaders across an organization, government, business, or the like.

We tend to generalize humans into two classifications: those that lead and those that follow. Everyone knows his or her place. As such, rigid role attributes are assigned to each group; followers tend to be submissive and leaders that control the hierarchy often quash any open sharing of individual thought and criticism to and of upper levels. The operating principle is that "the leader knows best."

What is generally overlooked is that collective intelligence and courage are what society needs to evolve and advance. Risk is a key factor in progress. Some risks have led to disastrous results, others have led to rapid advances that changed society with innovators worshipped as idols. What moves a paradigm change is courage across society and organizations with a shared purpose. Examples include a societal or business problem that requires a solution, human rights violations that need individuals to come together, and a natural disaster response where a collective needs to operate like a well-oiled machine to save lives, recover and re-establish some new normal.

Courageous Leaders in Action

Leaders are historically measured by their ability to deliver a bottom-line result to meet all stakeholders' expectations. Bottom-line results and expectations are reflected in employment contracts, performance plans, and an organization's strategic plan and goals. In a public company, the bottom line is essential to maintaining or growing the stock price to deliver a return on investment for the shareholders and takes precedence over all other activities and goals.

Generally speaking, executives, project teams and others set their baselines of performance measurements regardless of if these actions move the needle or not. However, managing expectations is the key to applying "benchmarks." There are a handful of courageous business leaders that we can look to for inspiration and consider as models of outstanding behavior. One example is Brian Cornell, CEO of Target who is a profile in courage in this arena. He announced to his board in 2016 that his pathway to a turnaround and accelerated growth was to commit $7 billion+ in capital investment. That meant people, processes, and culture. At the time, shares in Target fell in real-time as he announced the plan on an earnings call. But Cornell was courageous, he stuck to his guns and over-delivered after five years with a net income up 638%.

But there is more to the story on courage. According to Bill George, a senior fellow at Harvard Business School, "Courageous individuals take risks that go against the grain of their organizations.

They make decisions with the potential for revolutionary change in their markets. Their boldness inspires teams, energizes customers, and positions organizations as leaders in societal change (George, B (2017)."

Courage is not a skill learned in a classroom; it is mastered through life experiences of personal risk-taking. He adds, "If organizations are managed without courageous leadership and courageous individuals, then R&D programs, product pipelines, investments in emerging markets, and employees' commitment to the company's mission all wither. These organizations can slip into malaise and may eventually fail, even if their leaders move on to avoid being held accountable."

Courage is a necessity for organizational change and transformation. A culture undergoing transformation, including the shareholders and stakeholders (staff, managers, customers, clients), may often manifest signs of ambient anxiety and fear of change. This can result in individuals internalizing these feelings as a threat. Courage, therefore, is important at all levels in an organization to mitigate anxiety and stress while allowing forward movement.

So, why do some people lack courage?

- They focus solely on hitting their numbers and meeting their goals which is a short-term mentality.
- They focus on a personal professional gain that takes precedence over organizational progress.
- They avoid risk-taking that may make them look bad to peers, stakeholders, and the public.
- They don't want to look or sound stupid.
- They don't believe their voice will be valued.
- They fear retaliation.
- They fear criticism.
- They fear failure.

Courageous Individual Leadership

Nancy Koehn, professor at Harvard Business School believes, "Most of our lives, we're beset by crises. Courageous leaders and individuals are not cowed or intimidated. They realize that, amid turbulence, there lies an extraordinary opportunity to grow and rise (Gavin, M. (2020)." If leading through the trifecta of a global health crisis, disruptive financial markets, and civil discord doesn't require courage, what does?

So, what are the behaviors and beliefs of courageous leaders and individuals? Koehn believes there are five key characteristics (Gavin, M. (2020).":

1. Authenticity. "Authentic leadership serves as the strongest predictor of employees' job satisfaction, organizational commitment, and workplace happiness. Research also shows that organizations, which are comprised of leaders who are true to themselves, demonstrate improvements in both employee trust and performance." In short, authentic leadership necessitates continual self-improvement (Gavin, M. (2020)."

2. Resilience. "Resilience is the capacity to not only endure great challenges but to get stronger in the midst of them. A leader's ability to do this is profound, not only for him or herself but for the impact it exerts on others and the larger mission (Gavin, M. (2020)."

3. Emotional Intelligence. "A keen sense of EI is vital to being a leader who can collaborate with others to achieve organizational goals." Self-awareness is key and continuous iteration unlocks success. EI leaders practice self-management and social awareness. According to research by TalentSmart, "90% of top performers in the workplace have a high degree of emotional intelligence, compared to 20% of bottom performers (Bradberry, T. (Nd.).

4. Self-Discipline. "When facing a crisis, you need to be prepared to lead under pressure and remain composed. Realize that in the heat of the moment, nothing an individual leader can do can solve the whole situation, you're better off acting from your strongest, calmest self than you are taking the first reactive, immediate action. (Gavin, M. (2020)."

5. Commitment to Purpose. "We're looking for leaders who can help us make a leap of faith and be integral to creating a better world, and to believe this is worthy of doing and possible (Gavin, M. (2020)." A study by DDI, reports that purpose builds organizational resilience and improves long-term financial performance. Being purpose-driven leverages an organization's objectives to inspire a team with a sense of mission (Gavin, M. (2020)."

Why Courage Defines Leadership Today

Consider the circumstances of running an organization today. We operate in uncertain times with ambiguous outcomes. Employees are emotionally and psychologically exhausted. Career fulfillment is at an all-time low evidenced by the Great Resignation. We are suffering from Zoom/Teams fatigue and long for meaningful in-person experiences. Employees are looking for leadership to help them find a path forward. We can't plan in the conventional sense, but we can act with great deliberation at the moment. And that takes courage.

Executive coach Ken Jacobs says employees need leaders "to have the courage to listen to feedback about leadership performance." That means leaders need to listen with an open mind. He adds, "Think of your team as leaders in training who want to know how they can be better and hit their own standards of excellence." And even more important, he says "They need you to have the courage to continue developing as a leader, for the rest of your career (Jacobs, K. 2009)."

Courage must permeate an organization. That means it takes personal security in an organization for employees to have the bravery and courage to voice ways organizations can learn and improve. We are talking about everyday courage, not dramatic whistleblowing.

According to Jim Detert, the John L. Colley Professor of Business Administration at the University of Virginia's Darden School of Business and the author of "Choosing Courage: The Everyday Guide to Being Brave at Work (Detert, J. (Nd.)." and Evan Bruno a PhD. candidate in leadership and organizational behavior at the Darden School of Business, "Challenging bosses about strategic moves or operating policies, speaking honestly to peers or subordinates who aren't pulling their weight, making and owning bold decisions — are acts of workplace courage (Bruno, E. & Detert, J. (2021)."

Accountabilities

Accountability is critical at all levels in an organization. Deter and Bruno report, "Teams in which peers hold one another accountable are more likely than others to identify areas of improvement and increase both individual and group effectiveness. And taking on stretch assignments or championing a bold process change can be a significant driver of personal growth and learning for individuals — which, of course, also benefits the organization."

Taking a courageous stand has inherent risks, clearly revealed by the #metoo movement. It is often difficult to demonstrate courage if the workplace culture does not support any of these actions:

- Standing up to authority figures.
- Confronting peers.
- Tackling difficult interactions with stakeholders.
- Sacrificing personal security for the greater good.

Most individuals by nature do not like confrontation. Confrontation takes courage to execute and be able to accept the consequences. Deter and Bruno are quick to point out that courageous behaviors are "likely to be met with some resistance — from above, from peers, or external stakeholders. It stands to reason that people see them as risky and thus don't do them nearly enough, despite their potential value. But even when the target of action is a subordinate, holding that person accountable for undesirable choices and actions is rare because of the courage it requires. As hard as these conversations can be, managers who delay or avoid them inadvertently sacrifice organizational learning and growth. While many courageous behaviors are risky because they can alienate people with economic, organizational, or social power, others largely involve stretching or challenging one's sense of self."

Courage Matters

We need to consider the importance of everyday courage, particularly in times of increasing ambiguity and uncertainty. We need to enable open dialogue without judgment across organizations and society for change and transformation to be successful. Courage transcends obvious organizational leadership and needs to be supported across all activities, upstream, downstream, and cross-stream. Courage to share honest information, feedback, and constructive criticism.

Inflection points

What are the hot buttons that impact the structure and constructs of retooling a business model to thrive in a digital economy? What are the human factors that propel or prevent transformation? Many of these triggers fall into a negative domain but flip the conversation and there are opportunities to address these concerns with new patterns of management and empowerment.

- **Positional power**
- **Personal power**
- **Lack of empathy**
- **Leading with courage**
- **Living with ambiguity**
- **Preparing for the metaverse**

- **Radical thinking**
- **Creating trust**
- **Unintended consequences**
- **Subconscious bias**
- **Management myopia**

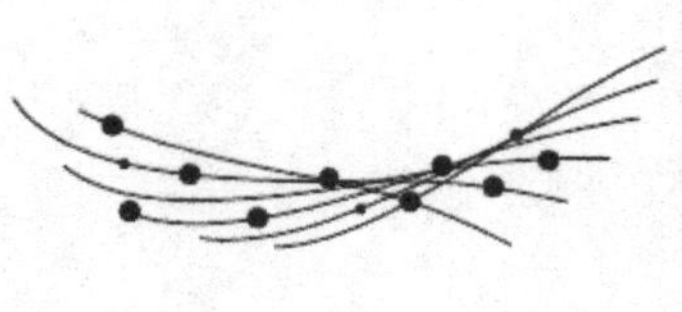

Part Four: Transformation Models

Introduction: Bridging Theory to Practice

The Truth About Transformation is filled with theory, anecdotes, field reports, and a massive amount of insight about the power of the human factor in any organizational journey of change and transformation. The information we have offered is based on real-life, in-the-trenches experience with a range of organizations representing a multitude of industry sectors. What they all have in common, regardless of the size of the operation, is that without an informed and empowered workforce aligned to an objective reality infused with shared purpose and contextually driven market orientation, any ambition to transform, change and pivot is destined to fail. A command-and-control approach is as antiquated as the silo model of an organization. Technology is not a quick cure; it enables possibilities. History and comparison to what others have done have their time and place and serve as potential input, but others' models and strategies should never be the foundation an organization builds for its own change or transformation by adapting to its current or target marketplace.

With that context, the following case studies (anonymous but very real) reveal that legacy mindsets, outdated leadership, operational models, and organizational dysfunction are alive and well. Enjoy learning from others' pain points and take a few moments to leverage what you have read in this book and answer the situational and field report questions in terms of what you might do based on what you have learned. And take these lessons to heart when you look at your own organization clearly in the eye.

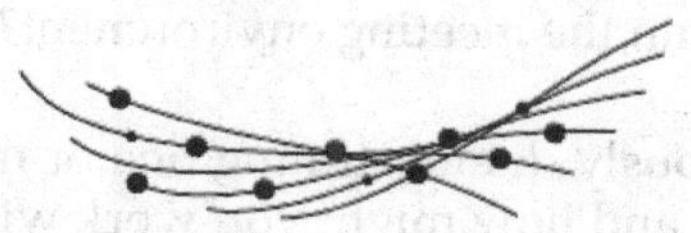

Chapter 37: Operational Breakdown

A small, niche B2B publisher went digital a decade ago. A daily article is transmitted to readers and its website has over 2,000 archived articles, including content from its former print editions. Ahead of its time, the staff works completely remotely, and all are long-time independent contractors. The founder lives in Florida, the editor in New York, the Gen Z social manager splits time between New York and Napa, the graphic designer is in Minnesota, the business development manager is in a suburb north of New York and the tech manager is a nomad, roaming the country experimenting with new places to live.

The team is predominantly female. They meet weekly on Zoom and communicate principally via email throughout the week. Phone calls rarely occur unless there is an immediate issue that needs to be resolved. This field report is about their systemic dysfunction.

Data Analytics

Larry, the tech manager, is self-trained, with a former career as a publisher and stockbroker. He has a task-focused work style, is literal, and over-communicates (likely due to his isolated lifestyle) in meetings and via email. He is a stickler about tech terminology, to the point of interrupting and correcting team members to redefine the terms they are using.

This infuriates the editor, Kate, who sees this as an unnecessary sidetrack that throws up an interruption-based barrier to conversation. The team isn't sure if Larry is attempting to deflect any potential discussion that may cause him to explain his tactics or if his behavior is a positional power play, particularly over the female members of the team. It has escalated to the point at which his interruptions are disruptive and derail meetings.

Critical Thinking Questions

- Is Larry right to repeatedly try to train his co-workers to use correct tech terms within the meeting environment?

- Is he unconsciously demonstrating one or more inherent biases? If so, which ones and how might you work with him to recognize his behavior?

- If Larry is attempting to exert positional power, how would you work with him to resolve such ongoing behavior?

- What tools, techniques, or approaches might the team members use to mitigate or eliminate Larry's disruptive behavior?

Communications

The number of emails among the team has escalated to an exponentially impossible level. Emails are getting lost, unseen, ignored, and deleted by accident. The team continually communicates that they are overwhelmed and fatigued with day-to-day work, and the volume of email only adds to their already-challenged emotional states. Larry has been begging the team to use Slack to track emails transparently as he attempts to solve the immediate problem. But he hasn't considered the potential larger operational and cultural issues within the team with his request.

The only members of the team that use Slack for content posts are the editor and designer, although they continue to use email to exchange requests, images and graphics, and general business information. Full transparency: the founder is 81 years old and tech-challenged.

Critical Thinking Questions

- Is this a familiar situation to you? Your team? Your organization? How effective can the organization be in meeting its shared purpose given the communications environment?

- What communication challenges might the organization be ignoring beyond the number of emails?

- Are there any generational dynamics at play? And if so, what might you do to help the team members?

- Is the organization promoting near-constant multitasking? Ineffective operational processes? Antiquated communications platforms?

- Is the organization functioning well for its size or can it scale with such a small team?

- What are opportunities for change and transformation?

Measuring Success

The business is funded principally by sponsors with comprehensive collaborative partnerships, banner advertising, content, and support of forums and podcasts. Responding to sponsor and partner digital performance reporting demands is becoming more and more critical. Larry uses WordPress data and Google Analytics to track page views and related data. This is a rudimentary practice that is not meeting the needs of sponsors and partners who want more and more detail on reach, the types of individuals reached and where, if at all, conversion is occurring. Sponsor and partner marketing budgets are tight as inflation has continued to chip away at their budgets, so comprehensive performance reports are essential.

Sponsors and partners are raising their voices and criticism louder and louder and threatening to move away from the publisher without more clarity about their investments. Gaining insight into reader engagement at a minimum is their biggest demand, but traditionally the organization has never cared nor focused much on engagement beyond click and anonymous visitor data. Basically, they don't have the analytics expertise (or team member) to deliver the results.

The readers of the organization's content are classified as older C-level executives who often depend on their staff to download and deliver the content directly to them. Of course, for the organization that is only an assumption based on random interaction with a few subscribers' administrative staff. With rudimentary data, the organization really has no way to identify its true audience or its demographic attributes.

The daily article is sent using a basic email marketing platform. This platform also serves as the customer/subscriber database platform, so the team has no clear data-oriented knowledge of individual subscriber behavior. Do they read every article sent?

Do they scan articles? Do they forward them along to others? Do they read other linked content (sponsors) and delve into the organization's archive? And most importantly to sponsors and partners, do the subscribers click or otherwise interact with their advertisements? Do they even read the sponsored content? Are they coming from the organization's website and converting? And if so, who are they?

The sponsors want transparent evidence of subscriber interaction with the content they are underwriting or advertising banners they are paying handsomely for.

The team is stressed because their jobs depend on the continuing revenue. They love the content they produce and care about the audience they serve. Performance-based data has always been nice to have but they really don't focus on it, it is more important to the staff to receive the occasional good job email from a subscriber. And as described, they have no analytics expert.

They know something needs to be done but they don't even know what options they have, particularly when the leadership, majorly tech challenged, isn't even seeking the input they need or willing to invest money into the business. Thoughts of any change or transformation to adapt to meet the sponsor and partner demands result in anxiety and fear. The staff feels an impending sense of doom.

Critical Thinking Questions

- With all they have going on, how would they seek to redefine their roles? Is that even something they should consider? Is it their responsibility to care?

- Is it possible for the organization to move to a data orientation in response to market demands? Can the culture change? If so, what steps might they need to take first?

- What options does the team have if leadership doesn't know or even a desire to lead them forward?

- Does the team need to redefine their own roles?

- Who should they hire and recast other roles and responsibilities?

- If the leader will not invest in the business, what might the team do, if anything?

- Are there any options to immediately meet the sponsor and partner demands and salvage what surely is revenue that is soon to go away?

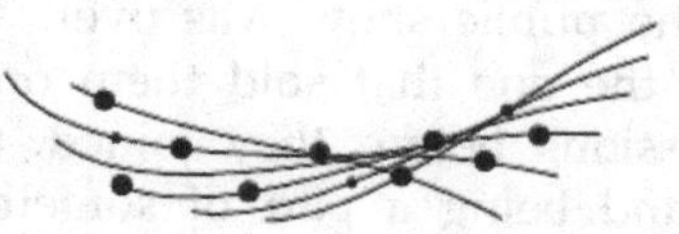

Chapter 38: Cultural Dysfunction

A B2B startup providing innovative business décor solutions online has received two waves of funding totaling $12 million. Although currently private, the company has an investor board that was attracted to the novel premise of the company and stands ready to grow the company as quickly as possible.

The first-time CEO, Hillary is charismatic and was highly successful in getting investors engaged and committed. She has used her attributes to attract a small staff of talented, capable professionals to the company. However, she has no prior experience in managing organizations—or even teams of individuals. She recruited a team of 18 experts across marketing, sales, and creative product development who have well-honed skills, having worked for successful companies with solid leaders. Each manager was enticed by Hillary with the promise of building a business from the ground up. They, too, are excited about the business proposition she has articulated.

The managers anticipated high-stress levels with long days the norm in the startup world. The hope was that Hillary's charisma would translate to her competencies as a leader and manager. Building a business in this way was new to them and they were excited to learn from her. Little did they know they were acting as children following the Pied Piper, and what they imagined their roles would be are very far from the truth.

In the early days, Hillary's lack of leadership and management skills came into focus as the team members sought her direction and/or input as they put their plans together while managing day-to-day operations.

Personality quirks in informal settings also started to emerge. The CEO they were getting to know better remained charismatic when interacting with the board members or potential customers but seemed to turn on a dime into someone else when the public show was over. The team was seeing a different person than the one that sold them on the company in their interviews and discussions before they joined. Still captivated by the promise of learning and being a part of something exciting, the team members started to talk among themselves and decided to continue in hopes of seeing improvement. They rationalize that perhaps Hillary is just overly stressed as she has a lot going on.

Hillary *is* stressed. Her ideas and ability to sell and convince others have now placed an incredible amount of responsibility on her shoulders to bring the company to life and create success. She has always felt she was entrepreneurial but now realizes she doesn't know what she needs to know to lead and operate the company. She also doesn't know how to lead her team or how to trust them to do their jobs. As a result, she is often defensive and operates in her own unstated power structure where she believes that only she knows what to do. Therefore, she micromanages everything and reviews everything the team members put in front of her. Her behavior is creating serious consequences that may prevent the company from meeting the investors' goals. To her team members, Hillary is increasingly seen as sinister because she truly believes she is empathetic and employee-centric. In truth, she is becoming more and more manipulative, driven by her own personal goals, and is largely unaware of her effect on her team.

Subversive Power Manipulation

Team members are forced to respond to her mercurial whims and moods, seeing no other alternative than appeasing her despite often believing that what she has demanded or decided is not useful. Hillary is not only unaware of her behavior but is also oblivious to the psychological and emotional effects she has on her team. She maintains double standards, takes no responsibility, and chastises individual team members for their work without setting any clear expectations. She never deviates from her own narrative, believing herself to be the smartest person in the room and dismisses the advice and recommendations of her experienced staff. Much of this behavior can be attributed to a sense of power position infallibility, never admitting that she could be wrong, being defensive but trying to present a strong front, and hiding behind that power to insulate her from the true reality. The behavior may also be manifesting as she is a highly insecure person.

The team members, as well as the investors, have a stake in ensuring the company's success. The investor board shares a fiduciary responsibility for the company. It is clear to the individual team members that some action must be taken, but they aren't sure who bears the responsibility or whom they should talk to first.

Critical Thinking Questions

- Would you, and if so, how would you, make the investor board aware of the CEO's behavior?

- As a dedicated team member who believes in the promise of the company, how would you work within the CEO's subversive power structure? Are there tactics or approaches that you might use to create awareness and alter the CEO's behavior indirectly?

- If you were on the executive management team, how would you balance protecting your team and managing up to the CEO to protect your own job and those on your team?

- Is this a no-win situation where a single personality will continue to set and influence the organization's culture? If so, can the team members ever be successful?

Market Orientation

The startup, flailing under its compromised leadership, pivoted from B2B to B2C with a new business model to rent home furnishings to any consumer. The ongoing decision-making of the CEO did not yield the results the team members or the investors hoped for. Therefore, given the infrastructure built for a B2B focus, the investors decided a focus on the consumer market may lead to more success. They don't want to give up on the B2B market but recognize additional market analysis is needed before spending more time and money marketing the offering to businesses.

With word spreading about the new innovative rental offering, the CEO is frequently interviewed and shares her passion and vision for a novel way to connect young, impressionable consumers with products they cannot yet afford. The CEO acquiesced to her investors and promises to be more accountable to them. She is considering scaling the business to offer the rental service nationally to designers, real estate developers, and theater and movie set designers, retooling and refocusing her initial B2B focus.

The marketing director on the team has experience in B2B marketing but limited B2C experience. After six months, it has become apparent that the change in focus came with no business strategy. The CEO continues with her behavior and micromanages the small details, constantly ignoring the big picture. The marketing director, despite considerable effort, is not getting the hoped-for results. There have been a few wins in certain regions of the country, but those wins have come because of a hefty spend of the marketing budget. The marketing director is frustrated as the CEO doesn't want to increase the marketing budget and is expecting the marketing director to pull the proverbial rabbit out of a hat. To make matters worse, the CEO in reporting to the board has inflated the revenue value of the few wins the company had to date.

Critical Thinking Questions

- As the company pivots, what information, data, and/or analysis is needed to clearly understand the new market potential?

- Is the new B2C focus a ruse to keep the business alive? Are there fundamental and foundational issues that are preventing any success for the company?

- How would you develop and define the company's shared purpose and true market orientation when the CEO is unable to?

- What business strategy, development, and planning need to occur?

- Does the company have the right workforce to make the pivot to a new business strategy?

- Does the company have the right CEO?

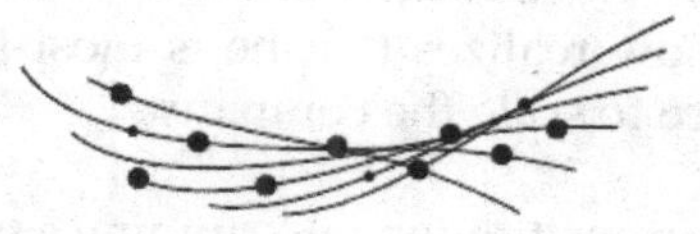

Chapter 39: Sidestepping Accountabilities

A young software technology company went public through a SPAC and overnight was infused with many millions of shareholder dollars. The CEO, Gabriel, co-founded his company 12 years ago and has been running the show alongside his original partners. As a public company, he now reports to a board of directors with direct fiduciary responsibility under regulatory oversight. Gabriel fired the chief revenue officer for criticizing the executive team in front of employees, among other reasons. Unhappy, the ex-sales director wrote a vengeful letter to the independent board members outlining a series of activities that he deemed negligent on the part of the CEO and executive management. The board had no choice but to open an internal investigation and retained a prestigious law firm (think, Mueller Investigation) to conduct it. Seven months and over $1.2 million in legal fees later, the executive management team was completely exonerated. The board, however, identified a hostile work culture that needed some immediate remediation, requiring that the CEO get some leadership coaching. It also put in place some additional board oversight and "guardrail" mechanisms to ensure that executive management brings about genuine workplace cultural change.

A Board Culture

Gabriel is experiencing growing pains adjusting to running a public company and being accountable to the board. He and his executive team have benefited from the infusion of over $60m and are now under pressure to execute his personal vision and the company's business plan. Gabriel is also chairman of the board. He only answered to himself and his partners before going public, now he is finding it anxiety-producing when the board routinely questions his judgment and actions.

Each of the board members is an established and highly qualified businessperson, and Gabriel knows there is much he can learn from them. Yet their routine questioning and advice have put him at times on the defensive. It's true that he launched and grew the business over the first dozen years, but he now realizes that he is most likely at the limit of his abilities and experience to scale the company.

Gabriel is conflicted in transitioning into running a public company. He only knows how to be the leader and owner of a private company. Above all, he is accustomed to making all the key decisions, and now, reporting to a board, he doesn't have the same control or financial purview that he once did. Stockholders, as partial owners of the company, share in its profit and loss. However, they often have little, if any, say in the business decisions of the company and they have no control over the everyday operations. Instead, it is the company's board of directors and not the CEO, that is charged with the decision-making responsibility and operational control.

Gabriel knows he must adapt his behavior. He also has to accept that he must meet objective goals, achieve agreed-upon outcomes, and follow established protocols, as stated by the board.

Having been the CEO of a private company all these years has led to Gabriel developing a strong ego and a quick temper. He believes that he has been able to manage his reactive behaviors with his team, but he is finding that he regresses when interacting with individual board members and the entire board. The pressures of strict GAAP financial accounting and legal oversight, brought on by his decision to fire the sales director, are only adding to his stress and defensive posturing with the board.

Critical Thinking Questions

- As a board director, how would you coach the CEO to adhere to established protocols and respect accountabilities without making him feel restrained or disempowered? What other advice could help the CEO?

- As one of Gabriel's direct reports, how would you encourage the CEO to practice self-evaluation to improve his work style and actively manage his default behaviors? Also, how do you help the CEO navigate his new role for the sake of the company's continued growth?

- How would you help the company adjust to its new shareholder accountability structure enabling it to meet the realistic annual growth goals it now must set?

- What does the company need to do to make Gabriel understand that he no longer runs the company by himself; he now reports to the board?

- As the company is going through change and transformation, what should the company consider and do to ensure success?

Advise and Dissent

In the ex-sales director's letter to the non-executive board members, he cited the CEO's intolerance for opinions and positions that run counter to his positions. Employees who disagreed were sidelined, fired, or voluntarily resigned. The board members, in their initial interactions with Gabriel, perceived a strong and competent leader. Yes, everyone has their faults, and running one's own business surely creates some strong personality traits. Savvy leaders, however, become self-aware of their own faults and actively keep them in check.

The phrase Gabriel used most often to describe problem employees was "You're not in alignment." This company-culture phase was often used to justify silencing any dissent from team members around the table. Morale at the company was already running low before the ex-sales director was fired and further eroded after his termination. Gabriel would catch chatter from time to time about the workplace culture and morale but would quickly dismiss it as not deserving any more thought. The staff (mostly engineers and sales development teams) were getting paid handsomely and needed to focus on the work to scale up the company. Gabriel didn't believe they needed to feel happy, and he didn't believe he bore any responsibility for making them happy.

The structure he created is typical for entrepreneurial owners: work hard, limit distractions and be totally committed ("aligned," as he puts it). He was convinced he knew best and controlling the company and its staff was his sole responsibility. The law firm conducting the review at the behest of the board interviewed 30 staff members across different departments, some of whom were Gabriel's direct reports and others with a direct or indirect role in the business development group. Across the interviews (and including key customers), the law firm heard the same criticisms of Gabriel over and over again.

According to the report from the law firm to the board, the CEO continues to be oblivious to the culture he is reinforcing. Although the report included only a handful of examples, the board in their private discussions found the report correlated to what they were seeing in their own interactions with Gabriel. He maintained a command-and-control structure over staff to ensure he was always the main idea- and decision-maker.

The board was seriously concerned that Gabriel fired the sales director without checking first with the board, as stipulated in the employment contract. He only informed the board after the fact with the lead general counsel assuring the board it was according to contractual protocols. However, the lead counsel resigned when the investigation started, implicitly stating some level of guilt.

The report also indicated that Gabriel intentionally did not adhere to the contract because he thought the board would veto the firing. The board is now questioning Gabriel's ethics. Since each board member has a fiduciary responsibility and can be held accountable, the members need to consider their own options. At this point, they do not want to fire Gabriel and replace him. He was the inventor of the tech solution and is the intellectual capital of the company. They decided to defer replacing him to avoid any negative press or nervousness from investors, particularly since the company is on the verge of closing a big deal. They have decided to put a list of recommendations to present to Gabriel and invest in him in the hopes they can help and coach him to become a better leader.

Critical Thinking Questions

- As a board director, what are your personal options? What known and underlying problems or issues need to be addressed to protect against any investor lawsuits?

- How would you present the list of recommendations to the CEO?

- Would you remove the CEO as executive chair of the board?

- Would you claw back any of Gabriel's annual bonus, which has not yet been approved by the board?
- How would you create a succession plan?

- How would you help create a culture that is non-toxic, open, and supportive of diverse opinions?

- How would you write the employee handbook to establish clear procedures and protocols? What would you write and codify in organizational policy and procedures, position descriptions, or team structures to ensure a healthy workplace culture?

- Are there other options that you could promote that facilitate the organization through this time of change and transition?

- How do you ensure a workplace that is open to constructive and critical thinking and dialog?

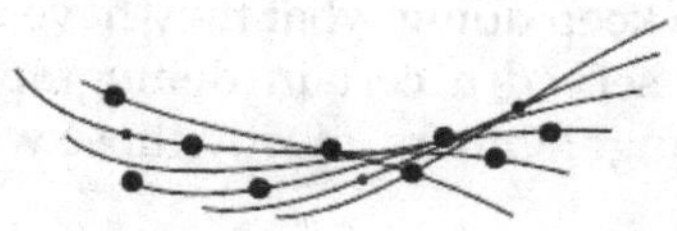

Chapter 40: Legacy Traps

A professional association has had a long successful history in serving its industry sector. Like many associations, the organization grew from a time when professionals and like-minded people with similar interests sought a way to come together in person to share a mutual set of challenges and solutions. Technology and the ability to extend an individual's reach didn't exist beyond printed magazines, journals, and a yearly conference.

The changes in its industry have been monumental based on new technologies, changes in professional roles, and educational requirements. The association has been challenged to match these technological advances in the field with relevant member benefits. The industry, like so many other industries, was required to transform enabled by technology to create efficiencies, new capabilities, and quicker ways to meet market demand. The association knows this and is playing catch-up to try to stay one step ahead of the needs of its members.

The association serves an industry sector that is also suffering from the fact that younger individuals do not see roles in this sector as attractive and lucrative career choices. The industry continues to be historically perceived as male-dominated, with prowess in mechanical solutions based on gut instinct decision-making. The parents of young students aren't helping. They want their children to seek high-level careers where their hands don't get dirty in old-fashioned work. The parents are seeking the value of an investment in college education in lucrative careers for their children. The companies in the sector are far too caught up in day-to-day management and trying to stay competitive. They have done little to attract young tech-savvy workers. Neither the companies nor the association has done much of anything to change the public's perception.

The association is apprehensive about spending money and effort to engage the public as they have no personal experience in branding or marketing. Internally, the staff disagrees on the actual problem to be solved. Some believe they just need to keep doing what they have always been doing; the association has always served a certain demographic with services and information, so why change? Others, mostly those who are data-driven, see the writing on the wall.

Alan, the CEO, is nearing retirement age and doesn't see the need to rock the boat. He'll leave the challenges to the next CEO to solve. He chooses not to go out on a note of potential failure and the criticism that would result. After all, the association isn't going to sink in just several months. Alan will just keep telling the board, and staff, what they want to hear. That will satisfy them for now.

The association's membership is shrinking faster than ever; the majority that remains are veterans in the field whom themselves are nearing retirement. The industry needs young, tech-savvy professionals to ensure the future of the sector and the association needs those younger professionals to stabilize and grow its membership. Without a significant number of diverse members, the association won't have the authority or credibility to represent or advocate for the profession. More to the point, they will not be able to command high dollars from industry companies for their educational products.

The data-driven staff members struggle with what they can do to get the CEO and their peers to see what is really going on. Why does Alan seemingly not care or share their concerns? How does the association stay on top of members' needs and attract a vital new generation of professionals? It continues to conduct an annual member survey, but the results don't provide enough insight as respondents are the core members who are in the late stages of their careers. However, the survey is an ingrained tool in decision-making and is interpreted as confirmatory to continue doing what has always been done. Only the high-level survey results are shared with the board, and leadership doesn't dig deeper into the findings to reveal possible solutions.

The association's board is comprised of mid-level practitioners who have never run an organization themselves as CEOs. The board historically has leaned on and relied on the association's CEO for needed insight and direction. They have significant technical knowledge gaps as they haven't integrated technology into their personal or professional lives unless they have been forced to do so.

Plus, they would rather not see the industry and companies they work for change any more than they need to. They believe that change is stressful, and that technology never works the way it's supposed to. Also, none of the current board members have experience in strategic planning. As a result, their decision-making strength is compromised and once again, reliant upon the CEO to tell them what they need to decide and do.

Critical Thinking Questions

- The association may be at a precipice. How would you help them determine how to change and transform? What do they need to do?

- How can you change the mindset of the CEO and help the board better understand what they need to know to determine the appropriate shared purpose?

- Context analysis would help. What are the factors and variables the association needs to understand?

- Has the association determined how its system, and therefore, its offerings align to Meso, Macro, and Micro viewpoints?

- As the board chair, would you suggest changing the composition of the board to bring on new expertise? How is that possible without upsetting the current board?

- How would you help the board exercise their critical thinking and active listening skills to move beyond their own biases?

- Can the association change the definition of its role as a convenor and value provider? Should it? If so, what is it currently not understanding?

- How would you bring the board up to date on technology and help them determine what the technology might afford the association in reaching the younger professionals with value?

Resistance to Change

The board recognizes the necessity to change and transform to meet the current and future needs of the individuals and industries they serve. They feel a palpable sense of urgency.

But they don't know where to start and believe that transformation is purely a simple technology fix (even though they are suspicious of technology in general). They think if only they could select and implement some silver-bullet technology platforms, their problems would be solved. With the wave of a magic tech wand, they would be able to reach the younger professionals, amp up member benefits and update the association's image—all at the same time. They would become relevant.

Alan recently hired a new Gen Z analyst to help close the association's technology gap. He did this partly in response to renegade managers who have been talking to board members independently, complaining about his lack of progressive leadership and knowledge. The rest of the team's reluctance to adapt has created roadblocks to change, believing that their decades of legacy industry knowledge transcend data and analytics. They pay lip service to change and are not themselves change agents.

Critical Thinking Questions

- How does the CEO change the workplace culture to introduce innovation? How does he sell new ideas to a team stuck in the past?

- How does the CEO empower his new data analyst and prevent the staff from roadblocking her new approaches and processes?

- How would you control managers who go to the board directly?

- How would you bring in new managers without losing critical institutional knowledge?

Inherent Bias

The biggest headache for the CEO is the manager who controls the CEU division. She is convinced she is the only person in the association with in-depth knowledge of the industry sector and as a result, holds other managers hostage to her opinions. She withholds information and controls the association's conference content, bypassing other members of the team. She also misses deadlines delivering content for the association's newsletter. Further, she makes it clear that she knows she is essential and continues to operate independently.

She has become a divisive influence on the management team, forcing them to adapt to her willful opinions and behavior. She has taken positional power to a new level by establishing her own rules for communications, shared knowledge, and perceptions of members' needs.

She uses gut instinct to make important decisions and resists insights revealed through data and analytics. She feels no need to change her tactics, no reason to change her demands on others or tolerate collaborative decision-making. She has been around a long time and to date, no one, not even the CEO or the board, has ever challenged her—or counseled her for that matter.

Critical Thinking Questions

- How would you deal with workplace disruptions caused by this one individual?

- How do you retain an expert with essential industry knowledge without her negatively impacting other members of the team?

- How would you create a system to protect institutional knowledge, so it is not dependent on just a few people?

- How would you help the CEU director to embrace data and analytics?

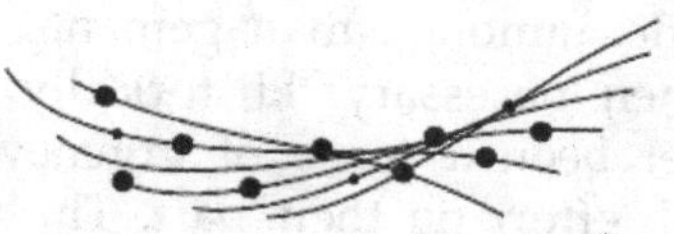

Chapter 41: Digital Transformation

The board of a professional association realizes that internal processes are woefully outdated, and the management team does not have enough objective-based information to plan for the future. Most of the managers have been with the organization for 20+ years and each department works within its own silo, further entrenching how work has always been accomplished, regardless of recognized failures and challenges in delivering timely customer service. Membership does not interface with marketing, there is no touch-point tracking of how members have engaged with the organization, the content team gets no input from member feedback—and none of the antiquated digital systems can communicate with each other. The organization has no real insight into how its value proposition accords with what its audience needs and wants.

The board wants an overhaul, starting with making the products and services it offers to members more valuable and contextually relevant. The board believes this shift will stabilize and grow the organization's credible presence to the professionals it represents and serves.

Membership revenues have continuously fallen over the past five years, and no one in management can explain why, other than simple guesswork. Conference attendance, pre-Covid, was already declining and impacted what exhibitors and sponsors were willing to pay to gain access to fewer attendees. Educational and publication product sales have also declined. If this continues, the organization will soon be existing only by tapping into its financial reserves.

Everyone on the management team is under pressure to reboot the association to be relevant and meaningful and transform itself to be competitive in a digital marketplace. But they don't know how to transform and change; they only know how to do what they have always done in the ways they have always done them.

Introducing Change

The prevailing attitude among management has been to make improvements only when necessary. Historically, based on their long tenures, there has never been a sense of urgency as situations always improved without much effort on their part. The recent shift in the 20-member board composition includes five new millennials, resulting in new noise and pressure. The management team is becoming increasingly concerned that this younger group's voice is going to become harder and harder to ignore. The board has made several recent decisions, including micromanaging staff hires which is out of the operational governance norm, but the CEO had to accede and support their involvement and ultimate choice of new hires.

One of the board-selected hires is a millennial manager named Gavin. He has just joined the team and the millennials on the board are in near-constant communication with Gavin to inform and direct him on how to change how the association operates. This confuses and annoys Gavin as he is not sure who is his boss. The CEO is planning to give Gavin a wider berth to protect him from having to contend with the board.

Gavin studied organizational culture and philosophy, as well as for analytics and data management. He is enthusiastic, well-trained, and impatient in implementing new systems to bring the association into the 21st century. He is light years ahead of the management team, speaks a different language infused with tech, and has a firm grasp of the power of data and analytics.

The management team, seeking to maintain their power positions and protect their territories, is becoming increasingly stressed as they aren't comfortable in a group or one-on-one with Gavin. They aren't sure how to block and tackle as they simply don't understand most of what Gavin bringing to the table.

Gavin has started to speak up more and more at management meetings about digital transformation and how new systems can immediately improve operations.

He has drafted a plan and is recommending that the association take $5 million immediately from the reserves to initiate it, procure new systems, then implement them. The management team has always attempted to stay above the operational fray and let their staff deal with and worry about day-to-day execution. The operational process problems Gavin keeps surfacing are foreign to them, so they cannot contribute or respond without the potential of embarrassing themselves. The group has never needed to talk about anything at this level of detail and depth.

Critical Thinking Questions

- What is your advice for Gavin in terms of introducing new ideas to a veteran team?

- How do you help people recognize what they don't know and understand what they don't know they don't know could be the lynchpin to transformation?

- How would Gavin best manage to transform the organization with digital strategies?

- How do you most effectively educate an analog mentality to understand and accept the benefits of a digital operational structure?

- How do you make people less anxious about change and what they may lose in the process?

Short-term Thinking

The board has asked for a comprehensive strategic plan that will provide a roadmap to digital transformation. The first draft of the plan (pre-Gavin) focused on short-term gains, majorly representing the replacement of existing technology systems and the implementation of several new systems. The plan included assumptions of how operations will improve and where efficiencies will be gained.

Gavin initially reviewed the plan and shared that there is a high potential to reduce the number of staff in certain departments as the new systems will automate many processes that are currently manual. However, the plan presented to the board doesn't speak to the long-term future or provide context as to how the parts of the plan contribute to long-term sustainability, relevance, and growth.

The board directs Gavin to help revise the original plan and work with staff across the organization to determine how to strengthen the long-term future of the association. Gavin is excited about the challenge but daunted by the fact that he is going to have to educate the management team and their staff and then work with each of them if he is going to put teeth into his plan. He needs to demonstrate, beyond the hype, real P/L estimates for stabilized and gained revenue, now and into the near (three-year) future.

The management team provides Gavin with a list of staff to work with and he finds the workers open to potential change — or at least that is what they are communicating to him in one-on-one discussions and group meetings. He tasks each department team to compile financial estimates of the new improvements, and within a couple of weeks, they present their findings. Given his data and analytics education, Gavin conducts a topline analysis of what they have provided, but he is not a finance guy and decides to take what they have provided him at face value. After all, they will have to own the revenue outcomes, not him.

Gavin develops the new plan reflecting the possible outcomes provided by the team. In the back of his mind, he worries he should have reviewed prior reports from previous years, but he is always in a hurry and quickly wipes those thoughts away. He plans to call on the staff representatives during the board meeting to field any questions. With one board meeting under his belt, Gavin feels he has a fairly good idea of how the revised presentation will go.

Gavin starts his presentation to the board, and with each section of the technology-focused roadmap, he brings forward the estimates the staff has provided. He notices some board members are raising their eyebrows or leaning over and talking among themselves. He also sees a few notes being passed to the non-executive board chair. The chair abruptly stops Gavin and opens the floor for questions. Immediately several hands go up.

The board members begin questioning the outcomes that Gavin has communicated. As the questions unfold, staff around the room begin squirming. Some board members raise previous reports they have received over the past few years. As the new plan details increases in membership and product sales and even projections to increase attendance at events based on marketing automation, it seems far out of line with the addressable market size available to the association.

It soon becomes clear that the Education Department frontloaded all their estimated gains. Membership looked at increasing their numbers with a wish list of programs that were not formulated for career-long membership. The Conference Department estimated projections by simply adding 20% gains on top of current performance without any connection to the market or how they would produce the increase.

The presentation became contentious, and the board dismissed the staff, including the CEO. They don't want to further discuss the issues publicly, as they bear responsibility for hiring Gavin. It appears to them that Gavin over-represented his knowledge and abilities to assess and develop plans for digital transformation holistically that are realistic and relevant. However, it is also possible that management and staff are seeking to sabotage Gavin, put the board back into its box, and get their hands out of hiring and operational decision-making.

The board has a very direct and frank discussion focused on their next steps. They have responsibility for the continued viability and relevance of the organization. They suspect sabotage in the numbers presented in the plan and question if the staff doesn't have the will to change, can Gavin be successful. What else can they do to address the current crisis? Two of the board members start to review the organization's bylaws to see what options they may have. They conclude that they must act quickly and substantively.

Critical Thinking Questions

- If you were on the board, what would you do? How can the board act, within their defined governance roles, to address the crisis?

- Would you replace the entire management team with those who have a better understanding of technology and its enabling potential?

- How would you ensure the strategic plan has diverse voices and inclusive input and represents realistic goals and outcomes?

- How would you research and create a long-term vision for an association that encapsulates technology enabling the association's aspirations for increased relevance and growth?

- What KPIs and outcomes for success would you establish for creating a viable long-term plan?

- How would you seek to instill support and enthusiasm in the management team and staff to change and transform?

- How would you help management and staff understand how they can transition?

- How would you create opportunities for all departments to work together in inter-connected systems under a shared purpose?

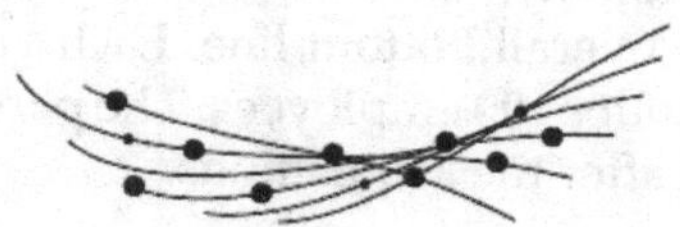

Chapter 42: Data-Driven Decision-Making

A large educational publishing company has been respectably successful over its 50- year history. For the first 40 years, the company was family-owned and decided in 2010 to go public. In the transition to public ownership, the diversity of experience across the board was expanded to include representatives who ran large, publicly traded companies to complement those members who are experienced in the publishing market.

For the past several years, the board and management have been seeking a way to transform in response to the industry shift to open-access publishing. For most of its history, the company's print products sold well and generated a solid level of ongoing revenue through reprints and copyright royalties. As physical books became less and less in demand, revenue has been decreasing.

The company currently manages a long list of digital platforms offering niche content. These digital platforms have historically produced substantial recurring revenue for the company, but since open access has become more and more respected, revenues have been declining. Without real clarity as to how to transform its existing print and digital products to continue to grow, the company decides growth via mergers and acquisitions is the way to go for the time being. The immediate increases in revenue resulting from the M/A activity will please investors and give the board and management more time to determine how to transform the business.

Based on the new M/A strategy, the company acquired four smaller companies, each highly specialized in delivering digital-based content and services.

Each of the acquisitions was a startup formed in the early 2000s and has tightly knit collegial cultures. Their solid performance and growth were what interested the company, and the board knew the results would immediately impact the overall bottom line. Each varies in the scale of its business, and each has under 100 employees. The parent has 800 employees, with 300 of those added after the acquisitions.

Little attention was paid to how the four acquisitions would be integrated into the overall company. The company was already underway with several large system replacements and any inclusion or integration with the four would elongate timelines and significantly increase costs. So, the board and management decided to delay formal integration and simply assign a company executive to oversee and guide the four acquisitions independently.

The board knew little about the cultural challenges that were emerging daily in the company, nor were they aware of the number of fractured and unconnected technological systems that existed and the cost to maintain them. Management continued to provide the board with regular reports that represented (or so they thought) performance data across the organization. Management spent considerable time manually compiling reports and checking data as the systems and the data within the systems were unreliable. Much of the operational expense for technology maintenance was hidden in budget line items and the personnel costs, attributed to manual manipulation of data and reports, were not measured or compensated.

To maximize sales and ensure the market remained pleased with the quarterly financial results, the board and CEO implemented new individual incentive plans and established metrics to maximize staff performance. Each employee was assigned a yearly bonus based on a percentage of salary and overall company performance.

Critical Thinking Questions

- Is a M/A strategy the best way to drive revenue growth?

- What are the considerations in startup acquisitions that ensure a frictionless process of integrating new companies onto a larger organization?

- How does a startup operation mentality meld into a performance-based organization?

- Would you place the CEOs of the acquisitions on the board?

- What needs to be implemented to transition manual reports to a more efficient system?

- Is the new incentive plan fair? Does it represent a shared purpose organizational model?

The Transformation Journey

Satisfied that financial performance would improve through the acquisitions and employee incentives, the board and management returned their attention to determining how to strategically transform the business in response to open access and the threat it presented to existing business lines. Traditionally operated as a B2B company, transformation included the need to focus on how to create expertise in managing, curating, and engaging a B2C audience. In open access, authors and creators are often individuals, not always representing an organization or business. B2C was unfamiliar territory and a significant challenge to contend with.

During the next quarterly board meeting, the non-executive board chair brought in a consultant to talk about the success data-driven organizations were experiencing, despite the market tumult. Technology enables businesses to change how they do business and continues to alter individuals and change how they seek, access, and interact with content, including educational-focused content.

The consultant's presentation was filled with hype and tons of buzzwords, which resulted in great excitement across the board with the promise of becoming a truly data-driven company. The focus would help it solve its near and future problems and challenges.

At the end of the meeting, the board moved into a non-executive session and invited the CEO to stay for the discussion. The board had already decided privately on a path to solve its problems and challenges and presented its decision to the CEO. By becoming a data-driven organization, the company would have the real-time insights it needs to determine where it is having success and how it can better apply its resources to maximize success. It would also have concrete insight into areas to divest and how to free up budget and resources to focus on innovations that were needed to adapt to open access and continue solid market performance.

The company subsequently reorganized with new internal teams reporting to the CEO. Some of the management teams were completely reassigned to focus on the project and relinquish their previous day-to-day responsibilities.

The teams worked diligently and enthusiastically to put together strategies and plans that would hopefully meet the board's goal of becoming a data-driven organization. The CEO felt the proposed strategies were appropriate, and after being approved by the board, it was time to socialize the plans across all divisions in the company.

The teams were excited about their work and eagerly began holding meetings with employees in each division. Once they presented the strategies, those attending started to ask questions. Many questions. The more questions that came, the more roadblocks came to light. Executives were concerned about the impact of the effort on the existing business lines and how the effort would distract staff from achieving their performance goals. Management and staff, regardless of the business line, took duck-and-cover positions as they didn't want any extra work since they were already contending with significant technology and process onboarding challenges. Others, never having worked outside their division before, didn't see the need to change or how it would help improve their own performance.

Deflated, the teams went back to the drawing board to think about how to get each area aligned. They decided to compile a list of priorities and activities and then have the members of the different divisions rank them in order of importance. The teams felt if each division contributed and felt their voices were heard, it would result in overall buy-in.

The ranking exercise was done twice, the first on a large set of initiatives and strategies, the second on a smaller list refined from the first ranking exercise. In subsequent meetings, the divisions continued to put forward more and more roadblocks. The pressure increased on the teams to get buy-in on the revised strategies and goals while recognizing the necessity for the divisions to achieve their own performance goals. The divisions continued to push back on the teams as the revenue goals alone were stress-inducing; there simply did not appear to be enough possibilities in the market to achieve the sales targets while also becoming a data-driven company.

As the realization came that the plan to become data-driven came at the same time as achieving increased sales targets that were limited by market constraints, the workforce became more and more stressed. Their personal bonuses were riding on achieving the increased goals: they saw family vacations canceled, new cars left on the lot, and contributions to the kids' college funds interrupted. They rebelled against the data-driven project and believed if they just continued to put up roadblocks, it would surely go away soon. The focus would then be maintained on achieving the sales goals and getting the big personal bonus.

Critical Thinking Questions

- If you were the CEO of the company, how would you handle the situation?

- How do you effectively introduce new ideas?

- How would you defuse the personal reactions across the workforce?

- What are the fundamental challenges that must be addressed first before introducing a data-driven model?

- What faulty premises may have been present in the board's and management's decision-making?

- Should organizational culture be ignored or respected? What steps would you take to improve the culture and have the workforce be recognized in the context of decision-making?

- What organizational elements are interdependent in moving to a data-driven organization?

- How do you know if a consultant's presentation is hype or realistic?

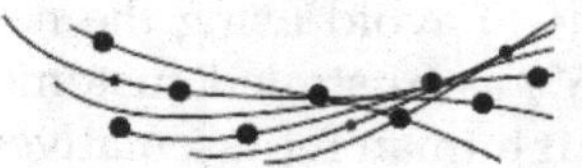

Chapter 43: The AI Implementation Disaster

A mid-sized insurance company with 800 employees decided to implement AI-powered chatbots and automated claims processing to reduce costs and improve customer response times. The C-suite, excited by vendor demonstrations, fast-tracked the implementation without involving any frontline claims adjusters, customer service representatives, or IT staff in the planning process.

The leadership team assumed the technology would simply replace repetitive tasks and that employees would naturally adapt, thereby liberating employees to focus on more meaningful work. They allocated $2.5 million to the project and set an aggressive six-month implementation timeline. The vendor promised a 40% reduction in processing time and 30% cost savings.

The Breakdown

Three months into the implementation, serious problems emerged. The AI system was trained on historical data that reflected the company's outdated claims processes and embedded undetected biases in decision-making. Claims adjusters discovered the AI was rejecting legitimate claims that fell outside narrow parameters, forcing manual overrides in 60% of cases — more work than before.

Customer service representatives found the chatbot couldn't handle nuanced questions and was directing customers to call the already overwhelmed customer service reps. The IT team, brought in too late, discovered the AI system couldn't integrate with the company's legacy database systems and required expensive custom development.

Employee morale plummeted. The claims department felt disrespected and feared job loss. Several experienced adjusters resigned, taking decades of institutional knowledge with them. The remaining staff became increasingly resistant, finding workarounds to avoid using the new system. Customer satisfaction scores dropped 25% as frustrated customers encountered both unhelpful bots and stressed-out human representatives.

Nonetheless, the leadership team doubled down (motivated by saving face), insisting employees just needed more training. They hired the tech vendor to conduct additional workshops, but attendance was poor and participants were openly hostile. Six months in, the company had spent $3.2 million with no measurable improvements—and new problems emerging daily.

Critical Thinking Questions

- How could the organization have better assessed whether AI was the right solution for their actual problems versus perceived problems?

- What fundamental mistakes did leadership make in their approach to technology adoption?

- How did the organization's failure to include diverse voices in planning contribute to the disaster?

- What role did confirmation bias play in leadership's continued investment despite clear failure signals?

- How would you have structured a pilot program to test AI implementation before full rollout?

- What steps would you take now to rebuild trust with employees and customers?

- What does this case reveal about the relationship between technology and the human factor in transformation?

- How would you redesign the implementation to honor both technological capability and human expertise?

Chapter 44: The Merger That Never Merged

Here's a fictional story, but one that is immediately relatable. Two regional healthcare systems, River Health (12 hospitals, urban-focused) and Stream Health Network (8 hospitals, rural-focused), announced a merger to create efficiencies, expand services, and better compete with national chains. On paper, the merger made perfect sense: complementary geographic coverage, minimal overlap, and combined purchasing power.

The boards of both organizations approved the merger enthusiastically. River Health's CEO, Sandra, a data-driven administrator with an MBA, was named CEO of the combined entity. Stream Health Network's CEO, Tom, a physician who had worked his way up through clinical ranks, was named Chief Medical Officer — technically a lateral move but one he perceived as a demotion.

Cultural Collision

The problems started immediately. River Health was built on technology, electronic health records, centralized decision-making, and metrics-driven performance management. Stream Health Network operated with decentralized authority, strong physician autonomy, and relationship-based decision-making that valued long-standing community connections.

Sandra immediately announced a standardization initiative: all facilities would adopt River Health's EHR system, supply chain processes, and performance metrics within 12 months. She believed standardization was essential for cost savings and quality improvements. The business case was sound, supported by a consulting firm analysis showing $45 million in annual savings.

Stream Health Network physicians and administrators were outraged. Their EHR system, while older, was customized to rural healthcare workflows. The standardized supply chain meant they'd lose relationships with local vendors who had provided flexibility during shortages. The performance metrics were designed for urban patient populations and didn't account for rural healthcare challenges, including transportation barriers and limited specialist access.

The Resistance

Rather than openly opposing the changes, Stream Health Network leaders engaged in passive resistance. They agreed to timelines in meetings but found endless reasons for delays. They attended training sessions but didn't implement new processes. They provided data when requested but framed it to reveal problems rather than solutions.

Three respected Stream Health Network physicians resigned, publicly citing "loss of clinical autonomy" and "corporate medicine priorities over patient care." Local media covered the story, and local business media began expressing concerns about the merger. Some patients started seeking care at competing facilities. With her academic training, Sandra viewed the resistance as predictable change management challenges that would resolve with time and persistence. Tom, caught between two worlds, tried to mediate with his team but was increasingly seen as having sold out by former Stream Health Network colleagues.

Eighteen months post-merger, the promised synergies hadn't materialized. Staff turnover at former Stream Health Network facilities reached 40%. Patient satisfaction scores were declining, and worse, the new board was questioning whether the merger was a mistake.

Critical Thinking Questions

- What cultural assessment should have occurred before the merger was finalized?

- How did Sandra's strengths as a data-driven leader become weaknesses in this context?

- What role did organizational identity and pride play in the resistance?

- How would you have structured the integration differently to honor both organizations' strengths?

- What decision-making process should have been used for standardization decisions?

- If you were Tom, how would you navigate your position between two cultures?

- How do you balance the need for operational efficiency with respect for localized expertise and relationships?

- What mechanisms could create shared purpose across two organizations with different histories and values?

- What early warning signs did leadership miss or dismiss?

Chapter 45: The Sustainability Pivot Breakdown

A 75-year-old manufacturing company producing industrial plastics announced a bold transformation to become a leader in sustainable materials. The CEO, motivated by both environmental concerns and market analysis showing growing demand for eco-friendly products, committed to transitioning 80% of production to bio-based and recycled materials within five years. The announcement generated positive press coverage and boosted stock prices. The board applauded the vision and influential customers expressed interest in sustainable alternatives. The company hired a Chief Sustainability Officer, expanded the R&D team, and began renovating facilities.

The Reality Gap

What the CEO didn't fully communicate — or perhaps understand — was that the transformation required fundamentally rethinking the entire business model and supply chain, not just swapping materials. The engineering team discovered that bio-based materials required different manufacturing processes, new equipment, and extensive testing. The existing workforce had deep expertise in traditional plastics but limited knowledge of sustainable alternatives.

The sales team faced a critical challenge: sustainable materials cost 40-60% more to produce. While some premium customers were willing to pay more, the company's largest customers — price-sensitive manufacturers — were not. The sales team, compensated on revenue, continued focusing on existing customer relationships and traditional products to meet their targets.

The R&D team made progress developing sustainable alternatives, but quality issues emerged. The new materials didn't perform identically to traditional plastics in many applications. Some early adopter customers experienced product failures, damaging the company's reputation for reliability.

The Chief Sustainability Officer, hired from a consulting background, created impressive reports and frameworks but struggled to translate a sustainable vision into operational reality that satisfied all stakeholders. She focused on obtaining sustainability certifications and marketing the company's mission statement while the engineering and production teams were stuck wrestled with daily practical challenges.

The Fracture

Within two years, the organization had effectively split into two camps: the "sustainability champions" led by the CSO and supported by marketing; and the "production realists" led by operations and sales who argued that the proposed transformation was happening too fast without adequate R&D and field testing. The production team felt pressured to meet unrealistic timelines risking quality and safety. The sales team resented being unable to sell what they were experts in, while being expected to sell higher-priced alternatives that weren't fully tested. The sustainability team felt the resistance was just old-school thinking and an unwillingness to change.

The CEO, frustrated by the lack of progress, increased the pressure and replaced several department heads. This only created more fear and resistance. Employee engagement scores dropped significantly. Some customers began to turn to alternative suppliers. Three years in, the company had achieved only 15% conversion to sustainable materials, well behind the plan's timeline. Financial performance had declined due to high R&D costs, production inefficiencies, and customer losses. The board was losing confidence in the transformation strategy.

Critical Thinking Questions

- What was the fundamental flaw in how the transformation was conceived and communicated?

- How did the company confuse aspirational vision with operational readiness?

- What stakeholder analysis should have occurred before making public commitments?

- How would you have structured a realistic timeline that balanced ambition with operational capability?

- What role did siloed decision-making play in the failures?

- How should the sales compensation and performance management systems have been redesigned to support the transformation?

- What pilot programs could have tested the transformation approach before full commitment?

- How do you balance the need for bold vision with practical implementation realities?

- What mechanisms would you create to ensure honest feedback reaches leadership without fear of retribution?

- If you were brought in as a consultant now, what would you recommend?

Critical Thinking Questions

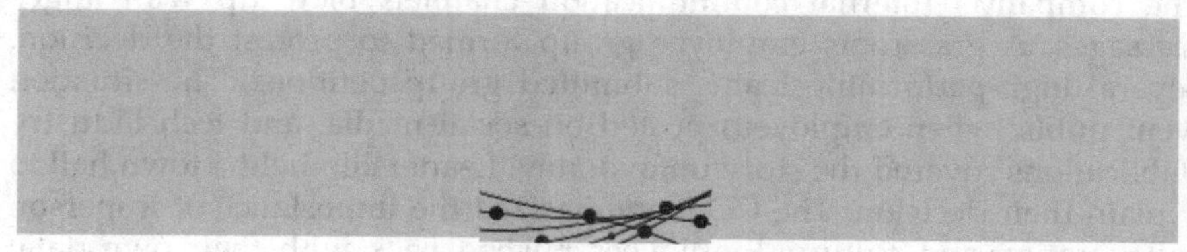

Chapter 46: The Remote Work Reversal

A technology services company with 2,500 employees successfully operated remotely during the pandemic. Productivity metrics improved, employee satisfaction reached all-time highs, and the company saved $8 million annually by reducing office space. Post-pandemic, leadership publicly celebrated becoming a "remote-first" company and used it as a recruitment advantage, attracting talent from across the country.

Two years later a new Chief Operating Officer joined from a traditional office-centric company. Within three months, he convinced the CEO and board that remote work was hindering innovation, weakening the culture, and making it difficult to mentor junior employees. He presented data showing that newly hired employees had longer onboarding times and cross-departmental collaboration had declined.

Based on the data, the leadership team announced a return-to-office mandate: All employees within 50 miles of an office location must work in-office four days per week, starting in 60 days. If they refused, they would be replaced. Leadership positioned the shift as "restoring our collaborative culture" and "investing in our future."

The Backlash

The reaction was immediate and severe. Over 60% of employees had specifically chosen this company for its remote flexibility. After joining, many had relocated to be near family, moved to lower cost-of-living areas, or made life decisions based on the "remote-first" model. Parents had arranged childcare and eldercare around flexible schedules. Employees with disabilities had thrived with remote accommodations.

The company's internal communication channels blew up with angry messages. A grassroots employee group formed to protest the decision. Several high-performing teams submitted group petitions. The situation went public when employees posted on social media, and tech industry publications covered the story unfavorably. Leadership held a town hall to explain their decision. The COO emphasized the importance of in-person collaboration and culture. Employees pushed back with their own data: productivity metrics, customer satisfaction scores, and project delivery timelines—all showing that remote work had been more successful.

The disconnect was stark: Leadership valued in-person presence and traditional collaboration models based on their personal preferences and past experience. Employees valued flexibility and their measured success. Neither side could understand the other's perspective. And as added pressure, the CEO now doubted her decision to listen to the new COO.

The Exodus

Within the 60-day notice period, 18% of the employees resigned including a disproportionately high number of high performers with in-demand skills. Exit interviews revealed common themes: broken trust ("they promised remote work"), feeling devalued ("our results don't matter"), and lifestyle disruption. As a result, the company had to offer significant salary increases and retention bonuses to reduce attrition, eliminating many of the cost savings from the return-to-office decision.

Recruitment also suffered. The company had to remove "remote-first" from job postings and struggled to compete for tech talent with companies offering flexibility. The CEO began actively questioning whether the return-to-office mandate was the right decision, but the COO insisted the short-term pain would yield long-term gains. The board was divided. Employee morale remained at record lows six months after implementation.

Critical Thinking Questions

- What decision-making process failures led to this situation?

- How did leadership's biases and personal preferences override empirical data?

- What change management principles were violated in how the decision was announced and implemented?

- How should the company have approached concerns about collaboration and culture while honoring employee expectations?

- What role did the COO's previous experience and confirmation bias play in his recommendations?

- If you were the CEO, how would you handle this situation now?

- What processes should exist to ensure leadership decisions consider diverse perspectives and potential consequences?

- How do organizations balance business needs with employee expectations when both sides have legitimate concerns?

- What does this case reveal about the importance of shared purpose and trust in transformation?

- How could the company rebuild trust with employees regardless of the final decision on remote work?

Chapter 47: The Customer Portal That Nobody Needed

A professional association with 45,000 members serving the architecture industry decided to launch a comprehensive digital customer portal. The vision was ambitious: members could access all services, content, continuing education, networking, and community features through a single integrated platform. The board approved a $1.8 million budget for a three-year development project.

The CEO, a forward-thinking leader who regularly attended technology conferences and studied innovation literature, believed the portal would position the association ahead of competitors and appeal to younger professionals. She hired a digital transformation director from the tech industry and assembled a project team including marketing, IT, and product development staff.

The Design Process

The project team conducted a member survey asking about desired features. The survey showed strong interest in mobile access, integrated learning, and networking capabilities. Armed with this data, the team developed detailed requirements and identified a vendor platform that could deliver the vision.

The team worked diligently for 18 months, holding regular meetings, reviewing mockups, and testing functionality. They created an impressive portal with a beautiful design, intuitive navigation (according to them), single sign-on, integrated payment systems, and extensive content organization. They developed training materials and planned a phased rollout.

What the team didn't do was show the portal during development to actual members or test whether their design decisions matched how members actually worked. The project team had become increasingly insular, proud of what they were building and overconfident that members would love it because it aligned with the original survey responses.

The Launch Disaster

The portal launched with significant fanfare: email announcements, videos, webinars, and promotional campaigns. Initial adoption was encouraging; 40% of members logged in during the first month. But then something went wrong. Usage metrics dropped sharply after initial exploration. Member services received hundreds of complaints. Social media posts were full of negative comments. The project team was baffled—they thought they had built exactly what members said they wanted.

The reality, the portal was designed around how the association thought members should engage, not how they actually did. Key issues emerged: Members didn't want to access everything through one portal—they had specific needs at specific times and found the comprehensive approach overwhelming. The navigation structure mirrored the association's internal organizational chart, not members' mental models of their own needs. Critical features members used regularly (conference registration, certification tracking) were buried under multiple clicks. Less-used features were prominently displayed. The mobile experience, while technically responsive, wasn't optimized for the quick transactions most members needed on mobile devices.

The portal required members to update their profiles extensively before full access—a barrier the team thought would improve data quality, but members experienced as excessive friction. Long-time members resented having to relearn systems that had worked fine for them. Most significantly, the portal reflected what young tech-savvy professionals might want, not what the association's current membership demographic (average age 48) actually needed. The team had confused aspirational membership with current membership.

The Aftermath

Nine months post-launch, only 22% of members used the portal regularly—mostly for basic functions like event registration. The association continued operating legacy systems in parallel because members demanded them. The portal became an expensive underutilized asset that still required ongoing maintenance and updates.

The CEO faced criticism from the board for the investment. The digital transformation director, defensive about the negative reception, argued that members "just need more education" and weren't ready for innovation. The organization was stuck with a portal that didn't serve its members well and had consumed massive resources.

Critical Thinking Questions

- What fundamental user research and testing failures occurred during development?

- How did the project team's assumptions and biases shape decisions without adequate validation?

- What is the difference between asking members what they want versus understanding what they actually need?

- How should the association have structured user involvement throughout the development process?

- What role did generational assumptions and aspirational thinking play in the design failures?

- How would you have structured a pilot program to test assumptions before full development?

- What mechanisms should exist to challenge team thinking and surface contrary evidence during long projects?

- If you were brought in to fix this situation, what would you do with the existing portal and remaining budget?

- How do organizations balance innovative vision with meeting current stakeholder needs?

- What does this case reveal about the importance of iterative development and user feedback in transformation projects?

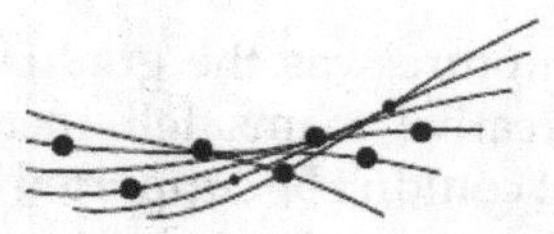

Chapter 48: The Data-Driven Culture That Killed Creativity

A mid-sized advertising agency known for creative excellence and award-winning campaigns was acquired by a global marketing conglomerate. The conglomerate's leadership believed the agency's informal, intuition-driven culture needed to "mature" and become more data-driven to improve efficiency and scalability.

They appointed a new managing director, Rachel, who came from a consulting background and had expertise in analytics and performance optimization. Rachel's mandate: implement data-driven decision-making across all agency operations while maintaining creative excellence.

The Transformation

Rachel moved quickly. She established KPIs for everything: billable hours, pitch-to-win ratios, client retention rates, creative concept testing scores, time spent in meetings, and even metrics for idea generation sessions. She implemented project management software that tracked every task and minute. She required data-backed justification for all creative decisions.

The agency invested heavily in marketing analytics tools and hired data scientists. Campaign pitches now required extensive consumer research, focus group testing, and predictive analytics before presentation to clients. Creative teams had to defend concepts with data showing likely performance based on similar past campaigns.

Rachel presented impressive reports to the parent company showing improved efficiency: projects were completed faster, resources were allocated more precisely, and profitability per project increased. The transformation appeared to be successful by every quantitative measure.

The Creative Collapse

What the data didn't capture was the gradual erosion of what made the agency special. The creative teams felt increasingly constrained. Bold, innovative concepts that couldn't be supported by historical data were killed in favor of measurable approaches. Creative directors spent more time justifying ideas than developing them. The agency's most senior creatives, who had built their reputations on intuitive breakthrough thinking, became frustrated. They felt the new process was designed to create competent work, not exceptional work. Several left for competitors or started their own agencies, taking key clients with them.

Junior creatives, who had joined the agency for its creative culture, found the environment increasingly mechanical. The focus on metrics and efficiency meant less mentorship, fewer experimental projects, and limited time for creative exploration. Innovation withered as teams focused on deliverables that met KPIs rather than pushing creative boundaries.

Clients began noticing a change. The agency's work became more formulaic, performative, and similar to every other agency. The campaigns were efficient and achieved reasonable results, but they weren't breaking through or winning awards. Long-standing clients whose loyalty was based on creative excellence began looking at other agencies.

The Crisis

Two years into the transformation, the agency lost three of its five largest accounts, representing 40% of revenue. Exit interviews with clients revealed a common theme: "You're not the agency we hired anymore. The work is acceptable, but it's no longer exceptional."

The parent company was confused. All the operational metrics had improved. Efficiency was up. Process compliance was high. Projects were delivered on time and on budget. Yet revenue was declining and the agency's market reputation was suffering.

Rachel doubled down, arguing that the client losses were due to market factors and that the agency needed even more rigorous data processes. But the remaining creative talent was unconvinced and demoralized. The agency's Glassdoor rating plummeted as current and former employees described a "soul-crushing" culture that had "abandoned creativity for spreadsheets."

The parent company faced a dilemma: The transformation had created quantifiable improvements in efficiency but qualitative deterioration in the very creativity that made the agency valuable.

Critical Thinking Questions

What was the fundamental misunderstanding about the relationship between data and creativity?

- How did the focus on measuring what is measurable lead to destroying what is valuable?

- What should Rachel have done differently to balance data-driven decisions with creative excellence?

- How do you measure and manage creative output without killing creativity?

- What role did Rachel's background and expertise play in how she approached the transformation?

- If you were the parent company CEO, how would you have structured the mandate differently?

- What mechanisms should exist to preserve cultural strengths during operational transformations?

- How do organizations balance efficiency and innovation when they often require different approaches?

- What early warning signs should have triggered a reassessment of the transformation approach?

- If you were brought in to recover the agency, what specific steps would you take?

The Last Word

Personal Notes on
Organizational Transformation

The Truth About Transformation is a field guide based on over 50 years combined of experience working with organizations of all sizes. For leaders, managers, the visionaries, and the innovators, it is the human factor that can propel or derail transformative change. Whether it is core values, deeply held beliefs, subconscious bias, or personal perceptions, people guide the future of organizational transformation. The "truth" in this case is an exploration of the many influences – most of which we are unaware of – that play into change.

This is not your typical business book on organizational aspirations. It is an unvarnished look at how organizations are dysfunctional in their attempt at transformation. It requires hard work and commitment to be open to the human factors that will actualize change. For leaders and managers, it means stepping out of their comfort zones and subordinating their egos, both of which are anxiety-provoking. We have brought forward behavioral and psychological insights that are often overlooked when considering organizational transformation. And yet, it is these human factors that will make or break your strategic plans.

Since the first edition of this book, the world has accelerated in ways few could have predicted. AI emerged from the edges of experimentation into the center of organizational life. Workforce expectations shifted permanently. Cultural tensions deepened. And leaders were forced to confront the uncomfortable reality that transformation is never about technology alone.

What has not changed is the truth at the center of every transformation: people determine the outcome. Human behavior—not AI, not strategy, not budget, not vision—is what makes change succeed or fail.

If anything, the last several years have reinforced the importance of understanding the Human Factor. Technology may redefine the tools we use, but it does not alter the psychology that drives human action. It does not resolve fear. It does not create trust. It does not inspire commitment. Only leaders — and the cultures they build — can do that.

This second edition is not simply an update. It reflects a world reshaped by disruption and possibility. But the core message endures: transformation begins and ends with humanity.

The Truth About Transformation then bridges theory into practice and opens the door to meaningful change that is sustainable for management, the workforce, and customers. Our intention is to change how individuals feel working together and our goal is to help anyone contemplating a transformative change to start the process with the right tools, mindset, and attitude.

Powered by empathy, an empowered organizational ecosystem can be built and sustained to meet the challenges of any disruptive, asymmetrical marketplace. It is the human factor that will determine your success ... or failure.

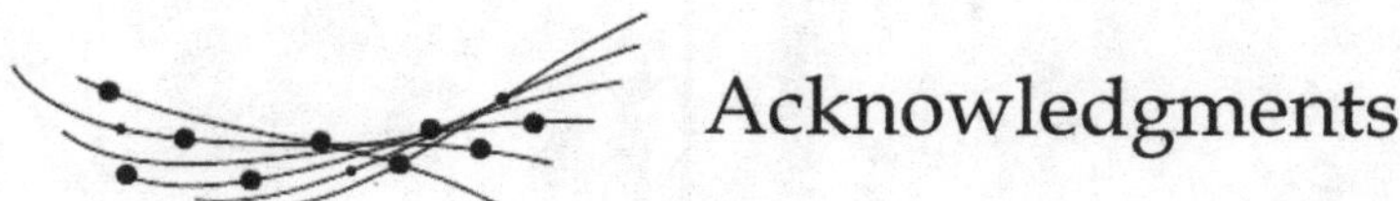 # Acknowledgments

It Takes a Village

I want to thank those that have supported me through the journey of writing this book and those who encouraged me to share everything I've learned in my career working, at this point, across dozens of organizations.

Thanks, with love, to my wife Lucia for always supporting me in my passions and encouraging me to stay committed to what I believe in, and for always pushing me out of my comfort zone.

To my boys Nicholas "Coty" and Zachary, thanks for trying to be the best you can be, always, and for not being afraid to follow your own passions and interests, always.

My work partners Elizabeth Stewart and Beth Bush Stansel who have been with me as part of 2040 Digital, taking the ride across so many interesting and inspiring client organizations and always rising to the occasion to set them on the right paths. Thanks for everything you both mean to me.

And finally, to my co-conspirator Deborah Patton, my deepest gratitude for taking this creative journey with me.

Kevin Novak

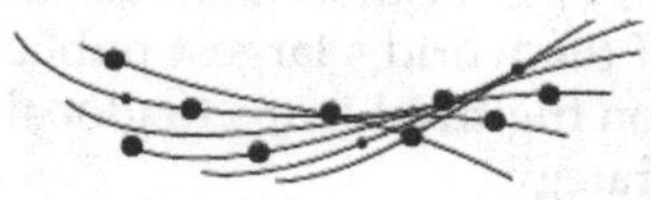

The Authors

Kevin Novak

Kevin Novak is the Founder and CEO of 2040 Digital, a consultancy specializing in organizational transformation, human behavior, digital strategy, and the psychology of change. With more than two decades of experience guiding complex organizations through disruption, he has advised global enterprises, associations, healthcare systems, and mission-driven institutions on navigating culture, identity, resistance, and the human dynamics that determine whether transformation succeeds or fails.

Kevin is also adjunct faculty at the University of Maryland, where he teaches courses on digital society and the impact of emerging technologies. His academic work reinforces his consulting practice, grounding the Human Factor Method™ in behavioral science, systems thinking, and real-world experience.

He is the author of The Truth About Transformation (First-Edition and Second-Edition), writes the long-running Ideas & Innovations weekly newsletter, and co-hosts The Human Factor Podcast, where he explores how identity, emotion, culture, and technology shape change and transformation. His work is grounded in a core conviction: transformation begins and ends with people, not systems.

Before founding 2040 Digital, Kevin held senior leadership roles across major institutions. As Vice President of New Business Development, Strategic Partnerships, and Digital Strategies for the American Institute of Architects, he led enterprise-wide modernization, digital transformation, and strategic growth initiatives.

Prior to that, as Chief Digital Officer and Director of Education Outreach at the U.S. Library of Congress, he oversaw one of the world's largest public digital programs, delivering more than 22 million digitized items to global audiences and shaping national digital access strategy.

He has served in multiple industry leadership positions, including Board Chair of the Business Information Association (BIA-Connectiv) and board roles with the Software & Information Industry Association (SIIA), the Business Press Education Foundation (BPEF), and the Specialty Information Publishers Association (SIPA). Kevin also co-chaired the W3C Open Data and W3C Open Government committees and was an industry data expert for the Obama Administration's Open Government Data Initiatives, collaborating with U.S. federal agencies to expand public access to government data.

Kevin holds an M.B.A. and an M.S. in Technology Management from the University of Maryland, and a B.A. in Social Sciences from the University of Pittsburgh.

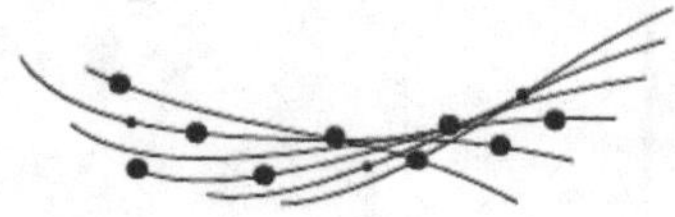

The Authors

Deborah Patton

Deborah Patton has made a career in publishing, marketing, creative services, and as an experiential event producer. As founder and executive director of Applied Brilliance, a thought leadership platform, she provides consulting services to promote innovation and creativity in companies and organizations seeking effective ways to convey to their customers, employees, and other stakeholders how emerging trends and major cultural shifts affect their businesses. She also serves as editor and COO of *The Robin Report*, a digital media platform serving C-level retail executives.

As an innovator in strategic marketing and communications, Deborah has helped top media brands manage change, sometimes tumultuous change, in the marketplace. She has helped revitalize traditional brands, re-launch media businesses, and create new brand identities for established media organizations. She believes that effective marketing and communications strategies are driven by mastering the art of listening from the customer's viewpoint, stepping outside one's own comfort zone and synthesizing the seemingly unconnected threads of emerging global trends as harbingers of cultural change.

With in-depth experience in a range of consumer markets, she has played leading roles at iconic media brands including Town & Country, House & Garden, Connoisseur, Modern Bride, and Seventeen. She has also led marketing and communications strategies for business media brands including Architecture, Interiors, Contract, The Hollywood Reporter, Billboard, Adweek, Brandweek, and Mediaweek.

Deborah holds a B.A. in art history and French from Pitzer College and studied at l'Ecole de Louvre in Paris.

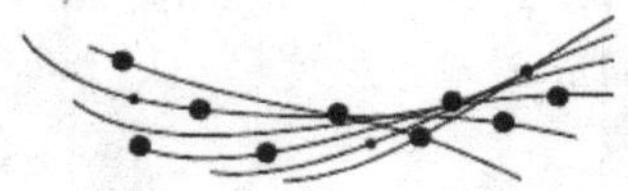 # References

Note: All references are cited in sequential order for each part of the book.

Part One

PR Newswire. (2020). *Impact of Covid 19 on the Global Manufacturing Industry.*
Retrieved from the web: https://www.prnewswire.com/news-releases/impact-of-covid-19-on-the-global-manufacturing-industry-2020

Wikipedia. (Nd.) *Technological Determinism.*
Retrieved from the web: https://en.wikipedia.org/wiki/Technological_determinism

Middle Berry Media Wiki. (2008). *Technological Determinism.*
Retrieved from the web:
https://mediawiki.middlebury.edu/MIDDMedia/Technological_Determinism

Yakobovitch, David. (2021). *The Diversity Problem In Technology With Dr. Jt Kostman, Data Scientist, Mathematician And Psychologist.*
Available via the web: https://www.humainpodcast.com/the-diversity-problem-in-technology-with-dr-jt-kostman-data-scientist-mathematician-and-psychologist/

Moazed, Alex. (Nd.). *What Is 'Innovation Theater'? A Definition, and How to Avoid It.* Applico Website.
Retrieved from the web: https://www.applicoinc.com/blog/what-is-innovation-theater-a-definition-and-how-to-avoid-it/

Blank, Steve. (2019). *Why Companies Do "Innovation Theater" Instead of Actual Innovation.*
Harvard Business Review. Harvard Business Publishing: Education.
Retrieved from the web: https://hbsp.harvard.edu/product/H0577T-PDF-ENG

Bezos, Jeffrey. (1997). *Letter to Shareholders.*
Retrieved from the web:
https://s2.q4cdn.com/299287126/files/doc_financials/annual/Shareholderletter97.pdf

Litchfield, Gideon. (2022). *Welcome to the New WIRED, The future begins here – again.*
Retrieved from the web: https://www.wired.com/story/welcome-to-the-new-wired/

Bricker, D. J., & Ibbitson, J. (2019). Empty Planet: The shock of global population decline.

United Nations. (Nd.). *Global Issues: Youth.*
Retrieved from the web: https://www.un.org/en/global-issues/youth

Niang, Thione. (2019). *Charts of the Week.* Brookings Institute.
Retrieved from the web: https://www.brookings.edu/blog/brookings-now/2019/01/18/charts-of-the-week-africas-changing-demographics/

United Nations. (Nd.). *Population.*
Retrieved from the web: https://www.un.org/en/global-issues/population

Worldometers. (Nd.). *World Population, United States Population.*
Retrieved from the web: https://www.worldometers.info

Worldometers. (Nd.). *Population Clock.*
Available on the web: World Population Clock at https://www.worldometers.info/world-population/

PEW Research Institute. (2022). *Most Americans say the declining share of White people in the U.S. is neither good nor bad for society.*
Retrieved from the web: https://www.pewresearch.org/fact-tank/2021/08/23/most-americans-say-the-declining-share-of-white-people-in-the-u-s-is-neither-good-nor-bad-for-society/

US Government, Census Bureau. (Nd.). *Census Data.*
Retrieved via the web: https://www.census.gov/data.html

Hinchcliff, Emma. (2021) *The female CEOs on this year's Fortune 500 just broke three all-time records.* Fortune Magazine.
Retrieved from the web: https://fortune.com/2021/06/02/female-ceos-fortune-500-2021-women-ceo-list-roz-brewer-walgreens-karen-lynch-cvs-thasuNda-brown-duckett-tiaa/

US Census Bureau. (2021). *Census Bureau Annual Business Survey.*
Retrieved via the web: https://www.census.gov/programs-surveys/abs.html

Finances Online. (2022). *52 Women in Technology Statistics: 2022 Data on Female Tech Employees.*
Retrieved via the web: https://financesonline.com/women-in-technology-statistics/

Zippia. (2022). *Nurse demographics and statistics in the US.*
Retrieved via the web: https://www.zippia.com/nurse-jobs/demographics/

Boyle, Patrick. AAMC (2021). *Nation's physician workforce evolves: more women, a bit older, and toward different specialties.*
Retrieved via the web: https://www.aamc.org/news-insights/nation-s-physician-workforce-evolves-more-women-bit-older-and-toward-different-specialties

Erudera College News. (2021). *Women Outnumber Men In US Colleges – Nearly 60% Of Students In 2020/21 Were Women.*
Retrieved via the web: https://collegenews.org/women-outnumber-men-in-us-colleges-nearly-60-of-students-in-2020-21-were-women/#:~:text=Data%20show%20that%2059.5%20percent,men%20decreasing%20by%2071%20percent.

UN Women Website. (2021). *Media Advisory: UN's Commission on the Status of Women highlights women's full and effective participation and decision-making in public life.*
Retrieved via the web: https://www.unwomen.org/en/news/stories/2021/3/media-advisory-csw65-commission-on-the-status-of-women-2021

Rosling, Hans., Rosling, Ola., Rönn Rosling, Anna. (2019). *Factfulness: 10 reasons we're wrong about the world – and why things are better than you think.*
Retrieved from the web: https://www.consilium.europa.eu/en/documents-publications/library/library-blog/posts/factfulness/

Donnelly, Grant., Whillans, Ashley. (2021). *Why Mentorship Programs don't Always Work*. Wall Street Journal.
Retrieved from the web: https://www.wsj.com/articles/why-mentorship-does-not-always-work-11635532464

Giurgea, Laura M., Whillans, Ashley V., and Yemiscigil, Ayse. (Nd.). *A multi-country perspective on gender differences in time use during COVID-19*.
Retrieved from the web: https://www.pnas.org/doi/pdf/10.1073/pnas.2018494118

Pandey, Erica. (2021). *Office politics move into the home*. Axios Finish Line, Axios Website.
Retrieved from the web: https://www.axios.com/2021/08/10/office-politics-home-remote-work

UN DESA. United Nations. (2018r). *Population Divisions*.
Retrieved from the web: https://www.un.org/development/desa/publications/2018-revision-of-world-urbanization-prospects.html

Indigenous Corporate Training, Inc. (2020). *What is the Seventh Generation Principle?*.
Retrieved from the web: https://www.ictinc.ca/blog/seventh-generation-principle

Huang, Zheping. (2017). *Alibaba billionaire Jack Ma gave a politician-like performance at the World Economic Forum*. Quartz.
Retrieved from the web: https://qz.com/889021/at-davos-alibabababas-jack-ma-just-wants-to-retire-early-because-hes-tired-of-the-tough-questions-about-china/

Economic Times. (2017). Jack Ma's 30-30-30 advice for the future.
Retrieved from the web: https://economictimes.indiatimes.com/magazines/panache/jack-mas-30-30-30-advice-for-thefuture/

Lu, Wei., Miller Lee J. (2018). *Gen Z Is Set to Outnumber Millennials Within a Year*. Bloomberg.
Retrieved from the web: https://www.bloomberg.com/news/articles/2018-08-20/gen-z-to-outnumber-millennials-within-a-year-demographic-treNds

Kulingowski, Kiely. (Nd.). *Business.com*.
Retrieved from the web: https://www.business.com/author/kiely-kuligowski/

Sackett, Heather. (2021). *The Bottom Line of Benefits for a 5 Generation Workforce*. Amwins Website.
Retrieved from the web: https://www.amwins.com/resources-insights/article/the-bottom-line-of-benefits-for-a-5-generation-workforce

Price Waterhouse Coopers (PWC). (2022). *Survey of over 52,000 workers indicates the Great Resignation is set to continue as pressure on pay mounts*.
Retrieved from the web: https://www.pwc.com/gx/en/news-room/press-releases/2022/global-workforce-hopes-and-fears-survey-2022.html

Harvard Pilgrim Healthcare. (2022). *Healthcare for Multiple Generations in Your Workforce*.
Retrieved from the web: https://www.harvardpilgrim.org/hapiguide/generation-employee-benefits/

Bridgeworks. (2019). *Generation Edge, 101*.
Retrieved from the web: https://www.generations.com/insights/generation-edge-101/

Chamberlin, Jamie. (2009). (Jeffrey Arnett) *Overgeneralizing the generations: As workplaces become increasingly age-diverse, psychologists are working to help people of all ages work together.* APA Monitor Website.
Retrieved from the web: https://www.apa.org/monitor/2009/06/workplaces

Waldman, Emma. (2021). (Megan Gerhardt) *How to Manage a Multi-Generational Team.* Harvard Business Review.
Retrieved from the web: https://hbr.org/2021/08/how-to-manage-a-multi-generational-team

Glasheen, Jasmine. (2021). *Verbal Interview via The Robin Report.*
More information available at: https://www.therobinreport.com/the-robin-report-annual-forum/jasmine-glasheen/

Deloitte. (2021). *The Deloitte Global 2022 Gen Z and Millennial Survey.*
Retrieved from the web: https://www2.deloitte.com/global/en/pages/about-deloitte/articles/genzmillennialsurvey.html

Beckler, Miles. (Nd.). *Miles Beckler Website.*
Retrieved from the web: https://www.milesbeckler.com

Kulingowski, Kiely. (2022). (Shabbar, Muhammad). *Hiring Tips for a Multigenerational Workforce: From Baby Boomers to Gen Z.* Business.com.
Retrieved from the web: https://www.business.com/articles/hiring-multigenerational-workforce/

Cunningham, Erin. (Nd.). *The Z List.* Refinery 29.
Retrieved from the web: https://www.refinery29.com/en-us/the-z-list/

Morris, Chris. (2018). *61 million Gen Zers are about to enter the US workforce and radically change it forever.* CNBC Website.
Retrieved from the web: https://www.cnbc.com/2018/05/01/61-million-gen-zers-about-to-enter-us-workforce-and-change-it.html

World Economic Forum. (2018). *Why Generation Z has a totally different approach to money.*
Retrieved from the web: https://www.weforum.org/ageNda/2018/11/why-gen-z-is-approaching-money-differently-than-other-generations-95032cb6-6046-4269-a38a-0763bd7909ff/

McCrindle, Mark., Fell, Ashley. (2020) *Understanding Generation Alpha.*
Retrieved from the web: https://generationalpha.com/wp-content/uploads/2020/02/UNderstanding-Generation-Alpha-McCriNdle.pdf

Ripplematch. (2021) *What Gen-Z Wants.*
Retrieved from the web:
https://f.hubspotusercontent20.net/hubfs/8139278/What%20Gen%20Z%20Wants%20-%20Building%20an%20Organization%20to%20Attract%20and%20Retain%20The%20Next%20Generation%20of%20Talent.pdf

Goldberg, Emma. (2021). *Do Generations Matter? Well, Maybe.* New York Times.
Retrieved from the web: https://www.nytimes.com/2021/11/04/insider/gen-z-millennial-workplace.html

Litt, Michael. (2018). *Gen-Z employees don't do email.* Fast Company.
Retrieved from the web: https://www.fastcompany.com/90261656/gen-z-employees-dont-do-email

Frick, Walter. (2021). *The next phase of remote work will be even more disruptive.* Quartz Website.
Retrieved from the web: https://qz.com/2079942/the-next-wave-of-remote-jobs-will-transform-the-economy/

Doyle, Allison. (2021). *How Long Should an Employee Stay at a Job?* The Balance Careers.
Retrieved from the web: https://www.thebalancecareers.com/how-long-should-an-employee-stay-at-a-job-2059796

Rinne, April. (2019). *The Flux Mindset.*
Retrieved from the web: https://fluxmindset.com/

Wikipedia. (Nd.). *Definition of Artificial Intelligence.*
Retrieved from the web: https://en.wikipedia.org/wiki/Artificial_intelligence

Parker, Ceri. (2018). *Google CEO − AI will be bigger than electricity or fire.*
Retrieved from the web: https://medium.com/world-economic-forum/google-ceo-ai-will-be-bigger-than-electricity-or-fire-d85d437687ed

The Economist Data Team. (2018). *A study finds nearly half of jobs are vulnerable to automation.*
Retrieved from the web: https://www.economist.com/graphic-detail/2018/04/24/a-study-fiNds-nearly-half-of-jobs-are-vulnerable-to-automation

Abril, Danielle., Harwell, Drew. (2021). *Keystroke tracking, screenshots, and facial recognition: The boss may be watching long after the pandemic ends.* Washington Post.
Retrieved from the web:
https://www.washingtonpost.com/technology/2021/09/24/remote-work-from-home-surveillance/

Kingston, Jennifer A. (2022). *Welcome to the summer of robots.* Axios.
Retrieved from the web: https://www.axios.com/2022/06/09/robots-kitchen-delivery-robotics

Rawsthorn, Alice. (2007). *John Maeda: Rethinking technology and the digital revolution.* New York Times.
Retrieved from the web: https://www.nytimes.com/2007/05/04/style/04iht-design7.1.5567585.html

Thrift, Scott. (Nd.). *The Present Website.*
Available via: https://thepresent.is

Brynjolfsson, Erik. (Nd.). *Biography.*
Available via: https://workofthefuture.mit.edu/team-member/erik-brynjolfsson/

Dorsey, Jason. (2021). *7 things you need to know about Generation Z.* MarketWatch Website.
Retrieved from the web: https://www.marketwatch.com/story/7-things-you-need-to-know-about-generation-z-2021-01-29

McKinsey. (2020). *Reimagining the pandemic organization.*
Retrieved via the web:
https://www.mckinsey.com/~/media/mckinsey/business%20functions/people%20and%20
organizational%20performance/our%20insights/reimagining%20the%20way%20businesses
%20operate/reimagining-the-postpandemic-organization.pdf

Dennis, Brady, Kaplan., Sarah, Adam., Karla., Booth, William., Westfall, Sammy., & Bhattarai,
Abha. (2021). *World leaders reach climate agreement at U.N. summit following two weeks of
negotiations.* The Washington Post.
Retrieved from the web: https://www.washingtonpost.com/climate-
environment/2021/11/13/cop26-glasgow-climate-deal/

Hoffower, Hillary. (2022). *Meet the typical baby boomer: Worth $206,000, they've been blamed for
ruining the economy for millennials and are in the midst of the 'gray tsunami'.* Business Insider.
Retrieved from the web: https://www.businessinsider.com/typical-baby-boomer-net-worth-
debt-real-estate-retirement-2021-12

Marketmix. (Nd.). *Wealthy Baby Boomers – Where Do They Live?*
Retrieved from web: https://resources.datadrivenmarketing.equifax.com/dyks-equifax-
ddm/wealthy-baby-boomers-where-do-they-live-2

Wikipedia. (Nd.). *The Paradox of Choice.*
Retrieved from the web: https://en.wikipedia.org/wiki/The_Paradox_of_Choice

Cole, Brandon. (2018). *Luxury Brands Prefer to Burn Millions of Dollars' Worth of Clothes To
Letting 'Wrong' Shoppers Buy Them At Discount.*
Retrieved from the web: https://www.newsweek.com/luxury-brands-prefer-burn-millions-
dollars-worth-clothes-over-letting-wrong-1032088

Part Two

Society for Human Resources Management. (Nd.). *Organizational Structures.*
Retrieved from the web: https://www.shrm.org/resourcesandtools/tools-and-
samples/toolkits/pages/understandingorganizationalstructures.aspx

Deloitte HBS Reference. (Nd.). *Purpose Premium POV.*
Retrieved from the web:
https://www2.deloitte.com/content/dam/Deloitte/us/Documents/process-and-
operations/purpose-premium-pov.pdf

Amber Cabral (2020). *Allies and Advocates.* Amber Cabral & Cabral Co.
Available via: https://www.ambercabral.com/allies-and-advocates-creating-an-inclusive-
and-equitable-culture/

Marcie Merriman, (2019). *Is Gen Z the spark we need to see the light?.* EY Website.
Retrieved from the web: https://www.ey.com/en_us/consulting/is-gen-z-the-spark-we-
need-to-see-the-light and
https://qz.com/work/1691633/will-tech-addiction-mean-the-rise-or-demise-of-gen-z/

Shared Knowledge Diagram. (Nd.). Coggle.it.
Retrieved from https://coggle.it/diagram/V2zinRA-mKZnnwJQ/t/how-do-ways-of-
knowing-in-personal-and-shared-knowledge

Kleiner, Art., Schwartz, Jeffrey., Thomson, Josie. (Nd). *The Wise Advocate; The Inner Voice of Strategic Leadership*. Columbia Business School Publishing.
Weblink: http://cup.columbia.edu/book/the-wise-advocate/9780231178044

Marketing General Incorporated. (2021) *The 2021 Membership Marketing Benchmarking Report*.
Retrieved from the web: https://go.marketinggeneral.com/2021mmbr

Coleman, Basha. (Nd). *How to Write a Great Value Proposition*. HubSpot Incorporated.
Retrieved from the web: https://blog.hubspot.com/marketing/write-value-proposition

Peleg, Elad. (2021). *Why legacy companies need to tap into their inner startup*. Fast Company.
Retrieved from the web: https://www.fastcompany.com/90651724/why-legacy-companies-need-to-tap-into-their-inner-startup

MarketingMo. (2021). *Strategic Planning: Customer Retention Strategy*. MarketingMo Website.
Retrieved from the web: http://www.marketingmo.com/strategic-planning/customer-retention-strategy/

Minsky, Jeff. (2019). *Quarterly Quotes 2cd Quarter 2019*. MediaVilliage.Com (Quotes used from Arthur Sadoun, John Wren, Mark Penn and Sundar Pichai).
Retrieved from the web: https://www.mediavillage.com/article/quarterly-quotes-q2-2019-featuring-omnicom-comcast-nbcuniversal-disney-and-more/

Winters, Jeanette. (2018). *Transformational Readiness Model: Improving the Likeliness of Change Success*. HR Exchange Network Website.
Retrieved from the web: https://www.hrexchangenetwork.com/hr-talent-management/articles/transformational-readiness-model-improving-the-likeliness-of-change-success

Jahn, Jens., Luiz, Manuel., Messenböck, Reinhard., Werner, Robert. (2020). *Are You Ready to Transform?*. Boston Consulting Group Website Blog.
Retrieved from the web: https://www.bcg.com/publications/2020/are-you-ready-to-transform

Smith, Christopher. (2020). *The New Normal: Quotes and Definitions. Change Management*. Change Management Blog.
Retrieved from the web: https://change.walkme.com/the-new-normal-quotes/

World Economic Forum. (Nd.) *The Future of Jobs Report*.
Retrieved from the web: https://reports.weforum.org/future-of-jobs-2016/chapter-1-the-future-of-jobs-and-skills/

Hewlitt, Andrew., Lyon, Jamie., and Pelino, Michele. (2021). *Improving Collaboration Tools Facilitates Creativity, Innovation, And Profitability Research Report*. A Report Commissioned by Lucid, Inc.
Retrieved from the web: https://www.lucidchart.com/pages/webinars/forrester-july-2021

Lehner, Stephen. (Nd.). *Transformation*.
Retrieved from the web: https://thevibrantfactory.wordpress.com/2016/12/08/eating-through-transformation/

BRIDGES, WILLIAM. Managing Transitions: Making the Most of Change. Reading, Mass: Addison-Wesley, 1991., (multiple pages).

Evans, Richard (2019). *Managing Transformation? Begin with 'Why'*.

Retrieved from the web: https://www.linkedin.com/pulse/managing-transformation-begin-why-richard-evans/

Miller, Cheryl. (2018). *The Continuum of Transformation*. Quantum Circles Press.
Book available: https://www.amazon.com/Continuum-Transformation-Cheryl-Miller/dp/0985954620

Vivify Scrum. (Nd.). *Agile Methodology*.
Retrieved from the web: https://www.vivifyscrum.com/how-it-works

Einhorn Strauss, Cheryl. (2021). *11 Myths About Decision-Making*. Harvard Business Review Online.
Retrieved from the web: https://hbr.org/2021/04/11-myths-about-decision-making

Korn Ferry Focus. (2015). *Leading Through Ambiguity*.
Retrieved from the web: https://focus.kornferry.com/leadership-and-talent/leading-through-ambiguity/

Smallwood, Norm. (2020). *Two Types of Leaders: Ambiguity Absorber and Ambiguity Amplifier*.
RBL Group Website.
Retrieved from the web: https://www.rbl.net/insights/articles/two-types-of-leaders-ambiguity-absorber-and-ambiguity-amplifier

Blum, Andrew. (2020). *Leading in the Face of Ambiguity and Uncertainty*. Thrive Website.
Retrieved from the web: https://thriveglobal.com/stories/leading-in-the-face-of-ambiguity-and-uncertainty/

Clegg, Judith., Reisman, Jane. (2000). *Outcomes for Success*. ORS Impact and Clegg Associates.
Retrieved from the web:
https://www.orsimpact.com/DirectoryAttachments/132018_31656_887_TEF-Outcomes-for-Success-2000-_-Part-1-for-website.pdf

Weaver, Jenna. (Nd.). *Strategic Planning*. Clearpoint Strategy.
Retrieved from the web: https://www.clearpointstrategy.com/author/jweaver/

Jamieson, Dave. (2022). *Amazon Fined For 'Knowingly Putting Workers At Risk' With Productivity Quotas*. Huffington Post.
Retrieved from the web: https://www.huffpost.com/entry/amazon-fined-for-knowingly-putting-workers-at-risk-with-productivity-quotas_n_6238f2a5e4b009ab92fc0603

Swain, Gabriel. (Nd.). Articles available via: https://www.linkedin.com/in/gabriel-swain-disruptive-growth-marketing/

Choudhary, Amit. (Nd.). *Data-driven versus intuitive leadership – which offers a decision-making advantage?*. Capgemini insights Blog.
Retrieved from the web: https://www.capgemini.com/insights/expert-perspectives/data-driven-versus-intuitive-leadership-which-offers-a-decision-making-advantage/

Inavero. (aka Clearly Rated, Inc.). (2019). *Third Annual "Future Workforce Report" Sheds Light on How Younger Generations are Reshaping the Future of Work*.
Retrieved from the web: https://www.bloomberg.com/press-releases/2019-03-05/third-annual-future-workforce-report-sheds-light-on-how-younger-generations-are-reshaping-the-future-of-work

Harvard Business Review Research Report. (Nd.). *Meet the New Decision Makers.* Available from ThoughtSpot website: https://go.thoughtspot.com/white-paper-hbr-new-decision-makers.html

Sroka, Jason. (2021). *Information vs. Intuition: Start today to build a 'Data-Driven' team.* https://blog.smartsense.co/information-vs.-intuition-start-today-to-build-a-data-driven-team

Huang, Laura. (2019). *When It's OK to Trust Your Gut on a Big Decision.* Harvard Business Review. Harvard Business Publishing: Education. Available via the web: https://www.hbsp.harvard.edu/product/H058DF-PDF-ENG

Ferenstein, Gregory. (2016). *Netflix CEO Explains Why "Gut" Decisions Still Rule In The Era Of Big Data.* Forbes Online. Retrieved from the web: https://www.forbes.com/sites/gregoryferenstein/2016/01/22/netflix-ceo-explains-why-gut-decisions-still-rule-in-the-era-of-big-data/?sh=6f3a3d1f1e09

Imam, Raazi. (2018). *Data Vs. Intuition- What Matters More When Making Big Decisions?.* Retrieved from the web: https://www.linkedin.com/pulse/data-vs-intuition-what-matters-more-when-making-big-decisions-imam/

Westfall, Chris. (2020). *How Storytelling Can Advance Your Career: 5 Ways To Improve Communication Skills.* Forbes Online. Retrieved from the web: https://www.forbes.com/sites/chriswestfall/2022/01/28/how-storytelling-can-advance-your-career-5-ways-to-improve-communication-skills/?sh=677f8ca62fa1

Monecarlo. (Nd.) Gartner Report. *The State of Data Quality Solutions: Augment, Automate and Simplify.* Gartner Website. Retrieved via the web: https://www.montecarlodata.com/new-gartner-report-the-state-of-data-quality-solutions

Bourne, Vanson. (SnapLogic). (2020). *The State of Data Management – Why Data Warehouse Projects Fail & The Impact of Data Distrust.* Available online at: https://www.vansonbourne.com/work/210120011h

Bansal, Manu. (2021). *Flying Blind: How Bad Data Undermines Business.* Forbes Technology Council/Forbes Online. Retrieved from the web: https://www.forbes.com/sites/forbestechcouncil/2021/10/14/flying-blind-how-bad-data-undermines-business/?sh=49d3ad3429e8

Stobierski, Tim. (Nd.). *A Beginner's Guide to Value-based Strategy.* Harvard Business School Online. Available via: https://online.hbs.edu/blog/post/value-based-strategy

Bean, Randy. (2014). *Big Data Fatigue?* Sloan Management Review. Retrieved from the web: https://sloanreview.mit.edu/article/big-data-fatigue/

Schneider, Meredith. (2021). *15 brands that were ruined by poor decisions.* Ladders Website. Retrieved from the web: https://www.theladders.com/career-advice/15-brands-that-were-ruined-by-poor-decisions

Falasca, M., Zhang, J., Conchar, M., & Li, L. (2017). *The impact of customer knowledge and marketing dynamic capability on innovation performance: an empirical analysis.* Journal of Business & Industrial Marketing, 32(7), 901-912.

Akroush, Mamoun N; Mahadin, Bushra K. (2019). *An intervariable approach to customer satisfaction and loyalty in the internet service market.* Internet Research; Bradford Vol. 29, Issue. 4.

Acosta, Alexandra & Herrero-Crespo, Ángel & Agudo, Jesús. (2018). *Effect of market orientation, network capability and entrepreneurial orientation on international performance of small and medium enterprises (SMEs).* International Business Review. 27. 10.1016/j.ibusrev.2018.04.004.

Kohli, A. K., & Jaworski, B. J. (1990). *Market Orientation: The Construct, Research Propositions, and Managerial Implications.* Journal of Marketing, 54(2), 1–18. https://doi.org/10.2307/1251866

Paul Murphy, Annie. (2021). *The Extended Mind.* Available via: https://anniemurphypaul.com/wp-content/uploads/2021/04/The-Extended-Mind-2-Free-Chapters.pdf and https://www.nytimes.com/2021/06/11/books/review/the-extended-mind-annie-murphy-paul.html

BrandCulture. (Nd.). *Shared Purpose – Uniting Brand and Culture to Drive Business Performance.* BrandCulture Website. Retrieved from the web: https://brandculture.com/insights/shared-purpose-uniting-brand-and-culture-to-drive-business-performance/

Edelman Trust Barometer. (2022). Retrieved from the web: https://www.edelman.com/trust/2022-trust-barometer

Schuyler, Shannon. (Pandy, Erica). (2021). *The C-suite job of the future: Chief purpose officer.* Axios Finish Line. Axios. Retrieved from the web: https://www.axios.com/2021/07/21/chief-purpose-office-corporate-responsibility

Eurasia Group. (2022). *Risk 9: Corporates losing the culture wars.* Eurasia Group Website. Retrieved from the web: https://www.eurasiagroup.net/live-post/top-risks-2022-9-corporates-losing-the-culture-wars

Addison, Mickey. (2016). *How to Build Shared Purpose in Your Team.* Mickey Addison Website. Retrieved from the web: http://www.mickeyaddison.com/2016/07/13/build-shared-purpose-team/

Renjen, Punit. (2021). *A conversation on organizational trust with Punit Renjen.* Deloitte Website. Retrieved from the web: https://www2.deloitte.com/us/en/insights/topics/leadership/open-conversation-with-punit-renjen-on-organizational-trust.html

Cooper, Jackie. (2012). *The People Want Business with a Purpose (Will Social Intrapreneurs Deliver?).* Ashoka Website. Retrieved from the web: https://www.ashoka.org/fr-aaw/story/people-want-business-purpose-will-social-intrapreneurs-deliver

Brimmer, Andrea. (Nd.) *Brand Purpose Playbook.* ANA. Retrieved from the web: https://www.ana.net/content/show/id/brand-purpose-playbook

Beaulieu, Ken. (Nd.) *Brand Purpose Playbook*. ANA.
Retrieved from the web: https://www.ana.net/content/show/id/brand-purpose-playbook

Porter Novelli. (2021). *The 2021 Porter Novelli Executive Influence Study*. Porter Novelli Website.
Retrieved from the web: https://www.porternovelli.com/findings/the-2021-porter-novelli-executive-influence-study/

Cooper, Kate. (2021). *The Darker Side Of 'Always On.'* Forbes Online.
Retrieved from the web: https://www.forbes.com/sites/katecooper/2021/10/15/the-darker-side-of-always-on/?sh=6a4f27432546

Kwasi Mitchell. (2021). *Interview with Kwasi Mitchell*. Leader Impact Website.
Retrieved from the web:
https://www.leadersmag.com/issues/2021.2_Apr/Purpose/LEADERS-Kwasi-Mitchell-Deloitte-US.html

BrandPie. (Nd.). *What CEOs Really Think About The Role Of Purpose In An Organization*.
BrandPie Website.
Retrieved from the web: https://www.brandpie.com/thinking/what-ceos-really-think-about-the-role-of-purpose-in-an-organization

Cone, Carol. (2020). *B2B Companies Face "Purpose Paradox"*. The Harris Poll Website. Retrieved
from the web: https://theharrispoll.com/briefs/b2b-companies-face-purpose-paradox/

Raleigh, Robert. (Nd.). *The Science, its why people do what they do*. PathSight Website. Retrieved
from the web: https://pathsight.com/the-science/

WTW (Watson Wyeth). (Nd.). *About WTW*. Retrieved via the web:
https://www.wtwco.com/en-US/About-Us/overview

Part Three

Tarallo, Mark. (2020). *How Managers Can Overcome Their Personal Biases*. SHRM.
Retrieved from the web: https://www.shrm.org/resourcesandtools/hr-topics/organizational-and-employee-development/pages/self-aware-managers.aspx

Childress, Rasheda. (2020). *Is Bias Affecting How You Lead?* American Society of Association
Executives, Winter Issue.
Retrieved from the web:
https://www.asaecenter.org/resources/articles/an_magazine/2020/winter/is-bias-affecting-how-you-lead

NeuroLeadership Institute. (2021). *Podcast Season 4*.
Retrieved via the web/podcast at: https://neuroleadership.com/podcast/season-4/

Childress, Rasheda. (2020). *Overcome Your Unconscious Bias*. Associations Now Magazine.
Retrieved from the web: https://associationsnow.com/2020/01/overcome-your-unconscious-bias/

Ashworth-Keppel, Tanya. (2021). *Four Cognitive Biases That Affect Your Leadership*. *Australian*
Institute of Business.
Retrieved via the web: https://www.aib.edu.au/blog/leadership/four-cognitive-biases-that-affect-your-leadership/

Drucker, Peter F. (2001). *Management Challenges for the 21st Century*. New York: Harper Business, 1999.

Choudhary, Amit. (Nd.). *Data-driven versus intuitive leadership – which offers a decision-making advantage?*. Capgemini Insights Blog.
Retrieved from the web: https://www.capgemini.com/insights/expert-perspectives/data-driven-versus-intuitive-leadership-which-offers-a-decision-making-advantage/

Swain, Gabriel. (Nd.). Articles available via: https://www.linkedin.com/in/gabriel-swain-disruptive-growth-marketing/

Baker, Jordan. (2021). *Origins of the Haudenosaunee (Iroquois) Confederacy*. World History Encyclopedia.
Retrieved from the web: https://www.worldhistory.org/article/1656/origins-of-the-haudenosaunee-iroquois-confederacy/

ABC-AU. (2021). *Our long-term battle with short-term thinking. Guest: Richard Fisher – Senior journalist*. BBC Future.
Reviewed on the web: https://www.abc.net.au/radionational/programs/futuretense/our-long-term-battle-with-short-term-thinking/13517570

Catenacci, Christina. (2017). *Workplace Organizational Behaviour Part II: Perception*.
Retrieved via the web:
https://blog.firstreference.com/workplace-organizational-behaviour-part-ii-perception/#.Yreaw-zMK9Y

Farnam Street Blog. (Jan. 16, 2021). *Brain Food Blog*.
Retrieved from the web: https://fs.blog/brain-food/january-16-2022/

Abrahams, Matt., Zimbardo, Philip. (2021). *Get Psyched: How Time and Situations Shape Our Communication*. Podcast.
Reviewed via audio and text transcript: https://www.gsb.stanford.edu/insights/get-psyched-how-time-situations-shape-communication

Schneier, Bruce. (Nd.). *Entries Tagged "security theater"*.
Retrieved via the web: https://www.schneier.com/tag/security-theater/page/6/

Catenacci-Francois, Lauren. (Nd.).
Retrieved via the web: https://sps.columbia.edu/faculty/lauren-catenacci and
https://academiccommons.columbia.edu/doi/10.7916/D8RF7BFZ

Papakostas, Thomas. (2015). *Business Fallacy: Perception is reality... Really?* Linked-In Pulse.
Retrieved via the web: https://www.linkedin.com/pulse/fallacy-perception-reality-really-thomas-papakostas/

Anaejionu, Regina. (Nd.). *Perception Vs. Reality in the Workplace*. CHRON.
Retrieved via the web: https://smallbusiness.chron.com/perception-vs-reality-workplace-11364.html

Blitz, David. (2020). *The Optics: Perception Matters More Than Reality in Business*. Forbes Online.
Retrieved from the web:
https://www.forbes.com/sites/forbesbusinesscouncil/2020/09/14/the-optics-perception-matters-more-than-reality-in-business/?sh=4567988b3726

Boris, Vanessa., Peterson, Lani. (2017). *What Makes Storytelling So Effective for Learning?*
Harvard Business Publishing: Corporate Learning.
Retrieved via the web: https://www.harvardbusiness.org/what-makes-storytelling-so-effective-for-learning/

Boris, Vanessa., Peterson, Lani. (2017). *The Science Behind the Art of Storytelling.* Harvard
Business Publishing: Corporate Learning.
Retrieved via the web: https://www.harvardbusiness.org/the-science-behind-the-art-of-storytelling/

Haven, Kendall. (Nd.). *Applying the science of story to the art of communication.*
Retrieved via the web: https://www.kendallhaven.com

Renken, Elena. (writer). Neeley, Liz (Host). (2020). *How Stories Connect and Persuade Us: Unleashing the Brain Power of Narrative.* National Public Radio.
Retrieved via transcript at: https://www.npr.org/sections/health-shots/2020/04/11/815573198/how-stories-connect-and-persuade-us-unleashing-the-brain-power-of-narrative

Covey, Stephen R. *The 7 Habits of Highly Effective People: Restoring the Character Ethic.* New
York: Free Press, 2004.

Hyacinth, Brigette. (2020). *Leading the Future of the Workforce.*
Available via: https://www.amazon.com/Leading-Workforce-Future-Inspiring-Innovation/dp/9769609242

Maryville University. (Nd.). *How to Be a Better Listener: Exploring 4 Types of Listening.*
Retrieved via the web: https://online.maryville.edu/blog/types-of-listening/

Conghui Su, Hui Zhou, Liangyu Gong, Binyu Teng, Fengji Geng, Yuzheng Hu. *Viewing personalized video clips recommended by TikTok activates default mode network and ventral tegmental area.* NeuroImage, Volume 237, 2021.

Guell, X., Gabrieli, J. D., & Schmahmann, J. D. (2018). *Triple representation of language, working memory, social and emotion processing in the cerebellum: convergent evidence from task and seed-based resting-state MRI analyses in a single large cohort.* Neuroimage, 172, 437-449.

Carta, I., Chen, C. H., Schott, A. L., Dorizan, S., & Khodakhah, K. (2019). *Cerebellar modulation of the reward circuitry and social behavior. Science,* 363(6424), eaav0581.

Evans, R. B. (1990). *William James, "The Principles of Psychology," and Experimental Psychology.*
The American Journal of Psychology, 103(4), 433–447. https://doi.org/10.2307/1423317

Bavelier, Daphne & Green, C & Dye, Matthew. (2010). *Children, Wired: For Better and for Worse.*
Neuron. 67. 692-701. 10.1016/j.neuron.2010.08.035.

Ophir, E., Nass, C., & Wagner, A.D. (2009). *Cognitive control in media multitaskers.* Proceedings
of the National Academy of Sciences, 106, 15583 - 15587.

Matusz, Pawel & Merkley, Rebecca & Faure, Michelle & Scerif, Gaia. (2018). *Expert Attention: Attentional allocation depends on the differential development of multisensory number representations.*
Cognition. in press. 10.1016/j.cognition.2019.01.013.

Pea, Roy., McCandliss, Bruce. (Nd.). *Syllabus.* Stanford Graduate School of Education. More
information available: https://ed.stanford.edu/ldt/ldt-faculty

Footnotes2Plato. (Whitehead North, Alfred.) (2019). *Who Is Alfred North Whitehead & What Is Process Philosophy?*.
Retrieved via the web: https://footnotes2plato.com/2019/02/07/who-is-alfred-north-whitehead-what-is-process-philosophy/

Cialdini, Robert B. *Influence: Science and Practice*. New York: Harper Collins College Publishers, 1993.

Cialdini, Robert. *The Psychology of Persuasion and Practice*. New and Expanded. Harper Collins College Publishers. 2021.

Chen, Angela. (2017). *Neuroscientist Lisa Feldman Barrett explains how emotions are made*.
Retrieved via the web: https://www.theverge.com/2017/4/10/15245690/how-emotions-are-made-neuroscience-lisa-feldman-barrett

Schwartz, Barry. *The Paradox of Choice: Why More Is Less*. New York: Ecco, 2004.

Peale, D. N. V. (1990). *The power of positive thinking*. Cedar Books.

Blige, Mary J. (2022) *Good Morning Gorgeous*. Music.

Gilbert, D. (2006). *Stumbling on happiness*. Alfred A. Knopf.

Hicks, Greg. (Nd.). *The Art and Science of Thriving*.
Available via: http://greghicks.com

Mayo Clinic. (Nd.). *Positive thinking: Stop negative self-talk to reduce stress*.
Retrieved via the web: https://www.mayoclinic.org/healthy-lifestyle/stress-management/in-depth/positive-thinking/art-20043950

Adler, Sarah Elizabeth. (2018). *The Power of Negative Thinking*. The Atlantic.
Retrieved via the web: https://www.theatlantic.com/magazine/archive/2018/01/the-power-of-negativity/546560/

Yamawaki, Niwako & Tschanz, Brian & Feick, David. (2004). *Defensive pessimism, self-esteem instability, and goal strivings*. Cognition and Emotion. 18. 233-249. 10.1080/02699930341000004.

Selig, Meg. (2019). *9 Positive Benefits of Negative Thinking. Psychology Today*.
Retrieved via the web:
https://www.psychologytoday.com/us/blog/changepower/201912/9-positive-benefits-negative-thinking

Burkeman, Oliver. (2012). *How to Harness the Positive Power of Negative Thinking*. Greater Good Magazine.
Retrieved via the web:
https://greatergood.berkeley.edu/article/item/how_to_harness_the_power_of_negative_thinking

Sarasvathy, Saras. (2008). *Effectuation: Elements of Entrepreneurial Expertise*. Effectuation: Elements of Entrepreneurial Expertise. 243. 10.4337/9781848440197.

Einstein, Albert. (Quote) Found in: Letter to Jost Winteler (1901), quoted in The Private Lives of Albert Einstein by Roger Highfield and Paul Carter (1993).

Locke, E. A., & Latham, G. P. (2002). *Building a practically useful theory of goal setting and task motivation: A 35-year odyssey.* American Psychologist, 57(9), 705–717. https://doi.org/10.1037/0003-066X.57.9.705

Riopel, Leslie. (Nd.). Professor Riopel Biography and Article Index. *Positive Psychology.* Retrieved via the web: https://positivepsychology.com/team/leslie-riopel/

Anderman, E. M., & Maehr, M. L. (1994). *Motivation and Schooling in the Middle Grades.* Review of Educational Research, 64(2), 287–309. https://doi.org/10.3102/00346543064002287

Teunissen, P., & Bok, H. (2013). *Believing is seeing: How people's beliefs influence goals, emotions and behaviour.* MEDICAL EDUCATION, 47, 1064–1072.
Retrieved from the web:
http://search.ebscohost.com.ezproxy.umgc.edu/login.aspx?direct=true&db=ehh&AN=90674679&site=ehost-live

Jackson, Terence. (2015). *7-Step Process for Goal Attainment.* Linked-In Pulse.
Retrieved via the web: https://www.linkedin.com/pulse/7-step-process-goal-attainment-terence-jackson-ph-d-/

Matthews, Gail. Dr. (Nd.). *The Science Behind Setting Goals (and Achieving Them).* Forbes Books Online.
Retrieved from the web: https://forbesbooks.com/the-science-behind-setting-goals-and-achieving-them/

Wall Street Journal. (2022). *How Is TikTok Changing Children's Brains?* (Podcast and Transcript).
Retrieved via the web: https://www.wsj.com/podcasts/google-news-update/how-is-tiktok-changing-childrens-brains/5063302b-754b-4548-80c1-6fe877119779

Van Steenburg, Eric, Nancy Spears, and Robert O. Fabrize (2013), *"Point of Purchase or Point of Frustration: Consumer Frustration Tendencies and Response in a Retail Setting,"* Journal of Consumer Behaviour, 12 (5), 389-400.

Malone, Noreen. (2021). *The Age of Anti-Ambition.* New York Times Magazine.
Retrieved via the web: https://www.nytimes.com/issue/magazine/2022/02/18/the-22022-issue

Euromonitor. (2022). *What are the top ten global consumer trends in 2022?.*
Retrieved via the web: https://www.euromonitor.com/article/what-are-the-10-global-consumer-trends-in-2022

Terrell, Kenneth (AARP). (2019). *Americans 50 and Older Would be World's Third-Largest Economy, AARP Study Finds.*
Retrieved via the web: https://www.aarp.org/politics-society/advocacy/info-2019/older-americans-economic-impact-growth.html

Bureau of Labor Statistics. (2021). *Number of people 75 and older in the labor force is expected to grow 96.5 percent by 2030.*
Retrieved via the web: https://www.bls.gov/opub/ted/2021/number-of-people-75-and-older-in-the-labor-force-is-expected-to-grow-96-5-percent-by-2030.htm

Goldberg, Emma. (2022). *The 37-Year-Olds Are Afraid of the 23-Year-Olds Who Work for Them.* New York Times.
Retrieved via the web: https://www.nytimes.com/2021/10/28/business/gen-z-workplace-culture.html

Carlson, Daniel L., Petts, Richard J., and Pepin, Joanna. (2021). *To Keep Women in the Workforce, Men Need to Do More at Home.* Harvard Business Review.
Retrieved via the web: https://hbr.org/2021/04/to-keep-women-in-the-workforce-men-need-to-do-more-at-home

Pandy, Erica. (2021). *Why working mothers are burning out.* The Finish Line, Axios.
Retrieved via the web: https://www.axios.com/2021/11/02/working-mothers-burnout-deadline-extensions

Age Wave. (2022). *Age Wave/Edward Jones Study Reveals a New Retirement.*
Retrieved via the web: https://agewave.com/age-wave-edward-jones-study-reveals-a-new-retirement/

Parity.org. (2022). *Gender Parity in the Workplace.*
Retrieved via the web: http://www.parity.org/gender-diversity/

World Economic Forum. (2019). *Global Gender Pay report 2020.*
Available via the web: https://www.weforum.org/reports/gender-gap-2020-report-100-years-pay-equality/

Dennis, Thom. (2021). *Why is ageism in the workplace increasing?* HR Director.
Retrieved via the web: https://www.thehrdirector.com/features/diversity-and-equality/ageism-in-the-workplace-spikes-due-to-covid-19/

Kita, Joe. (AARP). (2019). *Workplace Age Discrimination Still Flourishes in America.*
Retrieved via the web: https://www.aarp.org/work/age-discrimination/still-thrives-in-america/

DiMuccio, Sarah, PhD., Sattari, Negin, PhD., Shaffer, Emily, PhD., Cline, Jared. (Nd.).
Masculine Anxiety: An Overlooked Factor in Men's Reluctance to Interrupt Sexism. Catalyst.
Retrieved via the web: https://www.catalyst.org/reports/masculine-anxiety-workplace/

Brook, Katherine. (2012). *Job Career Calling Key to Happiness and Meaning at Work.* Psychology Today.
Retrieved via the web: https://www.psychologytoday.com/us/blog/career-transitions/201206/job-career-calling-key-happiness-and-meaning-work

Thompson, Derek. (2021). *The Great Resignation Is Accelerating.* The Atlantic.
Retrieved via the web: https://www.theatlantic.com/ideas/archive/2021/10/great-resignation-accelerating/620382/

Gandhi, Vipula., Robison, Jennifer. (2021). (Gallup). *The 'Great Resignation' Is Really the 'Great Discontent.'.*
Retrieved via the web: https://www.gallup.com/workplace/351545/great-resignation-really-great-discontent.aspx

Atkinson, Emma. (2022). *Google upgrades family leave perks for workers, brands flummoxed by the metaverse and Glossier lays off 80+ following 2021 expansion.* PR Daily.
Retrieved from the web: https://www.prdaily.com/google-upgrades-family-leave-perks-for-workers-brands-flummoxed-by-the-metaverse-and-glossier-lays-off-80-following-2021-expansion/

Liu, Jennifer (CNBC via Axios). (2021). (Shonna Waters' Quotes). *Do you actually like your job? Try the 15-5 method to find out.*
Retrieved via the web: https://www.cnbc.com/2021/11/19/this-15-minute-weekly-habit-tells-you-how-actually-feel-about-your-job.html

Huffington, Arianna. (2021). *The Entry Interview and the Great Resignation.* Thrive Global.
Retrieved via the web: https://thriveglobal.com/stories/arianna-huffington-entry-interviews-important-great-resignation/

Werber, Cassie. (2022). *What happens when colleagues know each other's salaries.* Quartz at Work.
Retrieved via the web: https://qz.com/work/2118866/the-pros-and-cons-of-salary-transparency/

Obloj, Tomasz & Zenger, Todd R. *Incentives, Social Comparison Costs, and the Proximity of Envy's Object* (March 5, 2015). HEC Paris Research Paper No. SPE-2015-1085.
Available at SSRN: https://ssrn.com/abstract=2574248 or
http://dx.doi.org/10.2139/ssrn.2574248

New York Times. (Malone) (2022). *Part-time Work During a Labor Shortage.*
Retrieved via the web: https://www.nytimes.com/2022/02/02/briefing/labor-shortage-part-time-workers-us.html

Ozimek, Adam. (Nd.). *The Great Resignation: From Full-Time to Freelance.* UpWork.
Retrieved via the web: https://www.upwork.com/research/the-great-resignation

Parker, Kim., Menasce Horowitz, Juliana, and Minkin, Rachel. (2022). *COVID-19 Pandemic Continues to Reshape Work in America.* PEW Research.
Retrieved via the web: https://www.pewresearch.org/social-trends/2022/02/16/covid-19-pandemic-continues-to-reshape-work-in-america/

Newman, Nic. (2021). *Changing Newsrooms 2021: Hybrid working and improving diversity remain twin challenges for publishers.* Reuters.
Retrieved via the web: https://reutersinstitute.politics.ox.ac.uk/changing-newsrooms-2021-hybrid-working-and-improving-diversity-remain-twin-challenges-publishers

Grant Thornton. (2022). *Grant Thornton survey: Over half of employees open to changing jobs; majority still want workplace flexibility.*
Retrieved via the web: https://www.grantthornton.com/library/press-releases/2022/april/gt-survey-half-employees-open-changing-jobs-majority-still-want-workplace-flexibility.aspx

Forbes Leadership Forum. (2013). *The Crucial Edge That Makes a Board Exceptional.*
Retrieved via the web:
https://www.forbes.com/sites/forbesleadershipforum/2013/06/13/the-crucial-edge-that-makes-a-board-exceptional/?sh=17e51ac37a86

McKinsey Quarterly. (2016). *The CEO Guide to Boards.*
Retrieved via the web: https://www.mckinsey.com/featured-insights/leadership/the-ceo-guide-to-boards

Charron, Paul. (Nd.). *Leading through change: A perspective from Paul Charron.* Kearney.
Retrieved via the web: https://www.kearney.com/web/thefutureconsumer/article/-/insights/leading-through-change-a-perspective-from-paul-charron

Dugatkin, Lee Alan. (2022). *Social Animals Seek Power in Surprisingly Complex Ways*. Scientific American.
Retrieved via the web: https://www.scientificamerican.com/article/social-animals-seek-power-in-surprisingly-complex-ways/

Dugatkin, Lee Alan (2022). *Power in the Wild. Book Excerpt*.
Available via: https://undark.org/2022/04/22/book-excerpt-power-in-the-wild/

Wikipedia. (Nd.). *Power Position*.
Retrieved via the web: https://en.wikipedia.org/wiki/Power_position

F Luthans, BC Luthans, KW Luthans. (2021). *Organizational Behavior: An Evidence-Based Approach* Fourteenth Edition. New York. McGraw-Hill Irwin.

Walker, Kim. (Nd.). *Questioning Four Types of Power*. Arabella Advisors.
Retrieved via the web: https://www.arabellaadvisors.com/blog/questioning-four-types-of-power/

Van Bommel, Tara, PHD. (2022) *Empathy Is a Force for Innovation, Flourishing, and Intent to Stay*. Catalyst Online.
Retrieved from the web: https://www.catalyst.org/reports/empathy-work-strategy-crisis/

Hanon, Keely. (2022). *5 pandemic trends leaders should leave behind – and one that's here to stay*. Fast Company.
Retrieved via the web: https://www.fastcompany.com/90728525/5-pandemic-trends-leaders-should-leave-behind-and-one-thats-here-to-stay

Dias, Laura Portolese. (2011). *Human Resource Management*. Derived from Creative Commons licensed edition published by Flat World Knowledge, ca. 2011.

Study.com. (2021). *Positional Power: Legitimate, Coercive & Reward Power*.
Retrieved via the web: https://study.com/academy/lesson/positional-power-personal-power.html

Tobaccowala, Rishad. (2022). *The Age of Creativity*.
Retrieved via the web: https://rishadtobaccowala.com/blog/the-age-of-creativity

Furr, Nathan., Shiplov, Andrew. (2022). *Making Quantum Computing a Reality*. Harvard Business Review.
Retrieved via the web: https://hbr.org/2022/04/making-quantum-computing-a-reality

Bakhshi, Naser., Duin, Stefan Van. (2017). *Part 1: Artificial Intelligence Defined*. Deloitte Blog.
Retrieved via the web: https://www2.deloitte.com/nl/nl/pages/data-analytics/articles/part-1-artificial-intelligence-defined.html

Zahira Jaser., Petrakaki, Dimitra., Starr, Rachel., and Oyarbide-Magaña, Ernesto. (2022). *Where Automated Job Interviews Fall Short*. Harvard Business Review.
Retrieved via the web: https://hbr.org/2022/01/where-automated-job-interviews-fall-short

Azaria, Adi. (2020). *Why voice technology is the future of business*. IT Pro Portal Website.
Retrieved via the web: https://www.itproportal.com/features/why-voice-technology-is-the-future-of-business/

Strum, Lara. (2019). *Tech-Proofing the Millennial Workplace.* BizTech Magazine. Retrieved via the web: https://biztechmagazine.com/article/2019/08/tech-proofing-millennial-workplace

Masterofcode. (Nd.). Master of Code Website. Available via: https://masterofcode.com

Guzenko, Ivan. (Nd.). SmartyAds.com Website. Available via: https://smartyads.com/blog/author/ivan-guzenko

Artillery Intelligence. (2022). *AR and VR Report.* Preview available via: https://artillry.co/artillry-intelligence/the-immersive-commerce-era-ar-shopping-collide/

PWC. (2022). *Virtual Reality (VR) and Augmented Reality (AR) have the potential to deliver a £1.4 trillion boost to the global economy by 2030.* Retrieved via the web: https://www.pwc.com/id/en/media-centre/press-release/2020/english/virtual-and-augmented-reality-could-deliver-a-p1-4trillion-boost.html

Holbrook, Sarah. (2022). *Let the Games Begin.* The Robin Report Website. Retrieved via the web: https://www.therobinreport.com/let-the-games-begin/

Wilson, Mark. (2019). *Snap's secret weapon speaks.* Wired Magazine. Retrieved via the web: https://www.fastcompany.com/90382260/snaps-secret-weapon-speaks

Stilson, Janet. (2022). *Creating a Fully Formed Metaverse.* MediaVillage. Retrieved via the web: https://www.mediavillage.com/article/creating-a-fully-formed-metaverse/print/

White, Andrew. (2022). *Really, What is Metaverse?.* Gartner Group Blogs. Retrieved via the web: https://blogs.gartner.com/andrew_white/2022/01/07/really-what-is-metaverse/

Galloway, Scott. (2022). *Unreal Estate.* Marker Medium. Retrieved via the web: https://marker.medium.com/virtual-real-estate-will-be-the-next-speculative-frenzy-43083d9638f8

Stock, Greg. (2022). Personal Interview conducted by Deborah Patton. https://www.gregorystock.net/gregs-cv-2

Wired Magazine, Gadget Lab Podcast. (2018). *Mary Lou Jepsen on AR, VR, and Reading Your Mind.* Retrieved via the web: https://www.wired.com/2018/10/gadget-lab-podcast-381/

O'Neill, Michael. (2021). *Avatar robots are beginning to stake out their place in the workforce, and Japan is leading the way.* Business Insider. Retrieved via the web: https://www.businessinsider.com/avatar-robots-are-beginning-to-stake-out-their-place-in-the-workforce-with-japan-leading-the-way-2021-3

Lee, Thomas. (2020). *Learning to Learn.* Berkeley University. Retrieved via the web: https://vcresearch.berkeley.edu/news/learning-learn

MacLellan, Lila. (2022). *For some workers, there's a whole life unfolding in the metaverse. Quartz Work From Home.*

Retrieved via the web: https://qz.com/work/2126161/three-ways-the-metaverse-could-change-future-of-work/

Dua, Suneet. (KQ Education Group). (2021). *Metaverse tops business leaders' list of technology trends.*
Retrieved via the web: https://kqeducationgroup.com/metaverse-tops-business-leaders-list-of-technology-trends/

Quito, Ann. (Schumacher, Patrik). (2022). *A Zaha Hadid-designed city in the metaverse captures the ambitions of Liberland. Quartz.*
Retrieved via the web: https://qz.com/2129329/zaha-hadid-in-liberland-architects-designing-in-the-metaverse/

Nguyen, Tuong H. (2021). *5 Impactful Technologies from the Gartner Emerging Technologies and Trends Impact Radar for 2022.* Gartner Website.
Retrieved from the web: https://www.gartner.com/en/articles/5-impactful-technologies-from-the-gartner-emerging-technologies-and-trends-impact-radar-for-2022

Thomas, Lee. (Abeel, Pieter). (2020). *Learning to Learn.* Berkeley Website.
Retrieved via the web: https://vcresearch.berkeley.edu/news/learning-learn

O'Neill, Michael. (2021). *Avatar robots are beginning to stake out their place in the workforce, and Japan is leading the way.* Tech Insider.
Retrieved via the web: https://www.businessinsider.com/avatar-robots-are-beginning-to-stake-out-their-place-in-the-workforce-with-japan-leading-the-way-2021-3

Ciardi, John. *How Does a Poem Mean?.* Boston: Houghton Mifflin, 1960.

Ezra Klein. (2022). *Covid Policy and Trust.* New York Times.
Retrieved via the web: https://www.nytimes.com/2022/02/06/opinion/covid-pandemic-policy-trust.html

Edelman, Richard. (2022). *Breaking the Vicious Cycle of Mistrust.* Edelman's 2022 Trust Barometer Review.
Retrieved via the web: https://www.edelman.com/trust/2022-trust-barometer/breaking-vicious-cycle-distrust

Kravosky, Maria. (2013). *Chip and Dan Heath: How to Make Better Choices in Life and Work.* Stanford Graduate School of Business.
Retrieved via the web: https://www.gsb.stanford.edu/insights/chip-dan-heath-how-make-better-choices-life-work

George, Bill. (2017). *Op-Ed: Courage: The Defining Characteristic of Great Leaders.* Harvard Business School.
Retrieved via the web: https://hbswk.hbs.edu/item/courage-the-defining-characteristic-of-great-leaders

Gerdeman, Dina. (2017). Leadership Under Fire. Review and excerpt of Nancy Koehn's Five Leaders Forged in Crisis, and What We Can Learn From Them. Harvard Business School.
Retrieved via the web: https://hbswk.hbs.edu/item/5-leaders-forged-in-crisis-and-what-we-can-learn-from-them

Bradberry, Travis Dr. (Nd.). *Emotional Intelligence Can Boost Your Career And Save Your Life.*
Retrieved via the web: https://www.talentsmarteq.com/articles/Emotional-Intelligence-Can-Boost-Your-Career-And-Save-Your-Life-915340665-p-1.html/

DDI. (2018). *Global Leadership Forecast 2018.*
Retrieved via the web: https://www.ddiworld.com/research/global-leadership-forecast-2018

Jacobs, Ken (2009). Thought Leaders LLC Website.
Available via: https://www.thoughtleadersllc.com/2009/03/acting-courageously-leadership-in-storm/

Heath, Chip. & Abrahams, Matt. (2022). *Make Numbers Count: How to Translate Data for Your Audience.* Insights by Stanford Business, Organizational Behavior Podcast.
Retrieved from the web/podcast: https://www.gsb.stanford.edu/insights/make-numbers-count-how-translate-data-your-audience

George, Bill. (2017). *Op-Ed: Courage: The Defining Characteristic of Great Leaders.* Working Knowledge, Harvard Business School.
Retrieved from the web: https://hbswk.hbs.edu/item/courage-the-defining-characteristic-of-great-leaders

Gavin, Matt. (2020). *5 characteristics of a courageous leader.* Harvard Business School Online.
Retrieved from the web: https://online.hbs.edu/blog/post/courageous-leadership

Detert, Jim. (Nd.). *Choosing Courage: The Everyday Guide to Being Brave at Work.*
Reviewed via: https://jimdetert.com

Bruno, Evan., Detert, Jim. *The Courage to Be Candid.* (2021). Sloan Management Review.
Retrieved from the web: https://sloanreview.mit.edu/article/the-courage-to-be-candid/

Bradberry, Travis. Dr. (Nd.). *Emotional Intelligence Can Boost Your Career And Save Your Life.*
Retrieved from the web: https://www.talentsmarteq.com/articles/Emotional-Intelligence-Can-Boost-Your-Career-And-Save-Your-Life-915340665-p-1.html/

2025 Update New References

Frontiers in Computer Science. (2025). Digital anthropomorphism and the psychology of trust in generative AI tutors: An opinion-based thematic synthesis. Frontiers in Computer Science, 7. https://www.frontiersin.org/articles/10.3389/fcomp.2025.1638657/full

Alabed, A., Javornik, A., & Gregory-Smith, D. (2022). AI anthropomorphism and its effect on users' self-congruence and self–AI integration: A theoretical framework and research agenda. Technological Forecasting and Social Change, 182, 121786. https://doi.org/10.1016/j.techfore.2022.121786

Roose, K., et al. (2025). The benefits and dangers of anthropomorphic conversational agents. Proceedings of the National Academy of Sciences, 122, e2415898122. https://www.pnas.org/doi/10.1073/pnas.2415898122

Mark, G. (2023). Attention span research findings. University of California, Irvine.

Betteridge, B., Chien, W., Hazels, E., & Simone, J. (2023). How does technology affect the attention spans of different age groups? Oxford Journal. https://www.oxjournal.org/how-does-technology-affect-the-attention-spans-of-different-age-groups/

King's College London. (2022). Are attention spans really collapsing? Policy Institute and Centre for Attention Studies. https://www.kcl.ac.uk/news/are-attention-spans-really-collapsing

Shanmugasundaram, M., & Tamilarasu, A. (2023). The impact of digital technology, social media, and artificial intelligence on cognitive functions: a review. Frontiers in Cognition, 2, 1203077. https://doi.org/10.3389/fcogn.2023.1203077

Zhai, C., Wibowo, S., & Li, L. D. (2024). The effects of over-reliance on AI dialogue systems on students' cognitive abilities: A systematic review. Smart Learning Environments, 11, 28. https://doi.org/10.1186/s40561-024-00316-7

Gerlich, M. (2025). AI Tools in Society: Impacts on Cognitive Offloading and the Future of Critical Thinking. Societies, 15(1), 6. https://doi.org/10.3390/soc15010006

Lee, H.-P., Sarkar, A., Tankelevitch, L., Drosos, I., Rintel, S., Banks, R., & Wilson, N. (2025). The impact of generative AI on critical thinking: Self-reported reductions in cognitive effort and confidence effects from a survey of knowledge workers. CHI Conference on Human Factors in Computing Systems. https://www.microsoft.com/en-us/research/wp-content/uploads/2025/01/lee_2025_ai_critical_thinking_survey.pdf

Leroy, S. (2009). Why is it so hard to do my work? The challenge of attention residue when switching between work tasks. Organizational Behavior and Human Decision Processes, 109(2), 168–181.

Bankins, S., Denisova-Schmidt, E., & Kmec, J. (2024). A multilevel review of artificial intelligence in organizations: Implications for organizational behavior research and practice. Journal of Organizational Behavior, 45(6), 891-908. https://doi.org/10.1002/job.2735

Park, S., Kim, J., & Lee, H. (2024). The mental health implications of artificial intelligence adoption: the crucial role of self-efficacy. Humanities and Social Sciences Communications, 11, 1448. https://doi.org/10.1038/s41599-024-04018-w

Ghani, U., et al. (2024). Exploring how AI adoption in the workplace affects employees: a bibliometric and systematic review. Frontiers in Artificial Intelligence, 7, 1473872. https://doi.org/10.3389/frai.2024.1473872

Wang, X., Zhang, Y., & Liu, M. (2025). Mitigating the effect of AI anxiety on employees' creativity: a social cognitive perspective. Journal of Digital Management, 2, 6. https://doi.org/10.1007/s44362-025-00006-5

American Psychological Association. (2024). Digital Wellness Study 2024: Post-pandemic trends in digital dependency and mental health correlations. APA Digital Health Initiative.

Center for Humane Technology. (2024). Annual Report: Persuasive Technology Amplification and Mental Health Impacts. Center for Humane Technology.

Digital Wellness Institute. (2024). Digital Detox Program Effectiveness Study: Long-term outcomes and relapse patterns. Digital Wellness Institute Research Division.

Chen, H., Dong, G., & Li, K. (2023). Overview on brain function enhancement of Internet addicts through exercise intervention: based on reward-execution-decision cycle. Frontiers in Psychiatry, 14, 1094583. https://doi.org/10.3389/fpsyt.2023.1094583

Messeri, L., & Crockett, M. (2024). Illusions of objectivity in AI systems. Nature. https://doi.org/10.1038/s41586-024-07240-6

Nature Human Behaviour. (2025). Large language models are more persuasive than humans in online debates. Nature Human Behaviour. https://www.nature.com/articles/s41562-025-01929-w

Meta Platforms. (2020–2025). Reality Labs segment reports (cumulative >$60B losses). Meta Investor Relations. https://investor.fb.com

World Health Organization. (2019). International Classification of Diseases 11th Revision (ICD-11): Gaming disorder. https://icd.who.int/

Recent reviews (2023–2024). Automation bias in healthcare decision support systems. See e.g., Frontiers in Digital Health, 2023.

Frontiers in Computer Science. (2025). Digital anthropomorphism and the psychology of trust in generative AI tutors: an opinion-based thematic synthesis. *Frontiers in Computer Science*, 7. https://www.frontiersin.org/journals/computer-science/articles/10.3389/fcomp.2025.1638657/full

Science Direct. (2024, June). Trust and reliance on AI — An experimental study on the extent and costs of overreliance on AI. *Computers in Human Behavior*. https://www.sciencedirect.com/science/article/pii/S0747563224002206